the DARK HUNTERS

VOLUME 3

SHERRILYN KENYON

ADAPTED BY
JOSHUA HALE FIALKOV

ART BY
CLAUDIA CAMPOS WITH
GLASSHOUSE GRAPHICS

PRODUCTION BY
ZACH MATHENY

St. Martin's Griffin
New York

This is a work of fiction. All of the characters,
organizations, and events portrayed in this novel are
either products of the author's imagination or
are used fictitiously.

Art by Claudia Campos with Glass House Graphics.
Adaptation by Joshua Hale Fialkov.
Lettering and additional design by Zach Matheny.

www.stmartins.com

ISBN 978-0-312-37688-8

First Edition: October 2010

10 9 8 7 6 5 4 3 2 1

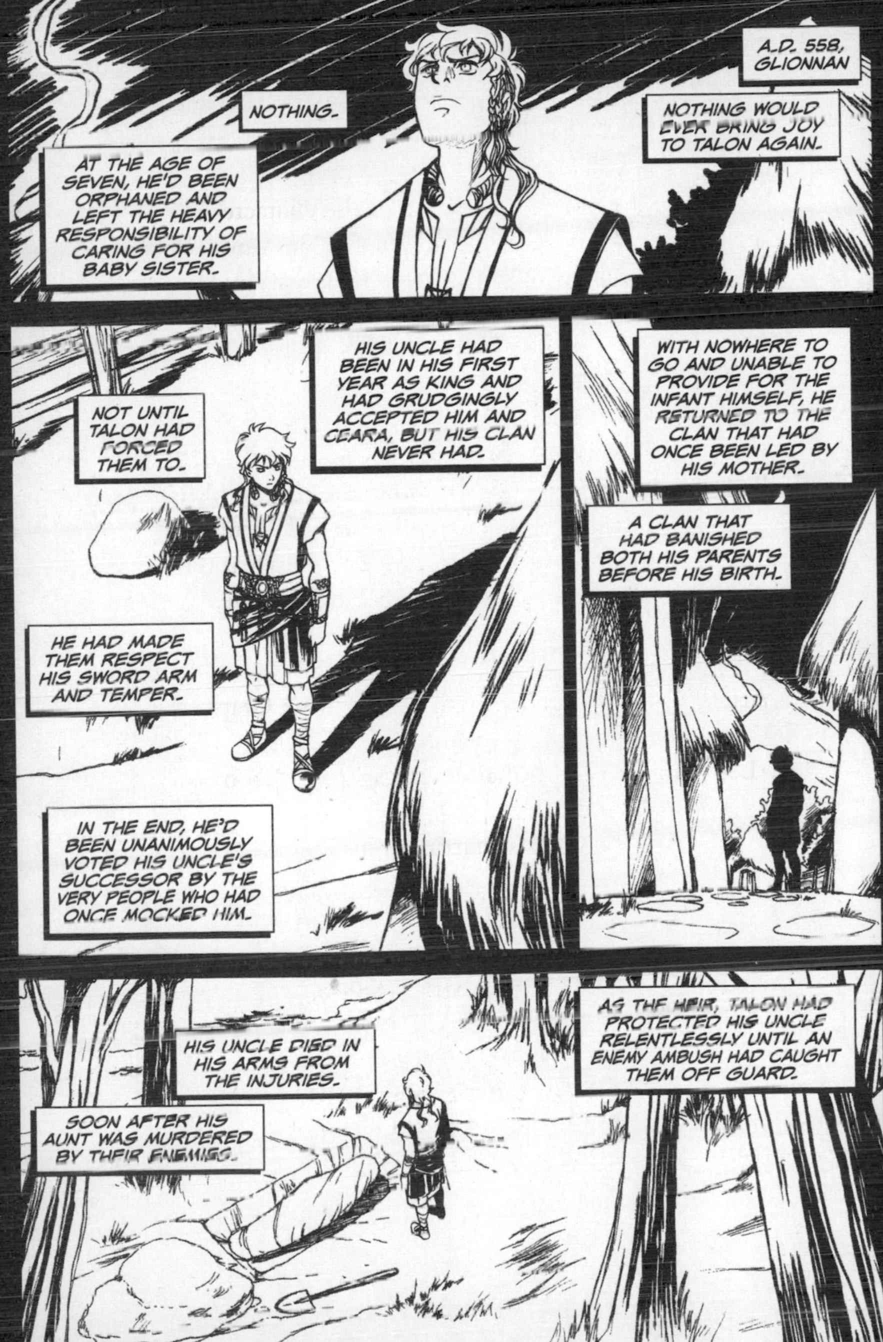
A.D. 558, GLIONNAN
NOTHING WOULD EVER BRING JOY TO TALON AGAIN.
NOTHING.
AT THE AGE OF SEVEN, HE'D BEEN ORPHANED AND LEFT THE HEAVY RESPONSIBILITY OF CARING FOR HIS BABY SISTER.
WITH NOWHERE TO GO AND UNABLE TO PROVIDE FOR THE INFANT HIMSELF, HE RETURNED TO THE CLAN THAT HAD ONCE BEEN LED BY HIS MOTHER.
A CLAN THAT HAD BANISHED BOTH HIS PARENTS BEFORE HIS BIRTH.
HIS UNCLE HAD BEEN IN HIS FIRST YEAR AS KING AND HAD GRUDGINGLY ACCEPTED HIM AND CEARA, BUT HIS CLAN NEVER HAD.
NOT UNTIL TALON HAD FORCED THEM TO.
HE HAD MADE THEM RESPECT HIS SWORD ARM AND TEMPER.
IN THE END, HE'D BEEN UNANIMOUSLY VOTED HIS UNCLE'S SUCCESSOR BY THE VERY PEOPLE WHO HAD ONCE MOCKED HIM.
AS THE HEIR, TALON HAD PROTECTED HIS UNCLE RELENTLESSLY UNTIL AN ENEMY AMBUSH HAD CAUGHT THEM OFF GUARD.
HIS UNCLE DIED IN HIS ARMS FROM THE INJURIES.
SOON AFTER HIS AUNT WAS MURDERED BY THEIR ENEMIES.

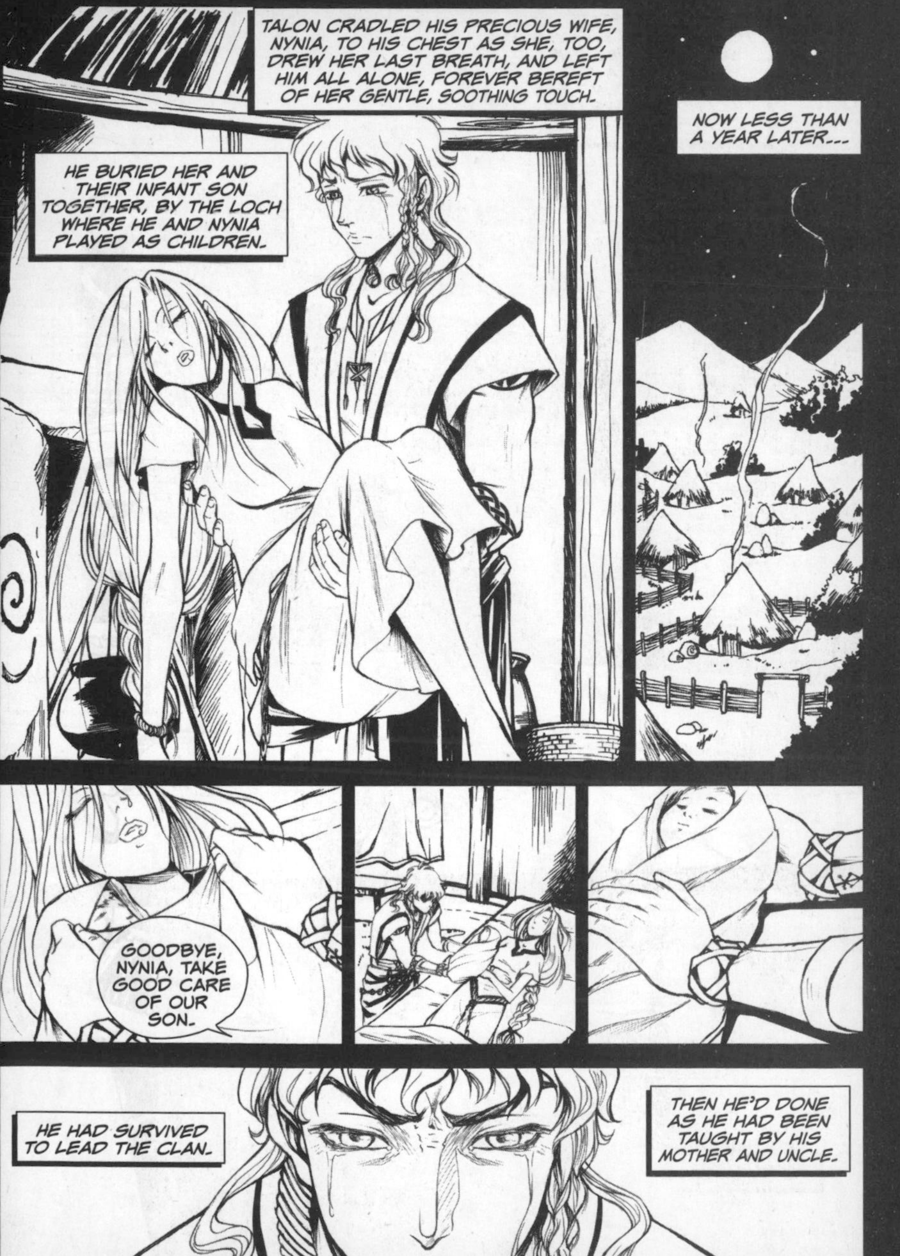
TALON CRADLED HIS PRECIOUS WIFE, NYNIA, TO HIS CHEST AS SHE, TOO, DREW HER LAST BREATH, AND LEFT HIM ALL ALONE, FOREVER BEREFT OF HER GENTLE, SOOTHING TOUCH.
HE BURIED HER AND THEIR INFANT SON TOGETHER, BY THE LOCH WHERE HE AND NYNIA PLAYED AS CHILDREN.
NOW LESS THAN A YEAR LATER...
GOODBYE, NYNIA, TAKE GOOD CARE OF OUR SON.
HE HAD SURVIVED TO LEAD THE CLAN.
THEN HE'D DONE AS HE HAD BEEN TAUGHT BY HIS MOTHER AND UNCLE.

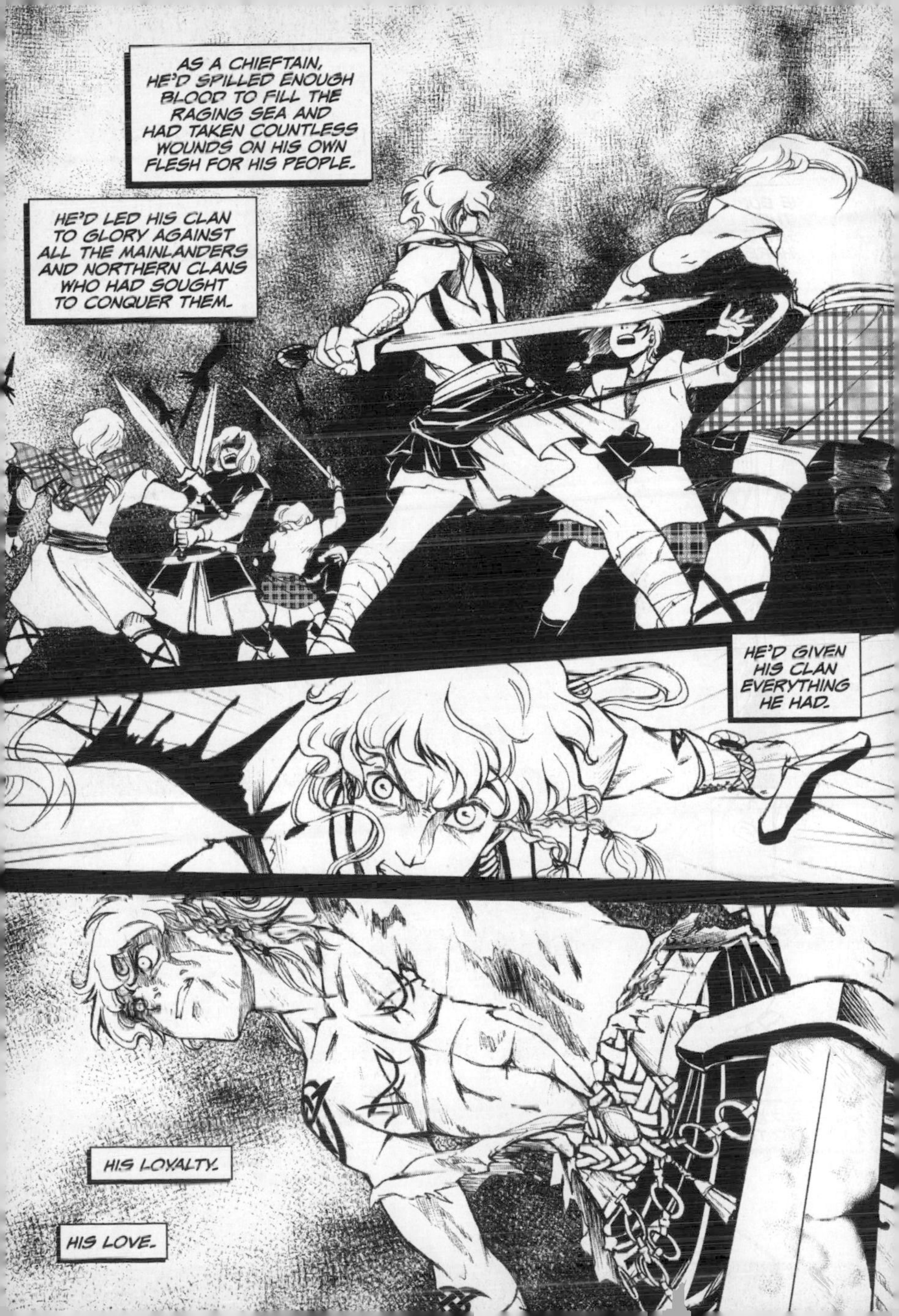
AS A CHIEFTAIN, HE'D SPILLED ENOUGH BLOOD TO FILL THE RAGING SEA AND HAD TAKEN COUNTLESS WOUNDS ON HIS OWN FLESH FOR HIS PEOPLE.
HE'D LED HIS CLAN TO GLORY AGAINST ALL THE MAINLANDERS AND NORTHERN CLANS WHO HAD SOUGHT TO CONQUER THEM.
HE'D GIVEN HIS CLAN EVERYTHING HE HAD.
HIS LOYALTY.
HIS LOVE.

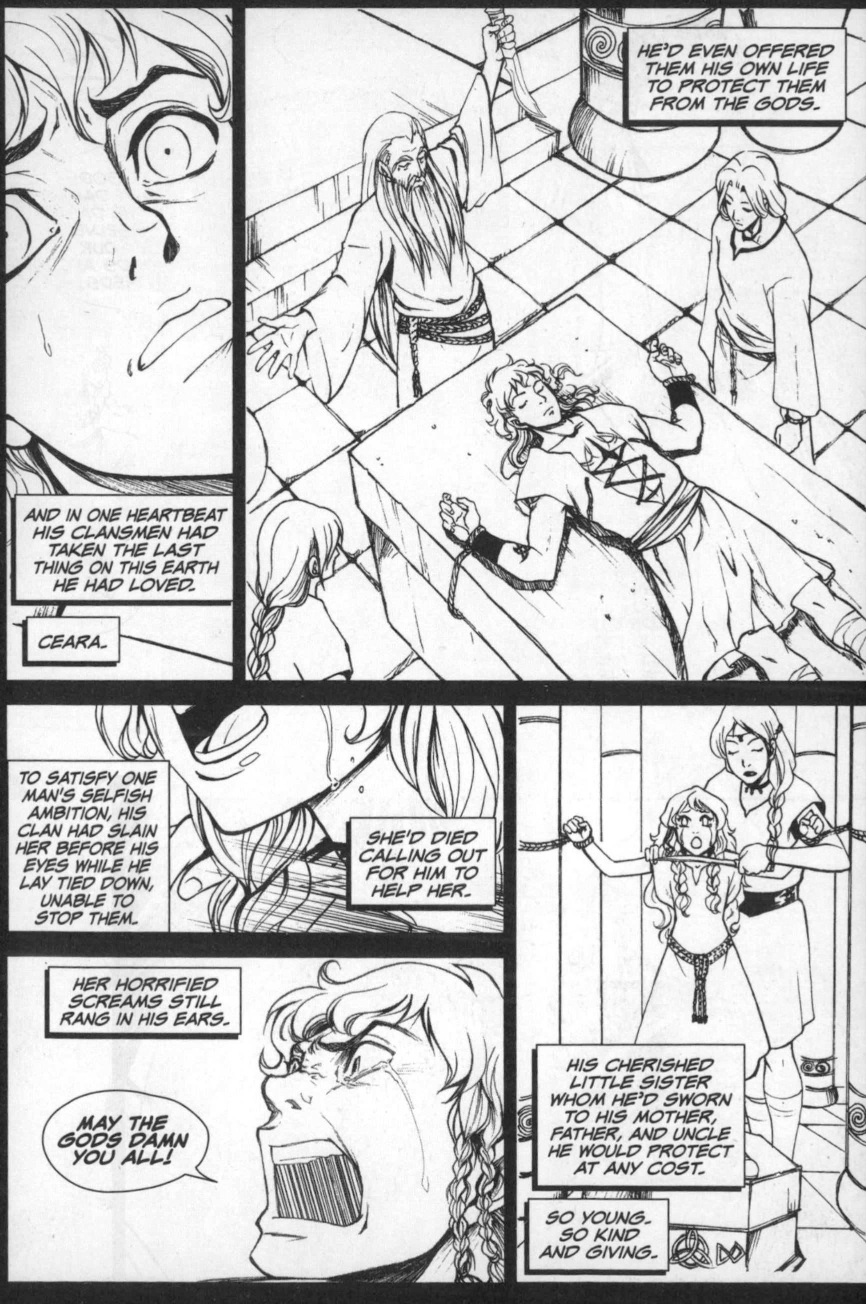
HE'D EVEN OFFERED THEM HIS OWN LIFE TO PROTECT THEM FROM THE GODS.
AND IN ONE HEARTBEAT HIS CLANSMEN HAD TAKEN THE LAST THING ON THIS EARTH HE HAD LOVED.
CEARA.
TO SATISFY ONE MAN'S SELFISH AMBITION, HIS CLAN HAD SLAIN HER BEFORE HIS EYES WHILE HE LAY TIED DOWN, UNABLE TO STOP THEM.
SHE'D DIED CALLING OUT FOR HIM TO HELP HER.
HER HORRIFIED SCREAMS STILL RANG IN HIS EARS.
MAY THE GODS DAMN YOU ALL!
HIS CHERISHED LITTLE SISTER WHOM HE'D SWORN TO HIS MOTHER, FATHER, AND UNCLE HE WOULD PROTECT AT ANY COST.
SO YOUNG. SO KIND AND GIVING.

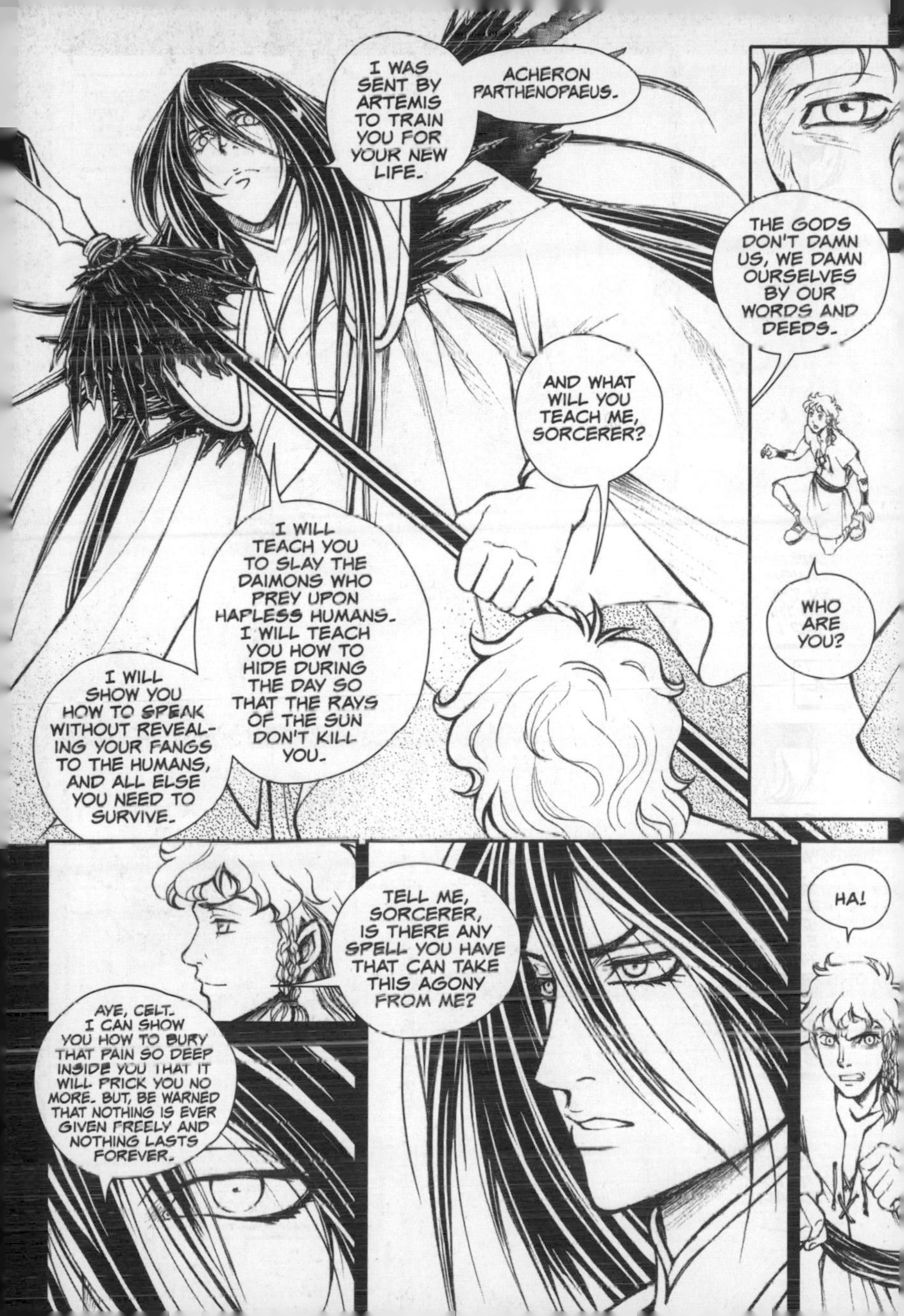
THE GODS DON'T DAMN US, WE DAMN OURSELVES BY OUR WORDS AND DEEDS.
WHO ARE YOU?
ACHERON PARTHENOPAEUS.
I WAS SENT BY ARTEMIS TO TRAIN YOU FOR YOUR NEW LIFE.
AND WHAT WILL YOU TEACH ME, SORCERER?
I WILL TEACH YOU TO SLAY THE DAIMONS WHO PREY UPON HAPLESS HUMANS. I WILL TEACH YOU HOW TO HIDE DURING THE DAY SO THAT THE RAYS OF THE SUN DON'T KILL YOU.
I WILL SHOW YOU HOW TO SPEAK WITHOUT REVEAL-ING YOUR FANGS TO THE HUMANS, AND ALL ELSE YOU NEED TO SURVIVE.
TELL ME, SORCERER, IS THERE ANY SPELL YOU HAVE THAT CAN TAKE THIS AGONY FROM ME?
AYE, CELT. I CAN SHOW YOU HOW TO BURY THAT PAIN SO DEEP INSIDE YOU THAT IT WILL PRICK YOU NO MORE. BUT, BE WARNED THAT NOTHING IS EVER GIVEN FREELY AND NOTHING LASTS FOREVER.
HA!

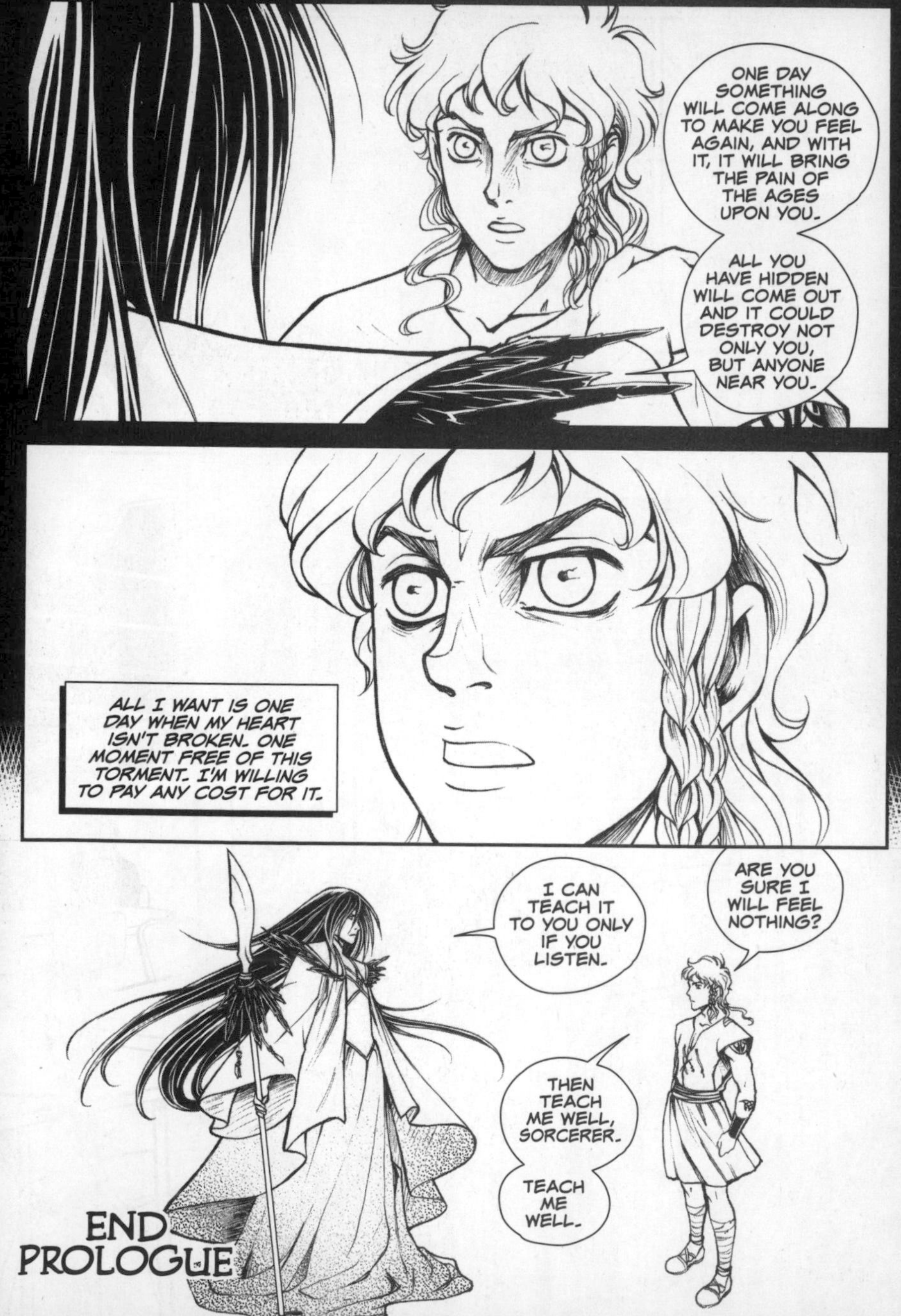

ONE DAY SOMETHING WILL COME ALONG TO MAKE YOU FEEL AGAIN, AND WITH IT, IT WILL BRING THE PAIN OF THE AGES UPON YOU.
ALL YOU HAVE HIDDEN WILL COME OUT AND IT COULD DESTROY NOT ONLY YOU, BUT ANYONE NEAR YOU.
ALL I WANT IS ONE DAY WHEN MY HEART ISN'T BROKEN. ONE MOMENT FREE OF THIS TORMENT. I'M WILLING TO PAY ANY COST FOR IT.
ARE YOU SURE I WILL FEEL NOTHING?
I CAN TEACH IT TO YOU ONLY IF YOU LISTEN.
THEN TEACH ME WELL, SORCERER.
TEACH ME WELL.
END PROLOGUE

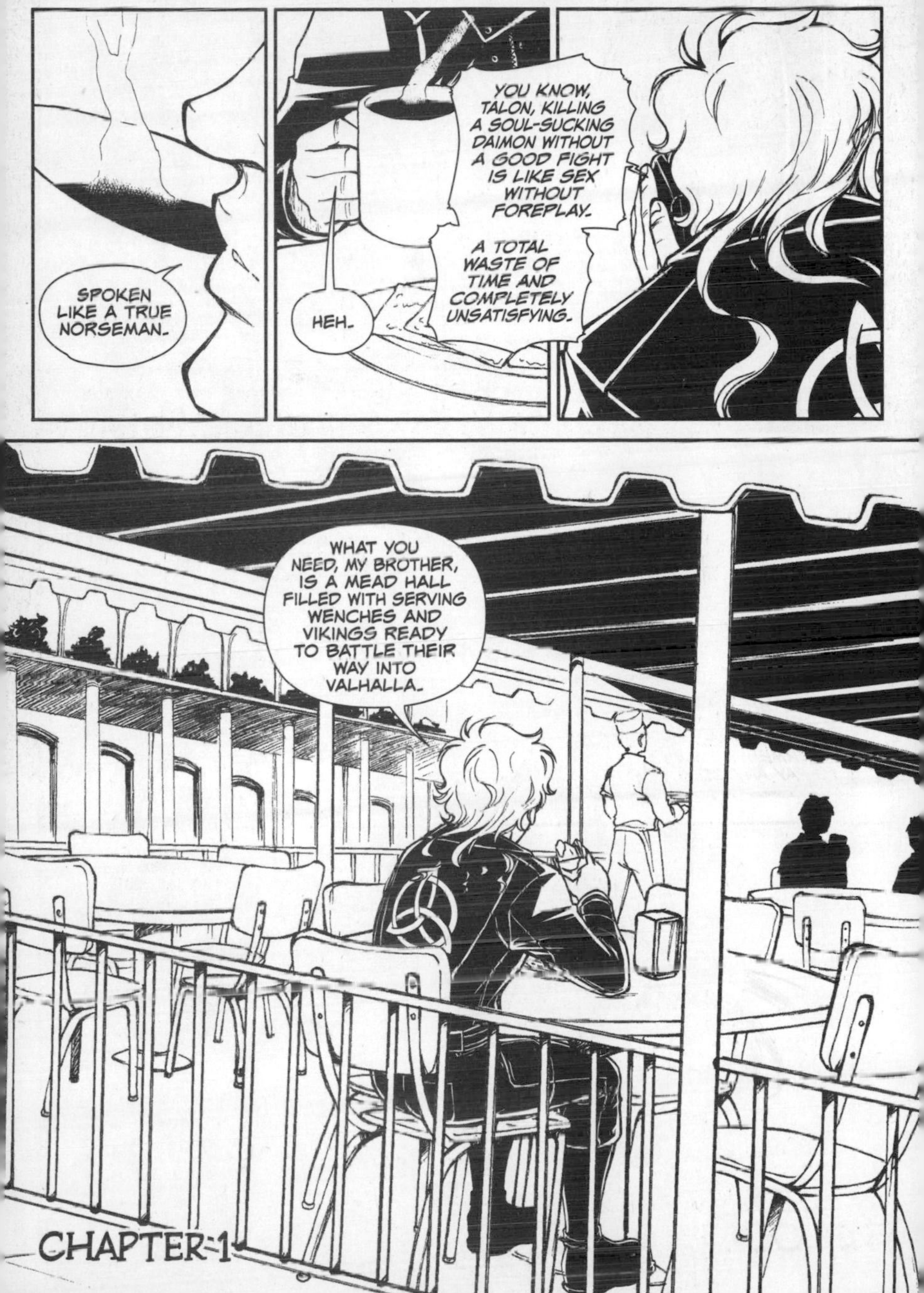
SPOKEN LIKE A TRUE NORSEMAN.
HEH.
YOU KNOW, TALON, KILLING A SOUL-SUCKING DAIMON WITHOUT A GOOD FIGHT IS LIKE SEX WITHOUT FOREPLAY.
A TOTAL WASTE OF TIME AND COMPLETELY UNSATISFYING.
WHAT YOU NEED, MY BROTHER, IS A MEAD HALL FILLED WITH SERVING WENCHES AND VIKINGS READY TO BATTLE THEIR WAY INTO VALHALLA.
CHAPTER 1

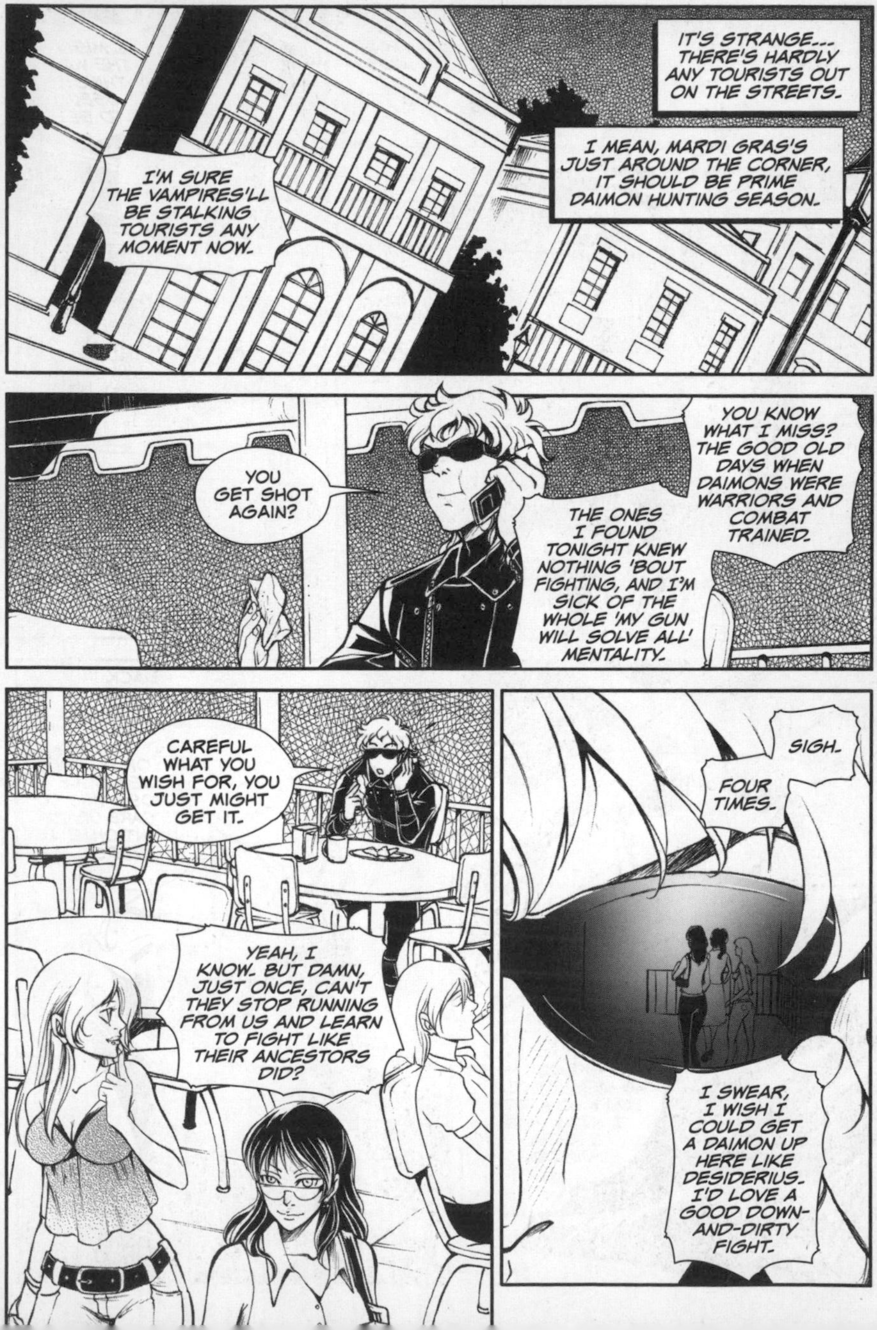
IT'S STRANGE... THERE'S HARDLY ANY TOURISTS OUT ON THE STREETS.
I MEAN, MARDI GRAS'S JUST AROUND THE CORNER, IT SHOULD BE PRIME DAIMON HUNTING SEASON.
I'M SURE THE VAMPIRES'LL BE STALKING TOURISTS ANY MOMENT NOW.
YOU KNOW WHAT I MISS? THE GOOD OLD DAYS WHEN DAIMONS WERE WARRIORS AND COMBAT TRAINED.
YOU GET SHOT AGAIN?
THE ONES I FOUND TONIGHT KNEW NOTHING 'BOUT FIGHTING, AND I'M SICK OF THE WHOLE 'MY GUN WILL SOLVE ALL' MENTALITY.
CAREFUL WHAT YOU WISH FOR, YOU JUST MIGHT GET IT.
YEAH, I KNOW. BUT DAMN, JUST ONCE, CAN'T THEY STOP RUNNING FROM US AND LEARN TO FIGHT LIKE THEIR ANCESTORS DID?
SIGH.
FOUR TIMES.
I SWEAR, I WISH I COULD GET A DAIMON UP HERE LIKE DESIDERIUS. I'D LOVE A GOOD DOWN-AND-DIRTY FIGHT.

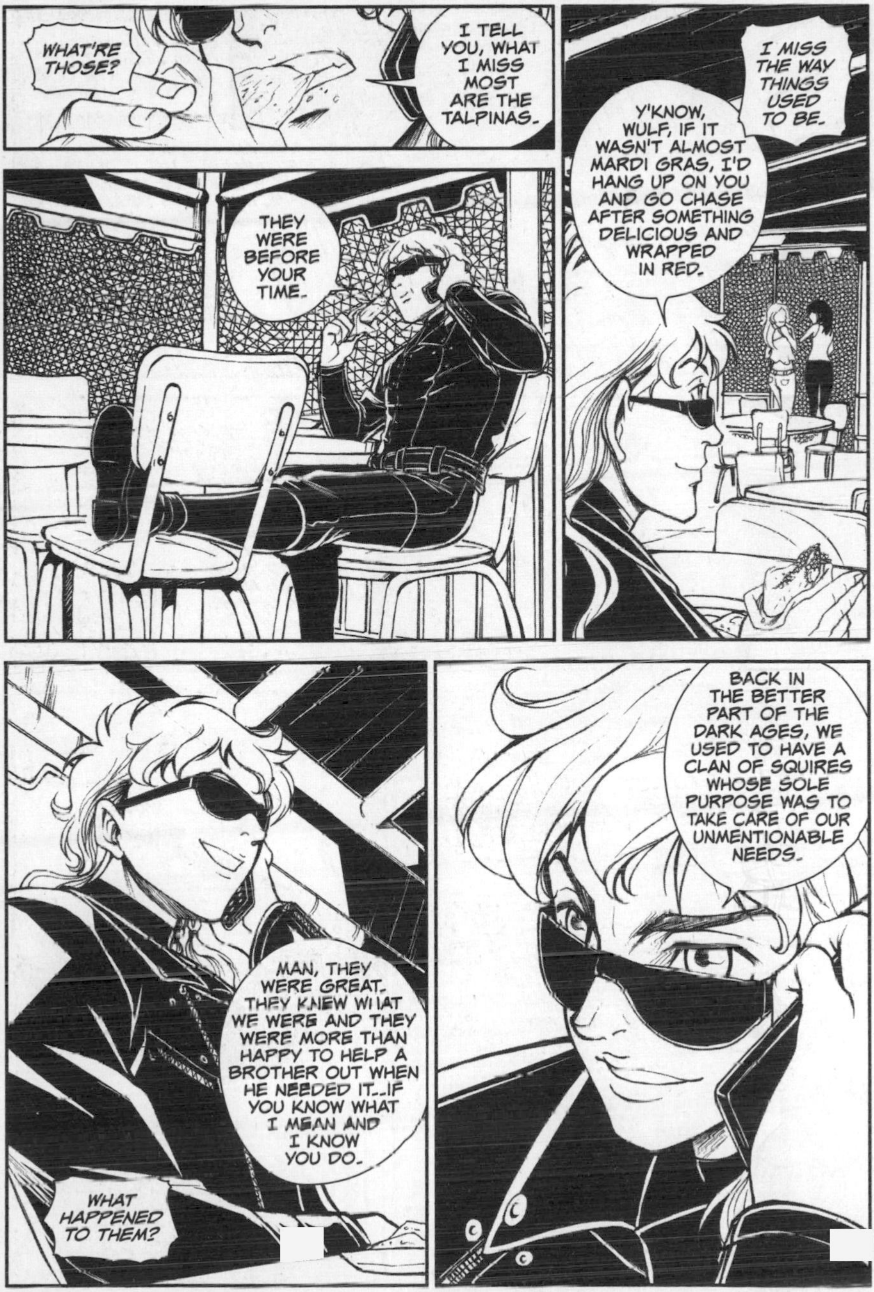
WHAT'RE THOSE?
I TELL YOU, WHAT I MISS MOST ARE THE TALPINAS.
THEY WERE BEFORE YOUR TIME.
I MISS THE WAY THINGS USED TO BE.
Y'KNOW, WULF, IF IT WASN'T ALMOST MARDI GRAS, I'D HANG UP ON YOU AND GO CHASE AFTER SOMETHING DELICIOUS AND WRAPPED IN RED.
MAN, THEY WERE GREAT. THEY KNEW WHAT WE WERE AND THEY WERE MORE THAN HAPPY TO HELP A BROTHER OUT WHEN HE NEEDED IT...IF YOU KNOW WHAT I MEAN AND I KNOW YOU DO.
WHAT HAPPENED TO THEM?
BACK IN THE BETTER PART OF THE DARK AGES, WE USED TO HAVE A CLAN OF SQUIRES WHOSE SOLE PURPOSE WAS TO TAKE CARE OF OUR UNMENTIONABLE NEEDS.

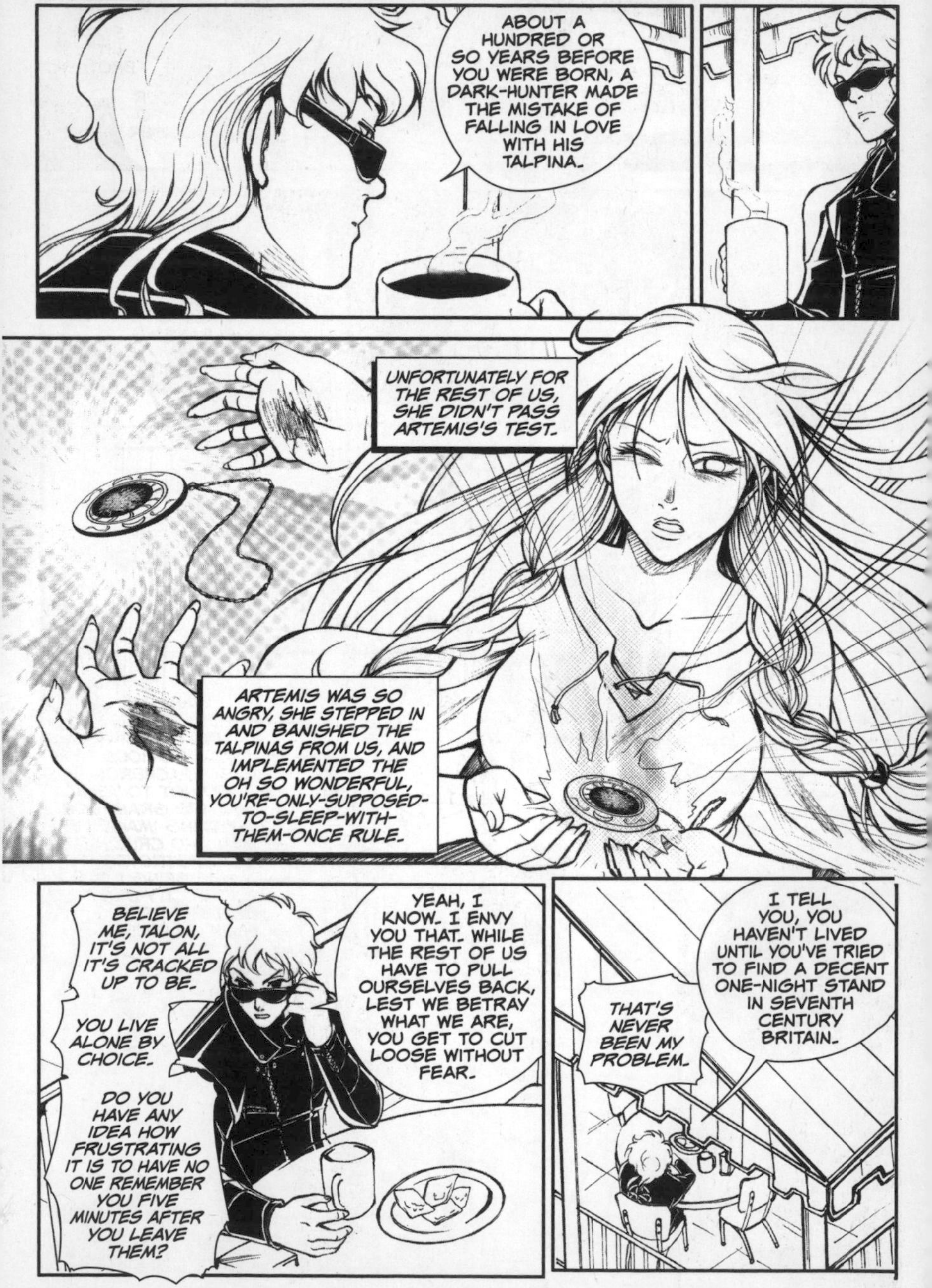

ABOUT A HUNDRED OR SO YEARS BEFORE YOU WERE BORN, A DARK-HUNTER MADE THE MISTAKE OF FALLING IN LOVE WITH HIS TALPINA.
UNFORTUNATELY FOR THE REST OF US, SHE DIDN'T PASS ARTEMIS'S TEST.
ARTEMIS WAS SO ANGRY, SHE STEPPED IN AND BANISHED THE TALPINAS FROM US, AND IMPLEMENTED THE OH SO WONDERFUL, YOU'RE-ONLY-SUPPOSED-TO-SLEEP-WITH-THEM-ONCE RULE.
YEAH, I KNOW. I ENVY YOU THAT. WHILE THE REST OF US HAVE TO PULL OURSELVES BACK, LEST WE BETRAY WHAT WE ARE, YOU GET TO CUT LOOSE WITHOUT FEAR.
BELIEVE ME, TALON, IT'S NOT ALL IT'S CRACKED UP TO BE.
YOU LIVE ALONE BY CHOICE.
DO YOU HAVE ANY IDEA HOW FRUSTRATING IT IS TO HAVE NO ONE REMEMBER YOU FIVE MINUTES AFTER YOU LEAVE THEM?
I TELL YOU, YOU HAVEN'T LIVED UNTIL YOU'VE TRIED TO FIND A DECENT ONE-NIGHT STAND IN SEVENTH CENTURY BRITAIN.
THAT'S NEVER BEEN MY PROBLEM.

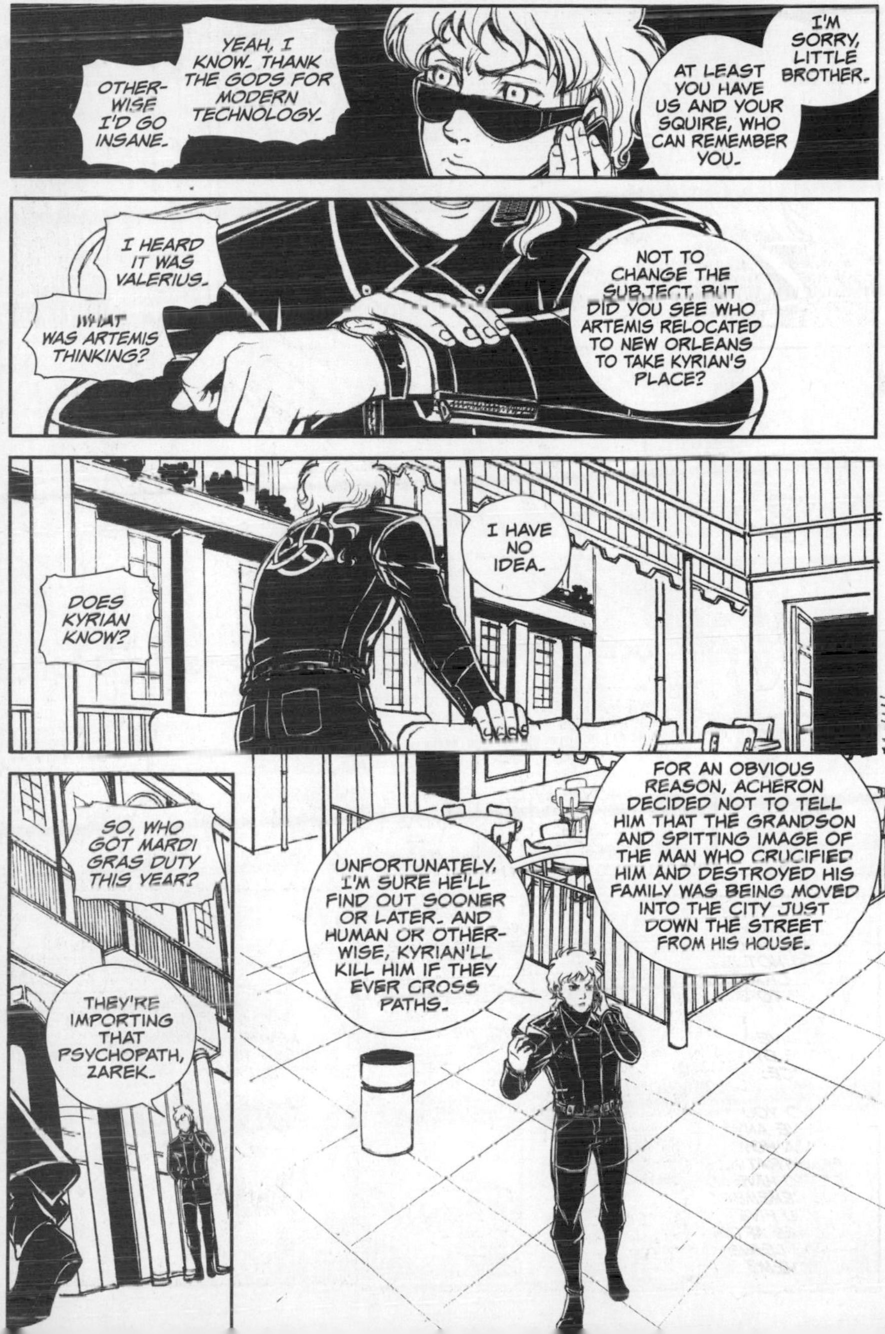
I'M SORRY, LITTLE BROTHER.
AT LEAST YOU HAVE US AND YOUR SQUIRE, WHO CAN REMEMBER YOU.
YEAH, I KNOW. THANK THE GODS FOR MODERN TECHNOLOGY.
OTHER-WISE I'D GO INSANE.
NOT TO CHANGE THE SUBJECT, BUT DID YOU SEE WHO ARTEMIS RELOCATED TO NEW ORLEANS TO TAKE KYRIAN'S PLACE?
I HEARD IT WAS VALERIUS.
WHAT WAS ARTEMIS THINKING?
I HAVE NO IDEA.
DOES KYRIAN KNOW?
FOR AN OBVIOUS REASON, ACHERON DECIDED NOT TO TELL HIM THAT THE GRANDSON AND SPITTING IMAGE OF THE MAN WHO CRUCIFIED HIM AND DESTROYED HIS FAMILY WAS BEING MOVED INTO THE CITY JUST DOWN THE STREET FROM HIS HOUSE.
UNFORTUNATELY, I'M SURE HE'LL FIND OUT SOONER OR LATER. AND HUMAN OR OTHER-WISE, KYRIAN'LL KILL HIM IF THEY EVER CROSS PATHS.
SO, WHO GOT MARDI GRAS DUTY THIS YEAR?
THEY'RE IMPORTING THAT PSYCHOPATH, ZAREK.

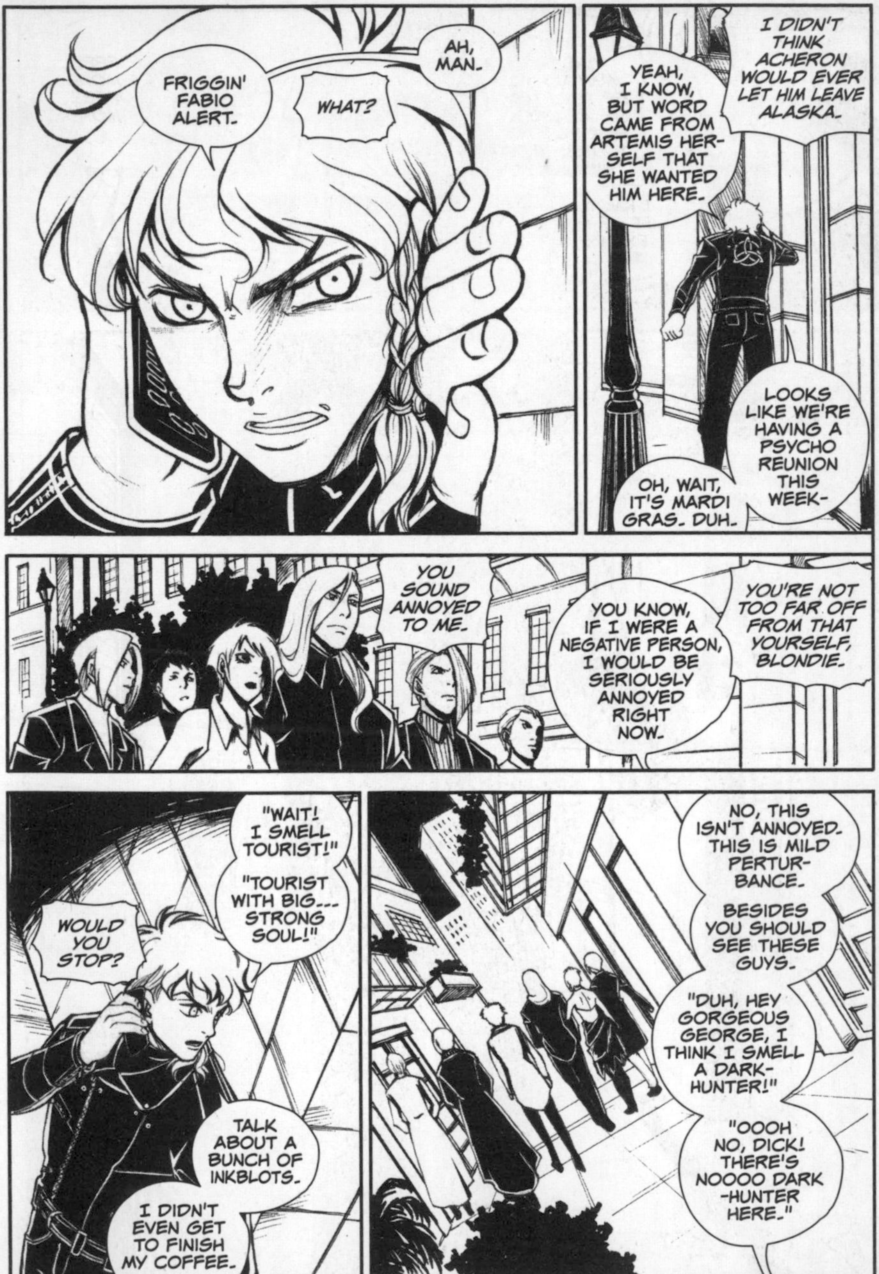

FRIGGIN' FABIO ALERT.
AH, MAN.
WHAT?
YEAH, I KNOW, BUT WORD CAME FROM ARTEMIS HER-SELF THAT SHE WANTED HIM HERE.
I DIDN'T THINK ACHERON WOULD EVER LET HIM LEAVE ALASKA.
LOOKS LIKE WE'RE HAVING A PSYCHO REUNION THIS WEEK-
OH, WAIT, IT'S MARDI GRAS. DUH.
YOU SOUND ANNOYED TO ME.
YOU KNOW, IF I WERE A NEGATIVE PERSON, I WOULD BE SERIOUSLY ANNOYED RIGHT NOW.
YOU'RE NOT TOO FAR OFF FROM THAT YOURSELF, BLONDIE.
"WAIT! I SMELL TOURIST!"
"TOURIST WITH BIG... STRONG SOUL!"
WOULD YOU STOP?
TALK ABOUT A BUNCH OF INKBLOTS.
I DIDN'T EVEN GET TO FINISH MY COFFEE.
NO, THIS ISN'T ANNOYED. THIS IS MILD PERTUR-BANCE.
BESIDES YOU SHOULD SEE THESE GUYS.
"DUH, HEY GORGEOUS GEORGE, I THINK I SMELL A DARK-HUNTER!"
"OOOH NO, DICK! THERE'S NOOOO DARK-HUNTER HERE."

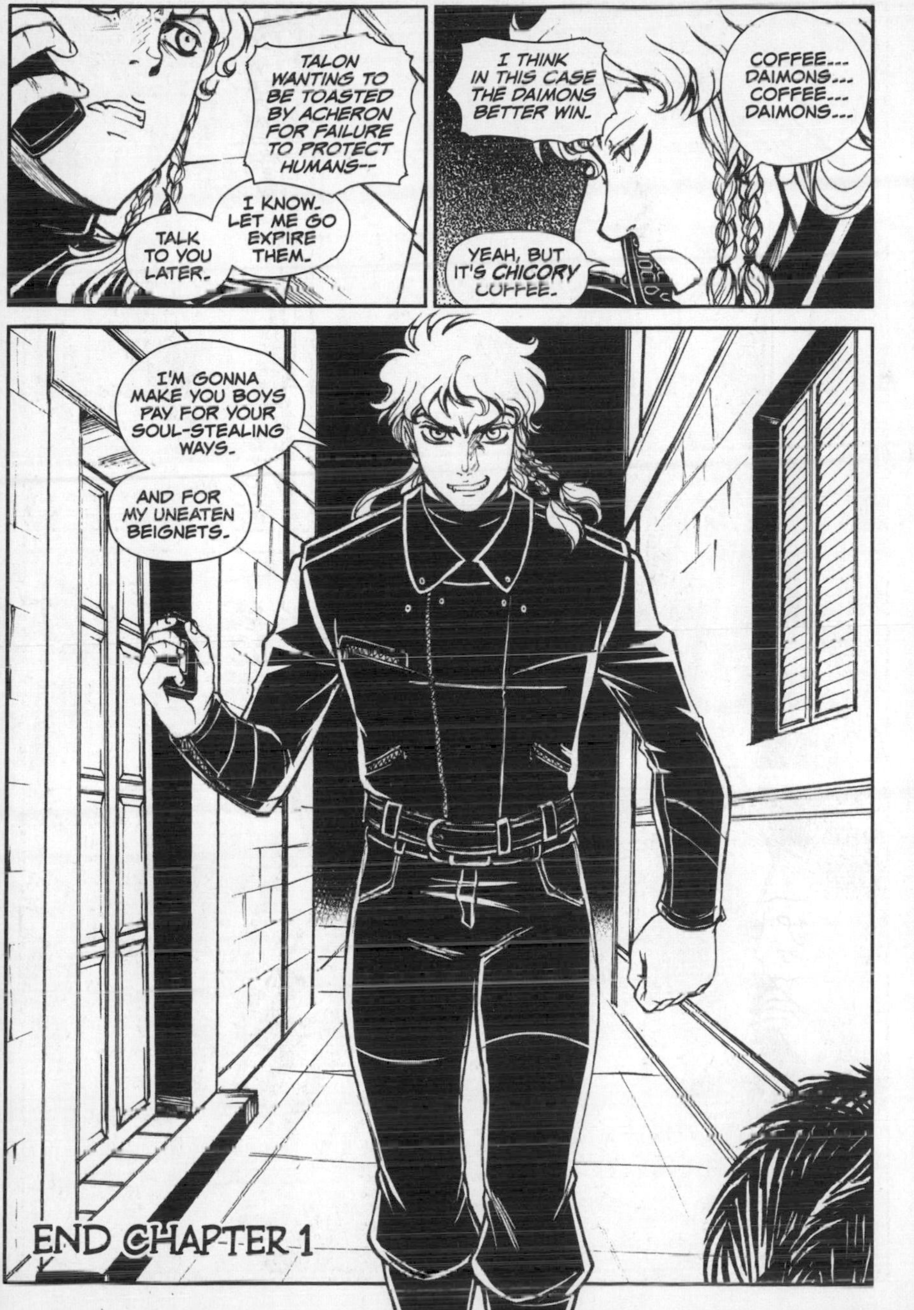
TALON WANTING TO BE TOASTED BY ACHERON FOR FAILURE TO PROTECT HUMANS--
I KNOW. LET ME GO EXPIRE THEM.
TALK TO YOU LATER.
I THINK IN THIS CASE THE DAIMONS BETTER WIN.
COFFEE... DAIMONS... COFFEE... DAIMONS...
YEAH, BUT IT'S CHICORY COFFEE.
I'M GONNA MAKE YOU BOYS PAY FOR YOUR SOUL-STEALING WAYS.
AND FOR MY UNEATEN BEIGNETS.
END CHAPTER 1

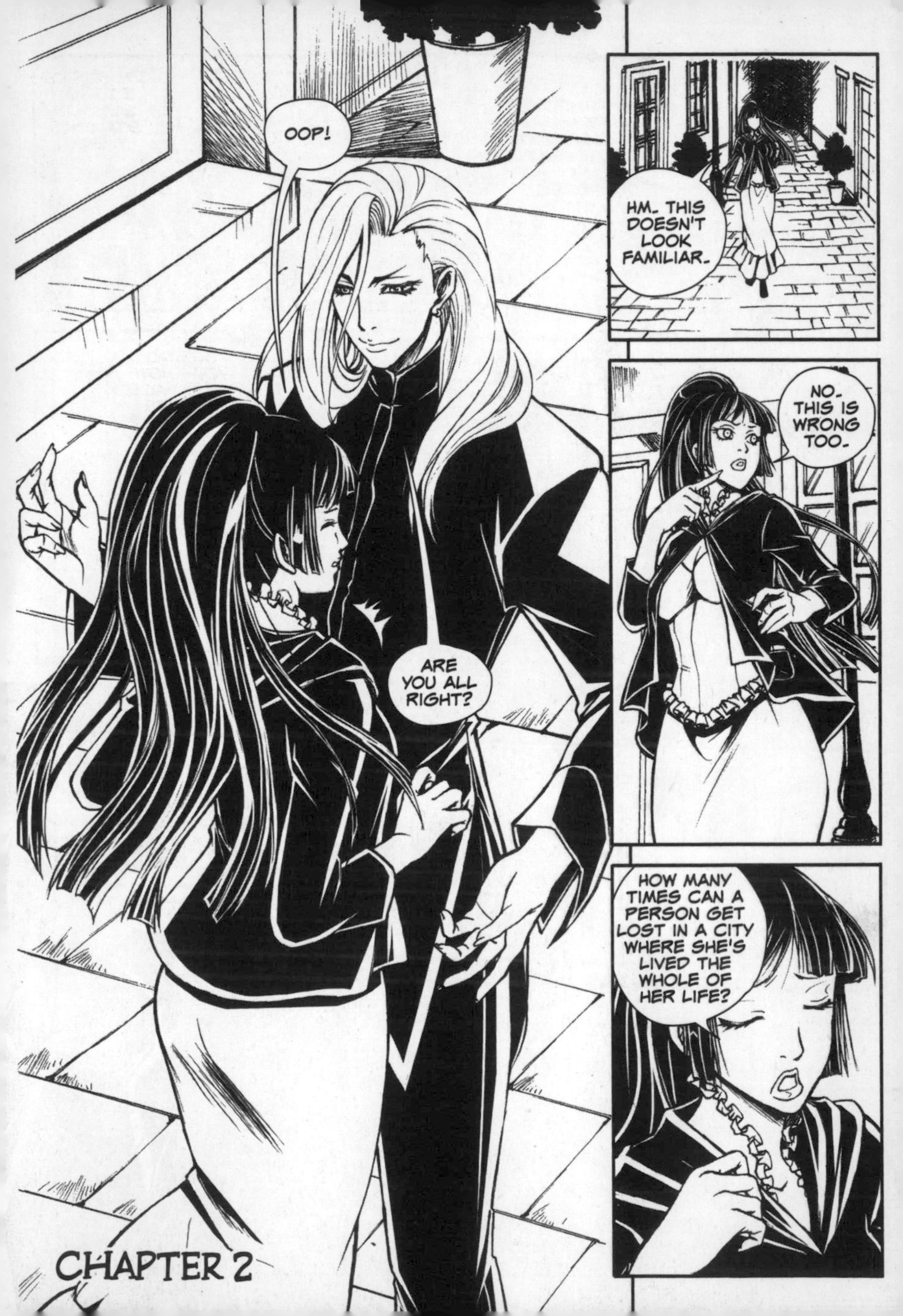
HM. THIS DOESN'T LOOK FAMILIAR.
NO. THIS IS WRONG TOO.
HOW MANY TIMES CAN A PERSON GET LOST IN A CITY WHERE SHE'S LIVED THE WHOLE OF HER LIFE?
OOP!
ARE YOU ALL RIGHT?
CHAPTER 2

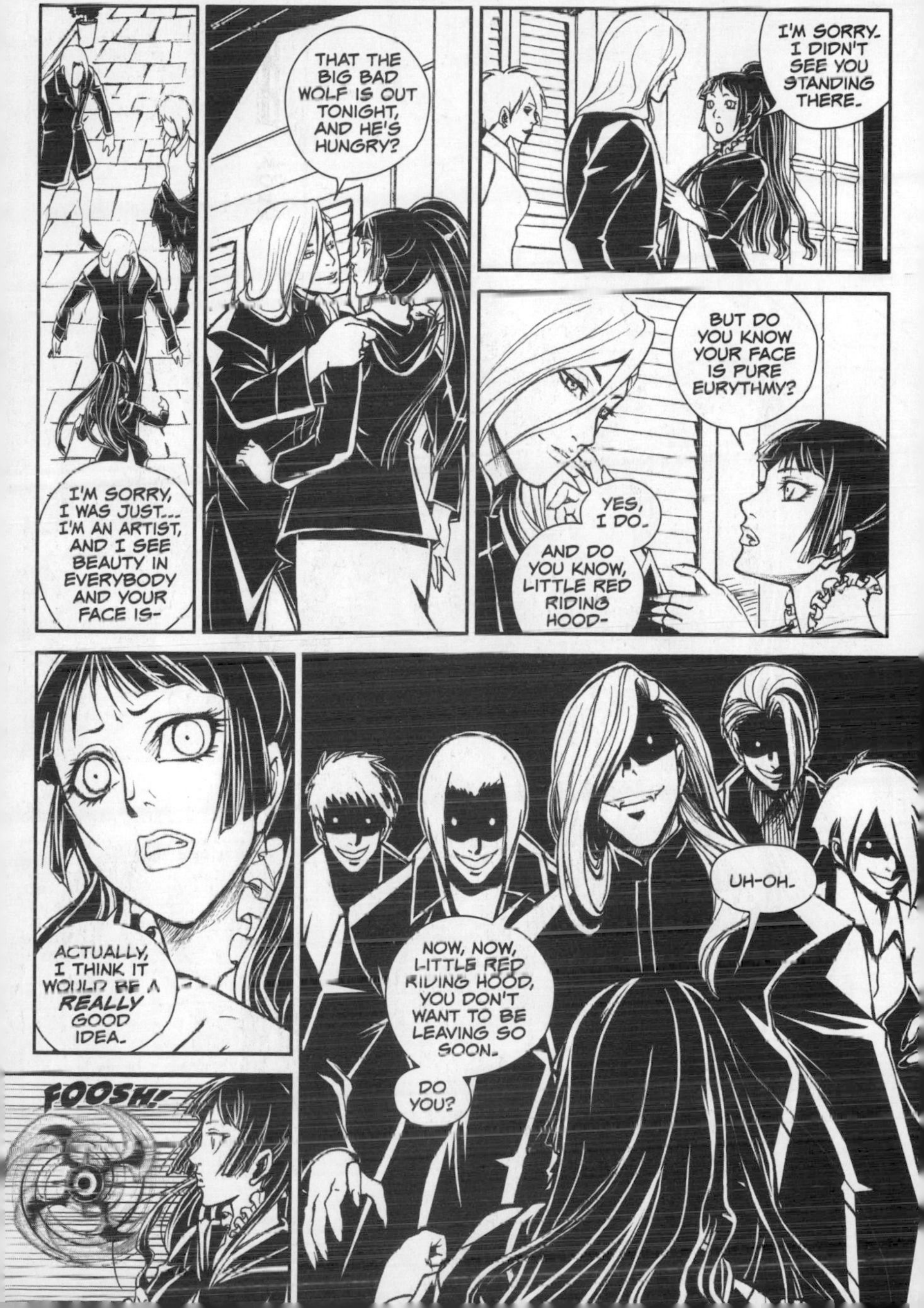
I'M SORRY, I WAS JUST... I'M AN ARTIST, AND I SEE BEAUTY IN EVERYBODY AND YOUR FACE IS-
THAT THE BIG BAD WOLF IS OUT TONIGHT, AND HE'S HUNGRY?
I'M SORRY. I DIDN'T SEE YOU STANDING THERE.
BUT DO YOU KNOW YOUR FACE IS PURE EURYTHMY?
YES, I DO.
AND DO YOU KNOW, LITTLE RED RIDING HOOD-
ACTUALLY, I THINK IT WOULD BE A REALLY GOOD IDEA.
FOOSH!
UH-OH.
NOW, NOW, LITTLE RED RIDING HOOD, YOU DON'T WANT TO BE LEAVING SO SOON.
DO YOU?

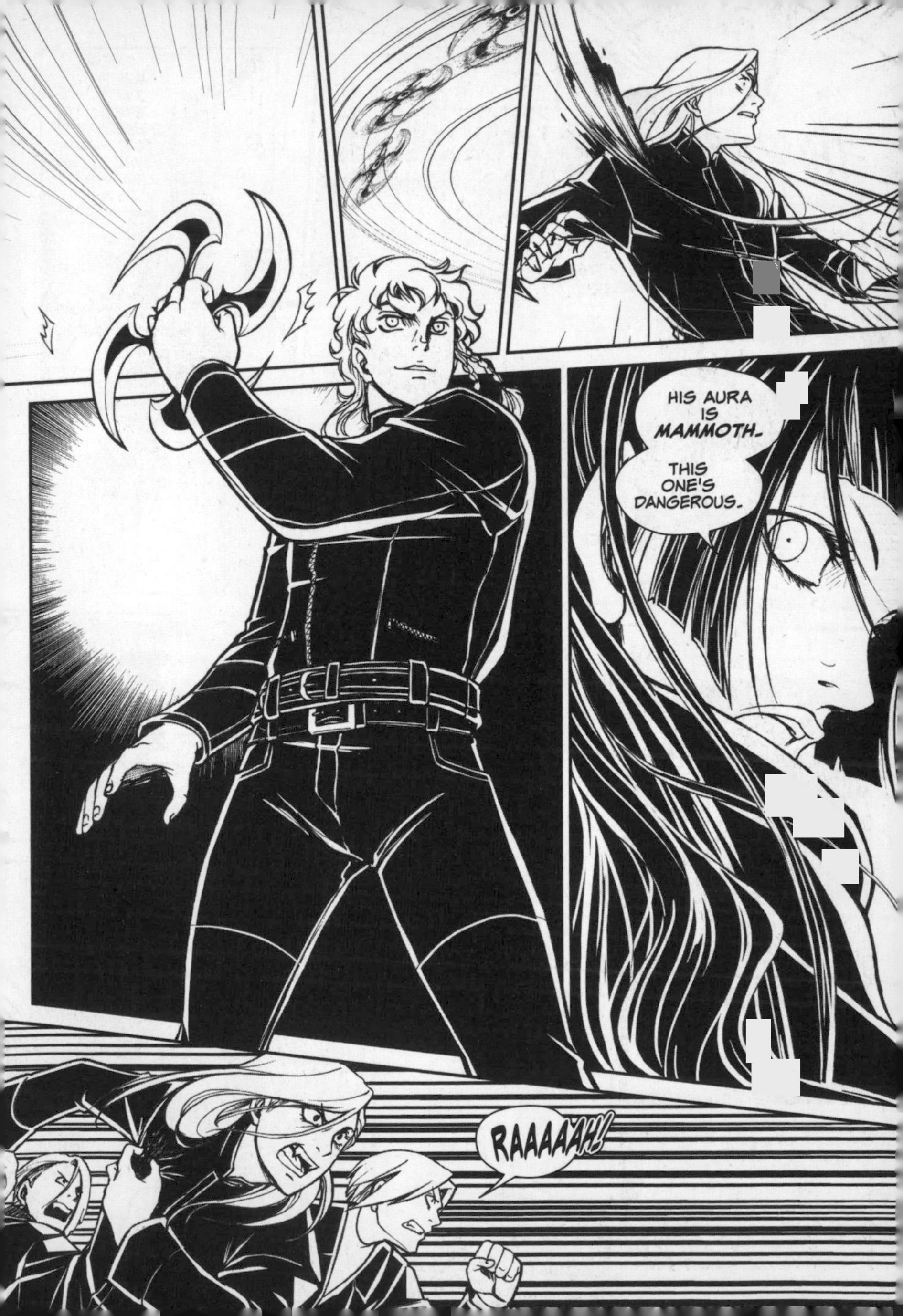
HIS AURA IS MAMMOTH.
THIS ONE'S DANGEROUS.
RAAAAAH!

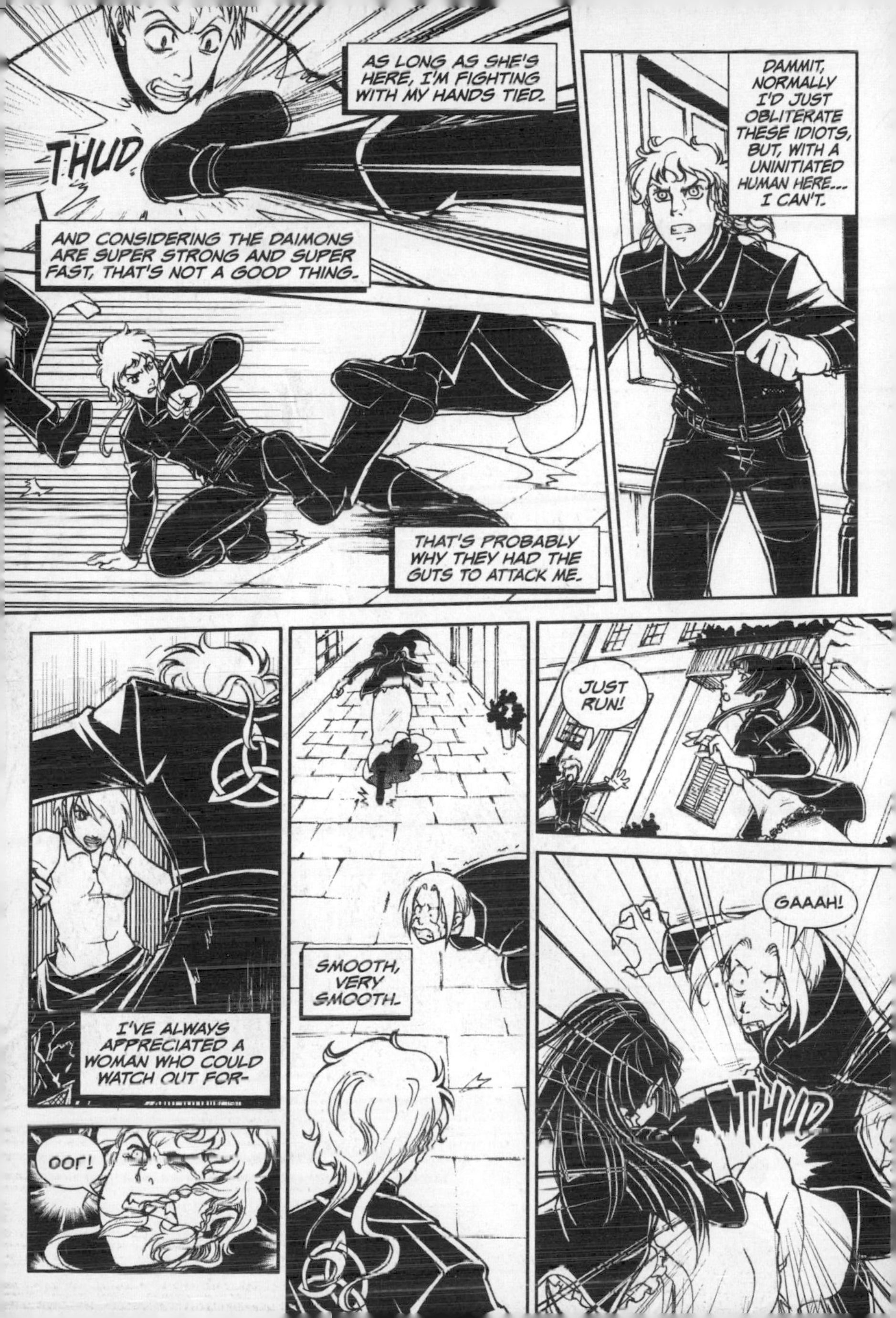
AS LONG AS SHE'S HERE, I'M FIGHTING WITH MY HANDS TIED.
THUD
AND CONSIDERING THE DAIMONS ARE SUPER STRONG AND SUPER FAST, THAT'S NOT A GOOD THING.
DAMMIT, NORMALLY I'D JUST OBLITERATE THESE IDIOTS, BUT, WITH A UNINITIATED HUMAN HERE... I CAN'T.
THAT'S PROBABLY WHY THEY HAD THE GUTS TO ATTACK ME.
I'VE ALWAYS APPRECIATED A WOMAN WHO COULD WATCH OUT FOR-
OOF!
SMOOTH, VERY SMOOTH.
JUST RUN!
GAAAH!
THUD

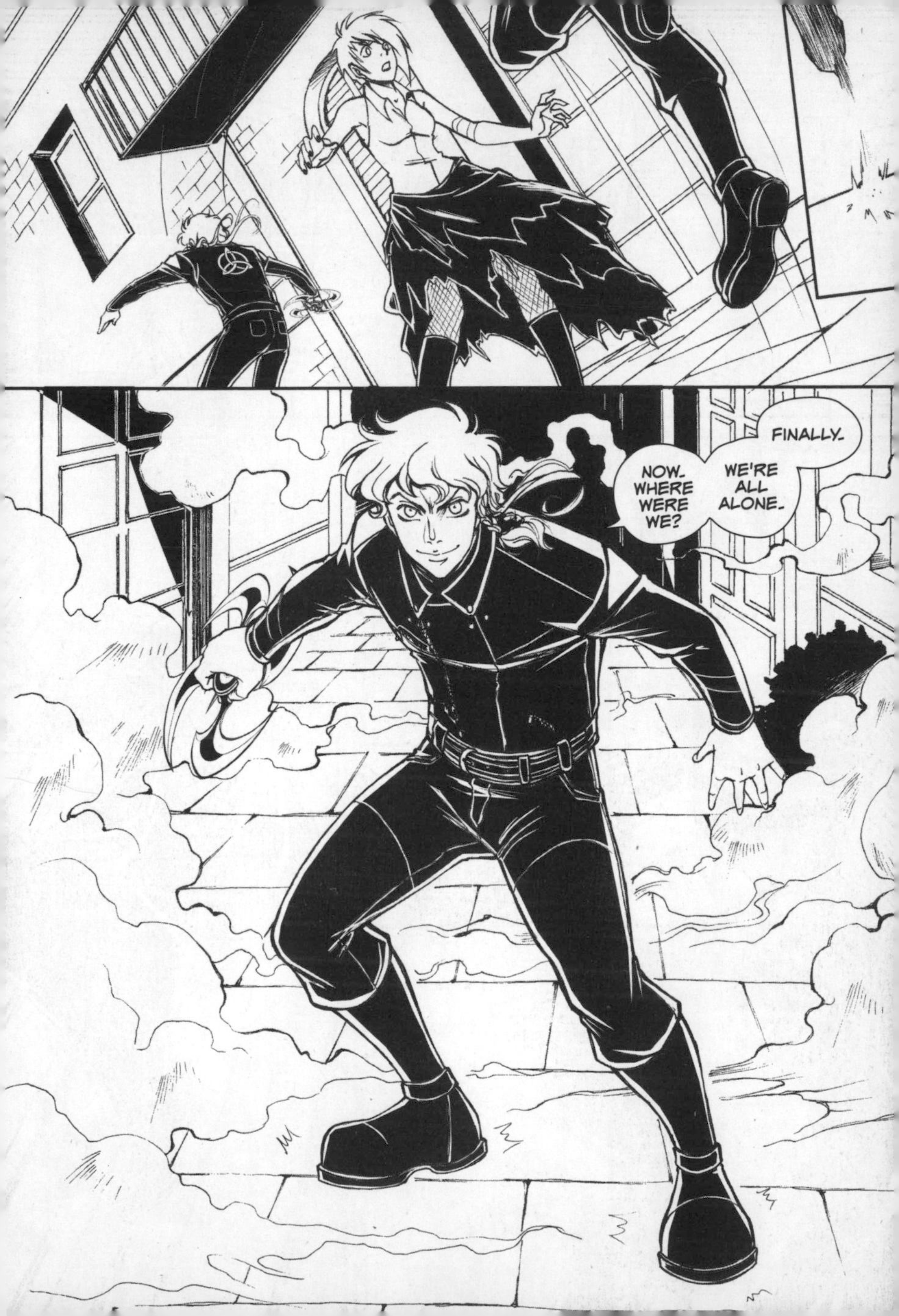
FINALLY. WE'RE ALL ALONE.
NOW. WHERE WERE WE?

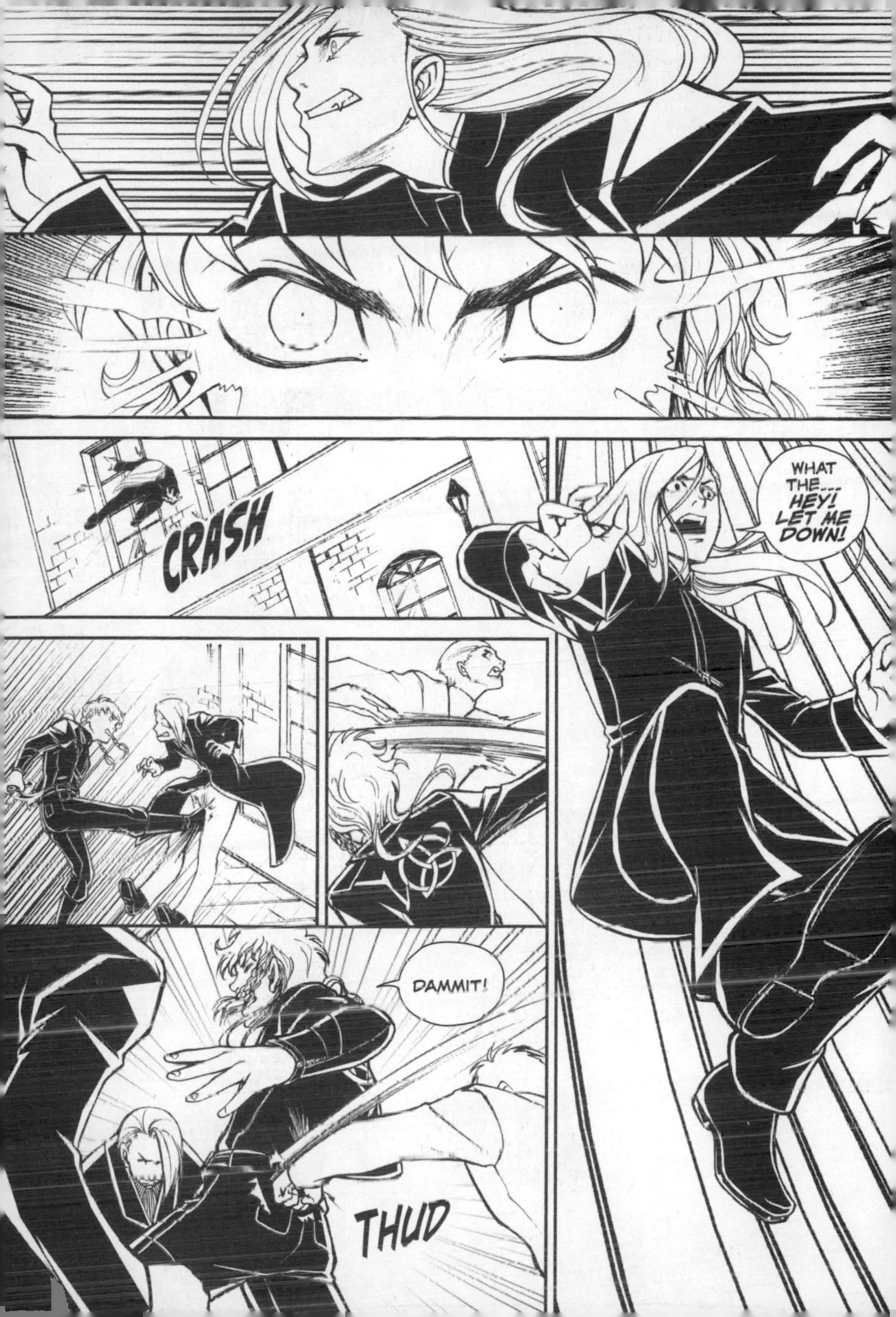

CRASH
WHAT THE... HEY! LET ME DOWN!
DAMMIT!
THUD

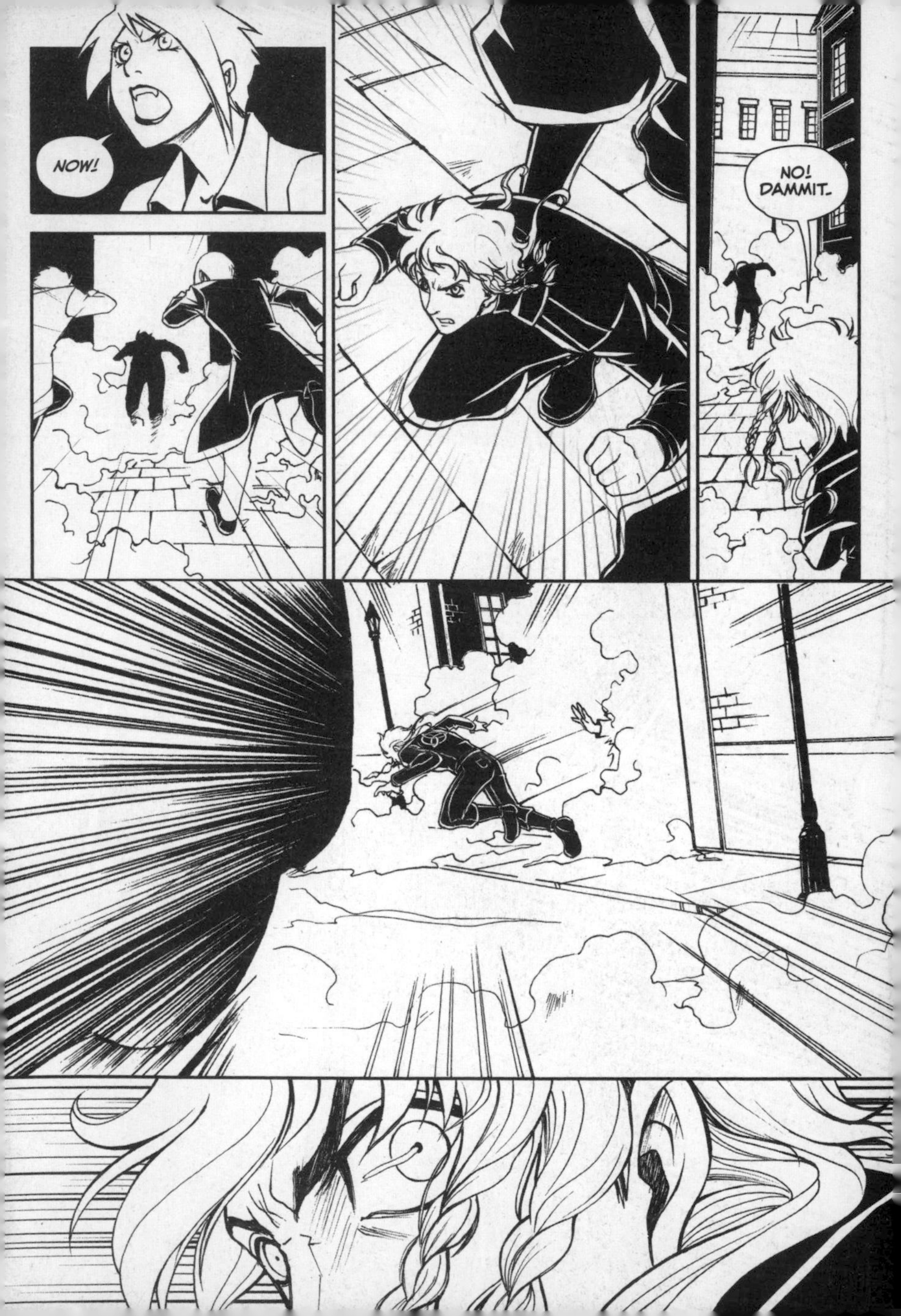
NOW!
NO! DAMMIT_

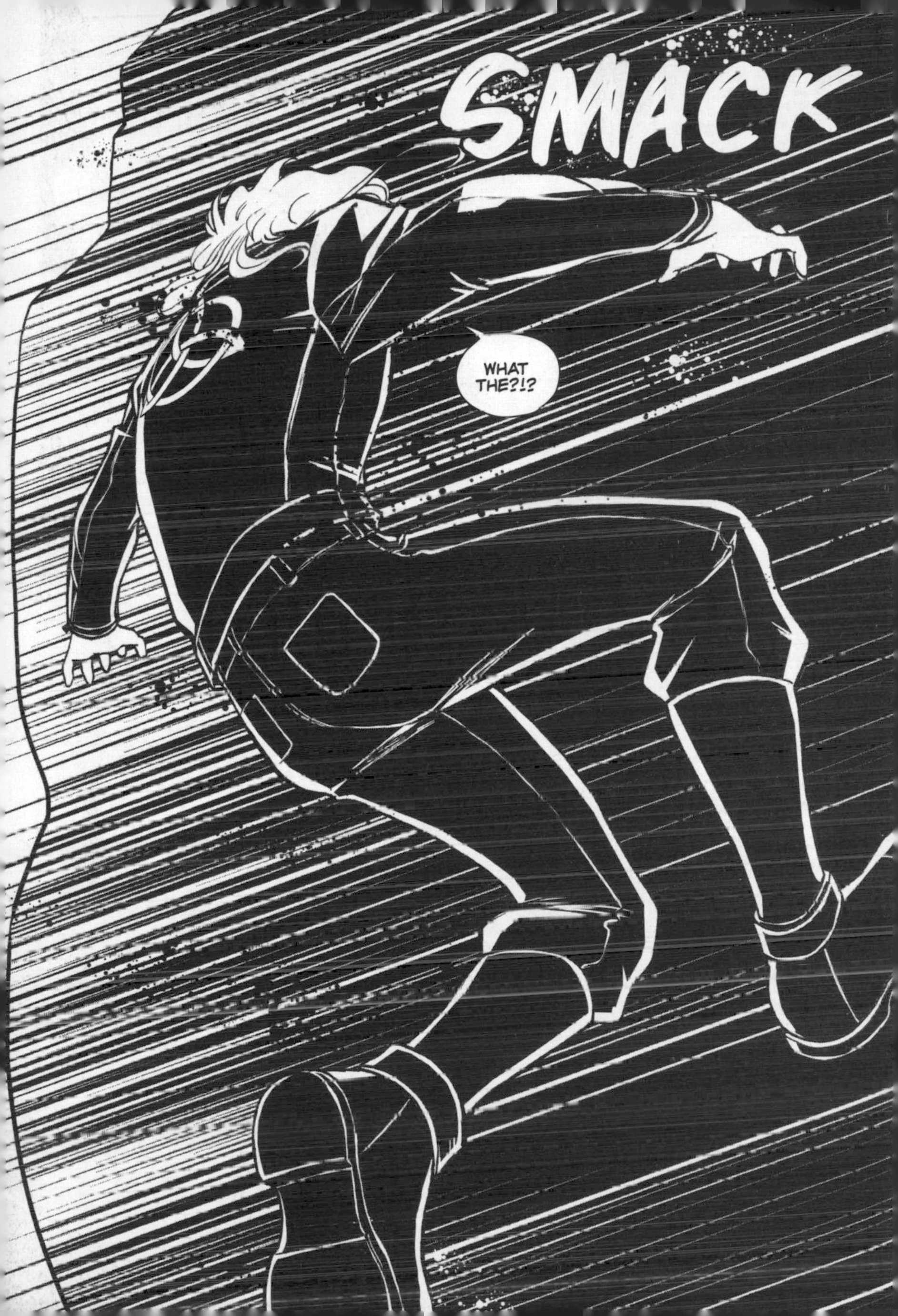
SMACK
WHAT THE?!?

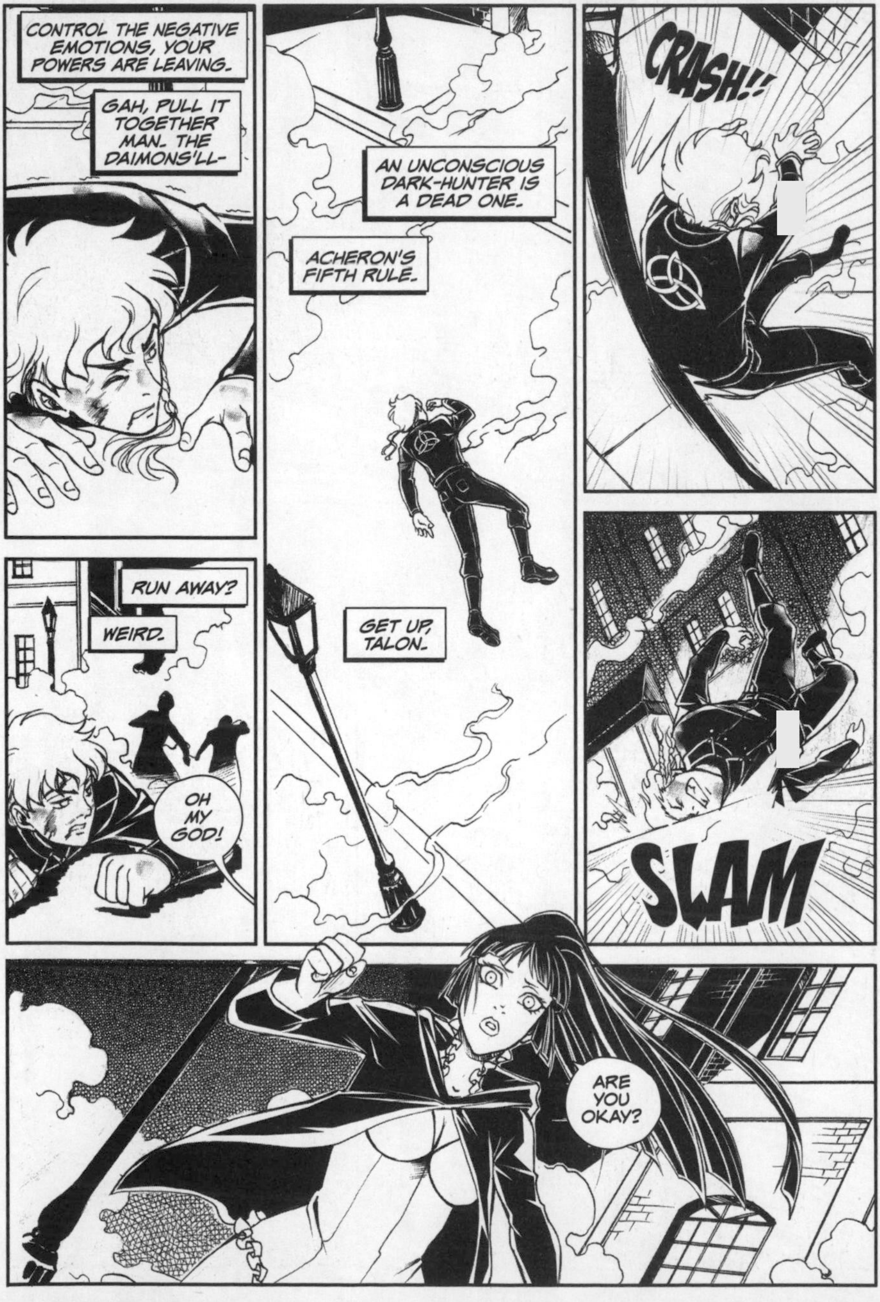
CONTROL THE NEGATIVE EMOTIONS, YOUR POWERS ARE LEAVING.
GAH, PULL IT TOGETHER MAN. THE DAIMONS'LL-
AN UNCONSCIOUS DARK-HUNTER IS A DEAD ONE.
ACHERON'S FIFTH RULE.
CRASH!!
SLAM
GET UP, TALON.
RUN AWAY?
WEIRD.
OH MY GOD!
ARE YOU OKAY?

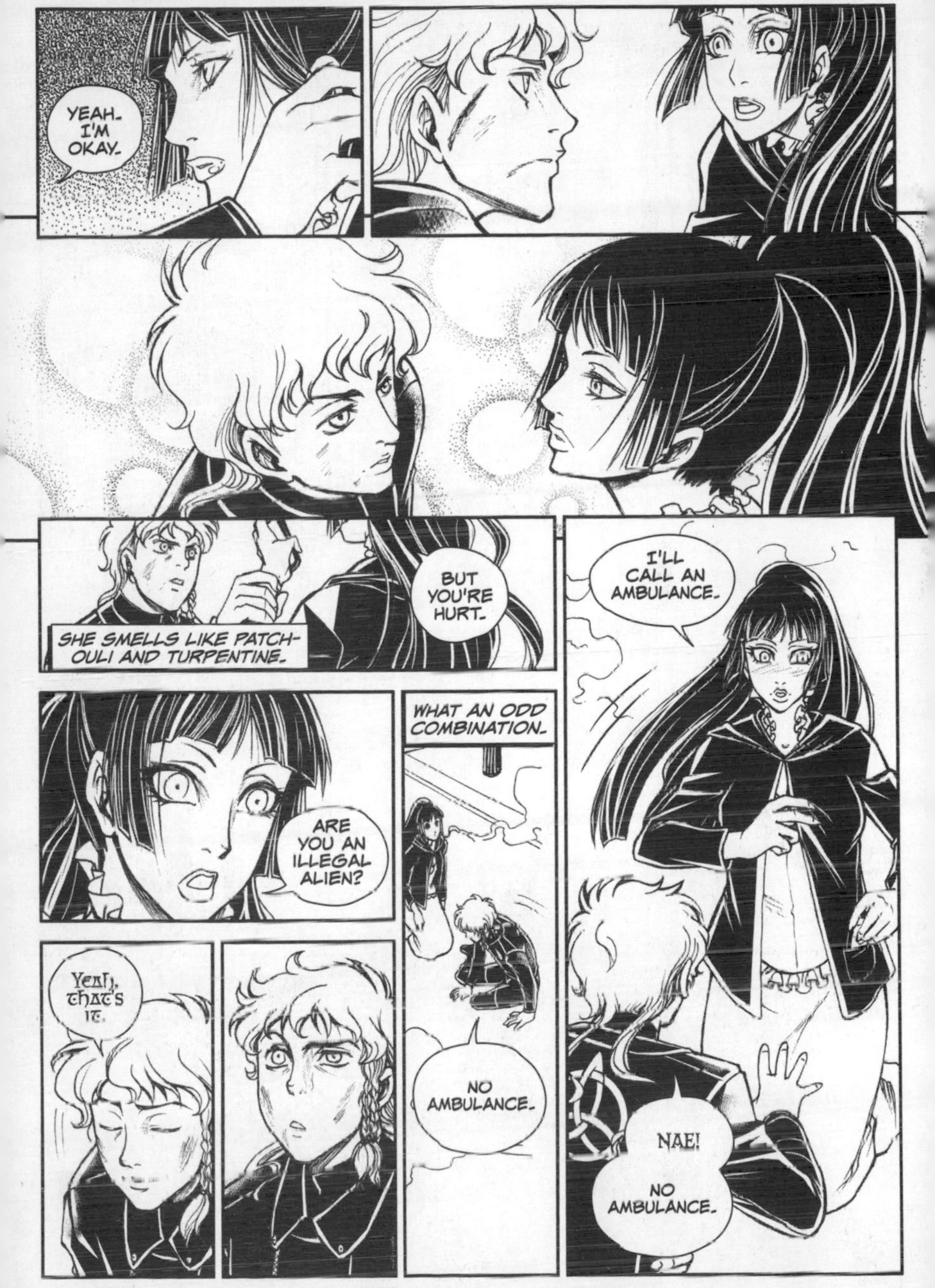
YEAH. I'M OKAY.
BUT YOU'RE HURT.
SHE SMELLS LIKE PATCH-OULI AND TURPENTINE.
I'LL CALL AN AMBULANCE.
ARE YOU AN ILLEGAL ALIEN?
WHAT AN ODD COMBINATION.
YEAH, THAT'S IT.
NO AMBULANCE.
NAE!
NO AMBULANCE.

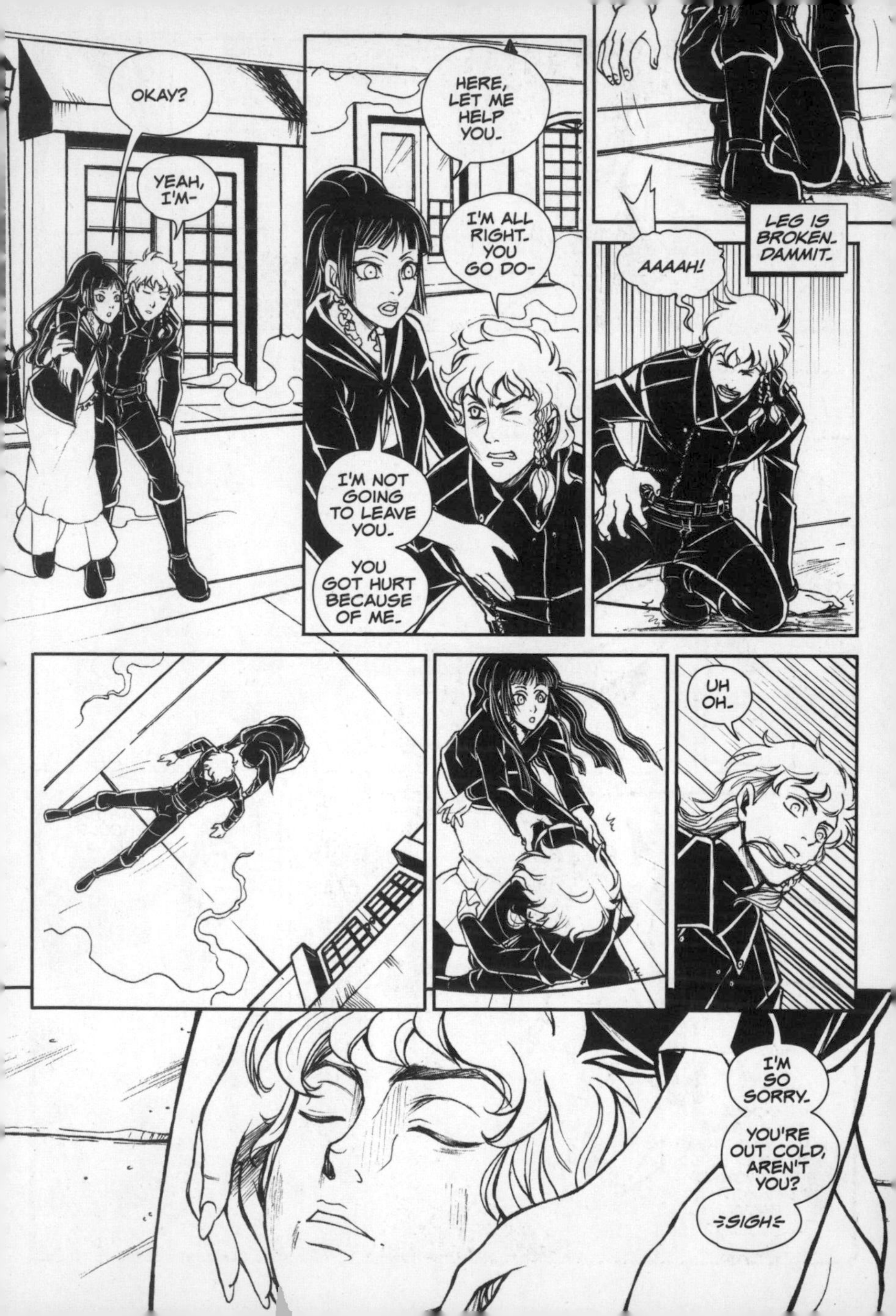

OKAY?
YEAH, I'M-
HERE, LET ME HELP YOU.
I'M ALL RIGHT. YOU GO DO-
I'M NOT GOING TO LEAVE YOU.
YOU GOT HURT BECAUSE OF ME.
LEG IS BROKEN. DAMMIT.
AAAAH!
UH OH.
I'M SO SORRY.
YOU'RE OUT COLD, AREN'T YOU?
=SIGH=

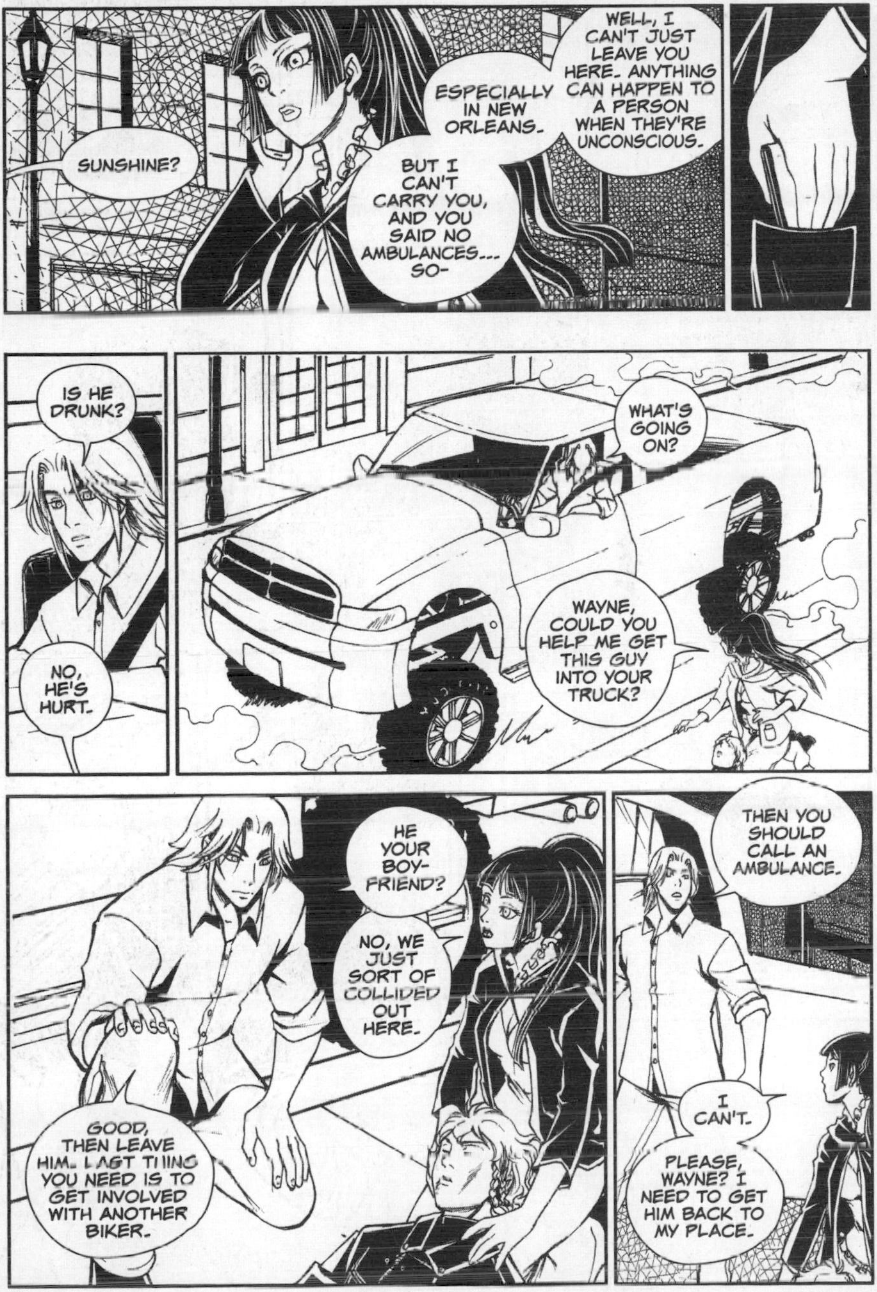
SUNSHINE?
BUT I CAN'T CARRY YOU, AND YOU SAID NO AMBULANCES... SO-
ESPECIALLY IN NEW ORLEANS.
WELL, I CAN'T JUST LEAVE YOU HERE. ANYTHING CAN HAPPEN TO A PERSON WHEN THEY'RE UNCONSCIOUS.
WHAT'S GOING ON?
WAYNE, COULD YOU HELP ME GET THIS GUY INTO YOUR TRUCK?
IS HE DRUNK?
NO, HE'S HURT.
HE YOUR BOY-FRIEND?
NO, WE JUST SORT OF COLLIDED OUT HERE.
GOOD, THEN LEAVE HIM. LAST THING YOU NEED IS TO GET INVOLVED WITH ANOTHER BIKER.
THEN YOU SHOULD CALL AN AMBULANCE.
I CAN'T.
PLEASE, WAYNE? I NEED TO GET HIM BACK TO MY PLACE.

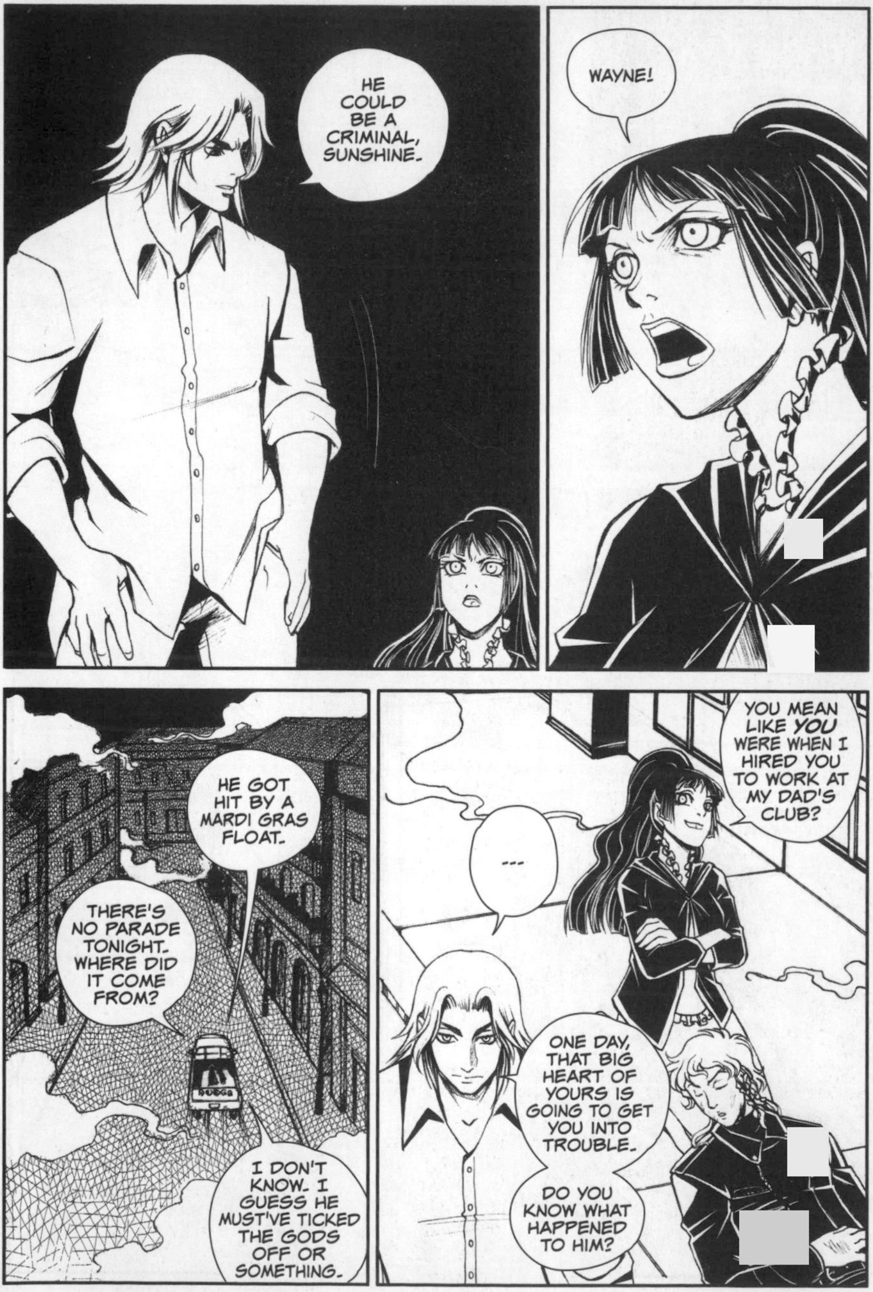
HE COULD BE A CRIMINAL, SUNSHINE.
WAYNE!
HE GOT HIT BY A MARDI GRAS FLOAT.
THERE'S NO PARADE TONIGHT. WHERE DID IT COME FROM?
I DON'T KNOW. I GUESS HE MUST'VE TICKED THE GODS OFF OR SOMETHING.
ONE DAY, THAT BIG HEART OF YOURS IS GOING TO GET YOU INTO TROUBLE.
YOU MEAN LIKE *YOU* WERE WHEN I HIRED YOU TO WORK AT MY DAD'S CLUB?
...
DO YOU KNOW WHAT HAPPENED TO HIM?

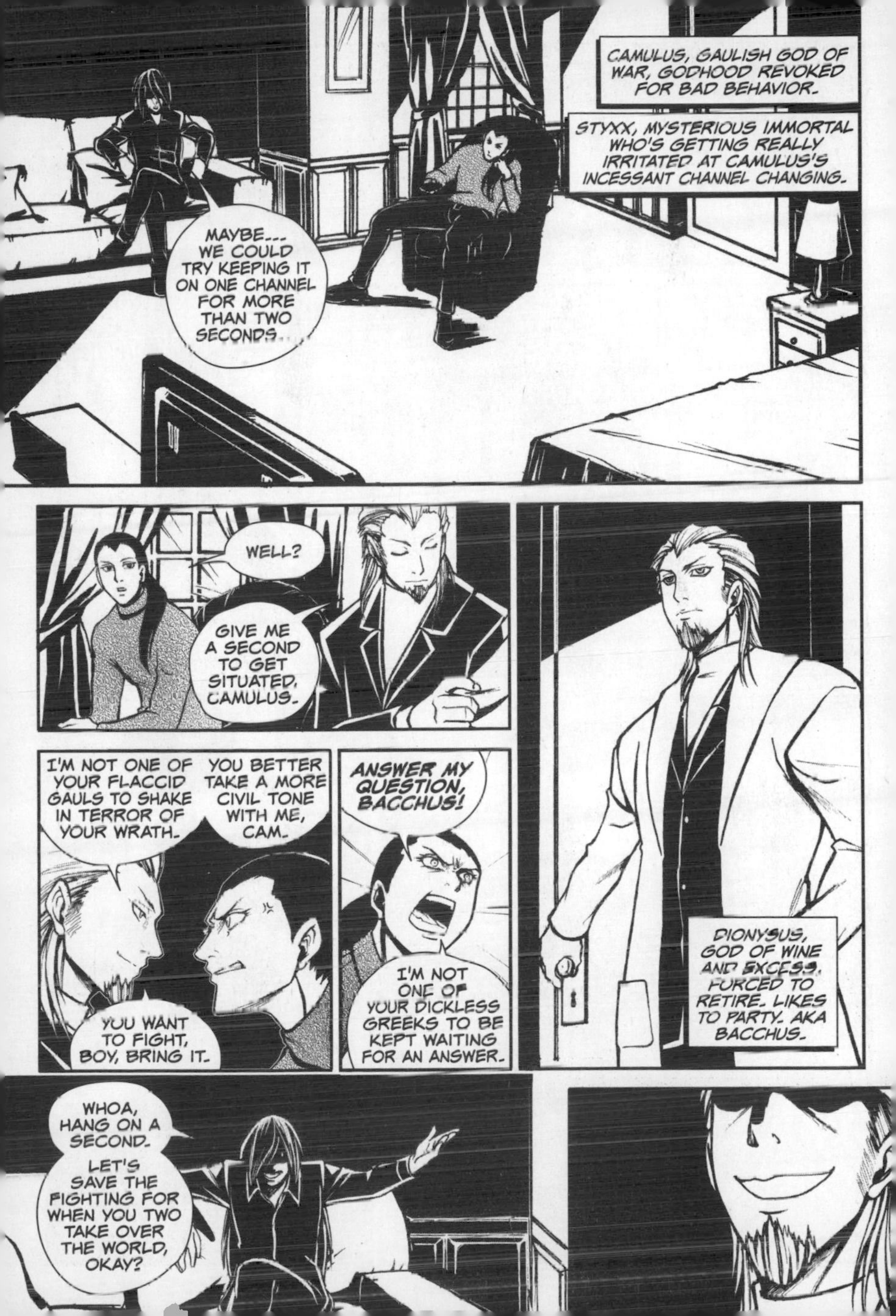
CAMULUS, GAULISH GOD OF WAR, GODHOOD REVOKED FOR BAD BEHAVIOR.
STYXX, MYSTERIOUS IMMORTAL WHO'S GETTING REALLY IRRITATED AT CAMULUS'S INCESSANT CHANNEL CHANGING.
MAYBE... WE COULD TRY KEEPING IT ON ONE CHANNEL FOR MORE THAN TWO SECONDS...
WELL?
GIVE ME A SECOND TO GET SITUATED, CAMULUS.
DIONYSUS, GOD OF WINE AND EXCESS. FORCED TO RETIRE. LIKES TO PARTY. AKA BACCHUS.
I'M NOT ONE OF YOUR FLACCID GAULS TO SHAKE IN TERROR OF YOUR WRATH.
YOU BETTER TAKE A MORE CIVIL TONE WITH ME, CAM.
YOU WANT TO FIGHT, BOY, BRING IT.
ANSWER MY QUESTION, BACCHUS!
I'M NOT ONE OF YOUR DICKLESS GREEKS TO BE KEPT WAITING FOR AN ANSWER.
WHOA, HANG ON A SECOND.
LET'S SAVE THE FIGHTING FOR WHEN YOU TWO TAKE OVER THE WORLD, OKAY?

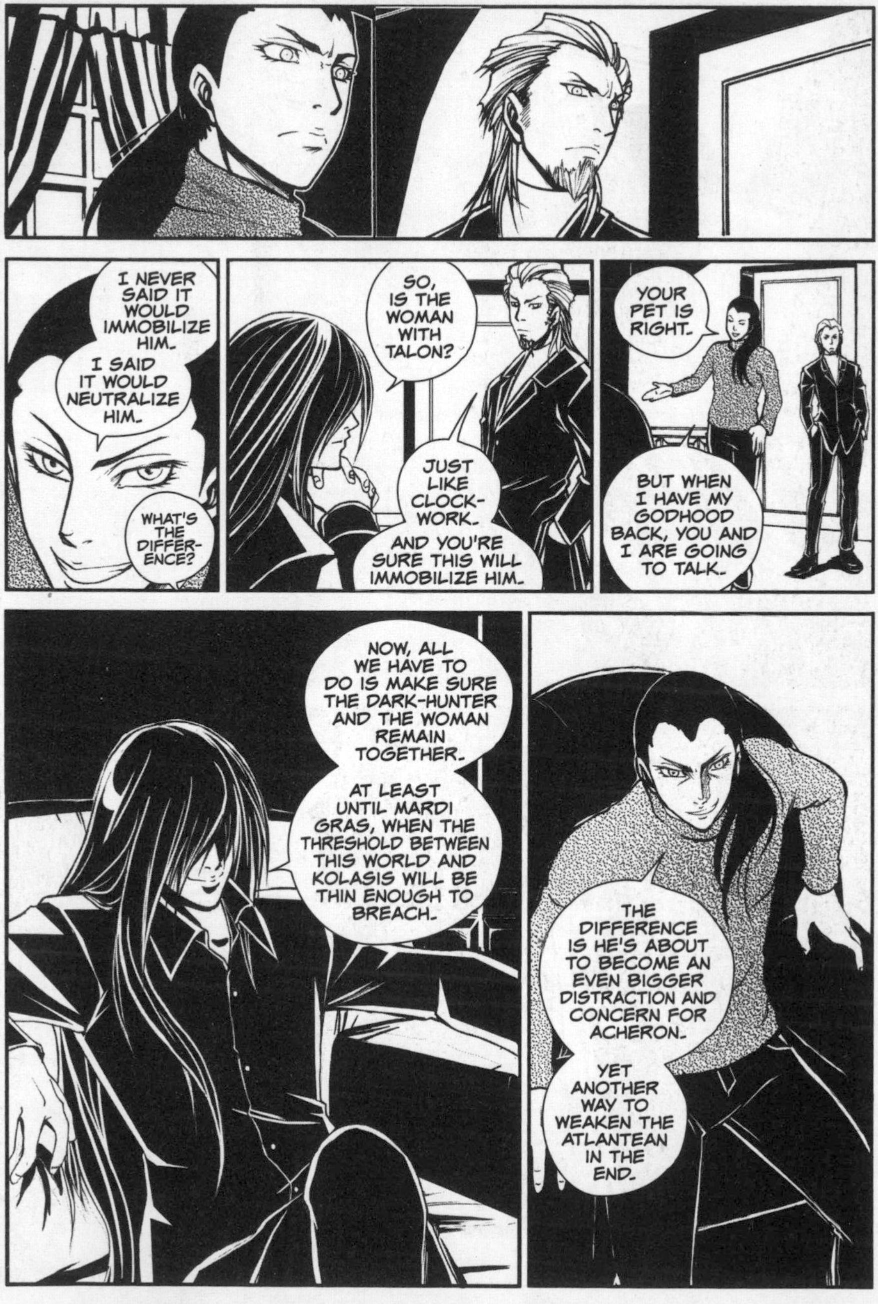

I NEVER SAID IT WOULD IMMOBILIZE HIM.
I SAID IT WOULD NEUTRALIZE HIM.
WHAT'S THE DIFFERENCE?
SO, IS THE WOMAN WITH TALON?
JUST LIKE CLOCKWORK.
AND YOU'RE SURE THIS WILL IMMOBILIZE HIM.
YOUR PET IS RIGHT.
BUT WHEN I HAVE MY GODHOOD BACK, YOU AND I ARE GOING TO TALK.
NOW, ALL WE HAVE TO DO IS MAKE SURE THE DARK-HUNTER AND THE WOMAN REMAIN TOGETHER.
AT LEAST UNTIL MARDI GRAS, WHEN THE THRESHOLD BETWEEN THIS WORLD AND KOLASIS WILL BE THIN ENOUGH TO BREACH.
THE DIFFERENCE IS HE'S ABOUT TO BECOME AN EVEN BIGGER DISTRACTION AND CONCERN FOR ACHERON.
YET ANOTHER WAY TO WEAKEN THE ATLANTEAN IN THE END.

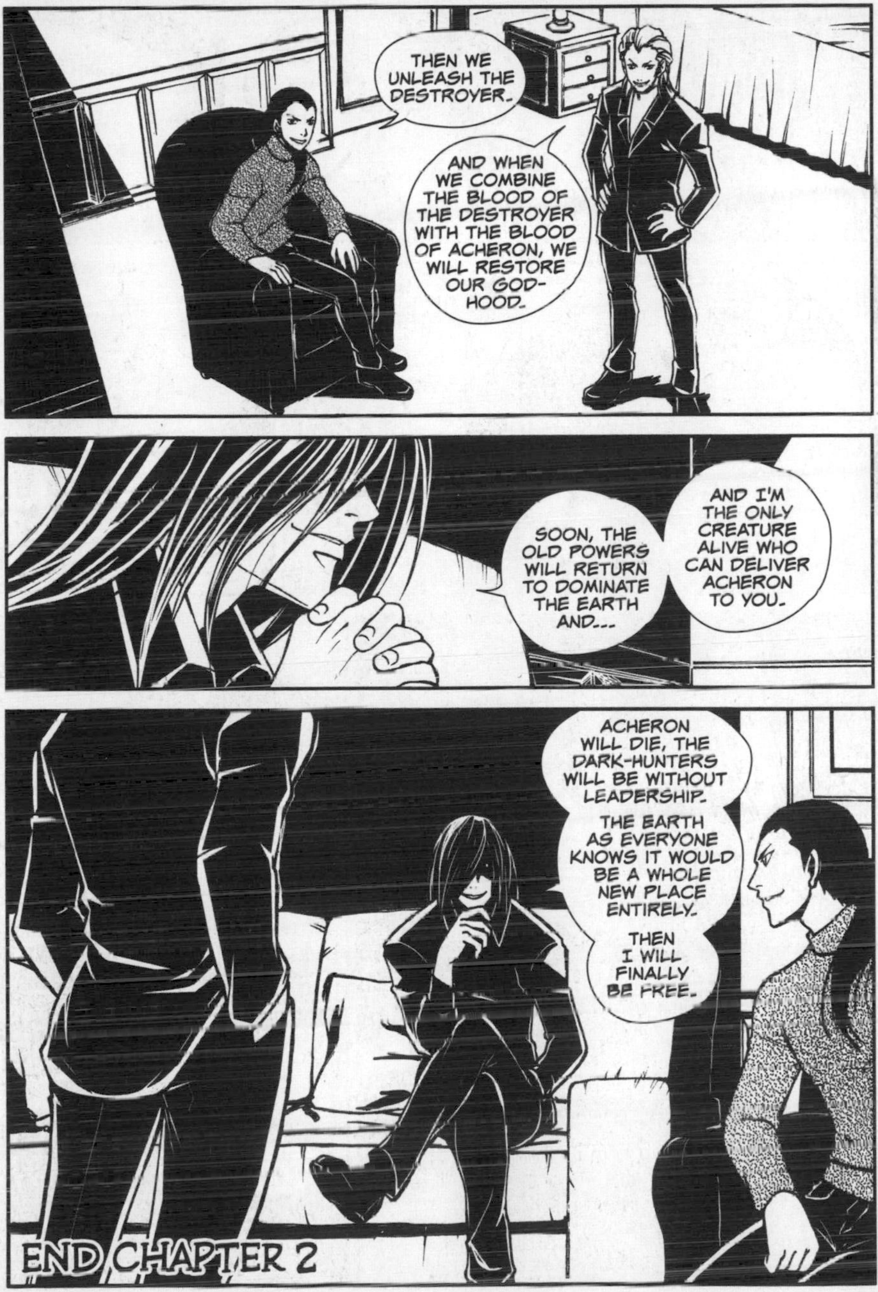
THEN WE UNLEASH THE DESTROYER.
AND WHEN WE COMBINE THE BLOOD OF THE DESTROYER WITH THE BLOOD OF ACHERON, WE WILL RESTORE OUR GOD-HOOD.
SOON, THE OLD POWERS WILL RETURN TO DOMINATE THE EARTH AND...
AND I'M THE ONLY CREATURE ALIVE WHO CAN DELIVER ACHERON TO YOU.
ACHERON WILL DIE, THE DARK-HUNTERS WILL BE WITHOUT LEADERSHIP.
THE EARTH AS EVERYONE KNOWS IT WOULD BE A WHOLE NEW PLACE ENTIRELY.
THEN I WILL FINALLY BE FREE.
END CHAPTER 2

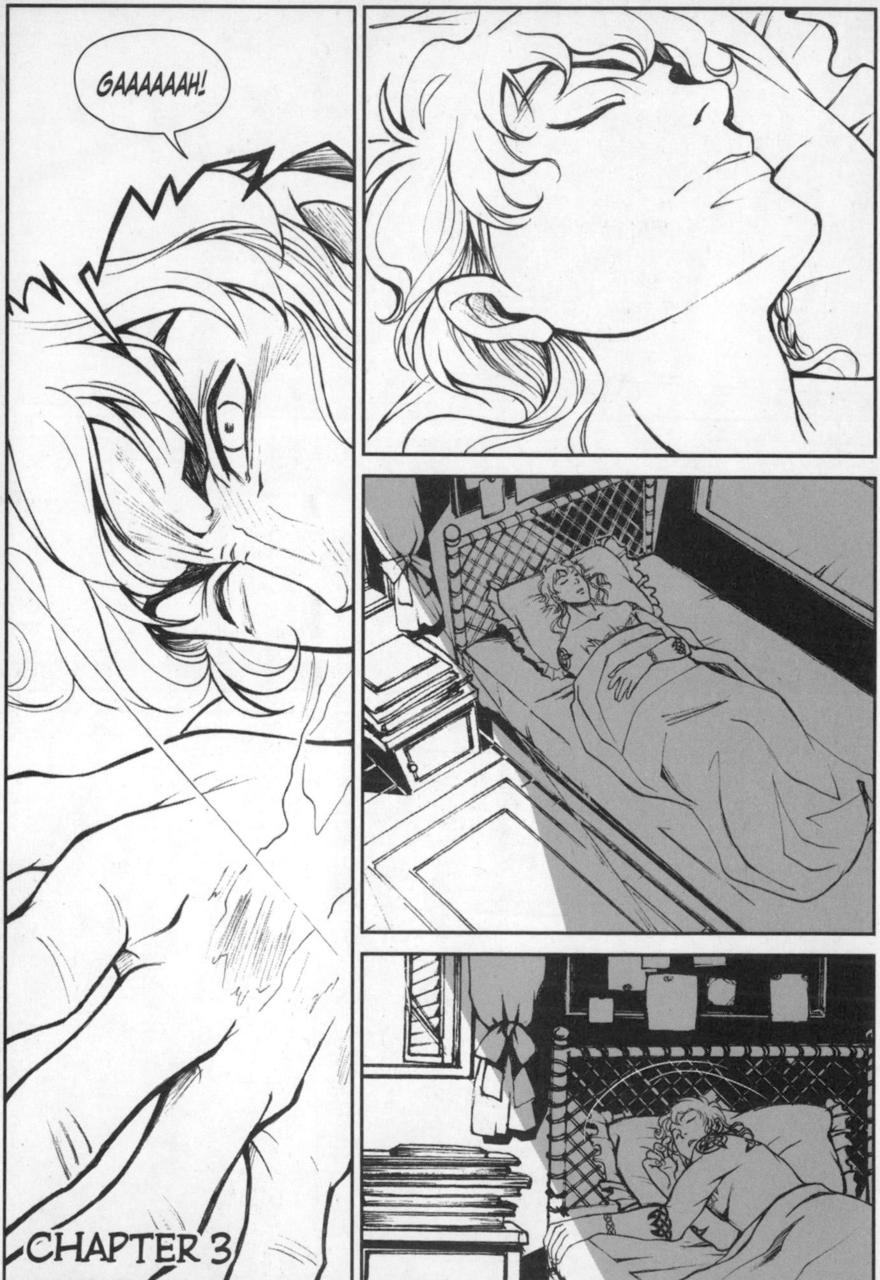
GAAAAAAH!
CHAPTER 3

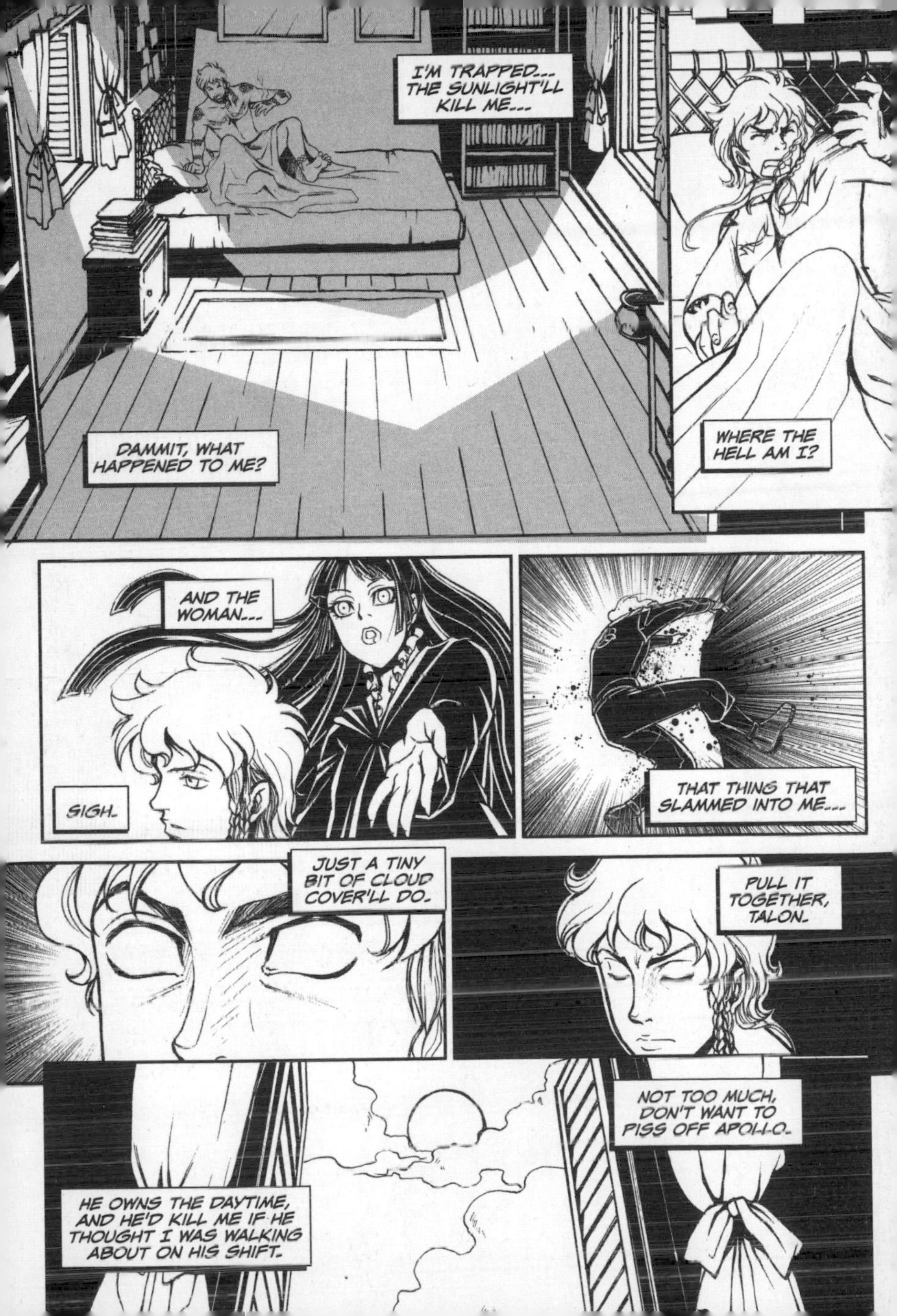
I'M TRAPPED... THE SUNLIGHT'LL KILL ME...
DAMMIT, WHAT HAPPENED TO ME?
WHERE THE HELL AM I?
AND THE WOMAN...
SIGH.
THAT THING THAT SLAMMED INTO ME...
JUST A TINY BIT OF CLOUD COVER'LL DO.
PULL IT TOGETHER, TALON.
NOT TOO MUCH, DON'T WANT TO PISS OFF APOLLO.
HE OWNS THE DAYTIME, AND HE'D KILL ME IF HE THOUGHT I WAS WALKING ABOUT ON HIS SHIFT.

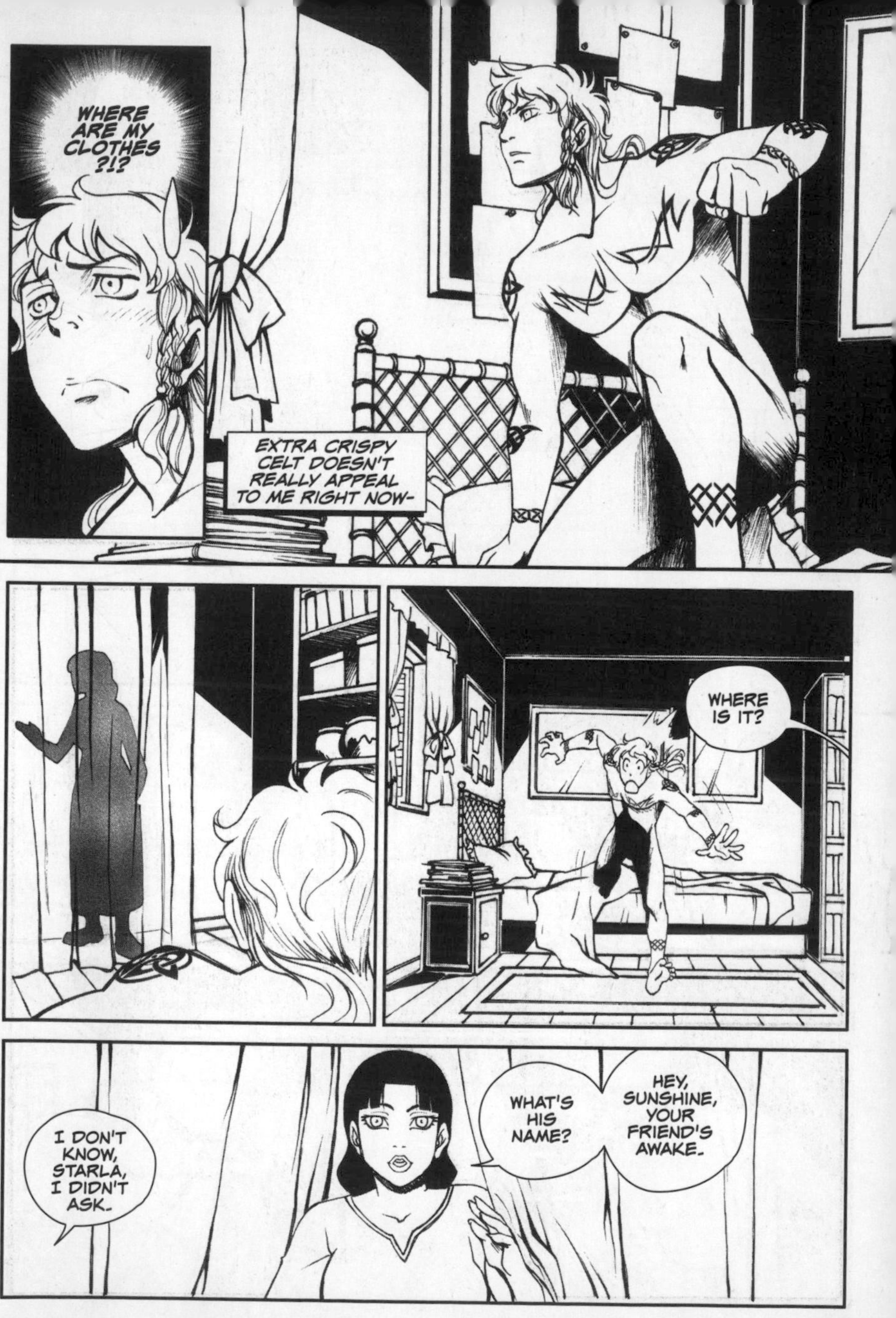
WHERE ARE MY CLOTHES ?!?
EXTRA CRISPY CELT DOESN'T REALLY APPEAL TO ME RIGHT NOW-
WHERE IS IT?
HEY, SUNSHINE, YOUR FRIEND'S AWAKE.
WHAT'S HIS NAME?
I DON'T KNOW, STARLA, I DIDN'T ASK.

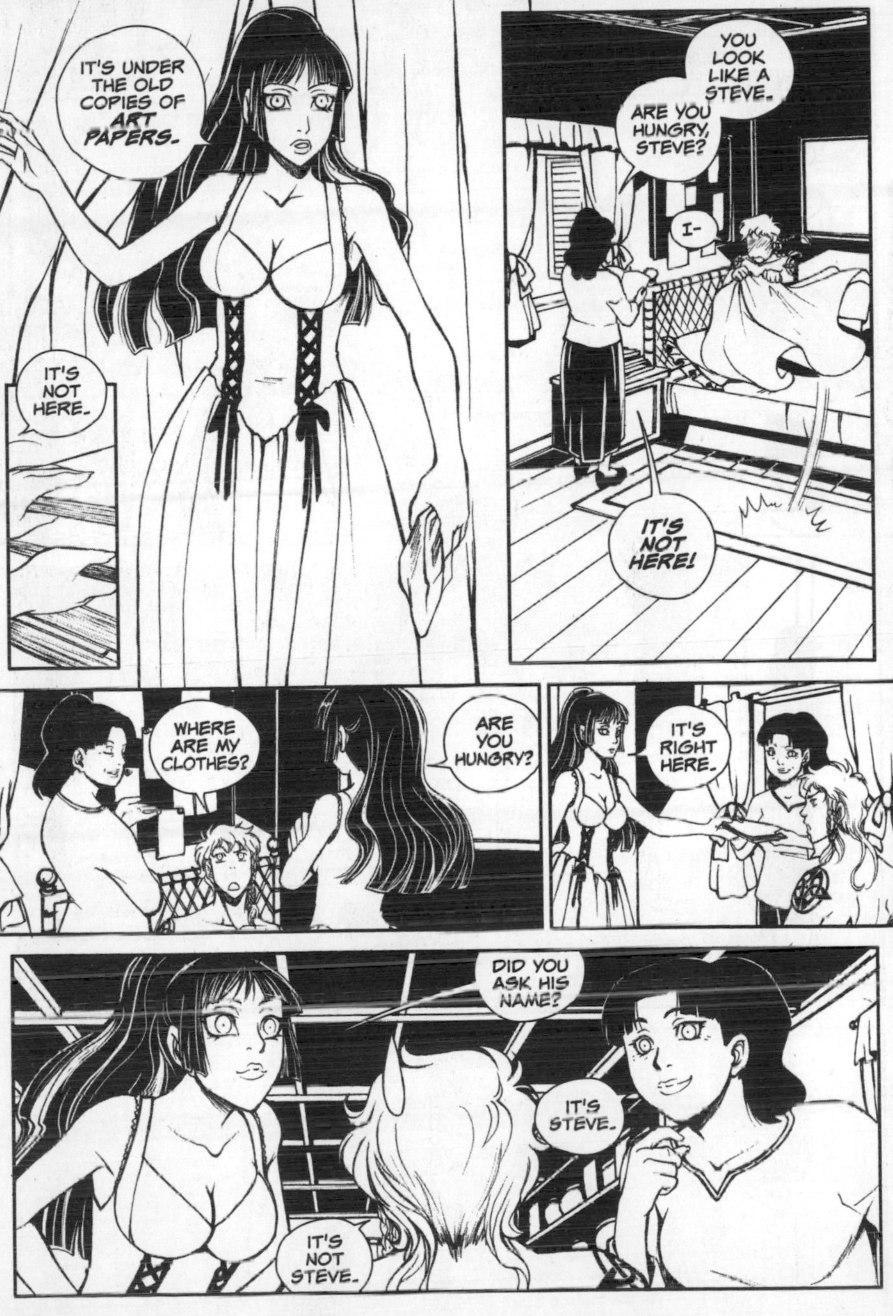

IT'S UNDER THE OLD COPIES OF ART PAPERS.
IT'S NOT HERE.
YOU LOOK LIKE A STEVE.
ARE YOU HUNGRY, STEVE?
I-
IT'S NOT HERE!
WHERE ARE MY CLOTHES?
ARE YOU HUNGRY?
IT'S RIGHT HERE.
DID YOU ASK HIS NAME?
IT'S STEVE.
IT'S NOT STEVE.

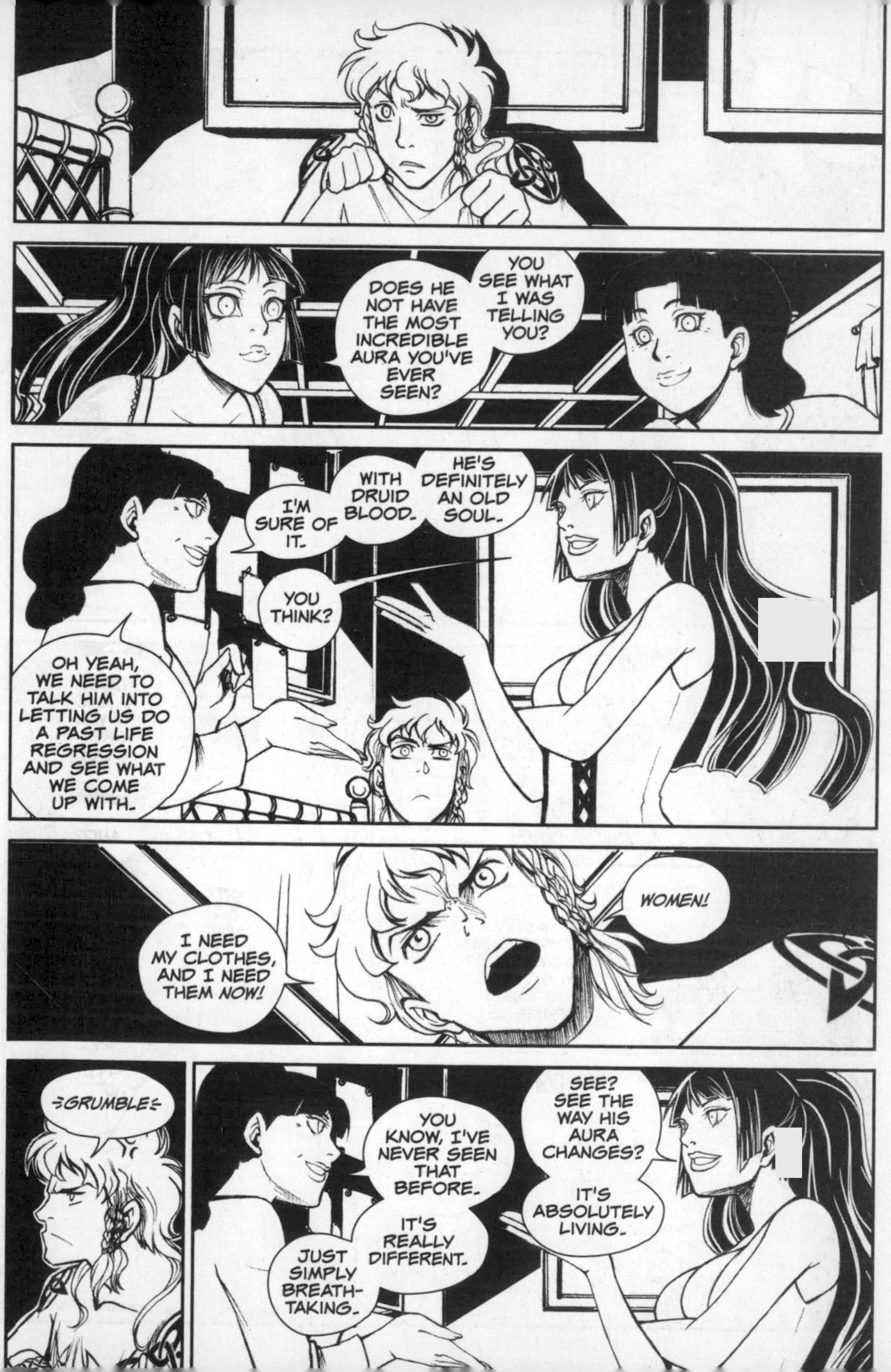
DOES HE NOT HAVE THE MOST INCREDIBLE AURA YOU'VE EVER SEEN?
YOU SEE WHAT I WAS TELLING YOU?
HE'S DEFINITELY AN OLD SOUL.
WITH DRUID BLOOD.
I'M SURE OF IT.
YOU THINK?
OH YEAH, WE NEED TO TALK HIM INTO LETTING US DO A PAST LIFE REGRESSION AND SEE WHAT WE COME UP WITH.
I NEED MY CLOTHES, AND I NEED THEM NOW!
WOMEN!
≈GRUMBLE≈
SEE? SEE THE WAY HIS AURA CHANGES?
IT'S ABSOLUTELY LIVING.
YOU KNOW, I'VE NEVER SEEN THAT BEFORE.
IT'S REALLY DIFFERENT.
JUST SIMPLY BREATH-TAKING.

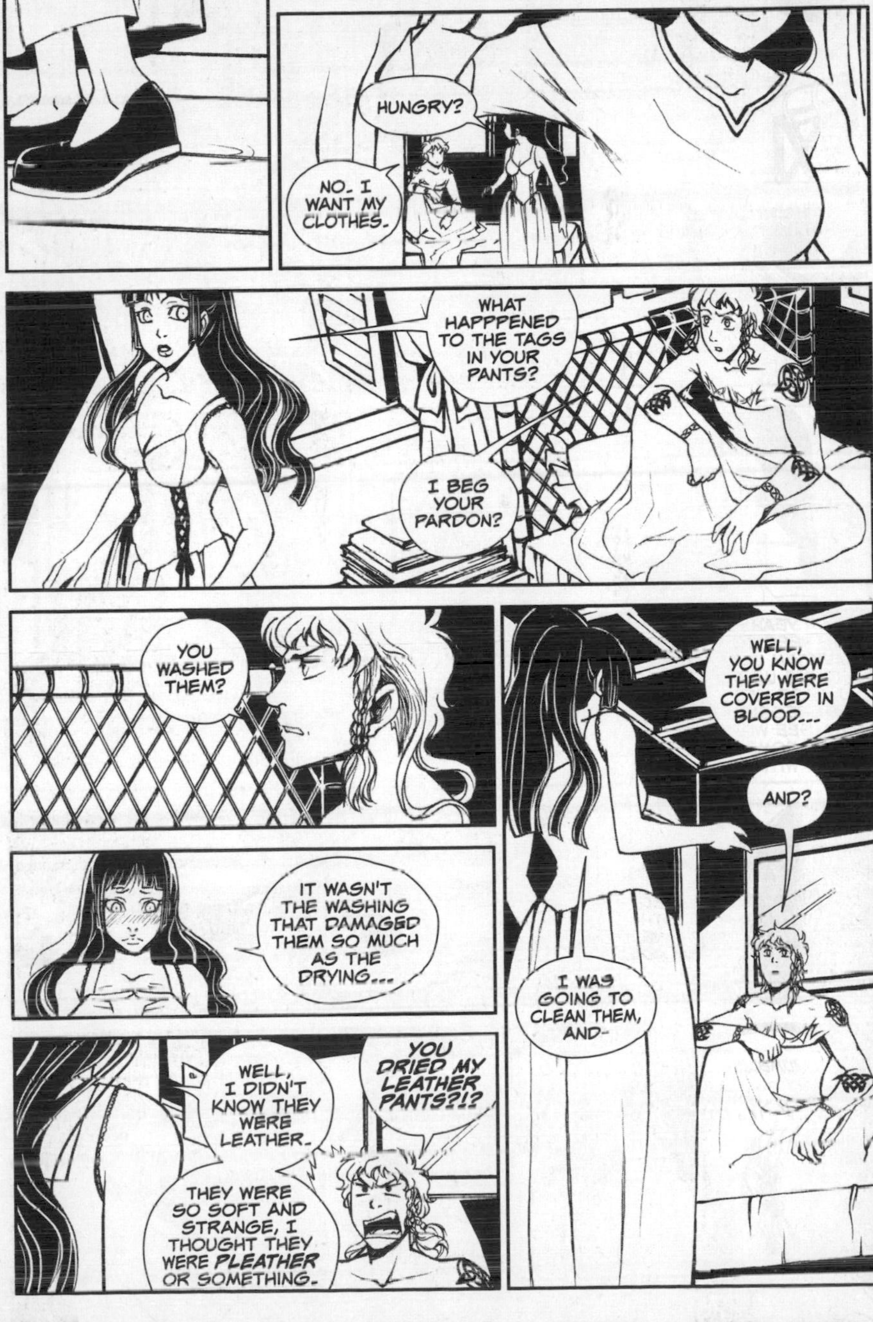
HUNGRY?
NO. I WANT MY CLOTHES.
WHAT HAPPPENED TO THE TAGS IN YOUR PANTS?
I BEG YOUR PARDON?
YOU WASHED THEM?
IT WASN'T THE WASHING THAT DAMAGED THEM SO MUCH AS THE DRYING...
YOU DRIED MY LEATHER PANTS?!?
WELL, I DIDN'T KNOW THEY WERE LEATHER.
THEY WERE SO SOFT AND STRANGE, I THOUGHT THEY WERE PLEATHER OR SOMETHING.
WELL, YOU KNOW THEY WERE COVERED IN BLOOD...
AND?
I WAS GOING TO CLEAN THEM, AND-

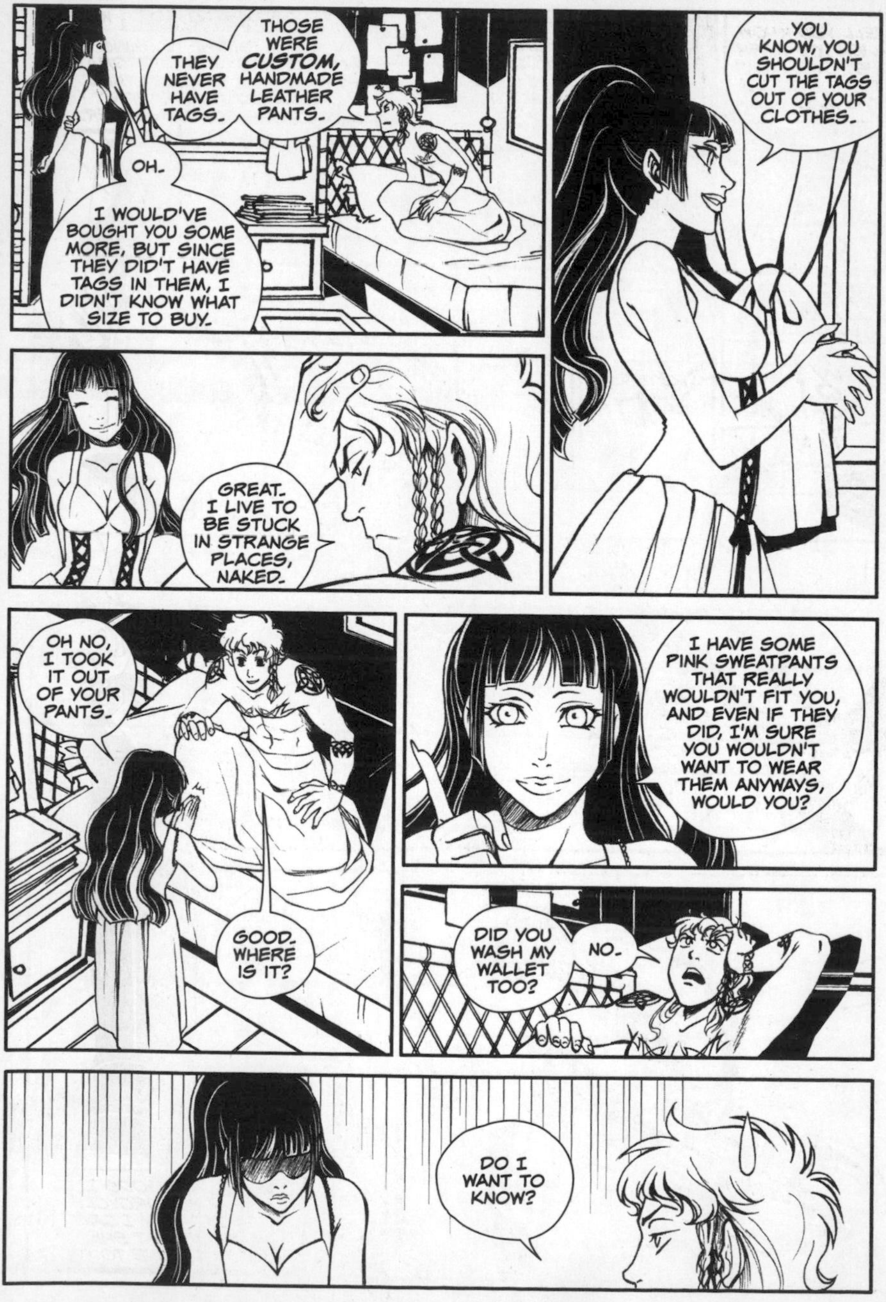
THOSE WERE CUSTOM, HANDMADE LEATHER PANTS.
THEY NEVER HAVE TAGS.
OH.
I WOULD'VE BOUGHT YOU SOME MORE, BUT SINCE THEY DID'T HAVE TAGS IN THEM, I DIDN'T KNOW WHAT SIZE TO BUY.
YOU KNOW, YOU SHOULDN'T CUT THE TAGS OUT OF YOUR CLOTHES.
GREAT. I LIVE TO BE STUCK IN STRANGE PLACES, NAKED.
OH NO, I TOOK IT OUT OF YOUR PANTS.
GOOD. WHERE IS IT?
I HAVE SOME PINK SWEATPANTS THAT REALLY WOULDN'T FIT YOU, AND EVEN IF THEY DID, I'M SURE YOU WOULDN'T WANT TO WEAR THEM ANYWAYS, WOULD YOU?
NO.
DID YOU WASH MY WALLET TOO?
DO I WANT TO KNOW?

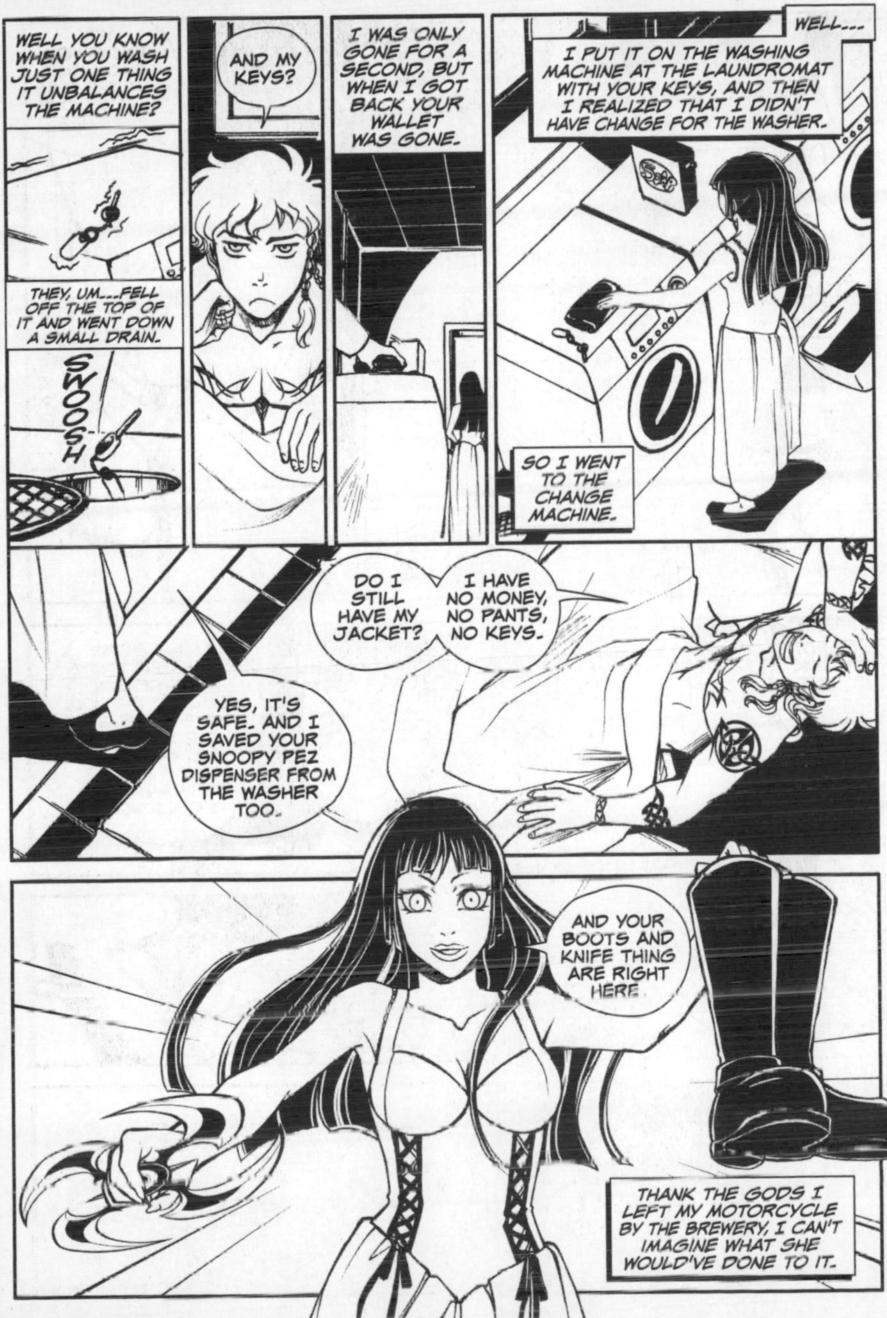
WELL YOU KNOW WHEN YOU WASH JUST ONE THING IT UNBALANCES THE MACHINE?
THEY, UM...FELL OFF THE TOP OF IT AND WENT DOWN A SMALL DRAIN.
SWOOSH
AND MY KEYS?
I WAS ONLY GONE FOR A SECOND, BUT WHEN I GOT BACK YOUR WALLET WAS GONE.
WELL...
I PUT IT ON THE WASHING MACHINE AT THE LAUNDROMAT WITH YOUR KEYS, AND THEN I REALIZED THAT I DIDN'T HAVE CHANGE FOR THE WASHER.
SO I WENT TO THE CHANGE MACHINE.
I HAVE NO MONEY, NO PANTS, NO KEYS.
DO I STILL HAVE MY JACKET?
YES, IT'S SAFE. AND I SAVED YOUR SNOOPY PEZ DISPENSER FROM THE WASHER TOO.
AND YOUR BOOTS AND KNIFE THING ARE RIGHT HERE.
THANK THE GODS I LEFT MY MOTORCYCLE BY THE BREWERY, I CAN'T IMAGINE WHAT SHE WOULD'VE DONE TO IT.

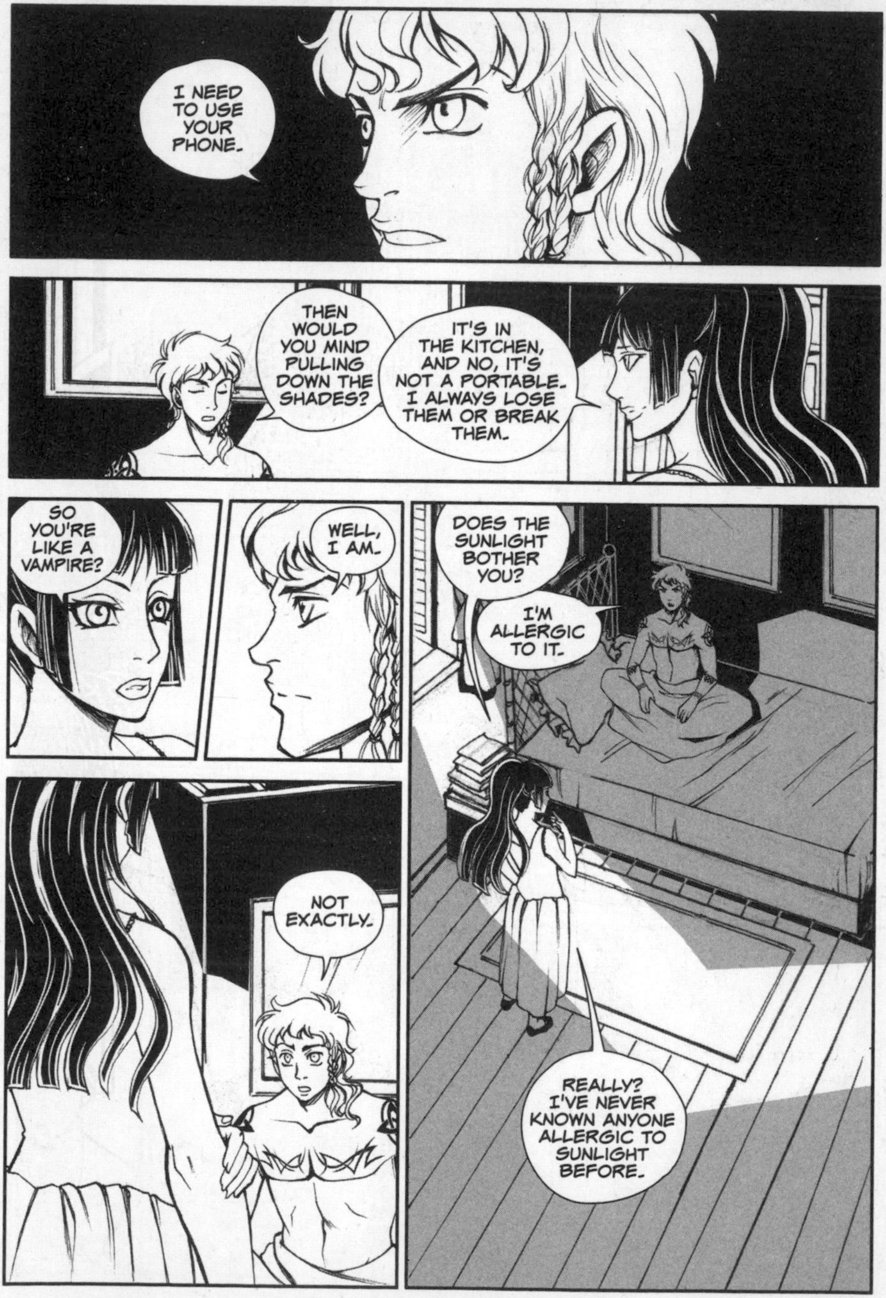
I NEED TO USE YOUR PHONE.
THEN WOULD YOU MIND PULLING DOWN THE SHADES?
IT'S IN THE KITCHEN, AND NO, IT'S NOT A PORTABLE. I ALWAYS LOSE THEM OR BREAK THEM.
SO YOU'RE LIKE A VAMPIRE?
WELL, I AM.
NOT EXACTLY.
DOES THE SUNLIGHT BOTHER YOU?
I'M ALLERGIC TO IT.
REALLY? I'VE NEVER KNOWN ANYONE ALLERGIC TO SUNLIGHT BEFORE.

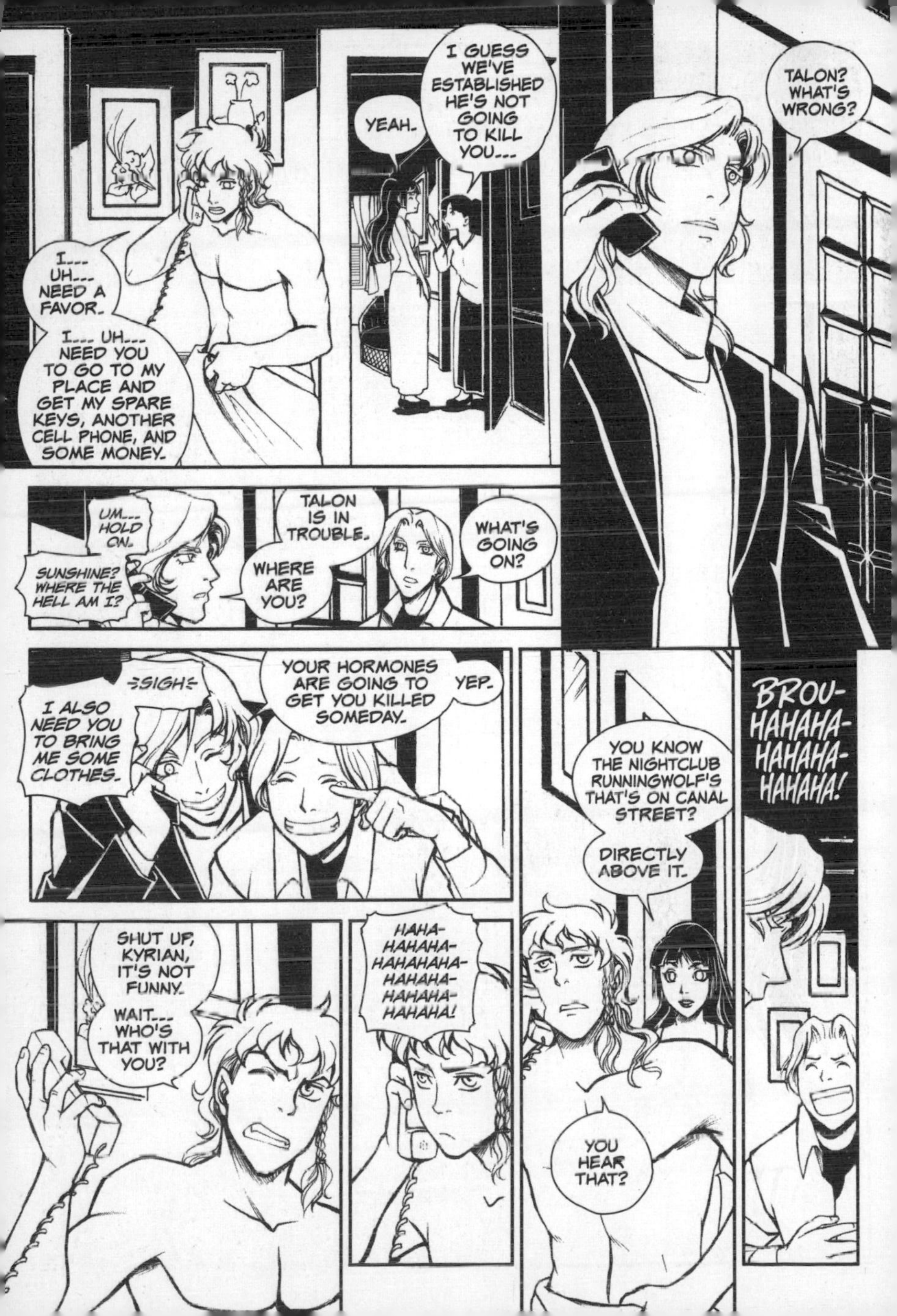

I... UH... NEED A FAVOR.
I... UH... NEED YOU TO GO TO MY PLACE AND GET MY SPARE KEYS, ANOTHER CELL PHONE, AND SOME MONEY.
YEAH.
I GUESS WE'VE ESTABLISHED HE'S NOT GOING TO KILL YOU...
TALON? WHAT'S WRONG?
UM... HOLD ON.
SUNSHINE? WHERE THE HELL AM I?
TALON IS IN TROUBLE.
WHERE ARE YOU?
WHAT'S GOING ON?
=SIGH=
I ALSO NEED YOU TO BRING ME SOME CLOTHES.
YOUR HORMONES ARE GOING TO GET YOU KILLED SOMEDAY.
YEP.
YOU KNOW THE NIGHTCLUB RUNNINGWOLF'S THAT'S ON CANAL STREET?
DIRECTLY ABOVE IT.
BROU-HAHAHA-HAHAHA-HAHAHA!
SHUT UP, KYRIAN, IT'S NOT FUNNY.
WAIT... WHO'S THAT WITH YOU?
HAHA-HAHAHA-HAHAHAHA-HAHAHA-HAHAHA-HAHAHA!
YOU HEAR THAT?

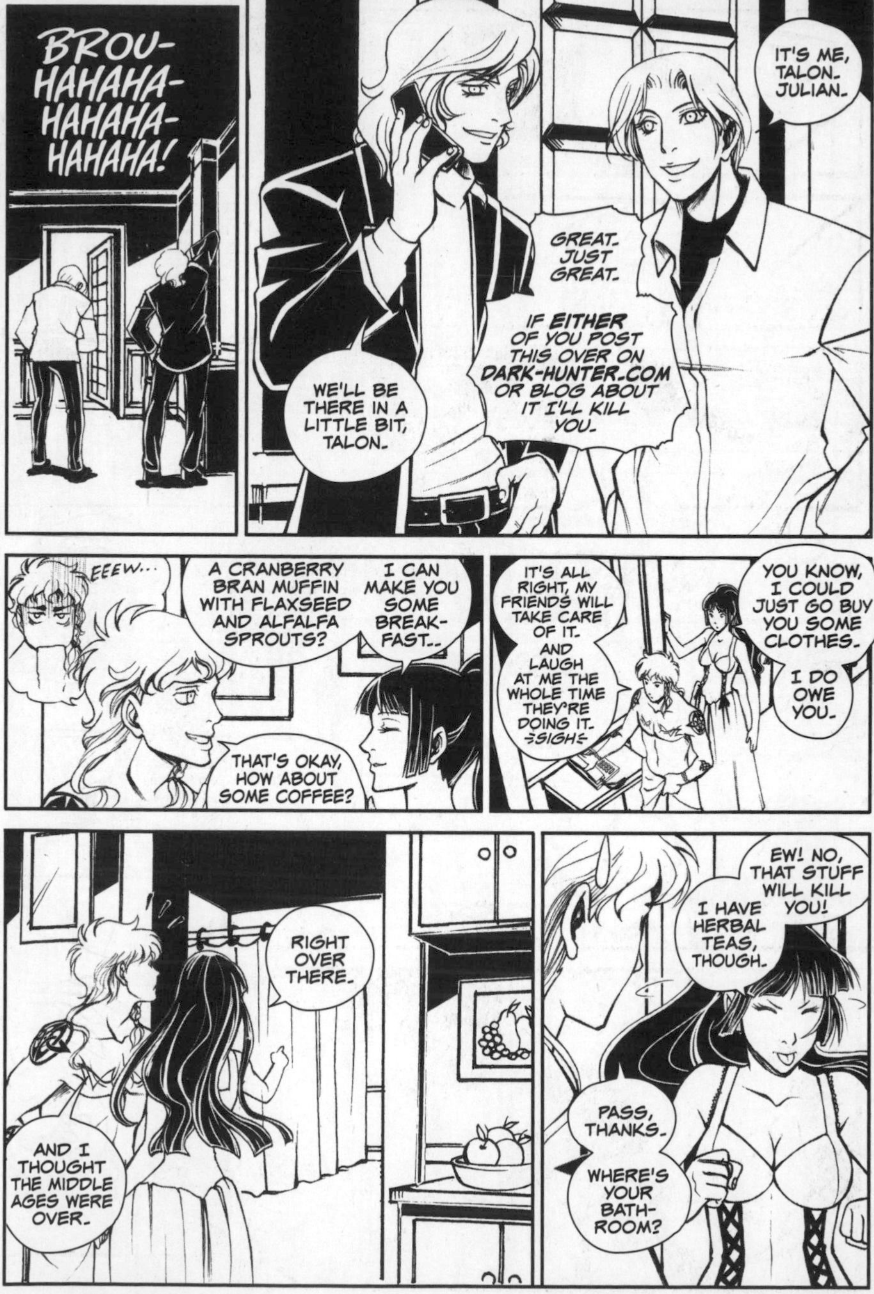
BROU-HAHAHA-HAHAHA-HAHAHA!
IT'S ME, TALON. JULIAN.
GREAT. JUST GREAT.
IF EITHER OF YOU POST THIS OVER ON DARK-HUNTER.COM OR BLOG ABOUT IT I'LL KILL YOU.
WE'LL BE THERE IN A LITTLE BIT, TALON.
EEEW...
A CRANBERRY BRAN MUFFIN WITH FLAXSEED AND ALFALFA SPROUTS?
I CAN MAKE YOU SOME BREAK-FAST..
THAT'S OKAY, HOW ABOUT SOME COFFEE?
IT'S ALL RIGHT, MY FRIENDS WILL TAKE CARE OF IT.
AND LAUGH AT ME THE WHOLE TIME THEY'RE DOING IT.
SIGH
YOU KNOW, I COULD JUST GO BUY YOU SOME CLOTHES.
I DO OWE YOU.
RIGHT OVER THERE.
AND I THOUGHT THE MIDDLE AGES WERE OVER.
EW! NO, THAT STUFF WILL KILL YOU!
I HAVE HERBAL TEAS, THOUGH.
PASS, THANKS.
WHERE'S YOUR BATH-ROOM?

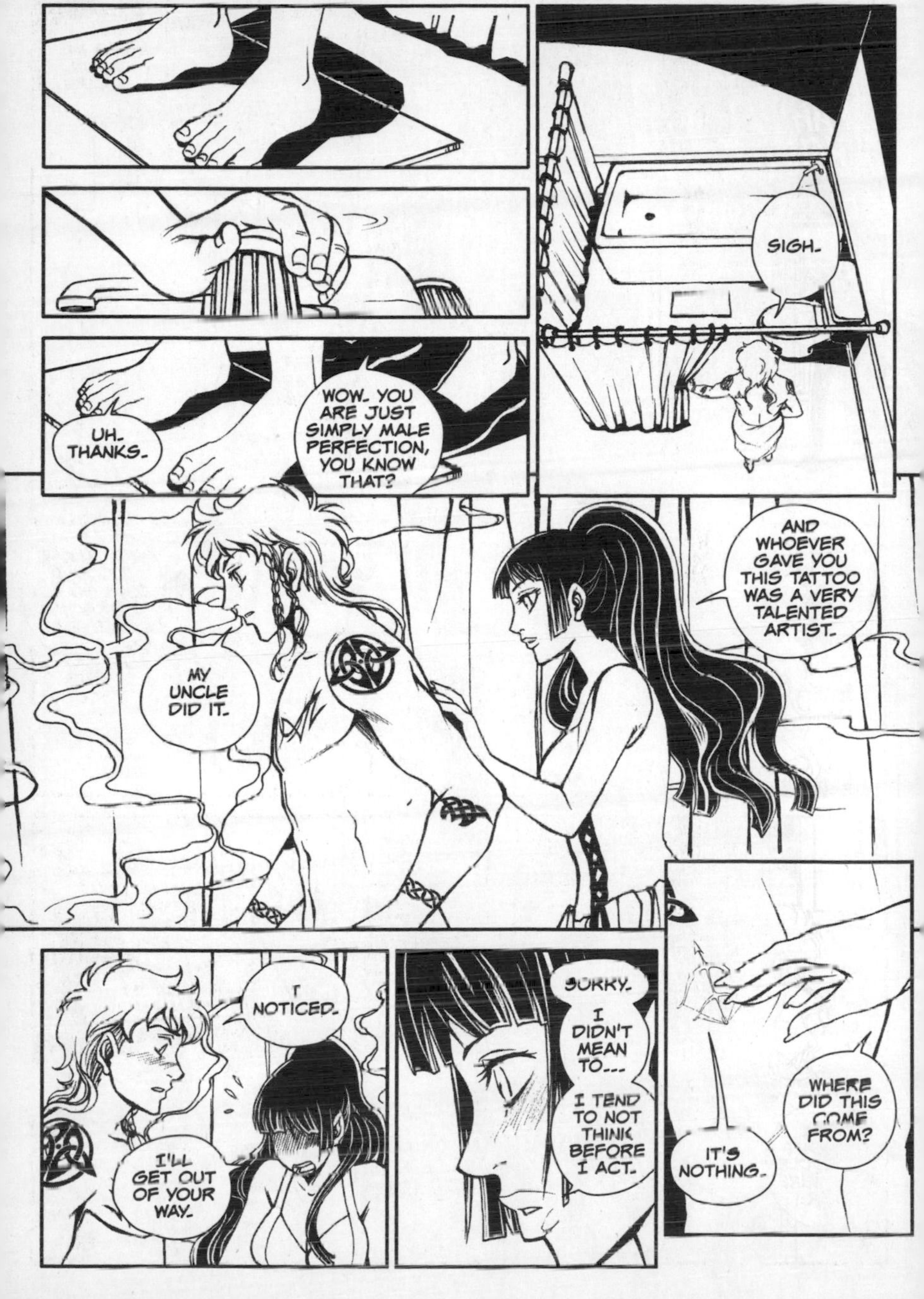

WOW. YOU ARE JUST SIMPLY MALE PERFECTION, YOU KNOW THAT?
UH. THANKS.
SIGH.
AND WHOEVER GAVE YOU THIS TATTOO WAS A VERY TALENTED ARTIST.
MY UNCLE DID IT.
I NOTICED.
I'LL GET OUT OF YOUR WAY.
SORRY.
I DIDN'T MEAN TO...
I TEND TO NOT THINK BEFORE I ACT.
WHERE DID THIS COME FROM?
IT'S NOTHING.

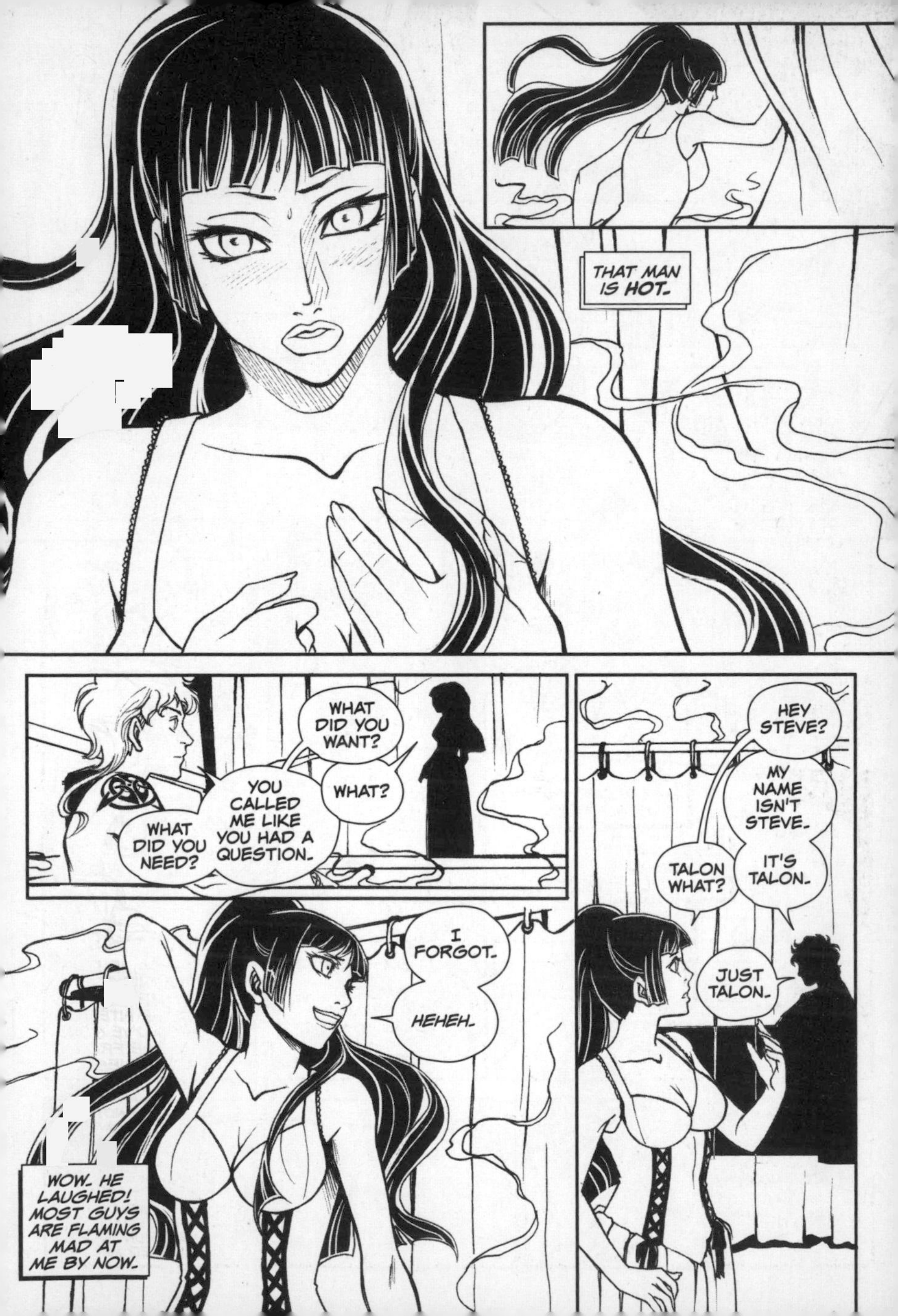
THAT MAN IS HOT.
WHAT DID YOU NEED?
YOU CALLED ME LIKE YOU HAD A QUESTION.
WHAT DID YOU WANT?
WHAT?
HEY STEVE?
MY NAME ISN'T STEVE.
IT'S TALON.
TALON WHAT?
JUST TALON.
I FORGOT.
HEHEH.
WOW. HE LAUGHED! MOST GUYS ARE FLAMING MAD AT ME BY NOW.

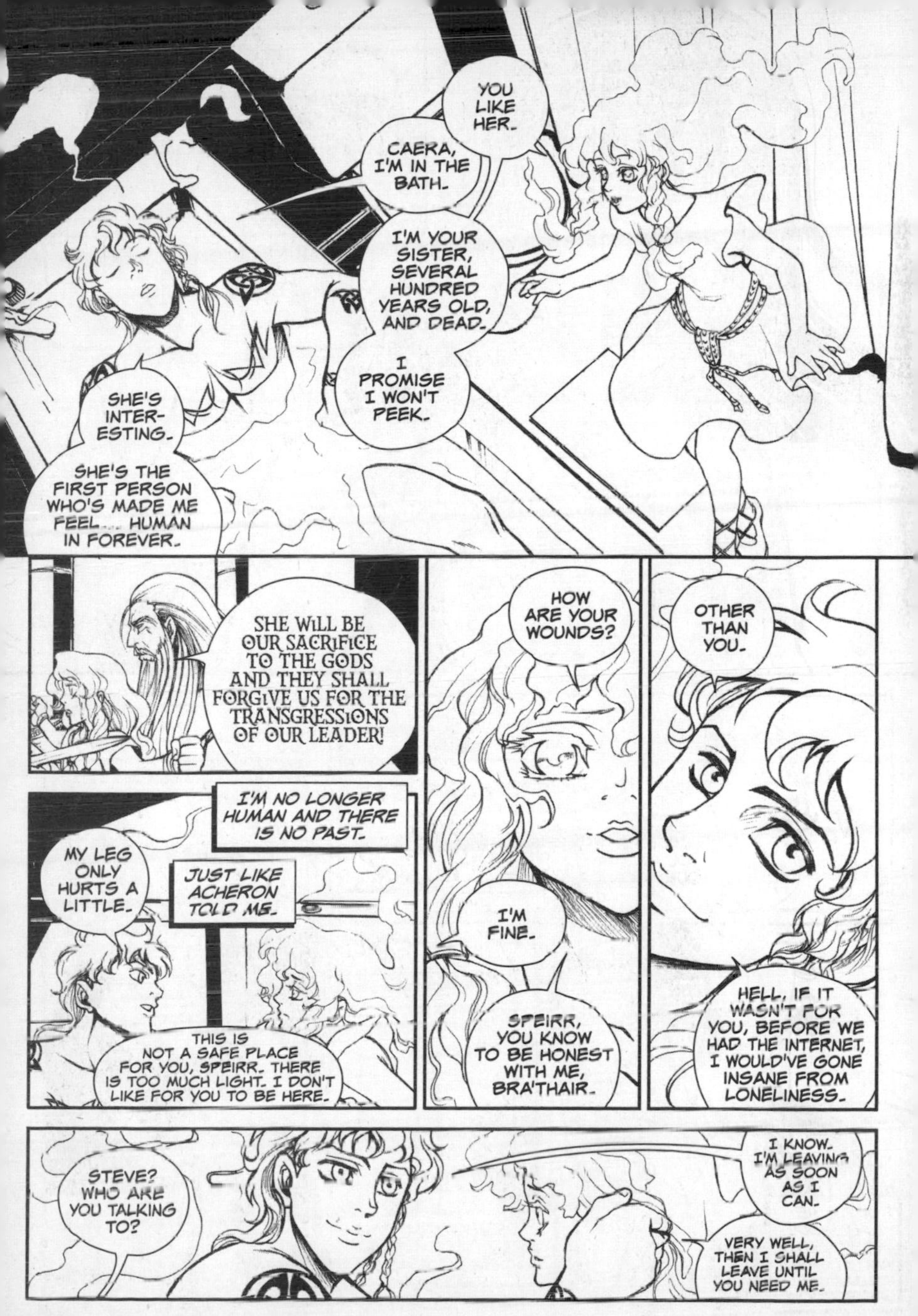

YOU LIKE HER.
CAERA, I'M IN THE BATH.
I'M YOUR SISTER, SEVERAL HUNDRED YEARS OLD, AND DEAD.
I PROMISE I WON'T PEEK.
SHE'S INTER-ESTING.
SHE'S THE FIRST PERSON WHO'S MADE ME FEEL... HUMAN IN FOREVER.
SHE WILL BE OUR SACRIFICE TO THE GODS AND THEY SHALL FORGIVE US FOR THE TRANSGRESSIONS OF OUR LEADER!
I'M NO LONGER HUMAN AND THERE IS NO PAST.
JUST LIKE ACHERON TOLD ME.
MY LEG ONLY HURTS A LITTLE.
THIS IS NOT A SAFE PLACE FOR YOU, SPEIRR. THERE IS TOO MUCH LIGHT. I DON'T LIKE FOR YOU TO BE HERE.
HOW ARE YOUR WOUNDS?
I'M FINE.
SPEIRR, YOU KNOW TO BE HONEST WITH ME, BRA'THAIR.
OTHER THAN YOU.
HELL, IF IT WASN'T FOR YOU, BEFORE WE HAD THE INTERNET, I WOULD'VE GONE INSANE FROM LONELINESS.
I KNOW. I'M LEAVING AS SOON AS I CAN.
VERY WELL, THEN I SHALL LEAVE UNTIL YOU NEED ME.
STEVE? WHO ARE YOU TALKING TO?

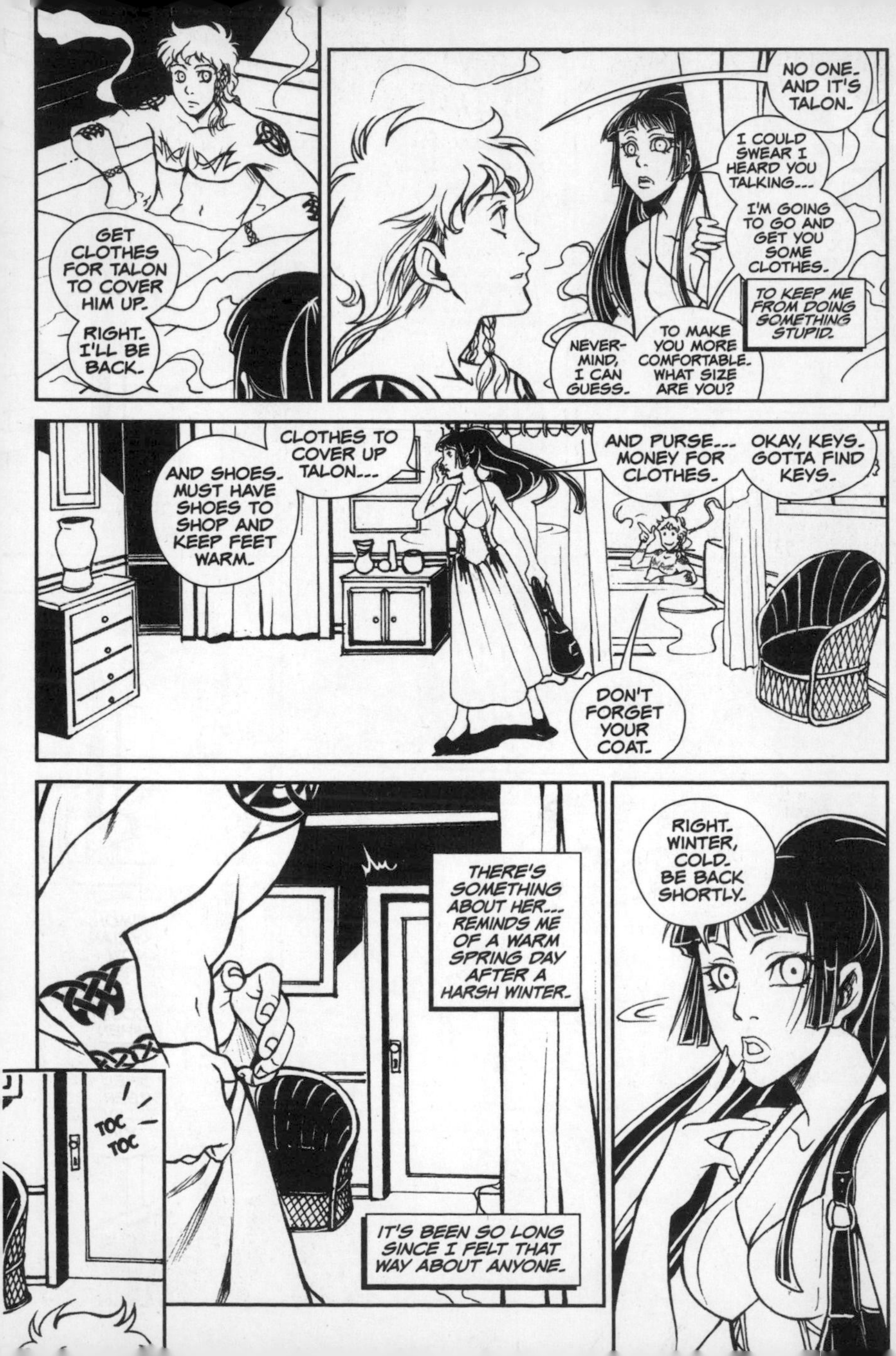
GET CLOTHES FOR TALON TO COVER HIM UP.
RIGHT. I'LL BE BACK.
NO ONE. AND IT'S TALON.
I COULD SWEAR I HEARD YOU TALKING...
I'M GOING TO GO AND GET YOU SOME CLOTHES.
TO KEEP ME FROM DOING SOMETHING STUPID.
TO MAKE YOU MORE COMFORTABLE. WHAT SIZE ARE YOU?
NEVER-MIND, I CAN GUESS.
CLOTHES TO COVER UP TALON...
AND SHOES. MUST HAVE SHOES TO SHOP AND KEEP FEET WARM.
AND PURSE... MONEY FOR CLOTHES.
OKAY, KEYS. GOTTA FIND KEYS.
DON'T FORGET YOUR COAT.
THERE'S SOMETHING ABOUT HER... REMINDS ME OF A WARM SPRING DAY AFTER A HARSH WINTER.
TOC TOC
IT'S BEEN SO LONG SINCE I FELT THAT WAY ABOUT ANYONE.
RIGHT. WINTER, COLD. BE BACK SHORTLY.

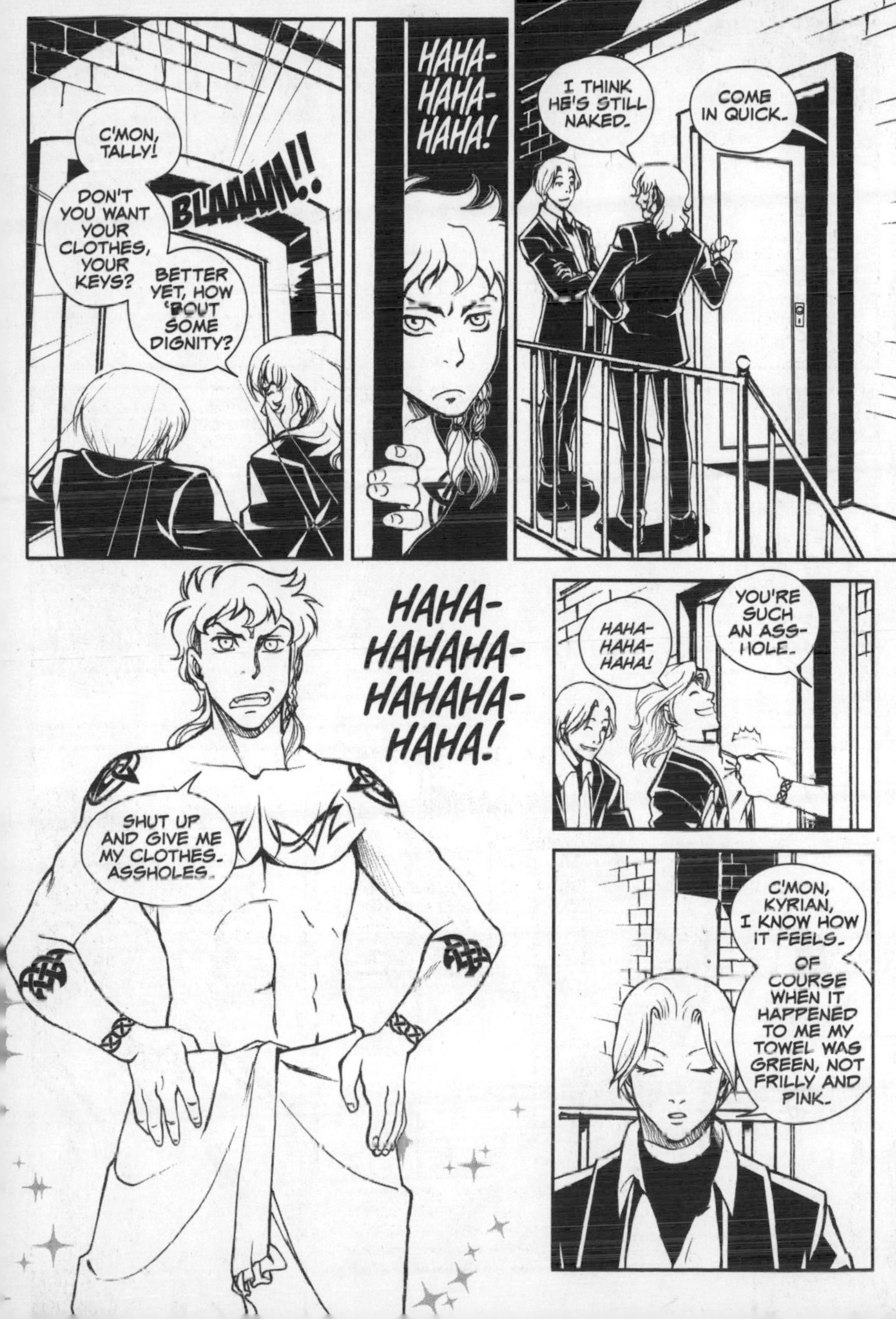

C'MON, TALLY!
DON'T YOU WANT YOUR CLOTHES, YOUR KEYS?
BLAAAM!!
BETTER YET, HOW 'BOUT SOME DIGNITY?
HAHA-HAHA-HAHA!
I THINK HE'S STILL NAKED.
COME IN QUICK.
SHUT UP AND GIVE ME MY CLOTHES. ASSHOLES.
HAHA-HAHAHA-HAHAHA-HAHA!
HAHA-HAHA-HAHA!
YOU'RE SUCH AN ASS-HOLE.
C'MON, KYRIAN, I KNOW HOW IT FEELS.
OF COURSE WHEN IT HAPPENED TO ME MY TOWEL WAS GREEN, NOT FRILLY AND PINK.

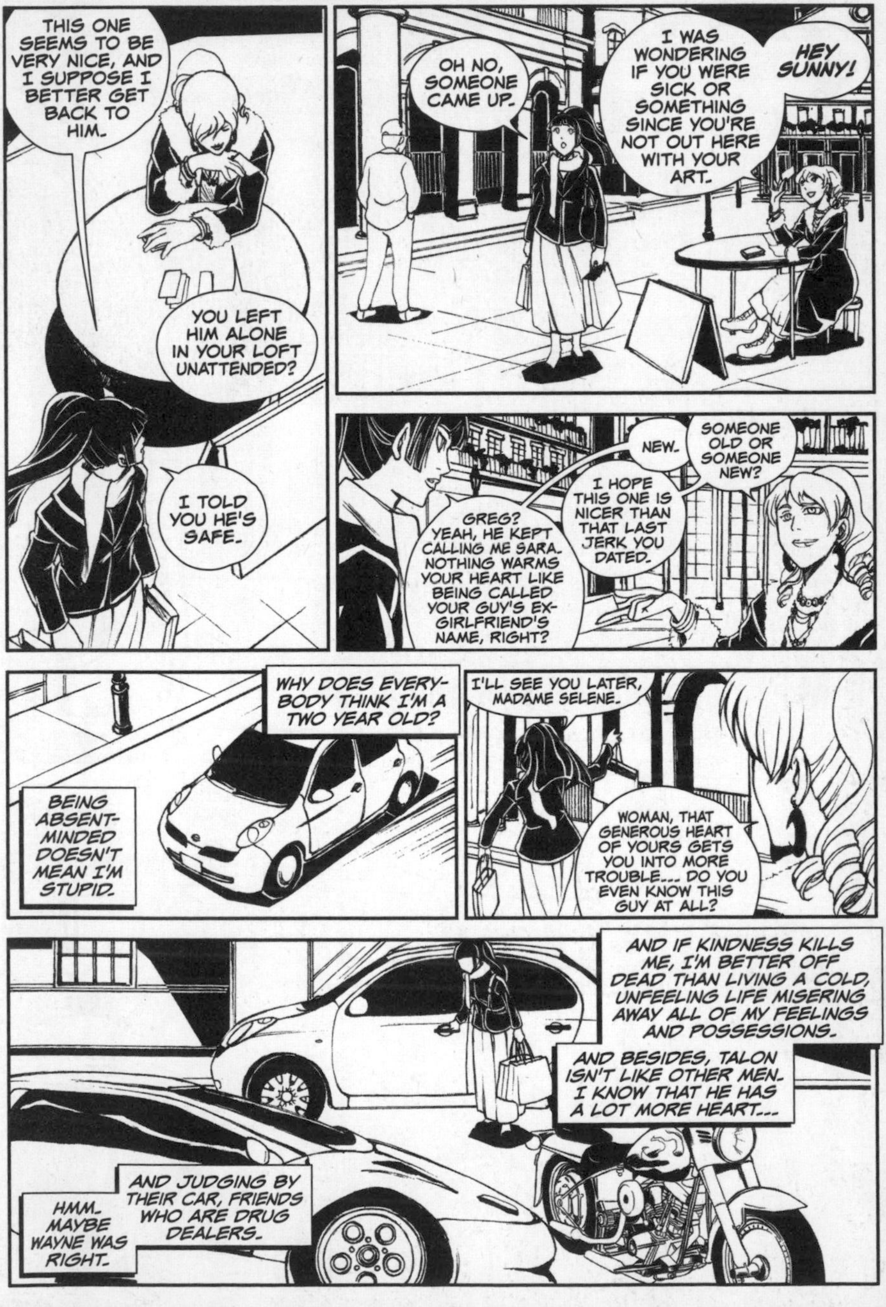
HEY SUNNY!
I WAS WONDERING IF YOU WERE SICK OR SOMETHING SINCE YOU'RE NOT OUT HERE WITH YOUR ART.
OH NO, SOMEONE CAME UP.
SOMEONE OLD OR SOMEONE NEW?
NEW.
I HOPE THIS ONE IS NICER THAN THAT LAST JERK YOU DATED.
GREG? YEAH, HE KEPT CALLING ME SARA. NOTHING WARMS YOUR HEART LIKE BEING CALLED YOUR GUY'S EX-GIRLFRIEND'S NAME, RIGHT?
THIS ONE SEEMS TO BE VERY NICE, AND I SUPPOSE I BETTER GET BACK TO HIM.
YOU LEFT HIM ALONE IN YOUR LOFT UNATTENDED?
I TOLD YOU HE'S SAFE.
I'LL SEE YOU LATER, MADAME SELENE.
WOMAN, THAT GENEROUS HEART OF YOURS GETS YOU INTO MORE TROUBLE... DO YOU EVEN KNOW THIS GUY AT ALL?
WHY DOES EVERYBODY THINK I'M A TWO YEAR OLD?
BEING ABSENT-MINDED DOESN'T MEAN I'M STUPID.
AND IF KINDNESS KILLS ME, I'M BETTER OFF DEAD THAN LIVING A COLD, UNFEELING LIFE MISERING AWAY ALL OF MY FEELINGS AND POSSESSIONS.
AND BESIDES, TALON ISN'T LIKE OTHER MEN. I KNOW THAT HE HAS A LOT MORE HEART...
AND JUDGING BY THEIR CAR, FRIENDS WHO ARE DRUG DEALERS.
HMM. MAYBE WAYNE WAS RIGHT.

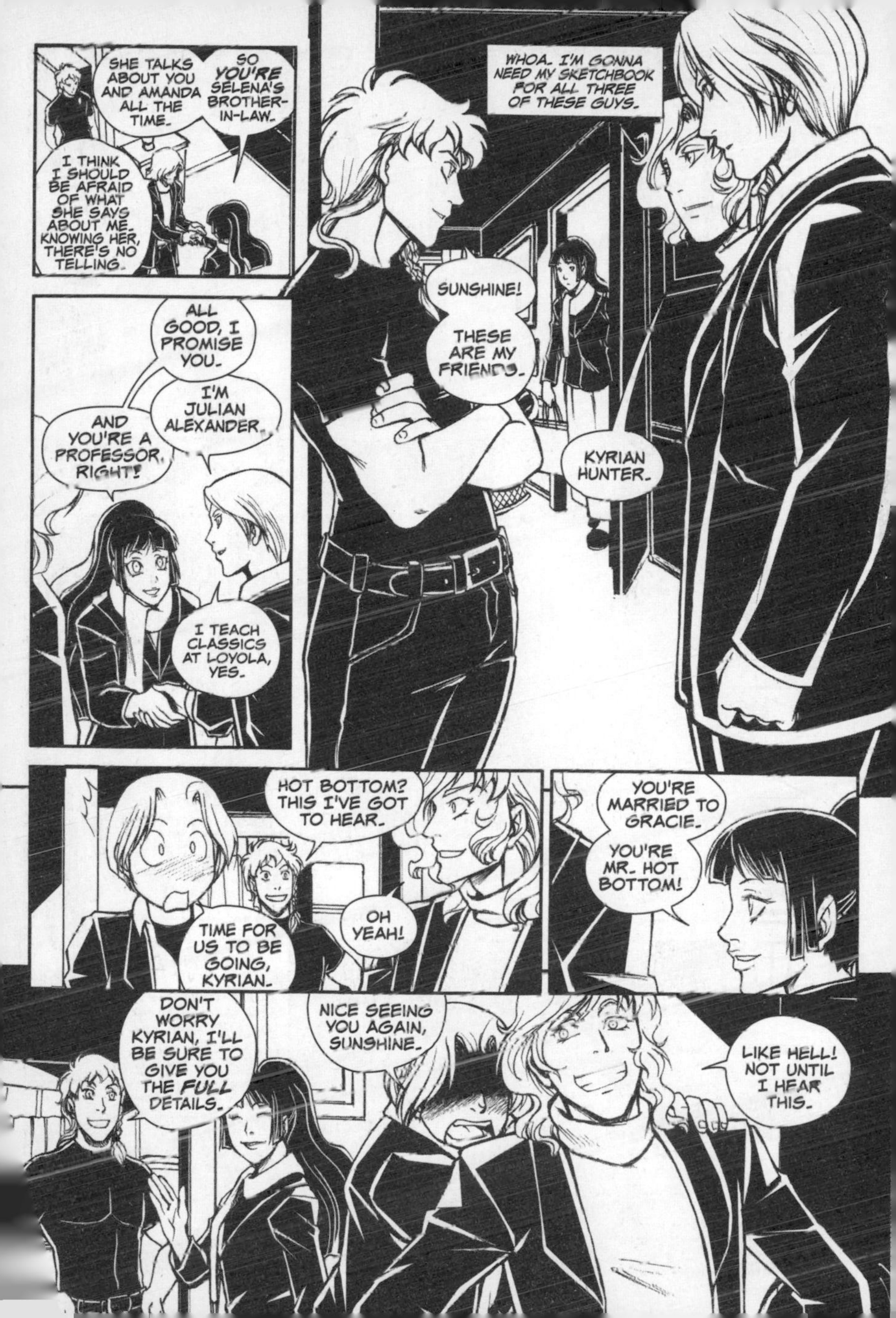
SO YOU'RE SELENA'S BROTHER-IN-LAW.
SHE TALKS ABOUT YOU AND AMANDA ALL THE TIME.
I THINK I SHOULD BE AFRAID OF WHAT SHE SAYS ABOUT ME. KNOWING HER, THERE'S NO TELLING.
WHOA. I'M GONNA NEED MY SKETCHBOOK FOR ALL THREE OF THESE GUYS.
SUNSHINE!
THESE ARE MY FRIENDS.
ALL GOOD, I PROMISE YOU.
I'M JULIAN ALEXANDER.
AND YOU'RE A PROFESSOR, RIGHT?
KYRIAN HUNTER.
I TEACH CLASSICS AT LOYOLA, YES.
YOU'RE MARRIED TO GRACIE.
YOU'RE MR. HOT BOTTOM!
HOT BOTTOM? THIS I'VE GOT TO HEAR.
OH YEAH!
TIME FOR US TO BE GOING, KYRIAN.
NICE SEEING YOU AGAIN, SUNSHINE.
LIKE HELL! NOT UNTIL I HEAR THIS.
DON'T WORRY KYRIAN, I'LL BE SURE TO GIVE YOU THE FULL DETAILS.

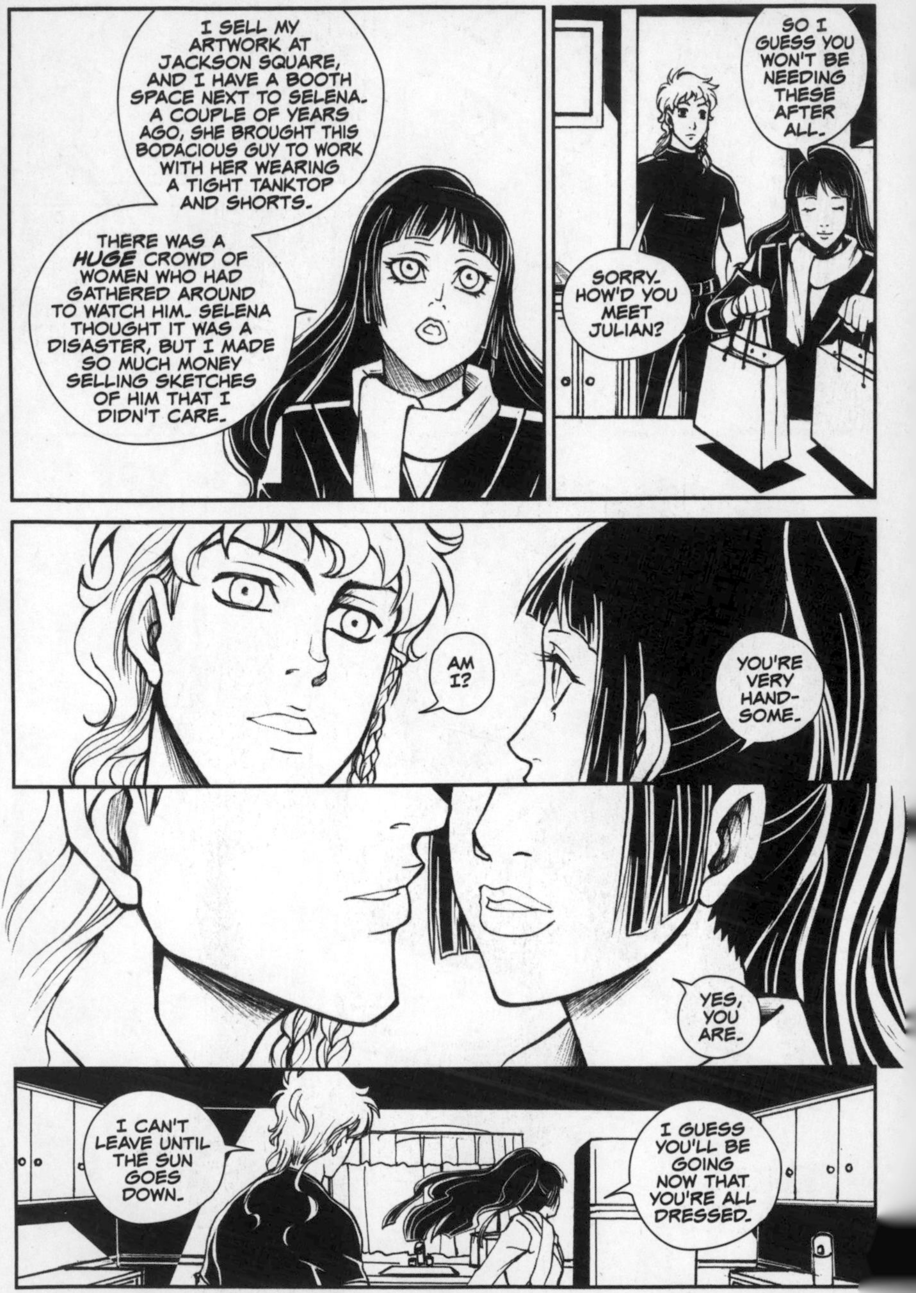
I SELL MY ARTWORK AT JACKSON SQUARE, AND I HAVE A BOOTH SPACE NEXT TO SELENA. A COUPLE OF YEARS AGO, SHE BROUGHT THIS BODACIOUS GUY TO WORK WITH HER WEARING A TIGHT TANKTOP AND SHORTS.
THERE WAS A *HUGE* CROWD OF WOMEN WHO HAD GATHERED AROUND TO WATCH HIM. SELENA THOUGHT IT WAS A DISASTER, BUT I MADE SO MUCH MONEY SELLING SKETCHES OF HIM THAT I DIDN'T CARE.
SO I GUESS YOU WON'T BE NEEDING THESE AFTER ALL.
SORRY. HOW'D YOU MEET JULIAN?
YOU'RE VERY HAND-SOME.
AM I?
YES, YOU ARE.
I GUESS YOU'LL BE GOING NOW THAT YOU'RE ALL DRESSED.
I CAN'T LEAVE UNTIL THE SUN GOES DOWN.

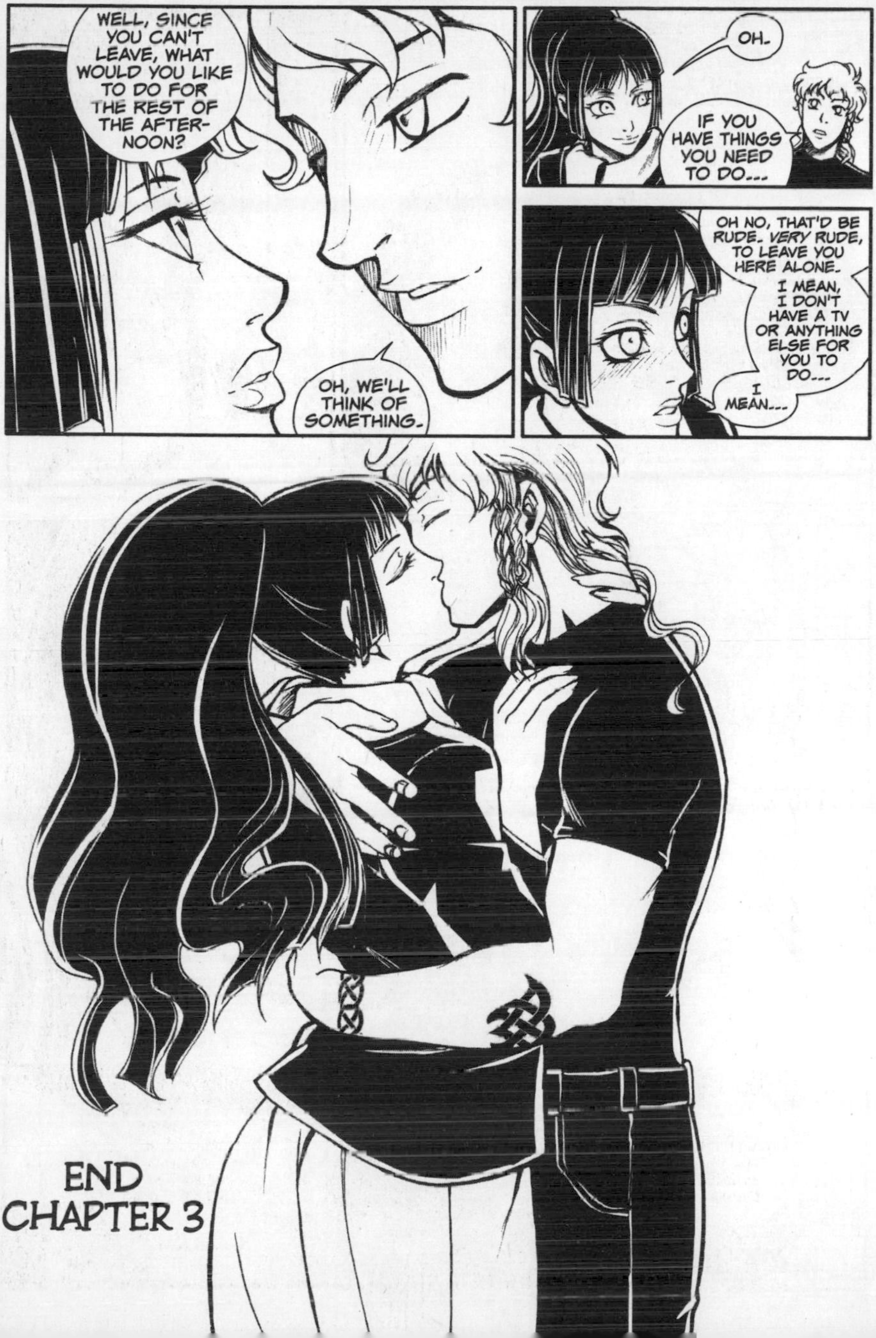
WELL, SINCE YOU CAN'T LEAVE, WHAT WOULD YOU LIKE TO DO FOR THE REST OF THE AFTER-NOON?
OH, WE'LL THINK OF SOMETHING.
OH.
IF YOU HAVE THINGS YOU NEED TO DO...
OH NO, THAT'D BE RUDE. *VERY* RUDE, TO LEAVE YOU HERE ALONE.
I MEAN, I DON'T HAVE A TV OR ANYTHING ELSE FOR YOU TO DO...
I MEAN...
END CHAPTER 3

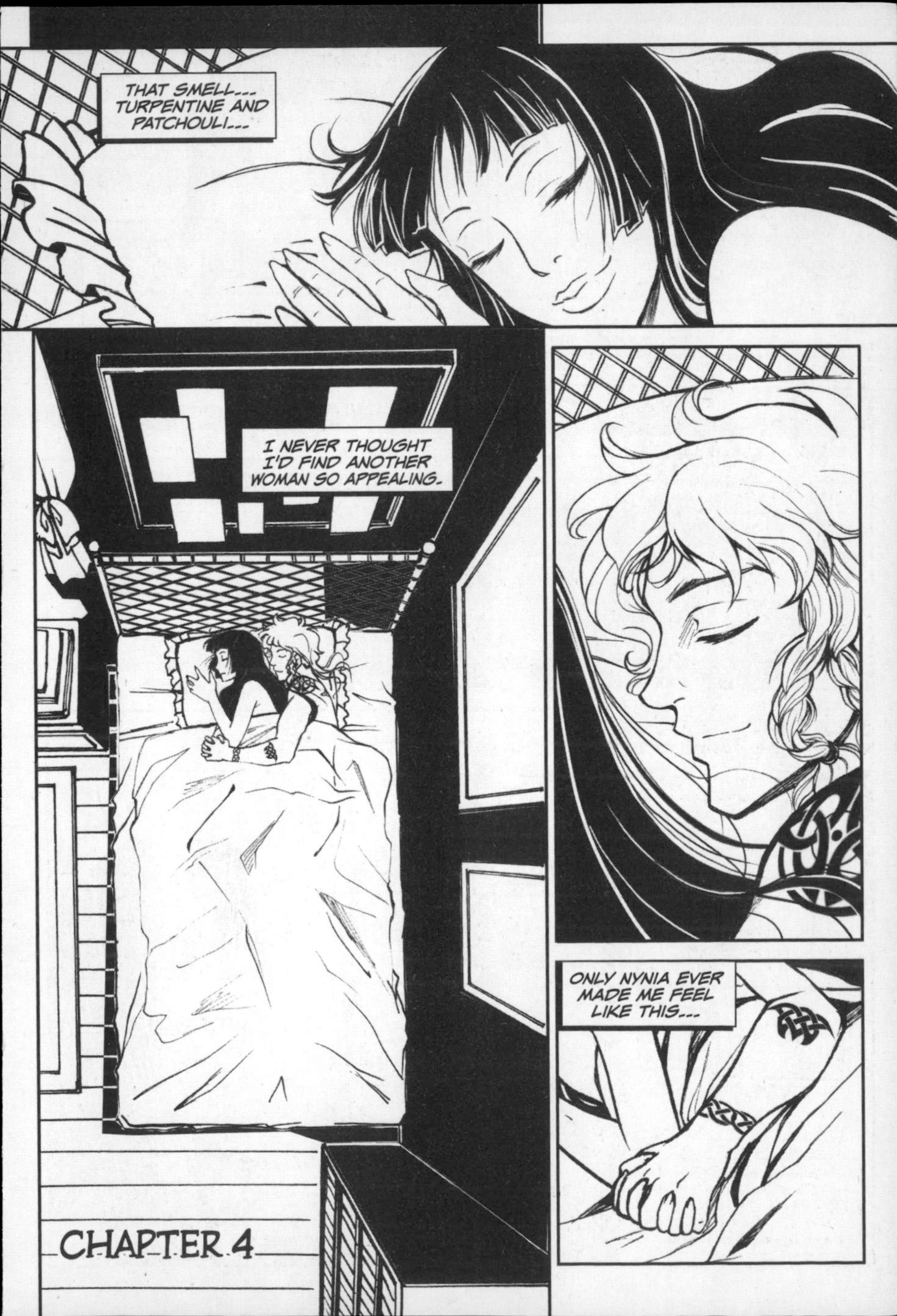
THAT SMELL... TURPENTINE AND PATCHOULI...
I NEVER THOUGHT I'D FIND ANOTHER WOMAN SO APPEALING.
ONLY NYNIA EVER MADE ME FEEL LIKE THIS...
CHAPTER 4

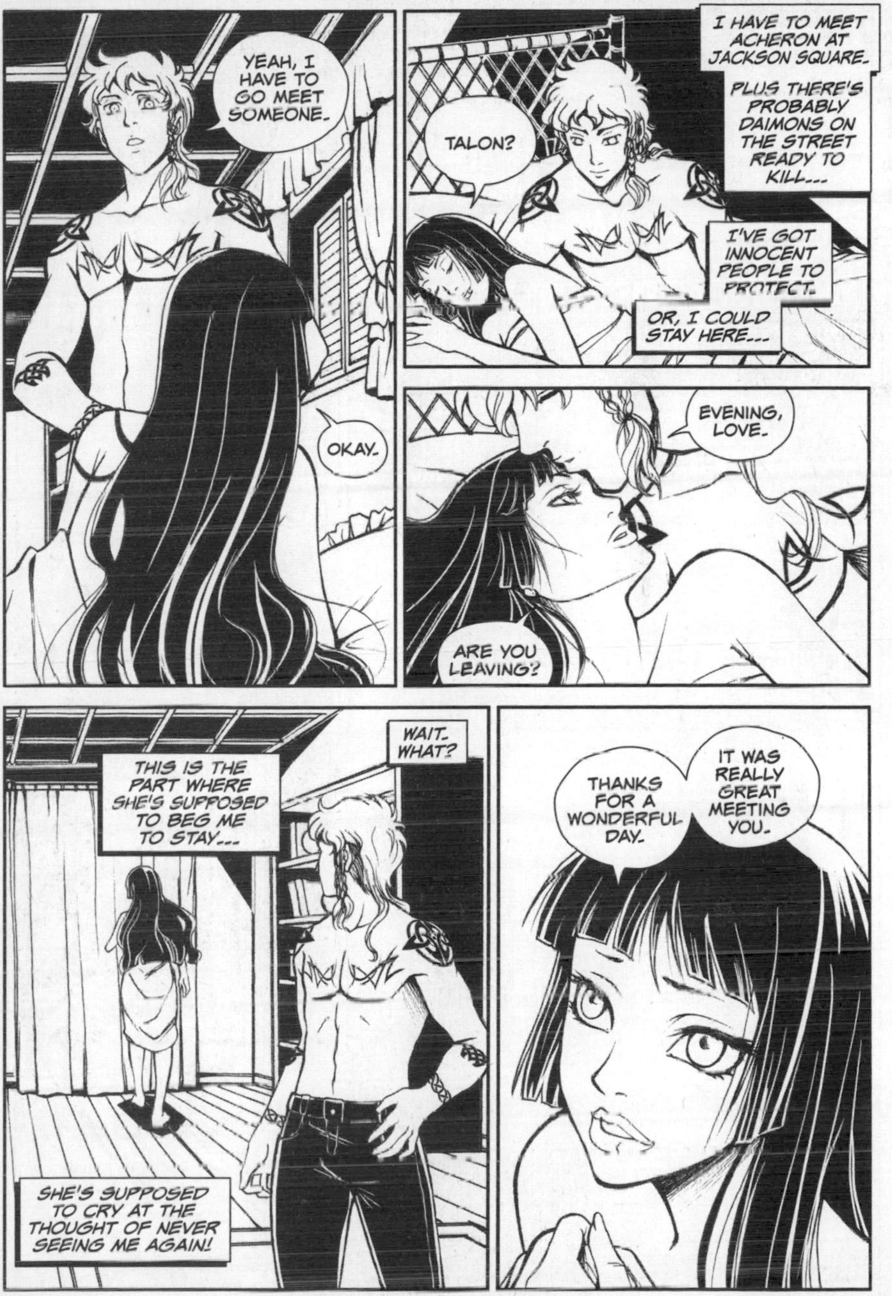
YEAH, I HAVE TO GO MEET SOMEONE.
OKAY.
I HAVE TO MEET ACHERON AT JACKSON SQUARE.
PLUS THERE'S PROBABLY DAIMONS ON THE STREET READY TO KILL...
TALON?
I'VE GOT INNOCENT PEOPLE TO PROTECT.
OR, I COULD STAY HERE...
EVENING, LOVE.
ARE YOU LEAVING?
WAIT. WHAT?
THIS IS THE PART WHERE SHE'S SUPPOSED TO BEG ME TO STAY...
SHE'S SUPPOSED TO CRY AT THE THOUGHT OF NEVER SEEING ME AGAIN!
THANKS FOR A WONDERFUL DAY.
IT WAS REALLY GREAT MEETING YOU.

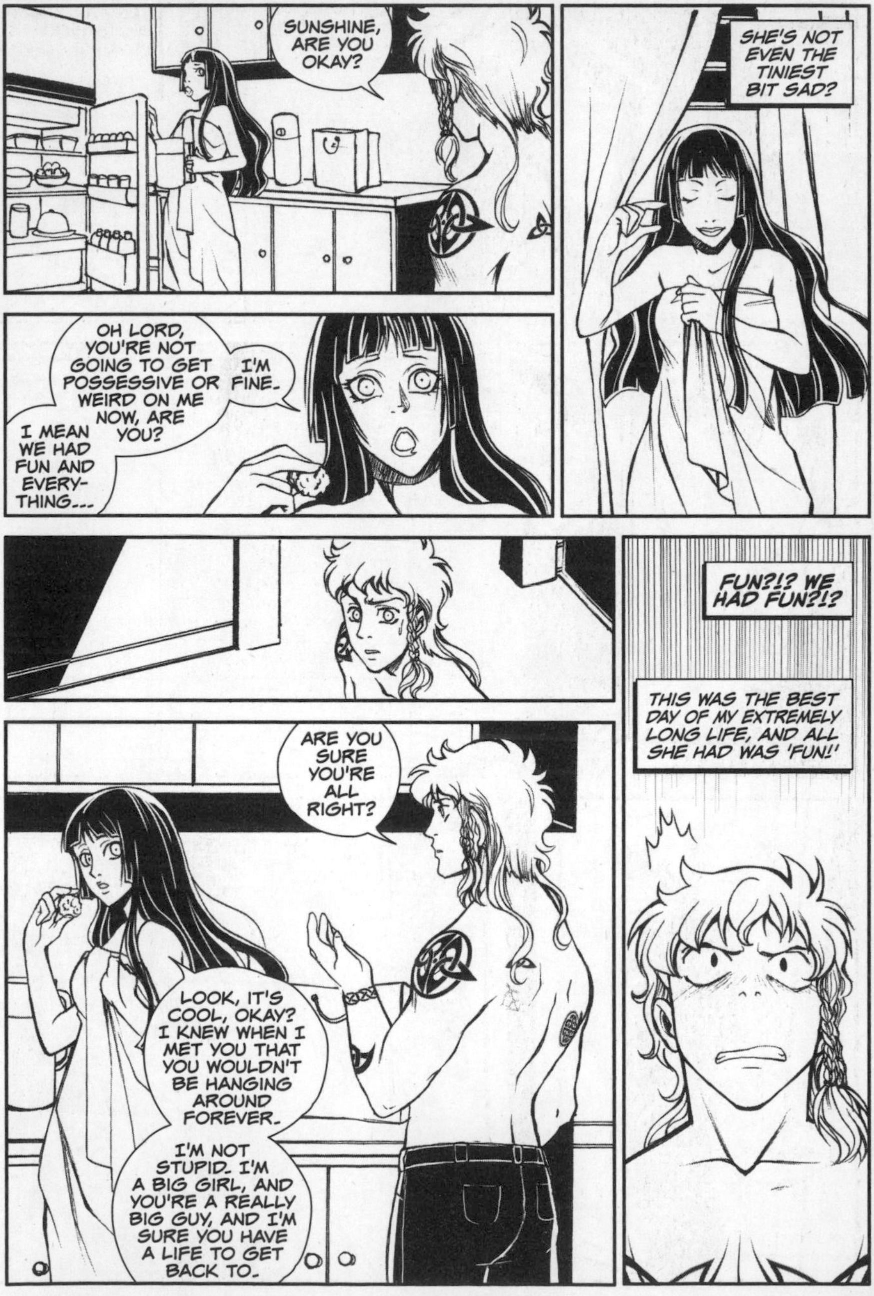
SUNSHINE, ARE YOU OKAY?
SHE'S NOT EVEN THE TINIEST BIT SAD?
I'M FINE.
OH LORD, YOU'RE NOT GOING TO GET POSSESSIVE OR WEIRD ON ME NOW, ARE YOU?
I MEAN WE HAD FUN AND EVERY-THING...
FUN?!? WE HAD FUN?!?
THIS WAS THE BEST DAY OF MY EXTREMELY LONG LIFE, AND ALL SHE HAD WAS 'FUN!'
ARE YOU SURE YOU'RE ALL RIGHT?
LOOK, IT'S COOL, OKAY? I KNEW WHEN I MET YOU THAT YOU WOULDN'T BE HANGING AROUND FOREVER.
I'M NOT STUPID. I'M A BIG GIRL, AND YOU'RE A REALLY BIG GUY, AND I'M SURE YOU HAVE A LIFE TO GET BACK TO.

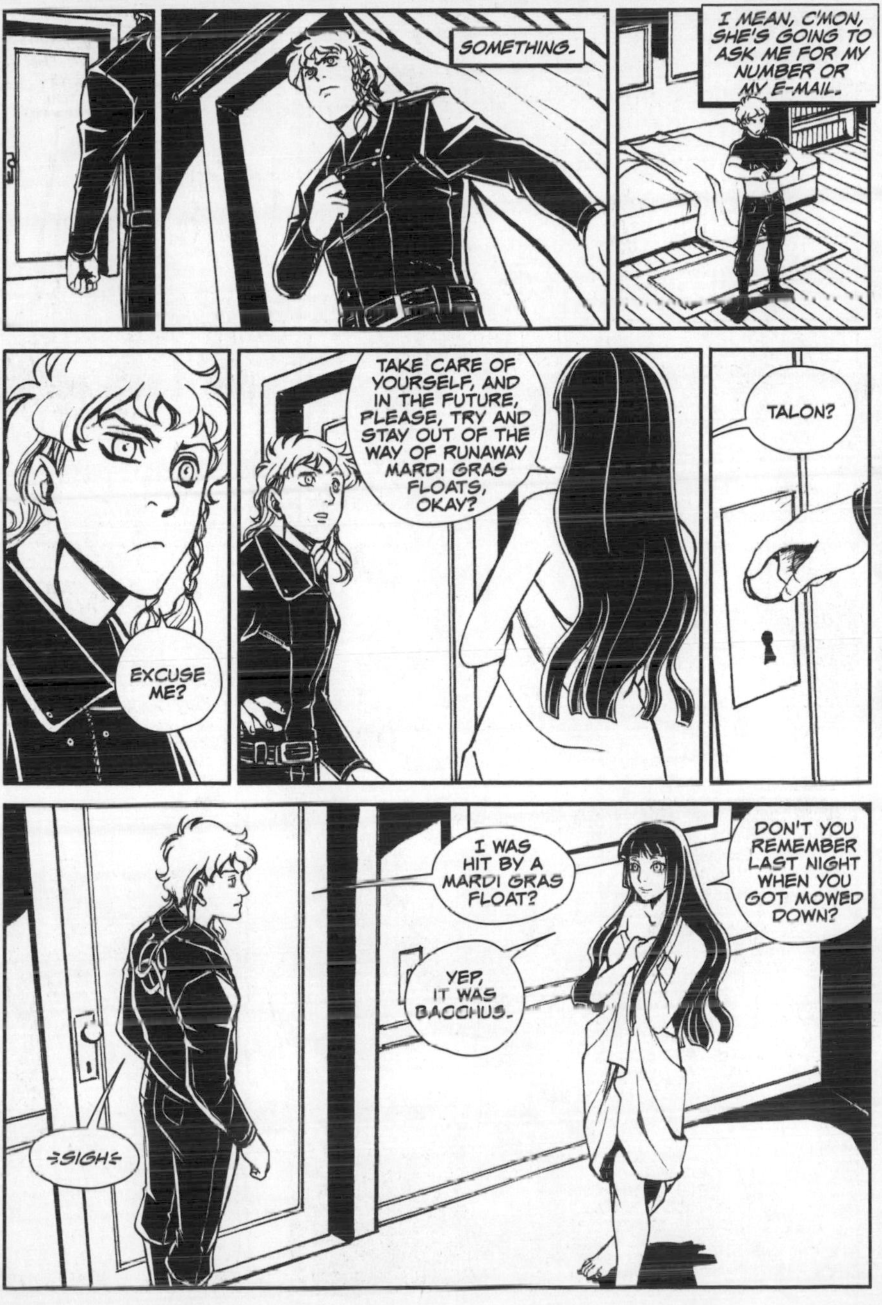
SOMETHING.
I MEAN, C'MON, SHE'S GOING TO ASK ME FOR MY NUMBER OR MY E-MAIL.
TAKE CARE OF YOURSELF, AND IN THE FUTURE, PLEASE, TRY AND STAY OUT OF THE WAY OF RUNAWAY MARDI GRAS FLOATS, OKAY?
EXCUSE ME?
TALON?
DON'T YOU REMEMBER LAST NIGHT WHEN YOU GOT MOWED DOWN?
I WAS HIT BY A MARDI GRAS FLOAT?
YEP, IT WAS BACCHUS.
=SIGH=

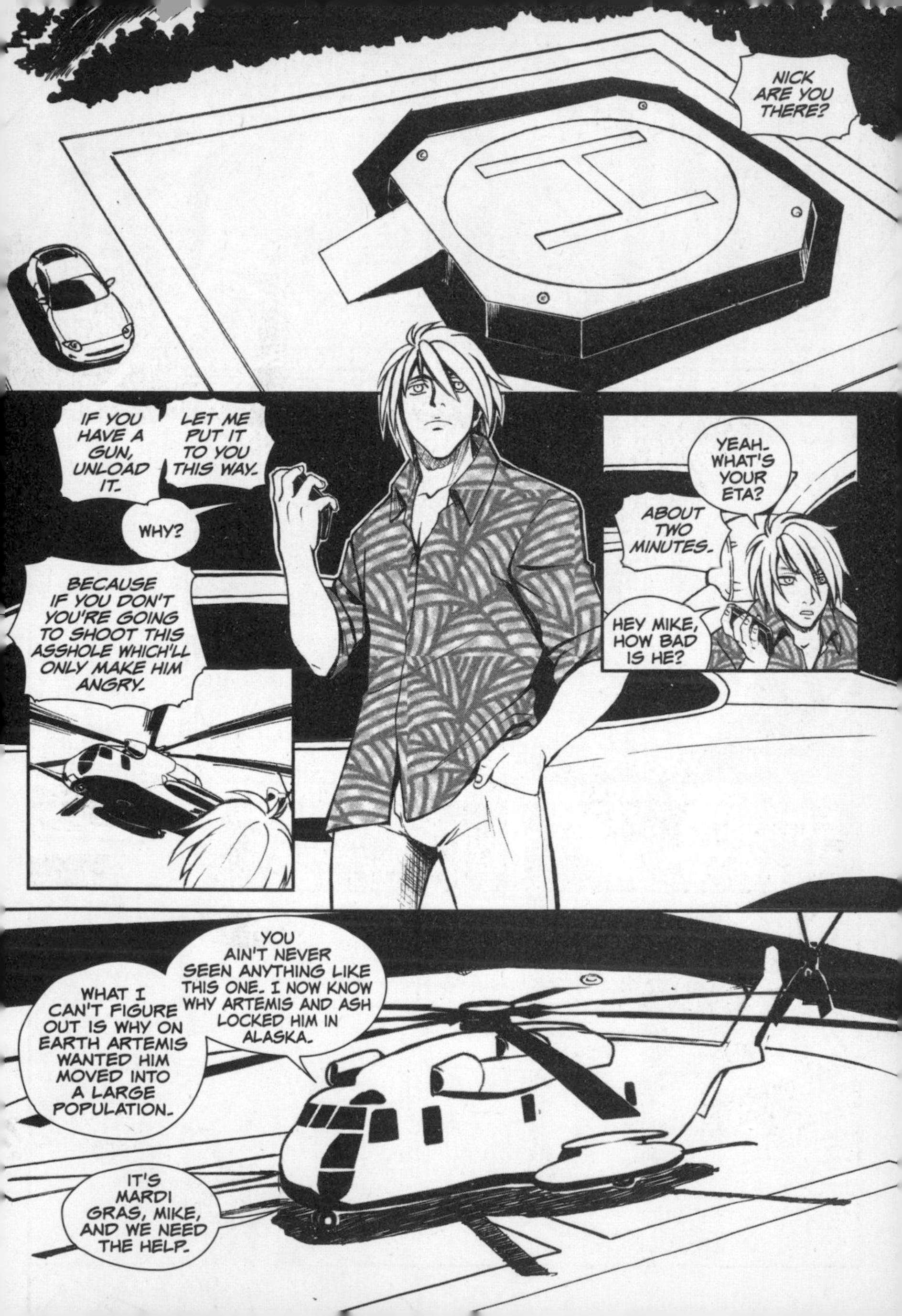
NICK ARE YOU THERE?
YEAH. WHAT'S YOUR ETA?
ABOUT TWO MINUTES.
HEY MIKE, HOW BAD IS HE?
LET ME PUT IT TO YOU THIS WAY.
IF YOU HAVE A GUN, UNLOAD IT.
WHY?
BECAUSE IF YOU DON'T YOU'RE GOING TO SHOOT THIS ASSHOLE WHICH'LL ONLY MAKE HIM ANGRY.
YOU AIN'T NEVER SEEN ANYTHING LIKE THIS ONE. I NOW KNOW WHY ARTEMIS AND ASH LOCKED HIM IN ALASKA.
WHAT I CAN'T FIGURE OUT IS WHY ON EARTH ARTEMIS WANTED HIM MOVED INTO A LARGE POPULATION.
IT'S MARDI GRAS, MIKE, AND WE NEED THE HELP.

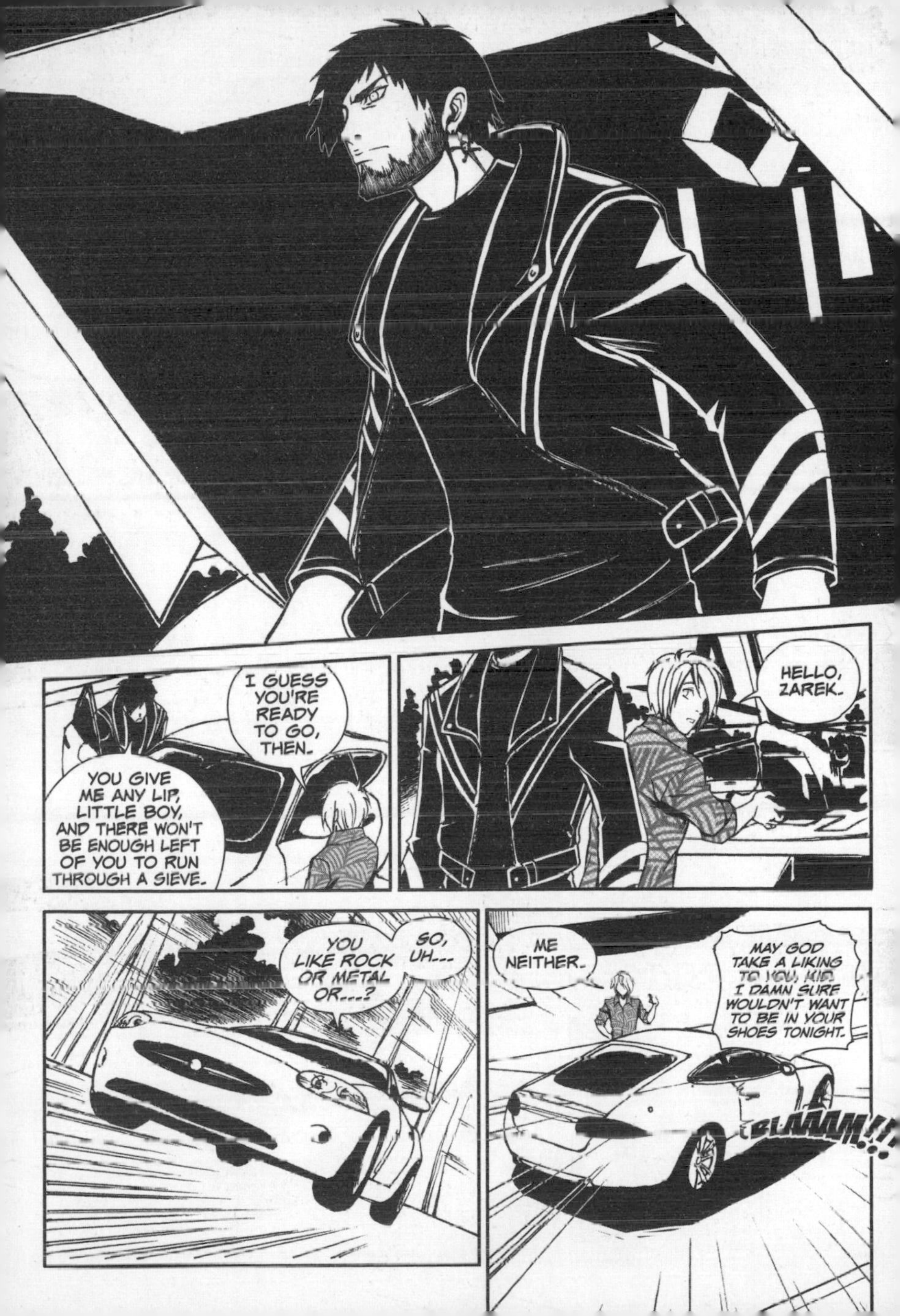
I GUESS YOU'RE READY TO GO, THEN.
YOU GIVE ME ANY LIP, LITTLE BOY, AND THERE WON'T BE ENOUGH LEFT OF YOU TO RUN THROUGH A SIEVE.
HELLO, ZAREK.
SO, UH...
YOU LIKE ROCK OR METAL OR...?
ME NEITHER.
MAY GOD TAKE A LIKING TO YOU, KID. I DAMN SURE WOULDN'T WANT TO BE IN YOUR SHOES TONIGHT.

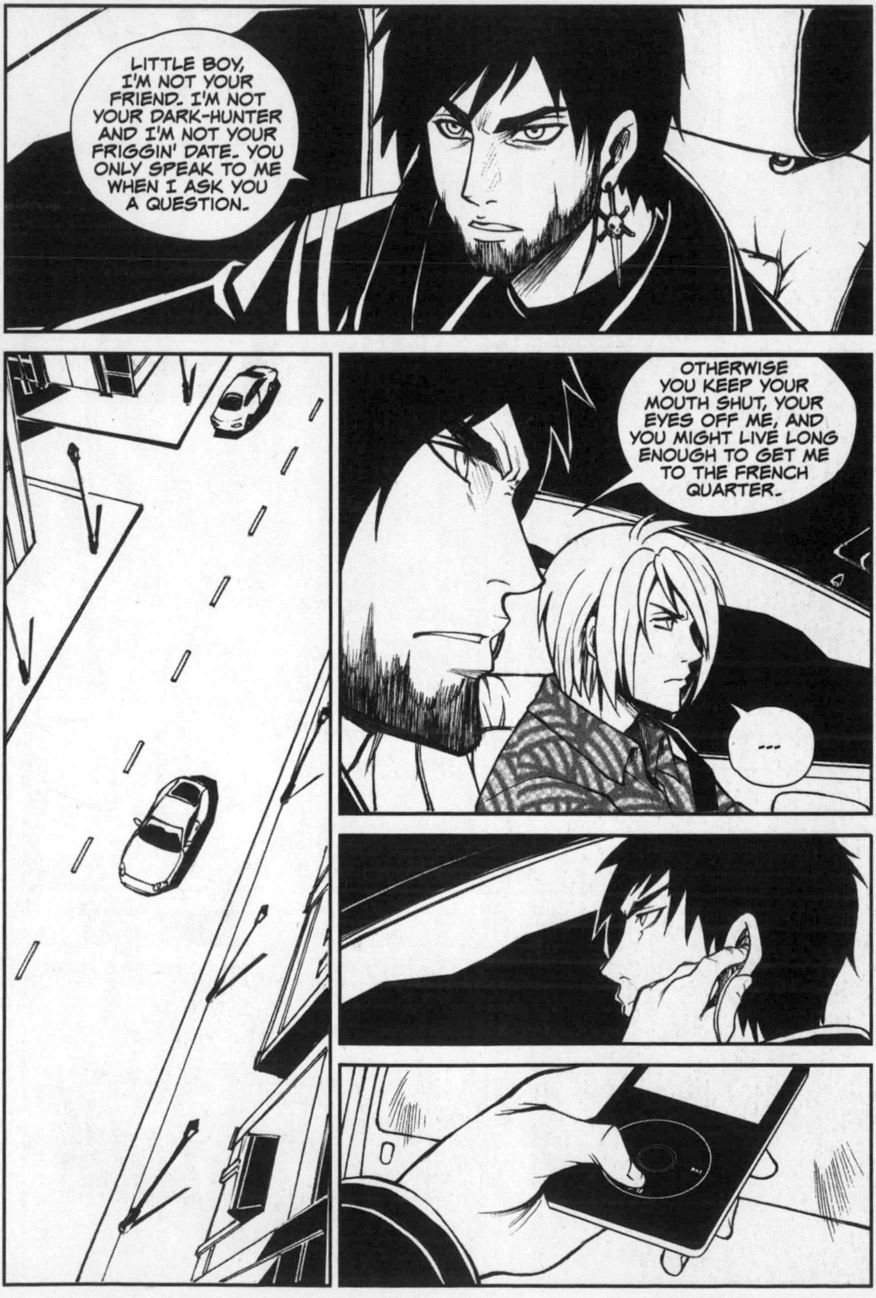
LITTLE BOY, I'M NOT YOUR FRIEND. I'M NOT YOUR DARK-HUNTER AND I'M NOT YOUR FRIGGIN' DATE. YOU ONLY SPEAK TO ME WHEN I ASK YOU A QUESTION.
OTHERWISE YOU KEEP YOUR MOUTH SHUT, YOUR EYES OFF ME, AND YOU MIGHT LIVE LONG ENOUGH TO GET ME TO THE FRENCH QUARTER.
...

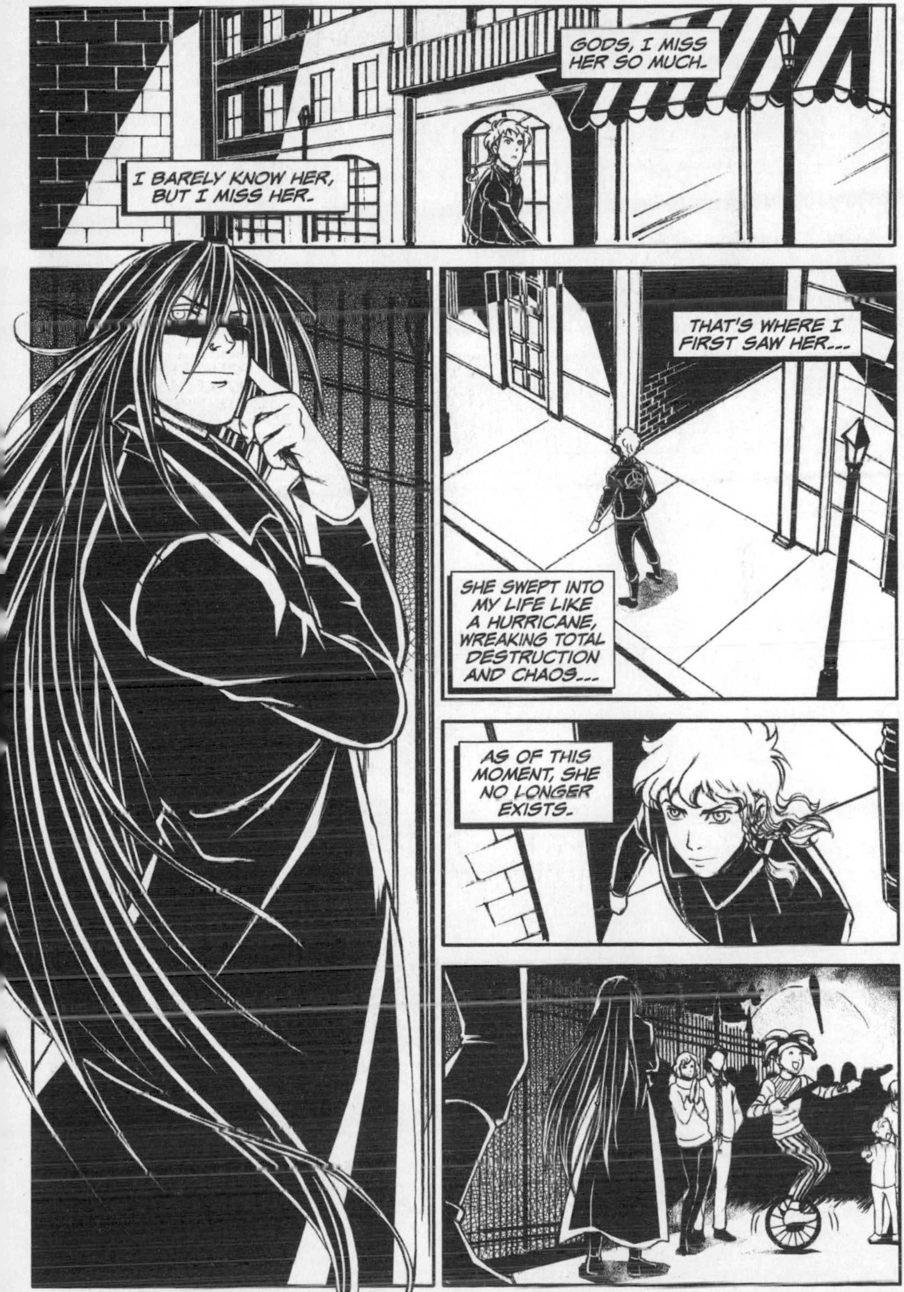
GODS, I MISS HER SO MUCH.
I BARELY KNOW HER, BUT I MISS HER.
THAT'S WHERE I FIRST SAW HER...
SHE SWEPT INTO MY LIFE LIKE A HURRICANE, WREAKING TOTAL DESTRUCTION AND CHAOS...
AS OF THIS MOMENT, SHE NO LONGER EXISTS.

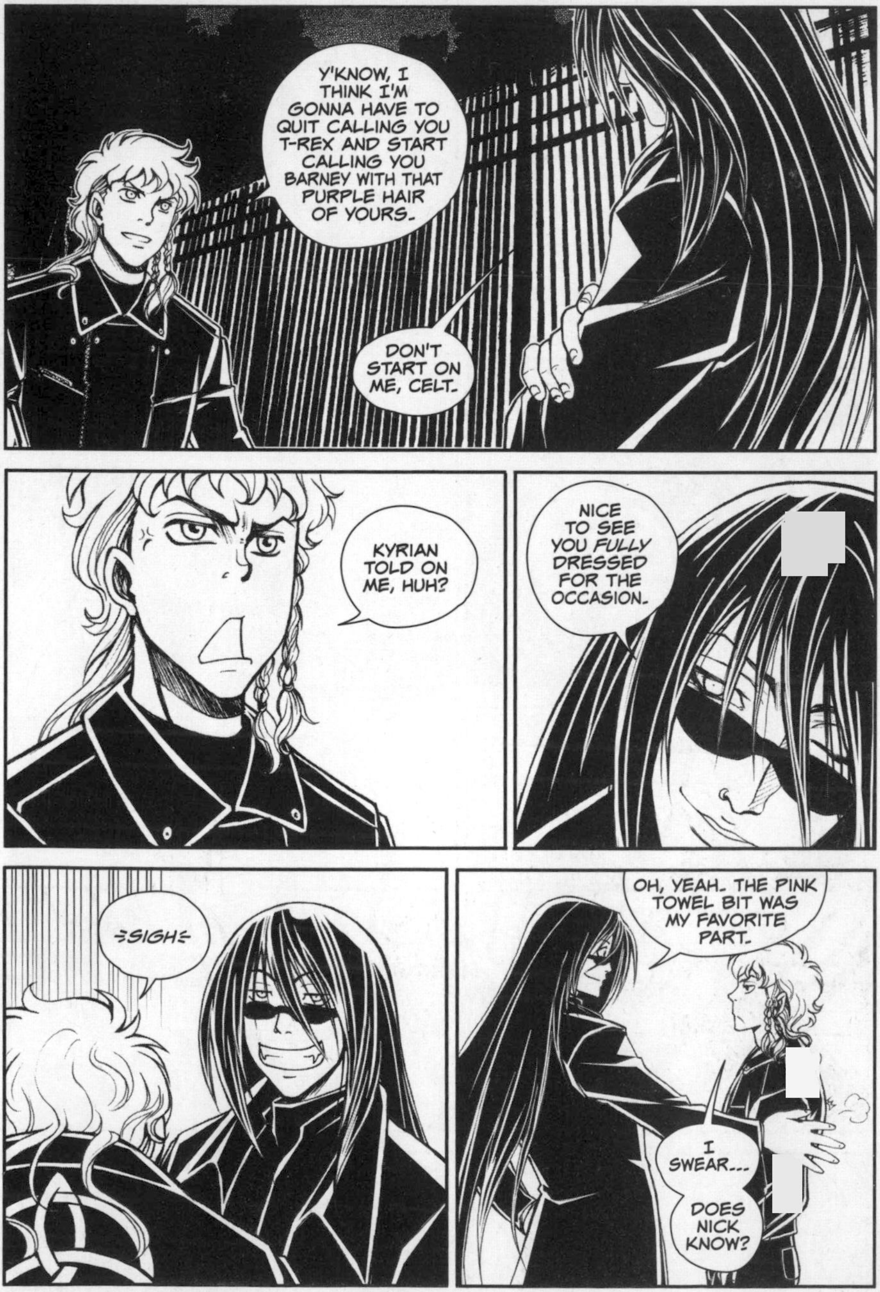
Y'KNOW, I THINK I'M GONNA HAVE TO QUIT CALLING YOU T-REX AND START CALLING YOU BARNEY WITH THAT PURPLE HAIR OF YOURS.
DON'T START ON ME, CELT.
KYRIAN TOLD ON ME, HUH?
NICE TO SEE YOU *FULLY* DRESSED FOR THE OCCASION.
=SIGH=
OH, YEAH. THE PINK TOWEL BIT WAS MY FAVORITE PART.
I SWEAR...
DOES NICK KNOW?

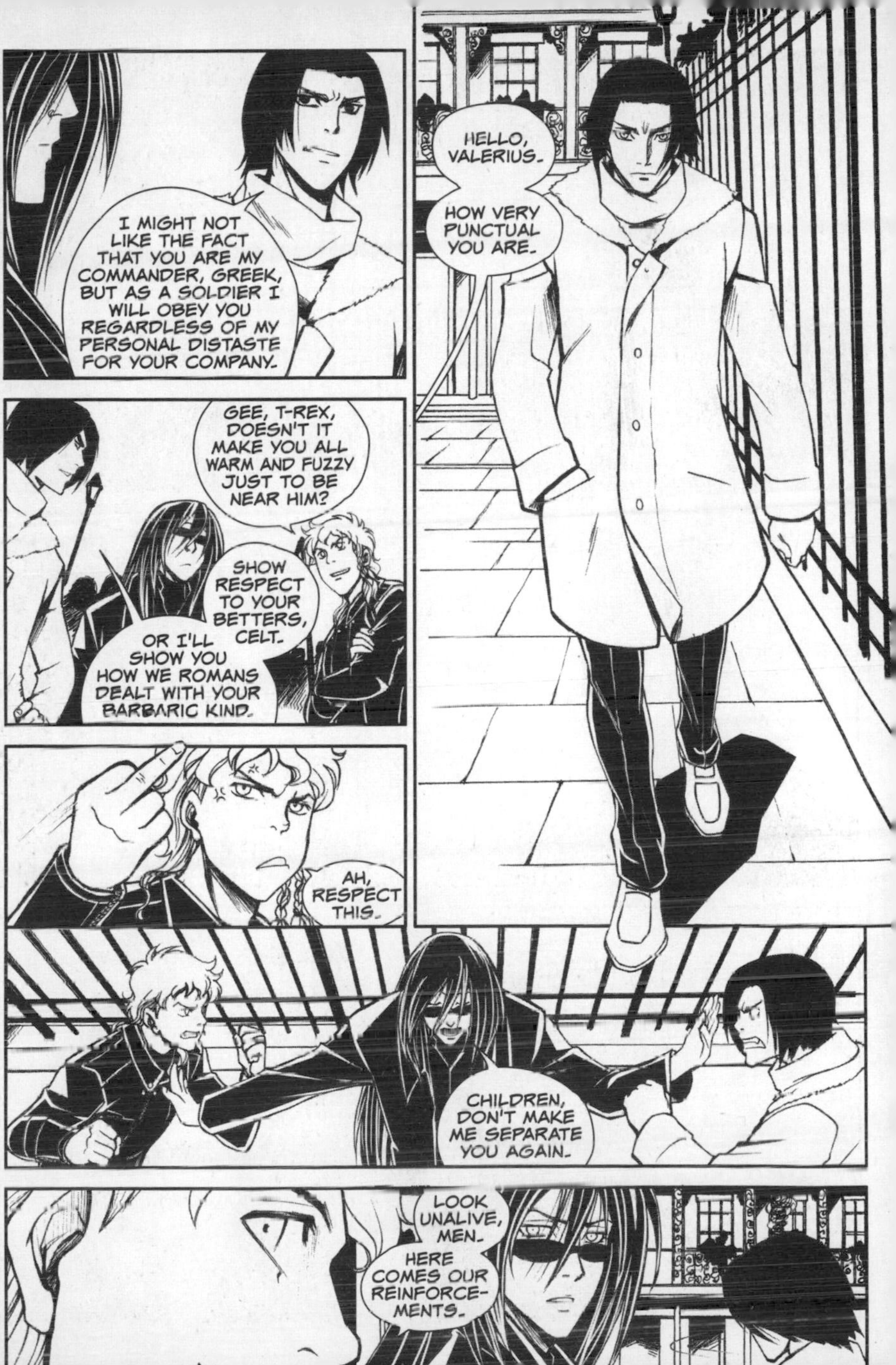
I MIGHT NOT LIKE THE FACT THAT YOU ARE MY COMMANDER, GREEK, BUT AS A SOLDIER I WILL OBEY YOU REGARDLESS OF MY PERSONAL DISTASTE FOR YOUR COMPANY.
GEE, T-REX, DOESN'T IT MAKE YOU ALL WARM AND FUZZY JUST TO BE NEAR HIM?
SHOW RESPECT TO YOUR BETTERS, CELT.
OR I'LL SHOW YOU HOW WE ROMANS DEALT WITH YOUR BARBARIC KIND.
AH, RESPECT THIS.
HELLO, VALERIUS.
HOW VERY PUNCTUAL YOU ARE.
CHILDREN, DON'T MAKE ME SEPARATE YOU AGAIN.
LOOK UNALIVE, MEN.
HERE COMES OUR REINFORCEMENTS.

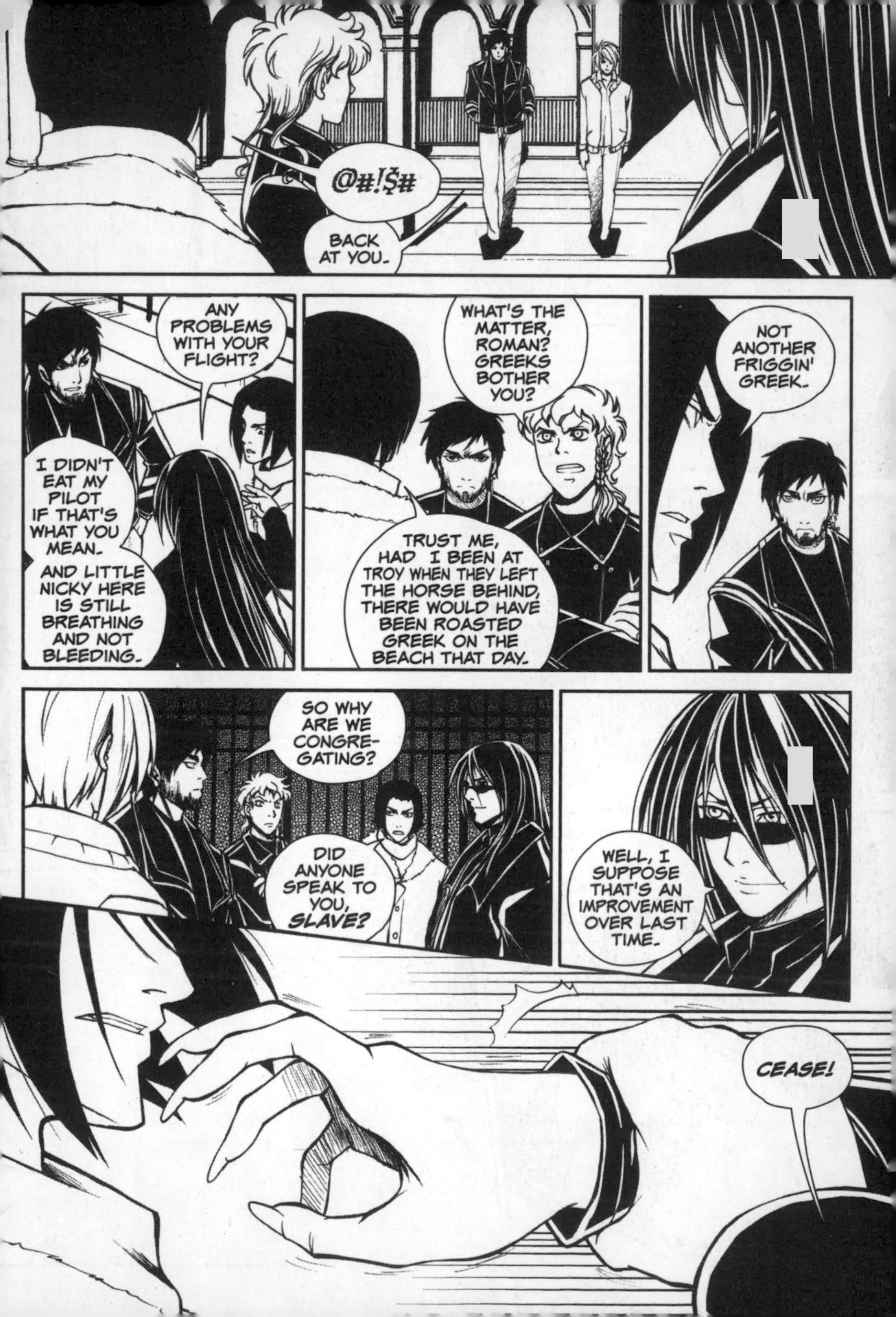
@#!$#
BACK AT YOU.
ANY PROBLEMS WITH YOUR FLIGHT?
I DIDN'T EAT MY PILOT IF THAT'S WHAT YOU MEAN.
AND LITTLE NICKY HERE IS STILL BREATHING AND NOT BLEEDING.
WHAT'S THE MATTER, ROMAN? GREEKS BOTHER YOU?
TRUST ME, HAD I BEEN AT TROY WHEN THEY LEFT THE HORSE BEHIND, THERE WOULD HAVE BEEN ROASTED GREEK ON THE BEACH THAT DAY.
NOT ANOTHER FRIGGIN' GREEK.
SO WHY ARE WE CONGREGATING?
DID ANYONE SPEAK TO YOU, SLAVE?
WELL, I SUPPOSE THAT'S AN IMPROVEMENT OVER LAST TIME.
CEASE!

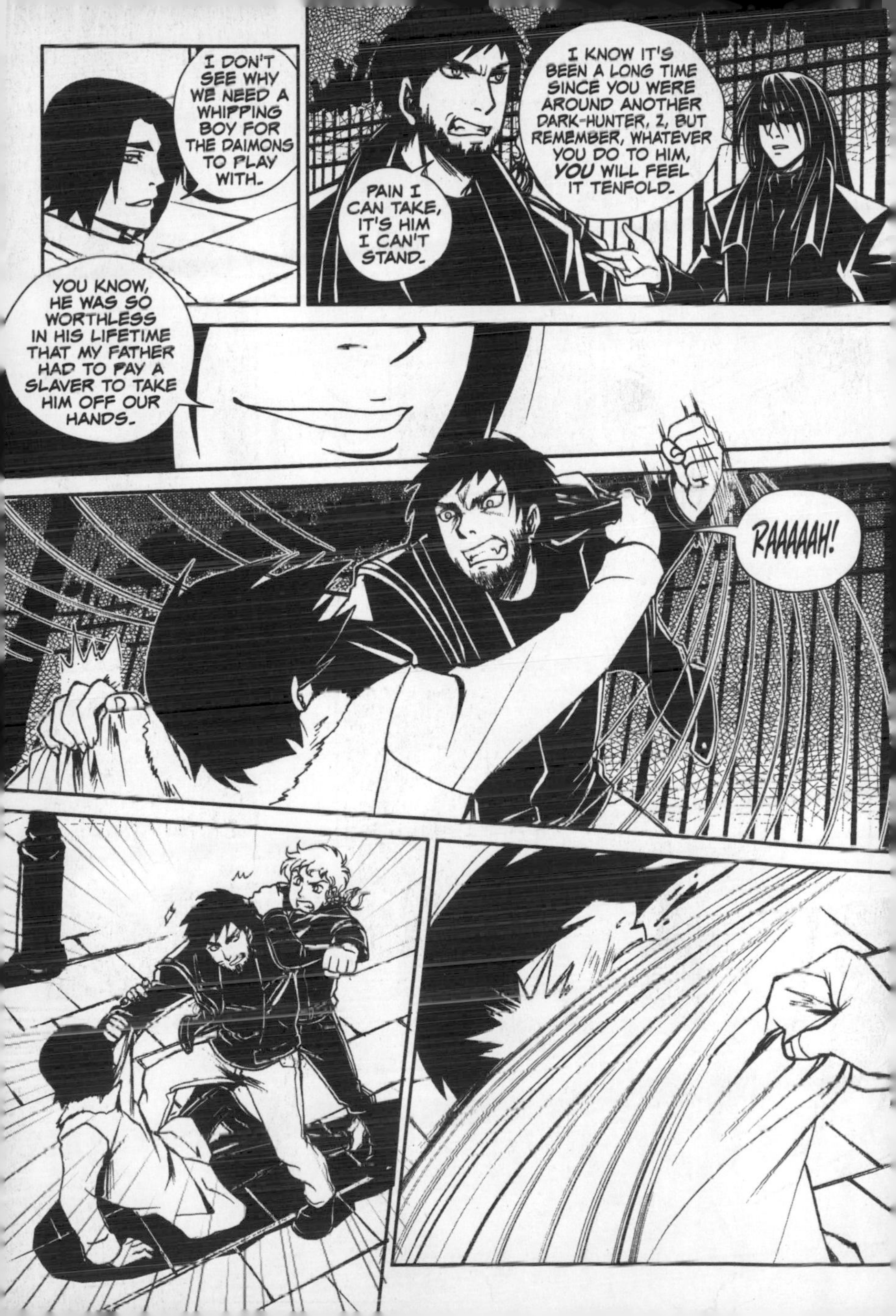
I DON'T SEE WHY WE NEED A WHIPPING BOY FOR THE DAIMONS TO PLAY WITH.
PAIN I CAN TAKE, IT'S HIM I CAN'T STAND.
I KNOW IT'S BEEN A LONG TIME SINCE YOU WERE AROUND ANOTHER DARK-HUNTER, Z, BUT REMEMBER, WHATEVER YOU DO TO HIM, YOU WILL FEEL IT TENFOLD.
YOU KNOW, HE WAS SO WORTHLESS IN HIS LIFETIME THAT MY FATHER HAD TO PAY A SLAVER TO TAKE HIM OFF OUR HANDS.
RAAAAAH!

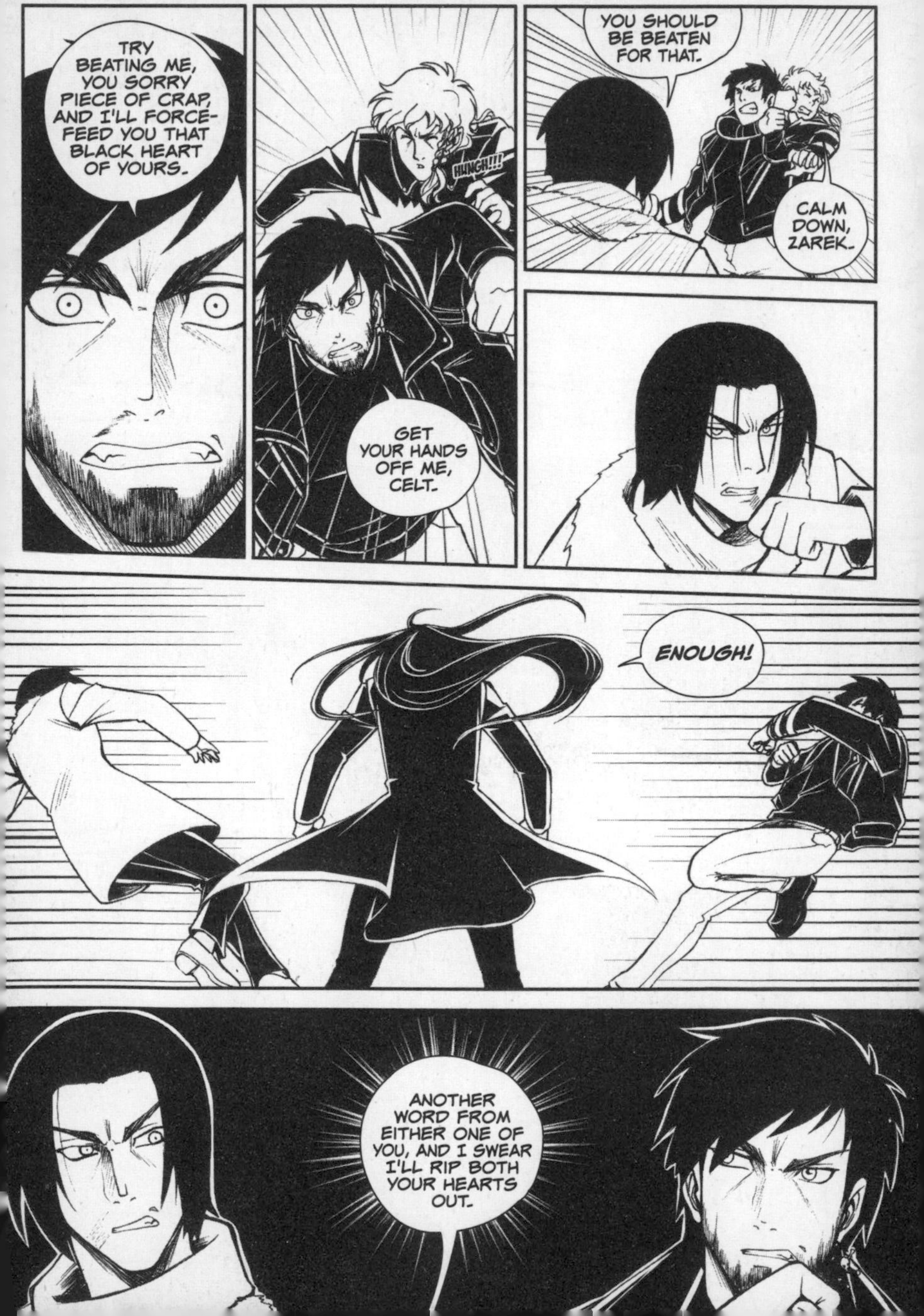
TRY BEATING ME, YOU SORRY PIECE OF CRAP, AND I'LL FORCE-FEED YOU THAT BLACK HEART OF YOURS.
HUNGH!!!
GET YOUR HANDS OFF ME, CELT.
YOU SHOULD BE BEATEN FOR THAT.
CALM DOWN, ZAREK.
ENOUGH!
ANOTHER WORD FROM EITHER ONE OF YOU, AND I SWEAR I'LL RIP BOTH YOUR HEARTS OUT.

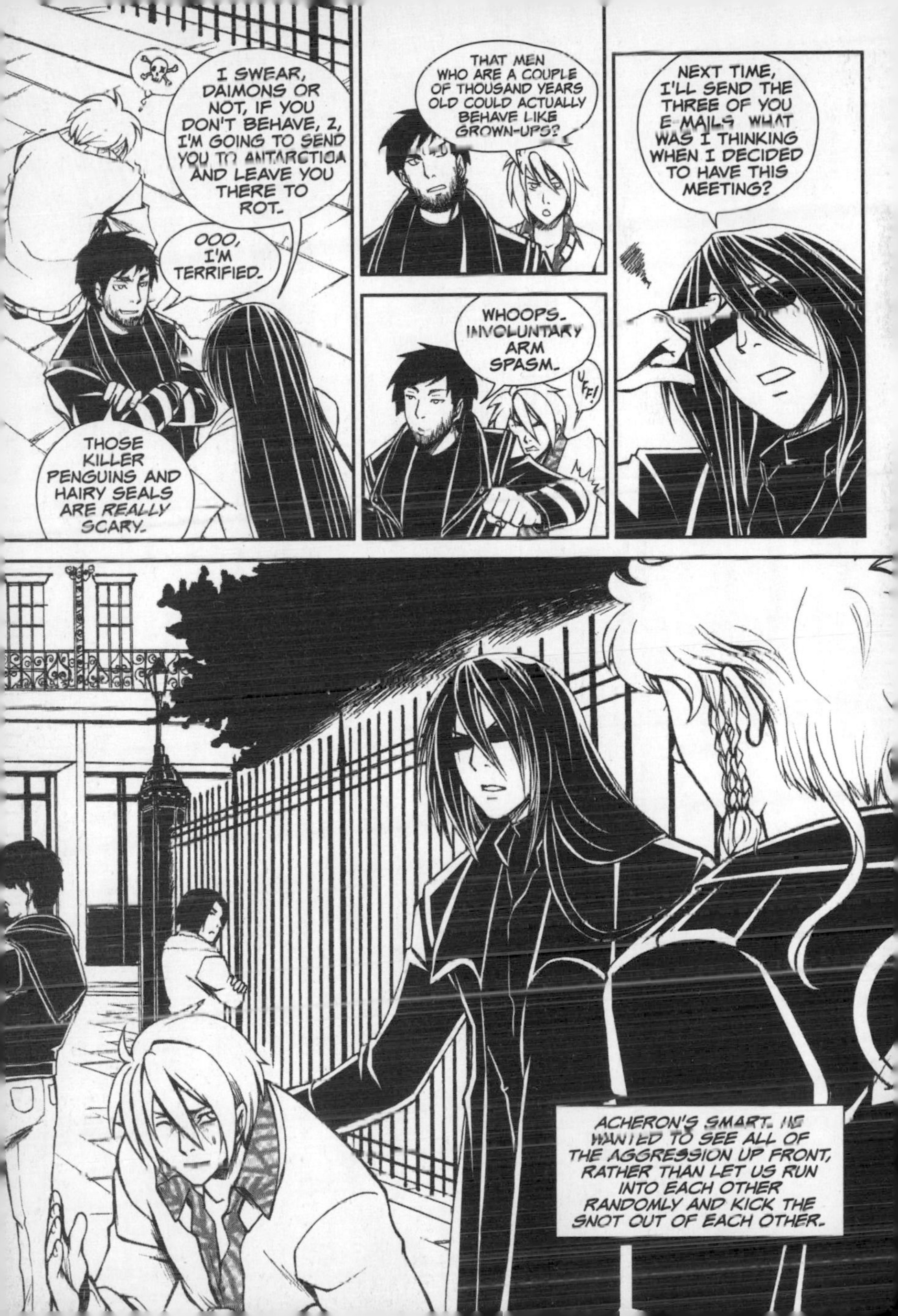
I SWEAR, DAIMONS OR NOT, IF YOU DON'T BEHAVE, Z, I'M GOING TO SEND YOU TO ANTARCTICA AND LEAVE YOU THERE TO ROT.
OOO, I'M TERRIFIED.
THOSE KILLER PENGUINS AND HAIRY SEALS ARE REALLY SCARY.
THAT MEN WHO ARE A COUPLE OF THOUSAND YEARS OLD COULD ACTUALLY BEHAVE LIKE GROWN-UPS?
WHOOPS. INVOLUNTARY ARM SPASM.
UFF!
NEXT TIME, I'LL SEND THE THREE OF YOU E-MAILS. WHAT WAS I THINKING WHEN I DECIDED TO HAVE THIS MEETING?
ACHERON'S SMART. HE WANTED TO SEE ALL OF THE AGGRESSION UP FRONT, RATHER THAN LET US RUN INTO EACH OTHER RANDOMLY AND KICK THE SNOT OUT OF EACH OTHER.

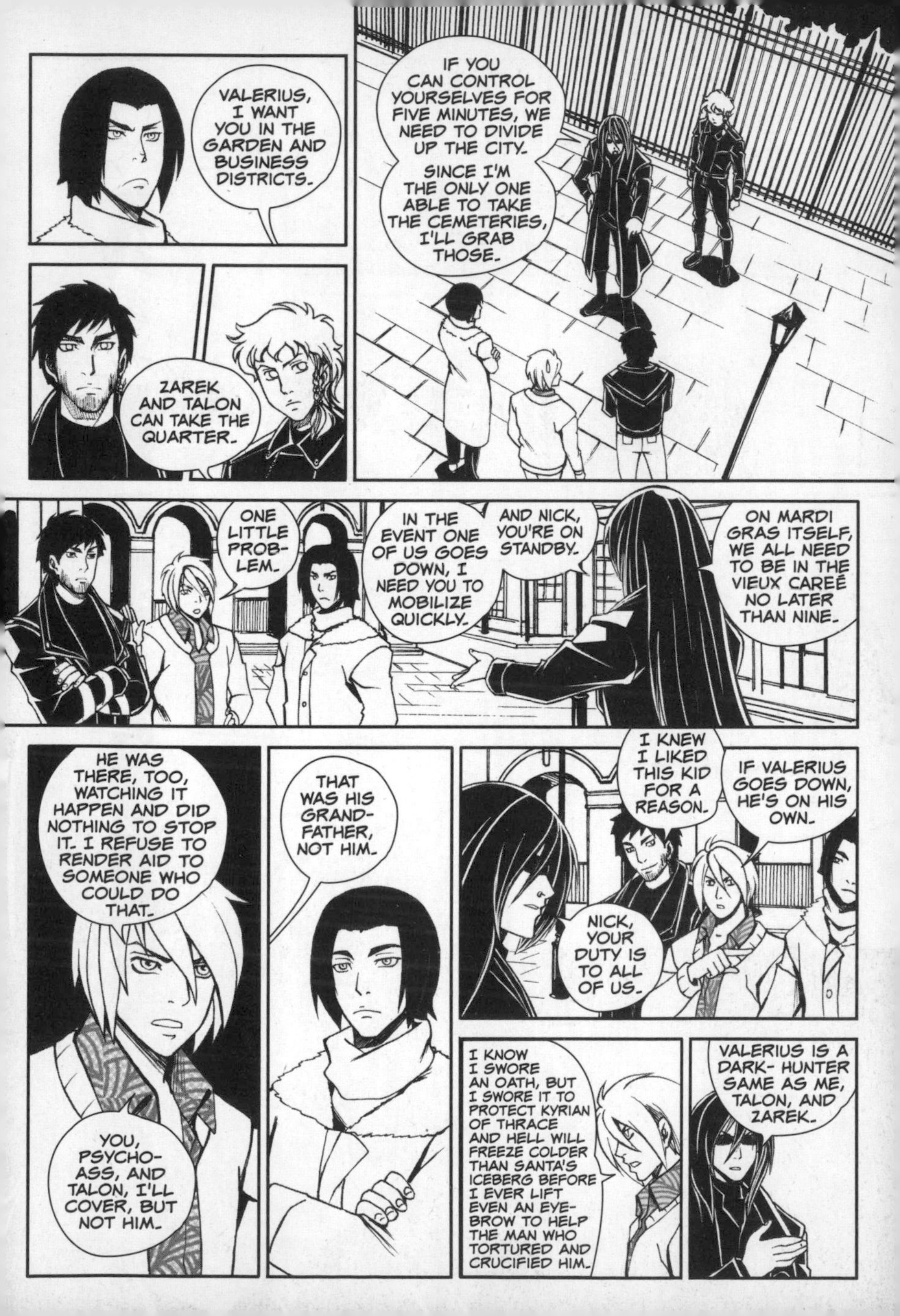
VALERIUS, I WANT YOU IN THE GARDEN AND BUSINESS DISTRICTS.
ZAREK AND TALON CAN TAKE THE QUARTER.
IF YOU CAN CONTROL YOURSELVES FOR FIVE MINUTES, WE NEED TO DIVIDE UP THE CITY.
SINCE I'M THE ONLY ONE ABLE TO TAKE THE CEMETERIES, I'LL GRAB THOSE.
ON MARDI GRAS ITSELF, WE ALL NEED TO BE IN THE VIEUX CAREÉ NO LATER THAN NINE.
AND NICK, YOU'RE ON STANDBY.
IN THE EVENT ONE OF US GOES DOWN, I NEED YOU TO MOBILIZE QUICKLY.
ONE LITTLE PROB-LEM.
HE WAS THERE, TOO, WATCHING IT HAPPEN AND DID NOTHING TO STOP IT. I REFUSE TO RENDER AID TO SOMEONE WHO COULD DO THAT.
YOU, PSYCHO-ASS, AND TALON, I'LL COVER, BUT NOT HIM.
THAT WAS HIS GRAND-FATHER, NOT HIM.
IF VALERIUS GOES DOWN, HE'S ON HIS OWN.
I KNEW I LIKED THIS KID FOR A REASON.
NICK, YOUR DUTY IS TO ALL OF US.
VALERIUS IS A DARK- HUNTER SAME AS ME, TALON, AND ZAREK.
I KNOW I SWORE AN OATH, BUT I SWORE IT TO PROTECT KYRIAN OF THRACE AND HELL WILL FREEZE COLDER THAN SANTA'S ICEBERG BEFORE I EVER LIFT EVEN AN EYE-BROW TO HELP THE MAN WHO TORTURED AND CRUCIFIED HIM.

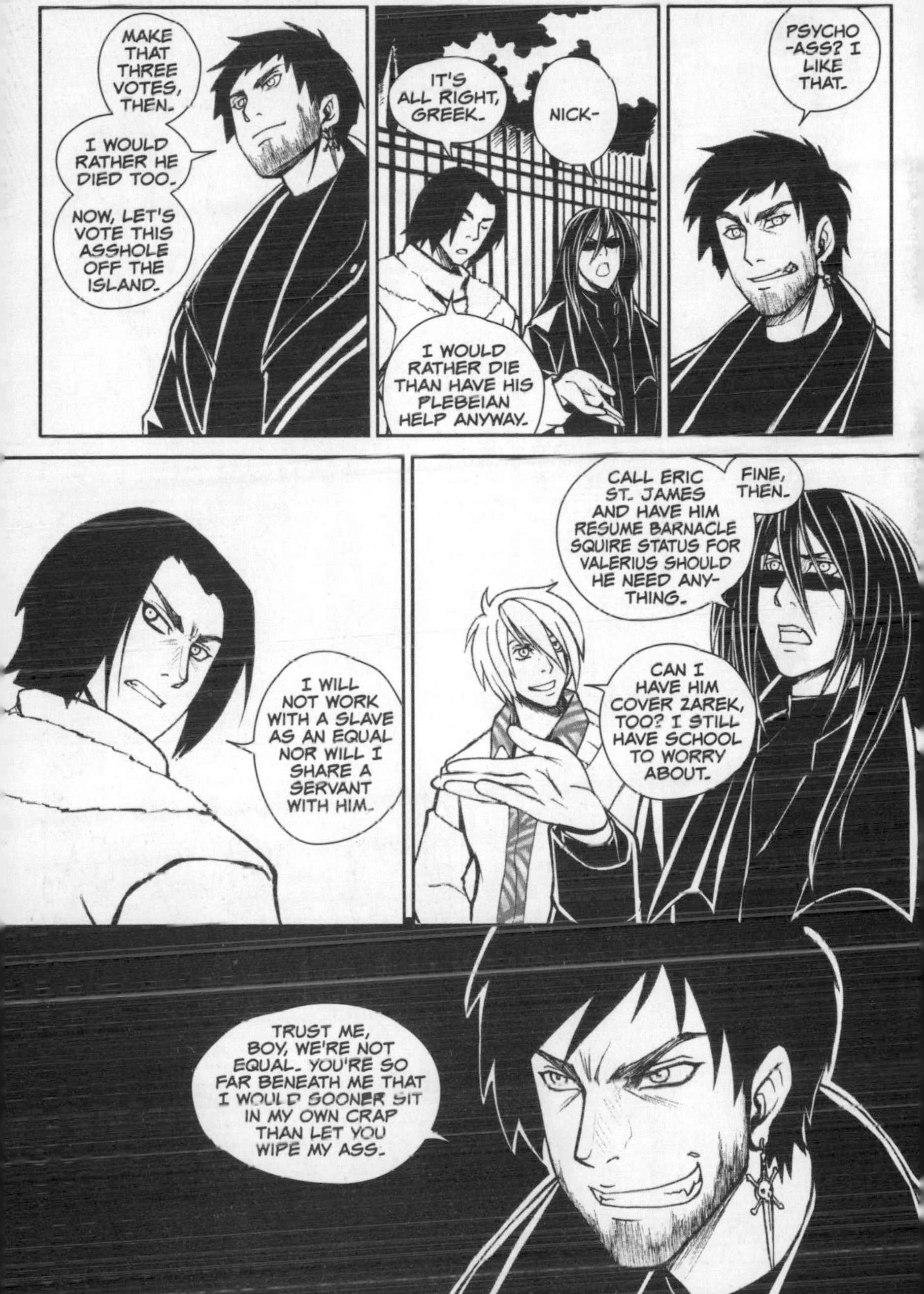

MAKE THAT THREE VOTES, THEN.
I WOULD RATHER HE DIED TOO.
NOW, LET'S VOTE THIS ASSHOLE OFF THE ISLAND.
IT'S ALL RIGHT, GREEK.
NICK-
I WOULD RATHER DIE THAN HAVE HIS PLEBEIAN HELP ANYWAY.
PSYCHO-ASS? I LIKE THAT.
I WILL NOT WORK WITH A SLAVE AS AN EQUAL NOR WILL I SHARE A SERVANT WITH HIM.
FINE, THEN.
CALL ERIC ST. JAMES AND HAVE HIM RESUME BARNACLE SQUIRE STATUS FOR VALERIUS SHOULD HE NEED ANYTHING.
CAN I HAVE HIM COVER ZAREK, TOO? I STILL HAVE SCHOOL TO WORRY ABOUT.
TRUST ME, BOY, WE'RE NOT EQUAL. YOU'RE SO FAR BENEATH ME THAT I WOULD SOONER SIT IN MY OWN CRAP THAN LET YOU WIPE MY ASS.

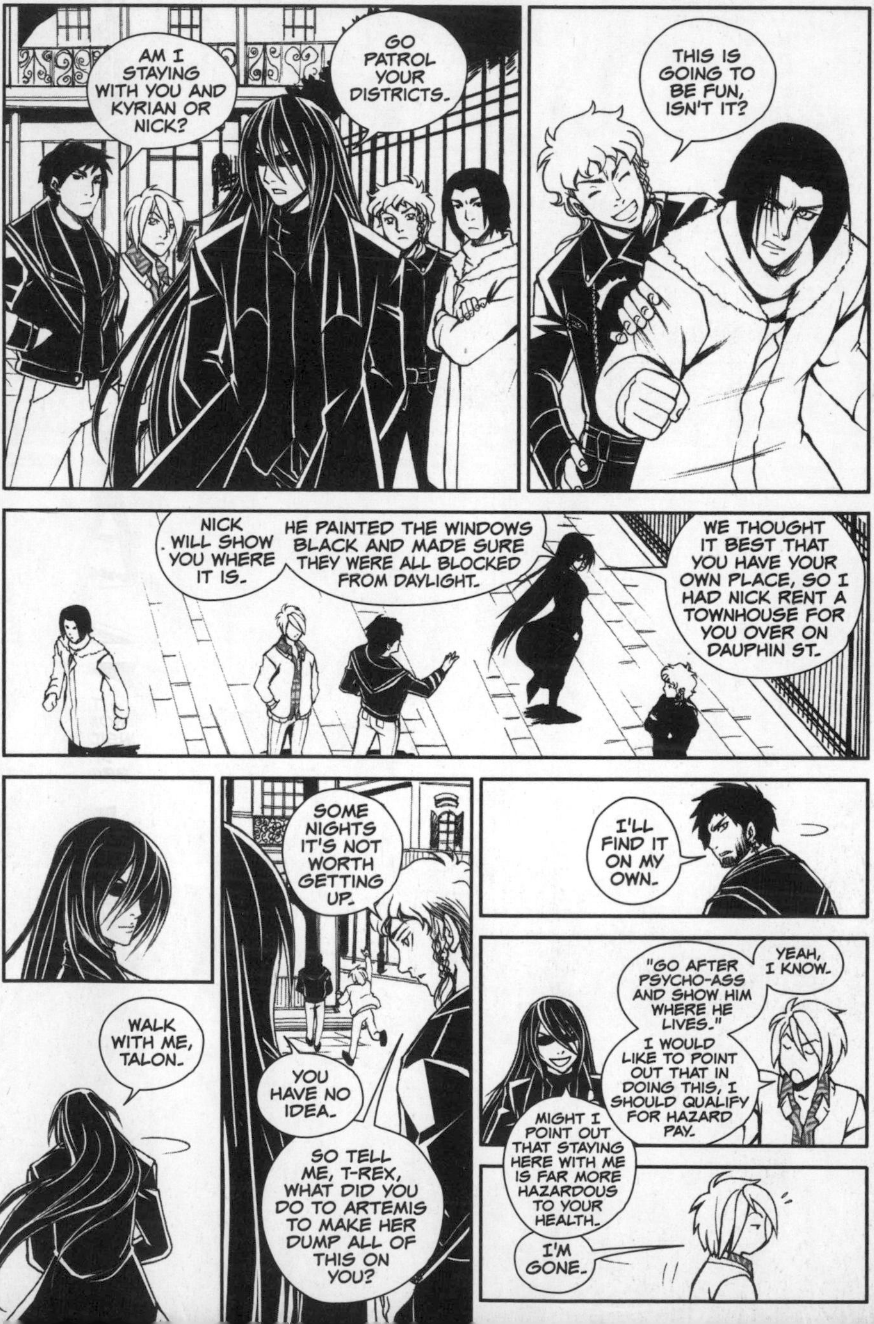

AM I STAYING WITH YOU AND KYRIAN OR NICK?
GO PATROL YOUR DISTRICTS.
THIS IS GOING TO BE FUN, ISN'T IT?
WE THOUGHT IT BEST THAT YOU HAVE YOUR OWN PLACE, SO I HAD NICK RENT A TOWNHOUSE FOR YOU OVER ON DAUPHIN ST.
HE PAINTED THE WINDOWS BLACK AND MADE SURE THEY WERE ALL BLOCKED FROM DAYLIGHT.
NICK WILL SHOW YOU WHERE IT IS.
I'LL FIND IT ON MY OWN.
"GO AFTER PSYCHO-ASS AND SHOW HIM WHERE HE LIVES."
YEAH, I KNOW.
I WOULD LIKE TO POINT OUT THAT IN DOING THIS, I SHOULD QUALIFY FOR HAZARD PAY.
MIGHT I POINT OUT THAT STAYING HERE WITH ME IS FAR MORE HAZARDOUS TO YOUR HEALTH.
I'M GONE.
WALK WITH ME, TALON.
SOME NIGHTS IT'S NOT WORTH GETTING UP.
YOU HAVE NO IDEA.
SO TELL ME, T-REX, WHAT DID YOU DO TO ARTEMIS TO MAKE HER DUMP ALL OF THIS ON YOU?

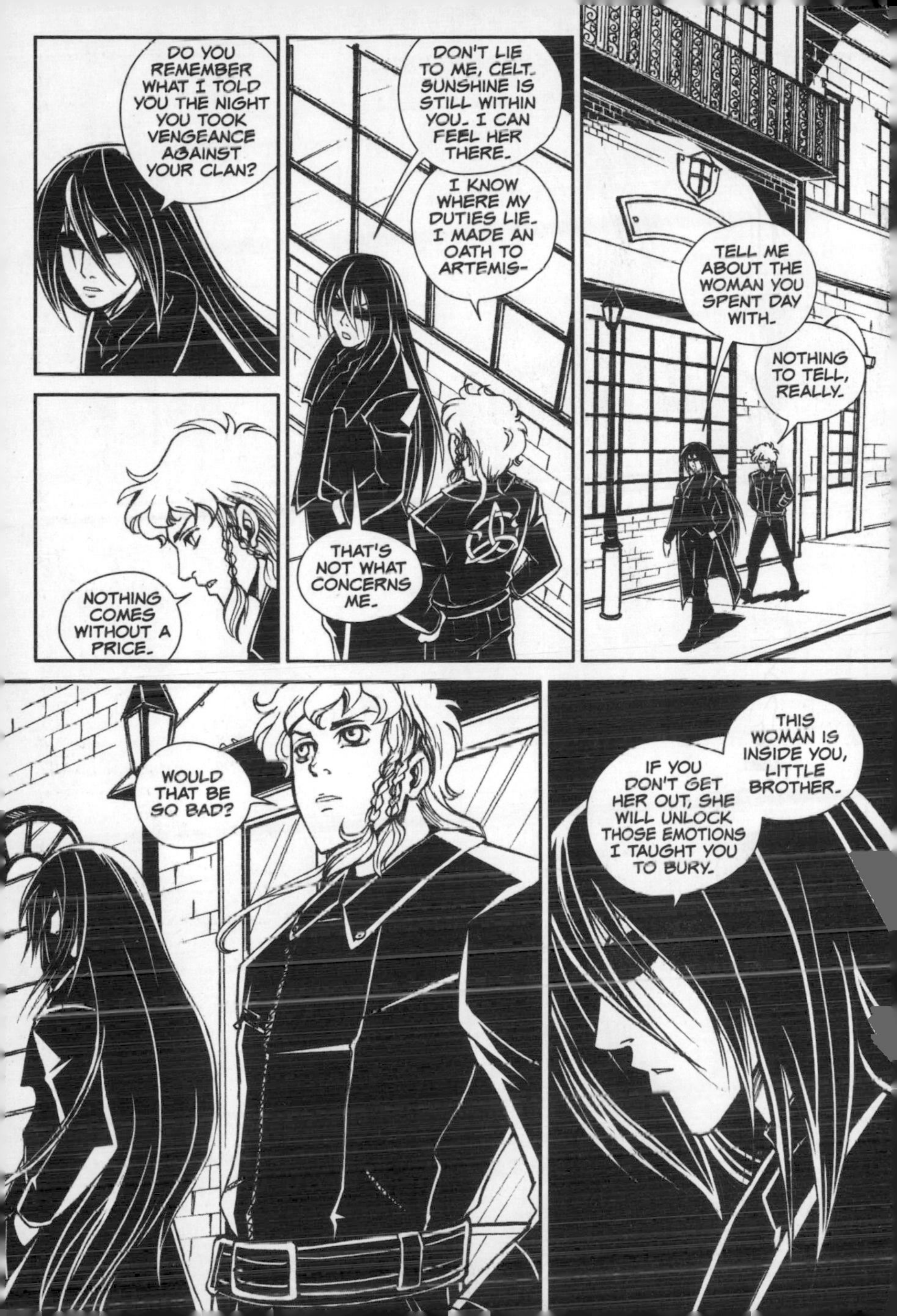
DO YOU REMEMBER WHAT I TOLD YOU THE NIGHT YOU TOOK VENGEANCE AGAINST YOUR CLAN?
NOTHING COMES WITHOUT A PRICE.
DON'T LIE TO ME, CELT. SUNSHINE IS STILL WITHIN YOU. I CAN FEEL HER THERE.
I KNOW WHERE MY DUTIES LIE. I MADE AN OATH TO ARTEMIS-
THAT'S NOT WHAT CONCERNS ME.
TELL ME ABOUT THE WOMAN YOU SPENT DAY WITH.
NOTHING TO TELL, REALLY.
WOULD THAT BE SO BAD?
THIS WOMAN IS INSIDE YOU, LITTLE BROTHER.
IF YOU DON'T GET HER OUT, SHE WILL UNLOCK THOSE EMOTIONS I TAUGHT YOU TO BURY.

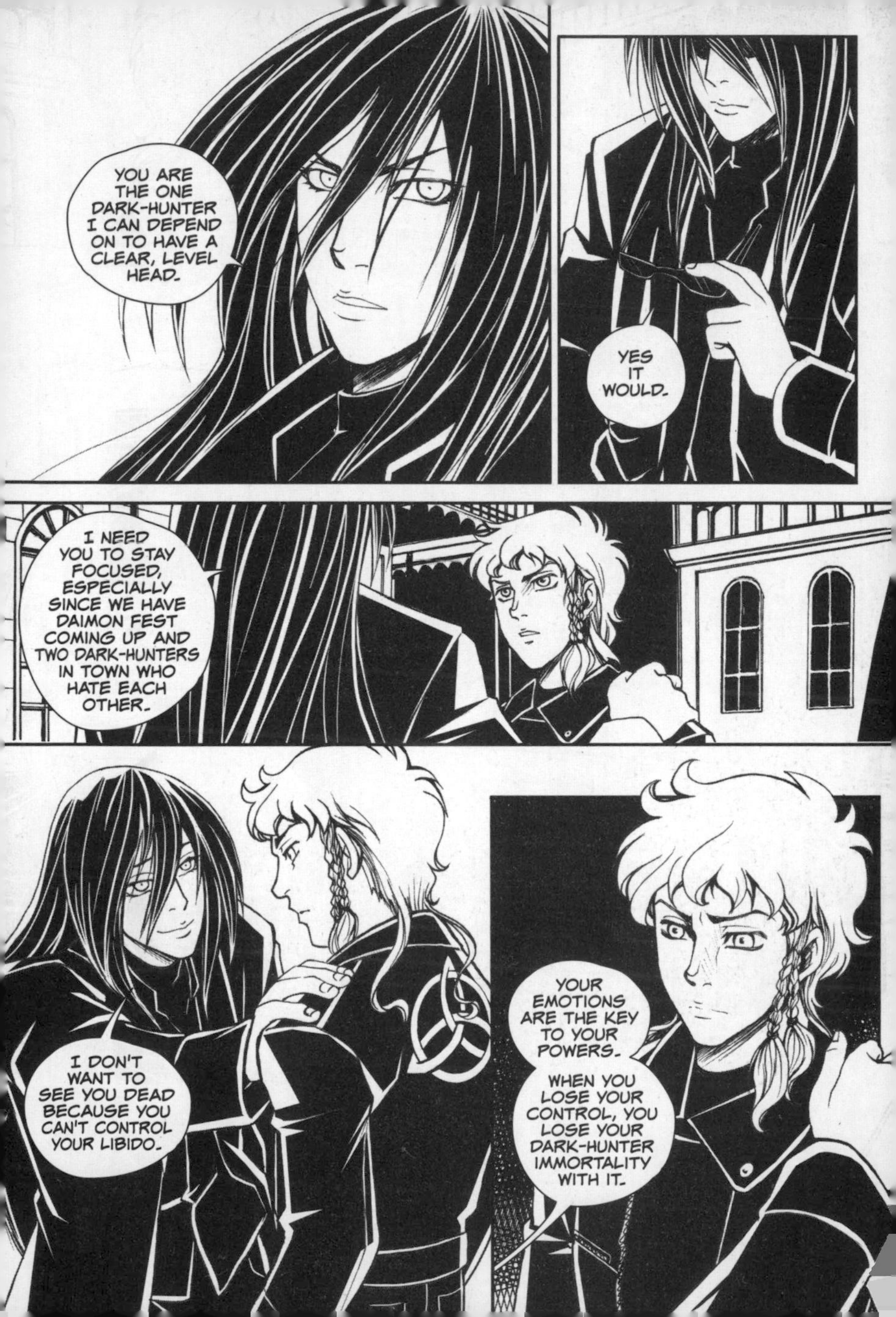
YOU ARE THE ONE DARK-HUNTER I CAN DEPEND ON TO HAVE A CLEAR, LEVEL HEAD.
YES IT WOULD.
I NEED YOU TO STAY FOCUSED, ESPECIALLY SINCE WE HAVE DAIMON FEST COMING UP AND TWO DARK-HUNTERS IN TOWN WHO HATE EACH OTHER.
I DON'T WANT TO SEE YOU DEAD BECAUSE YOU CAN'T CONTROL YOUR LIBIDO.
YOUR EMOTIONS ARE THE KEY TO YOUR POWERS.
WHEN YOU LOSE YOUR CONTROL, YOU LOSE YOUR DARK-HUNTER IMMORTALITY WITH IT.

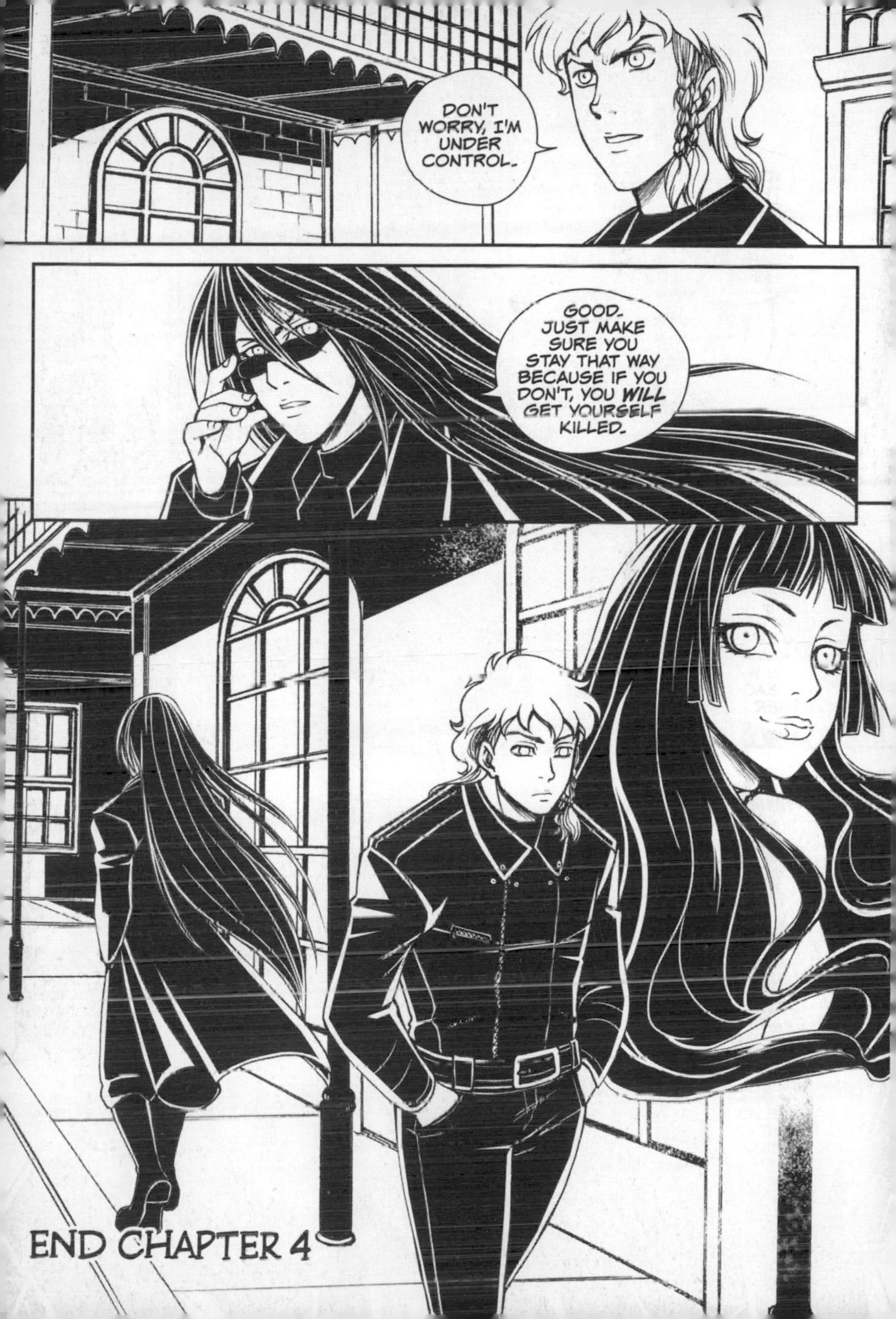
DON'T WORRY, I'M UNDER CONTROL.
GOOD. JUST MAKE SURE YOU STAY THAT WAY BECAUSE IF YOU DON'T, YOU WILL GET YOURSELF KILLED.
END CHAPTER 4

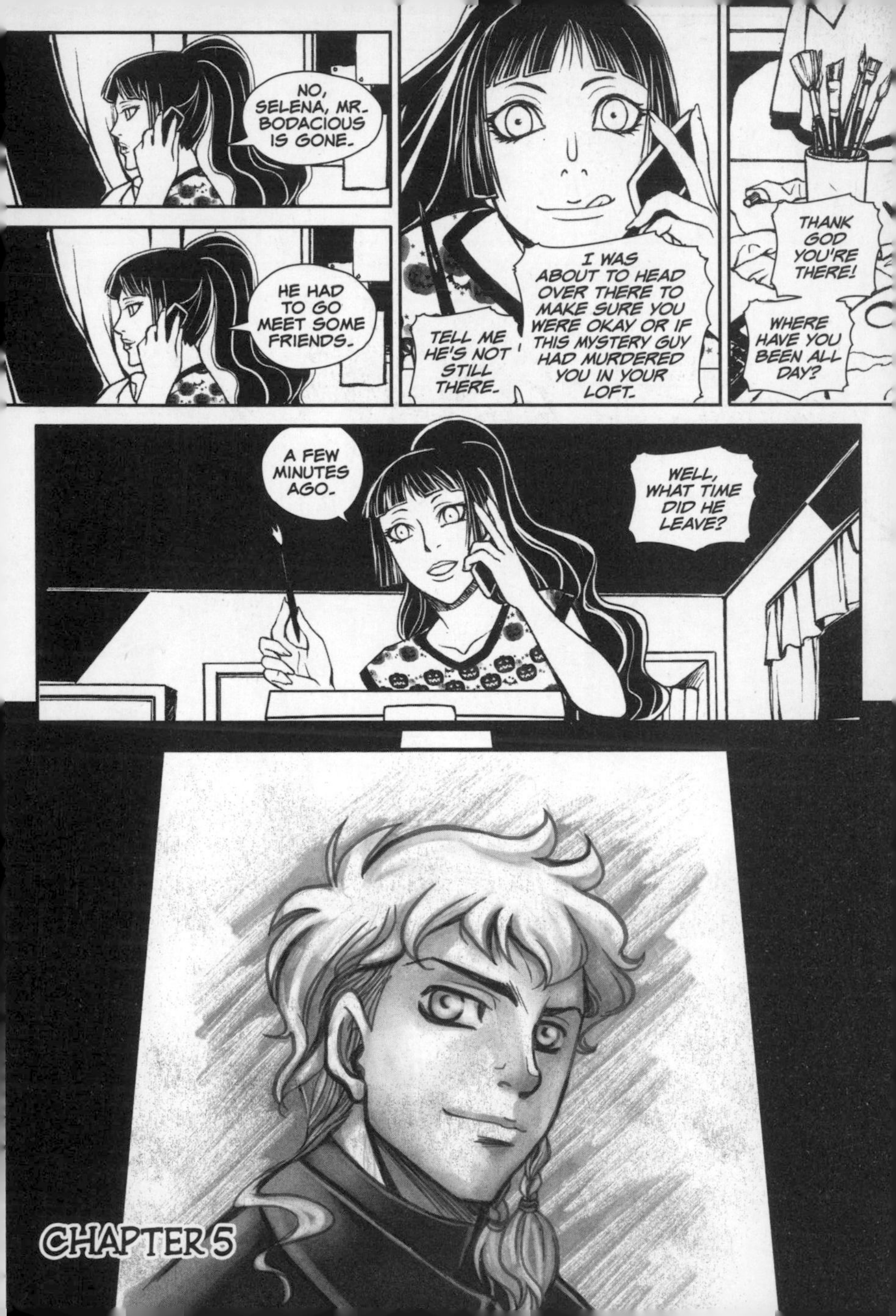
NO, SELENA, MR. BODACIOUS IS GONE.
HE HAD TO GO MEET SOME FRIENDS.
TELL ME HE'S NOT STILL THERE.
I WAS ABOUT TO HEAD OVER THERE TO MAKE SURE YOU WERE OKAY OR IF THIS MYSTERY GUY HAD MURDERED YOU IN YOUR LOFT.
THANK GOD YOU'RE THERE!
WHERE HAVE YOU BEEN ALL DAY?
WELL, WHAT TIME DID HE LEAVE?
A FEW MINUTES AGO.
CHAPTER 5

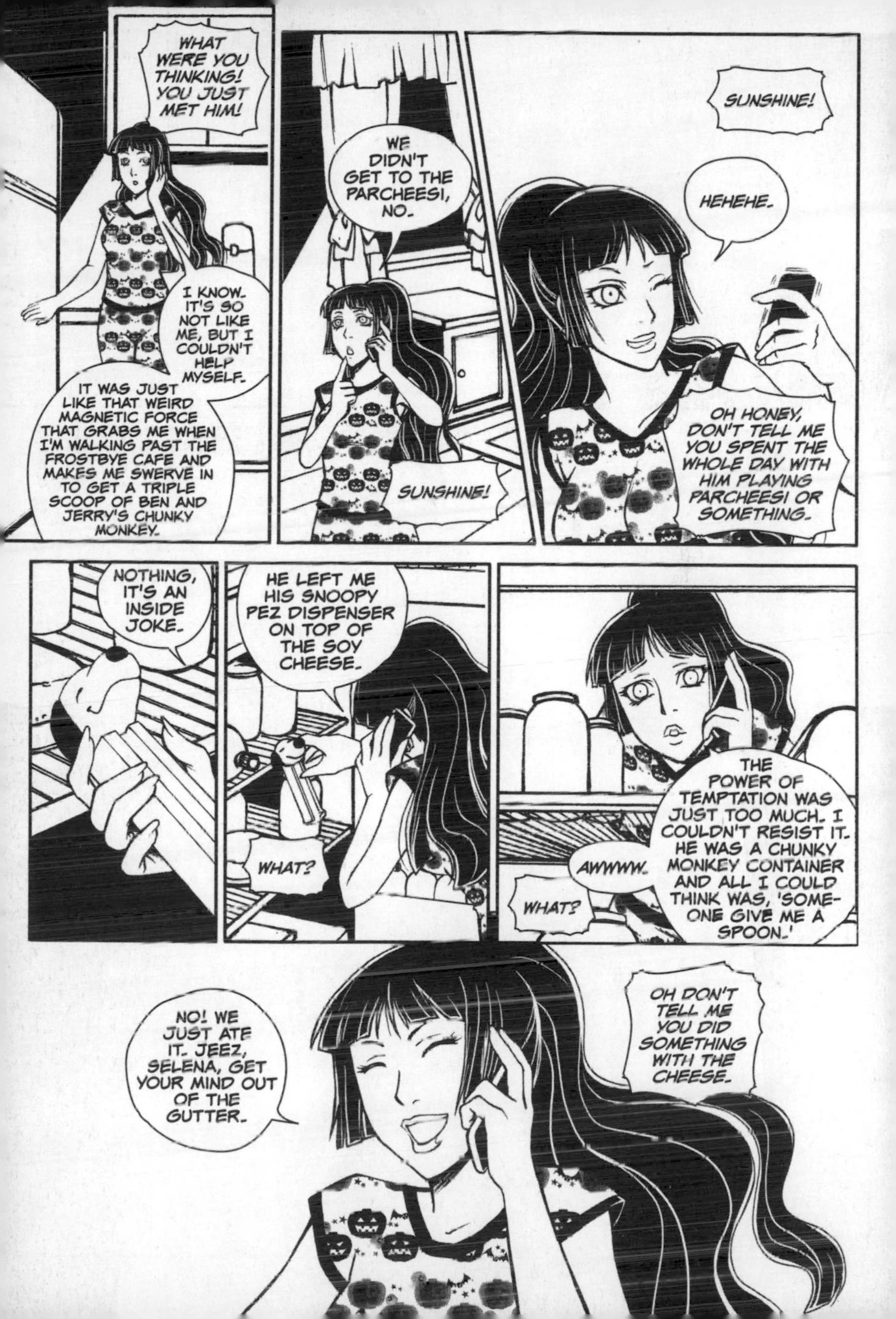
WHAT WERE YOU THINKING! YOU JUST MET HIM!
I KNOW. IT'S SO NOT LIKE ME, BUT I COULDN'T HELP MYSELF.
IT WAS JUST LIKE THAT WEIRD MAGNETIC FORCE THAT GRABS ME WHEN I'M WALKING PAST THE FROSTBYE CAFE AND MAKES ME SWERVE IN TO GET A TRIPLE SCOOP OF BEN AND JERRY'S CHUNKY MONKEY.
WE DIDN'T GET TO THE PARCHEESI, NO.
SUNSHINE!
SUNSHINE!
HEHEHE.
OH HONEY, DON'T TELL ME YOU SPENT THE WHOLE DAY WITH HIM PLAYING PARCHEESI OR SOMETHING.
NOTHING, IT'S AN INSIDE JOKE.
HE LEFT ME HIS SNOOPY PEZ DISPENSER ON TOP OF THE SOY CHEESE.
WHAT?
THE POWER OF TEMPTATION WAS JUST TOO MUCH. I COULDN'T RESIST IT. HE WAS A CHUNKY MONKEY CONTAINER AND ALL I COULD THINK WAS, 'SOME-ONE GIVE ME A SPOON.'
AWWWW.
WHAT?
OH DON'T TELL ME YOU DID SOMETHING WITH THE CHEESE.
NO! WE JUST ATE IT. JEEZ, SELENA, GET YOUR MIND OUT OF THE GUTTER.

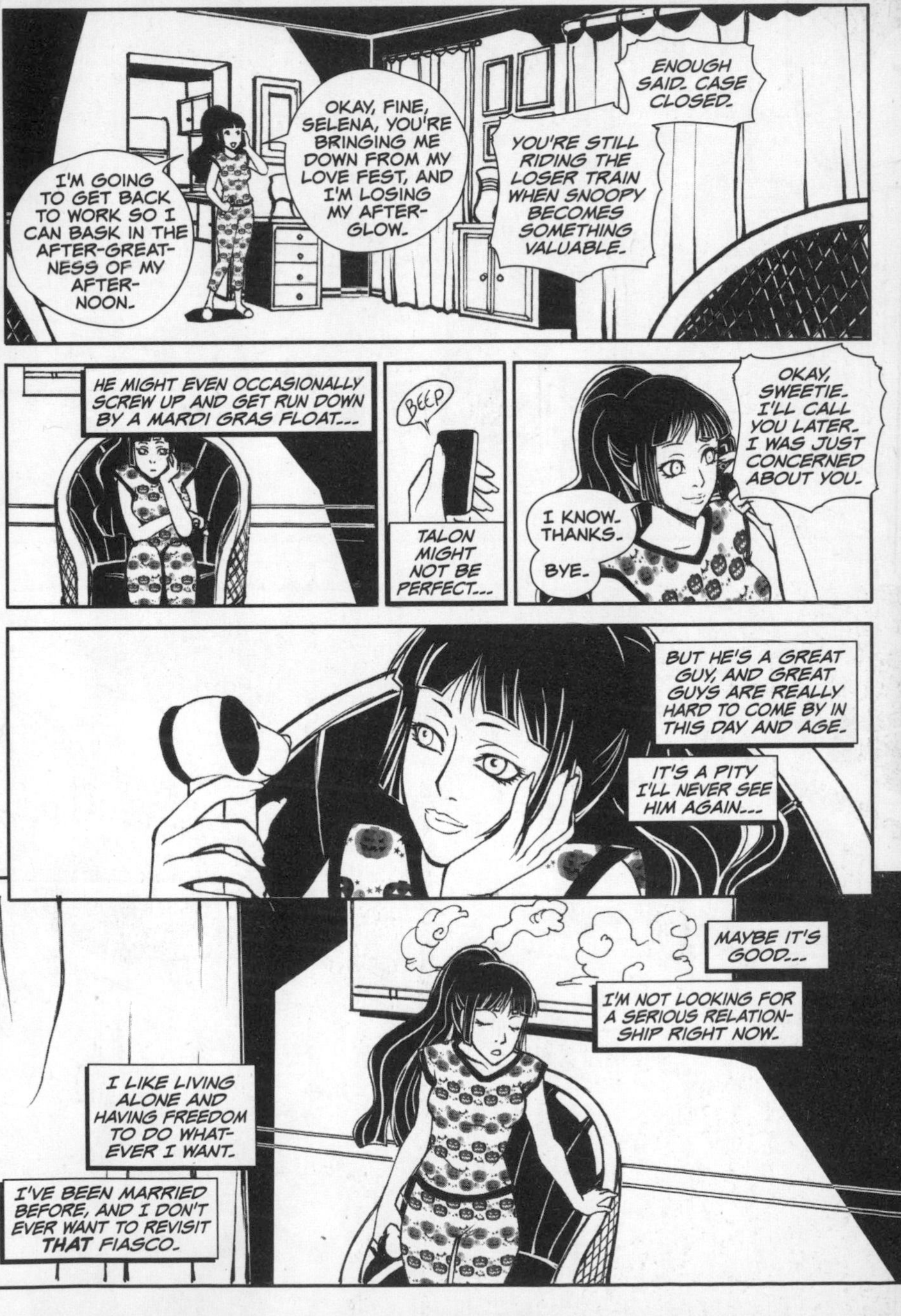

I'M GOING TO GET BACK TO WORK SO I CAN BASK IN THE AFTER-GREATNESS OF MY AFTERNOON.
OKAY, FINE, SELENA, YOU'RE BRINGING ME DOWN FROM MY LOVE FEST, AND I'M LOSING MY AFTER-GLOW.
ENOUGH SAID. CASE CLOSED.
YOU'RE STILL RIDING THE LOSER TRAIN WHEN SNOOPY BECOMES SOMETHING VALUABLE.
HE MIGHT EVEN OCCASIONALLY SCREW UP AND GET RUN DOWN BY A MARDI GRAS FLOAT...
BEEP
TALON MIGHT NOT BE PERFECT...
OKAY, SWEETIE. I'LL CALL YOU LATER. I WAS JUST CONCERNED ABOUT YOU.
I KNOW. THANKS.
BYE.
BUT HE'S A GREAT GUY, AND GREAT GUYS ARE REALLY HARD TO COME BY IN THIS DAY AND AGE.
IT'S A PITY I'LL NEVER SEE HIM AGAIN...
MAYBE IT'S GOOD...
I'M NOT LOOKING FOR A SERIOUS RELATIONSHIP RIGHT NOW.
I LIKE LIVING ALONE AND HAVING FREEDOM TO DO WHATEVER I WANT.
I'VE BEEN MARRIED BEFORE, AND I DON'T EVER WANT TO REVISIT THAT FIASCO.

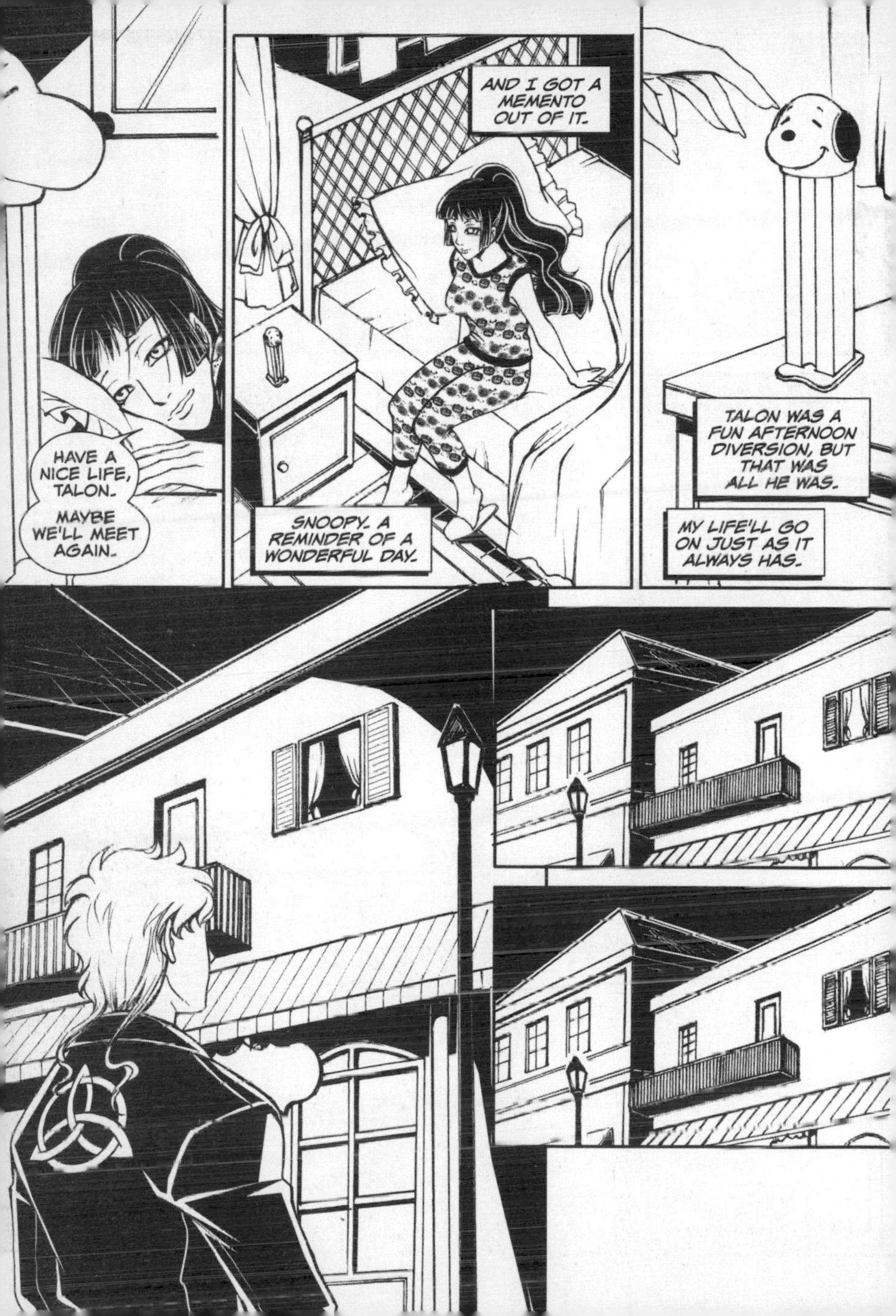
HAVE A NICE LIFE, TALON.
MAYBE WE'LL MEET AGAIN.
AND I GOT A MEMENTO OUT OF IT.
SNOOPY. A REMINDER OF A WONDERFUL DAY.
TALON WAS A FUN AFTERNOON DIVERSION, BUT THAT WAS ALL HE WAS.
MY LIFE'LL GO ON JUST AS IT ALWAYS HAS.

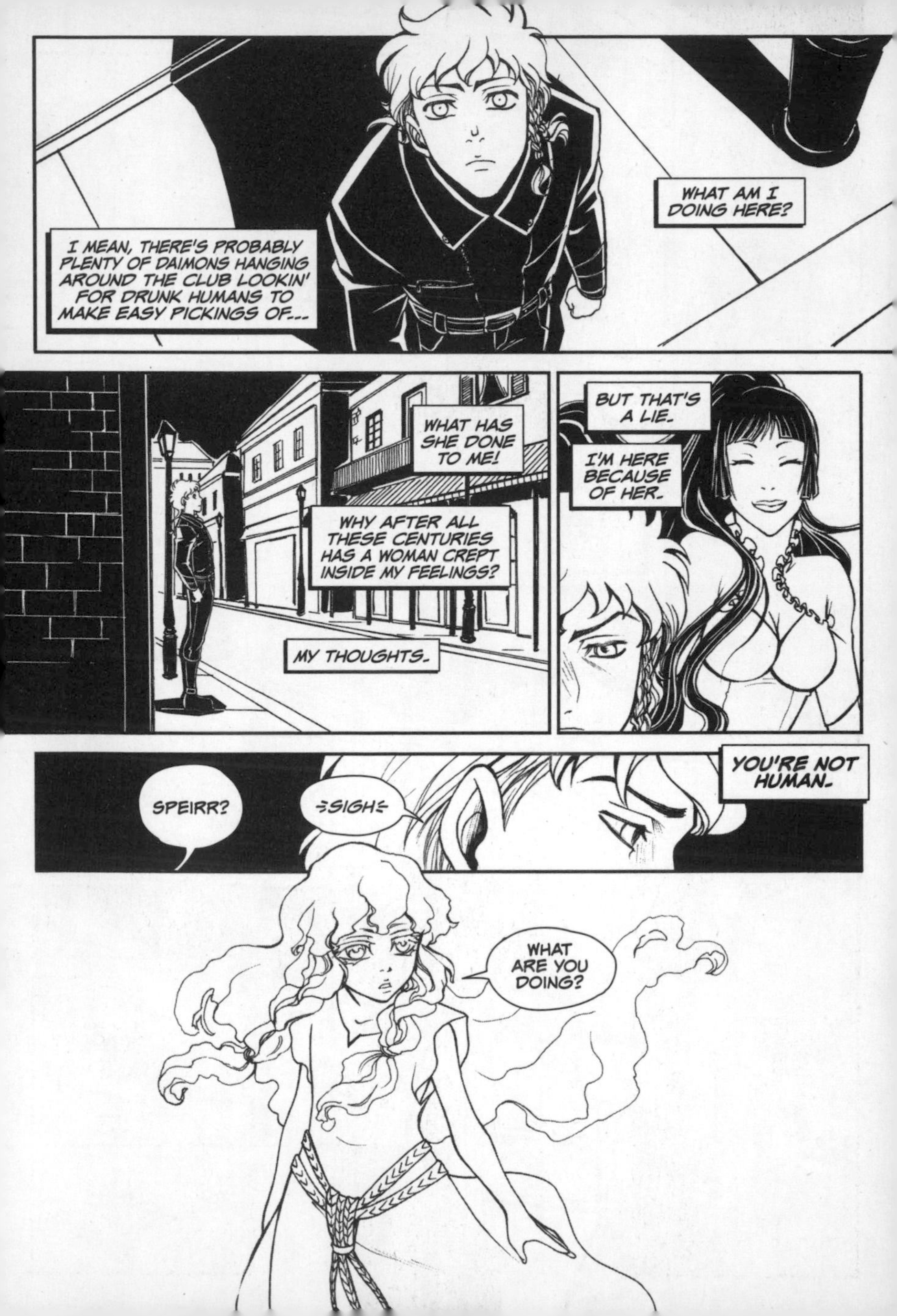
WHAT AM I DOING HERE?
I MEAN, THERE'S PROBABLY PLENTY OF DAIMONS HANGING AROUND THE CLUB LOOKIN' FOR DRUNK HUMANS TO MAKE EASY PICKINGS OF...
WHAT HAS SHE DONE TO ME!
WHY AFTER ALL THESE CENTURIES HAS A WOMAN CREPT INSIDE MY FEELINGS?
MY THOUGHTS.
BUT THAT'S A LIE.
I'M HERE BECAUSE OF HER.
YOU'RE NOT HUMAN.
=SIGH=
SPEIRR?
WHAT ARE YOU DOING?

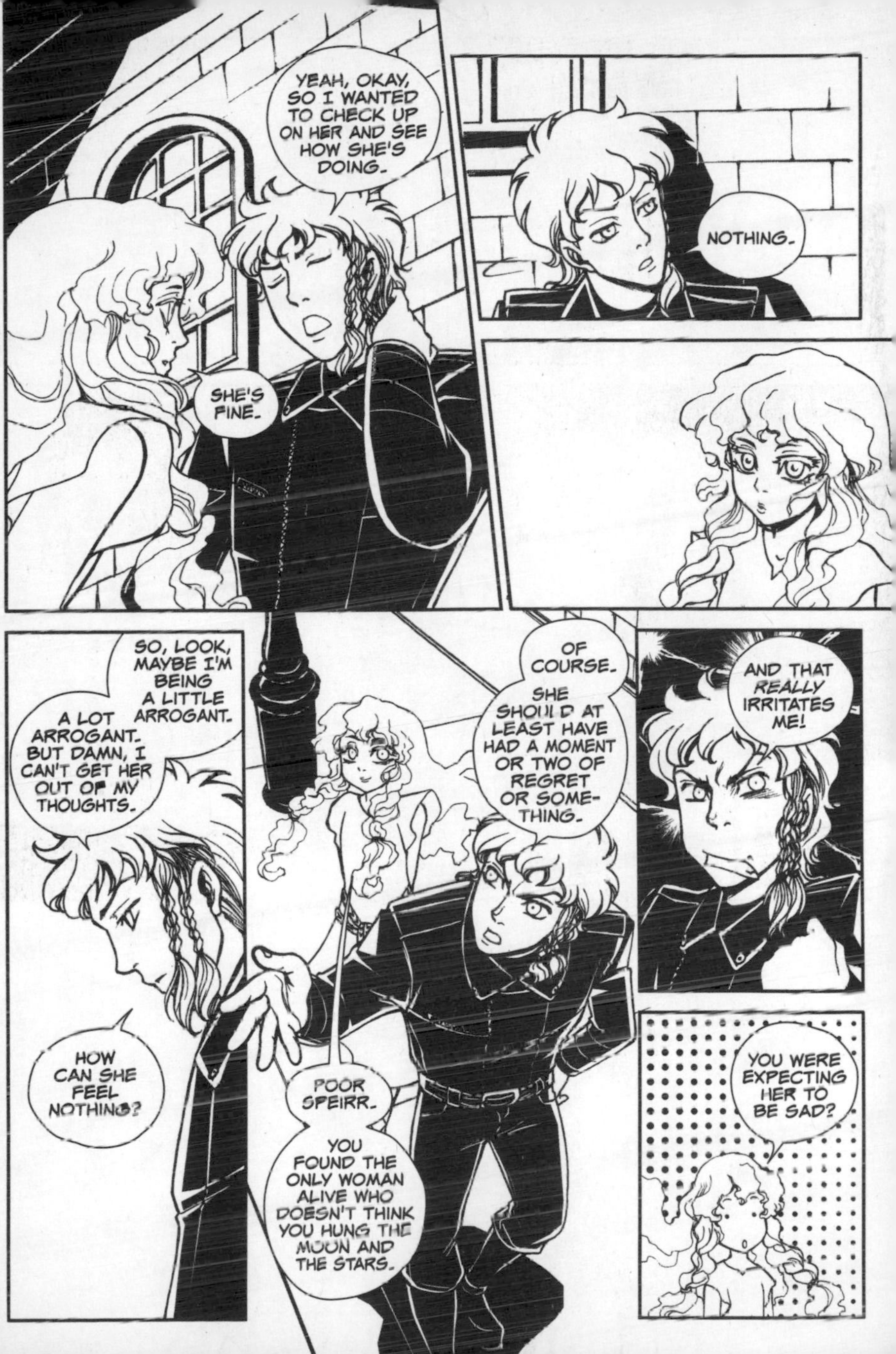
YEAH, OKAY, SO I WANTED TO CHECK UP ON HER AND SEE HOW SHE'S DOING.
SHE'S FINE.
NOTHING.
SO, LOOK, MAYBE I'M BEING A LITTLE ARROGANT.
A LOT ARROGANT. BUT DAMN, I CAN'T GET HER OUT OF MY THOUGHTS.
HOW CAN SHE FEEL NOTHING?
POOR SPEIRR.
YOU FOUND THE ONLY WOMAN ALIVE WHO DOESN'T THINK YOU HUNG THE MOON AND THE STARS.
OF COURSE.
SHE SHOULD AT LEAST HAVE HAD A MOMENT OR TWO OF REGRET OR SOMETHING.
AND THAT REALLY IRRITATES ME!
YOU WERE EXPECTING HER TO BE SAD?

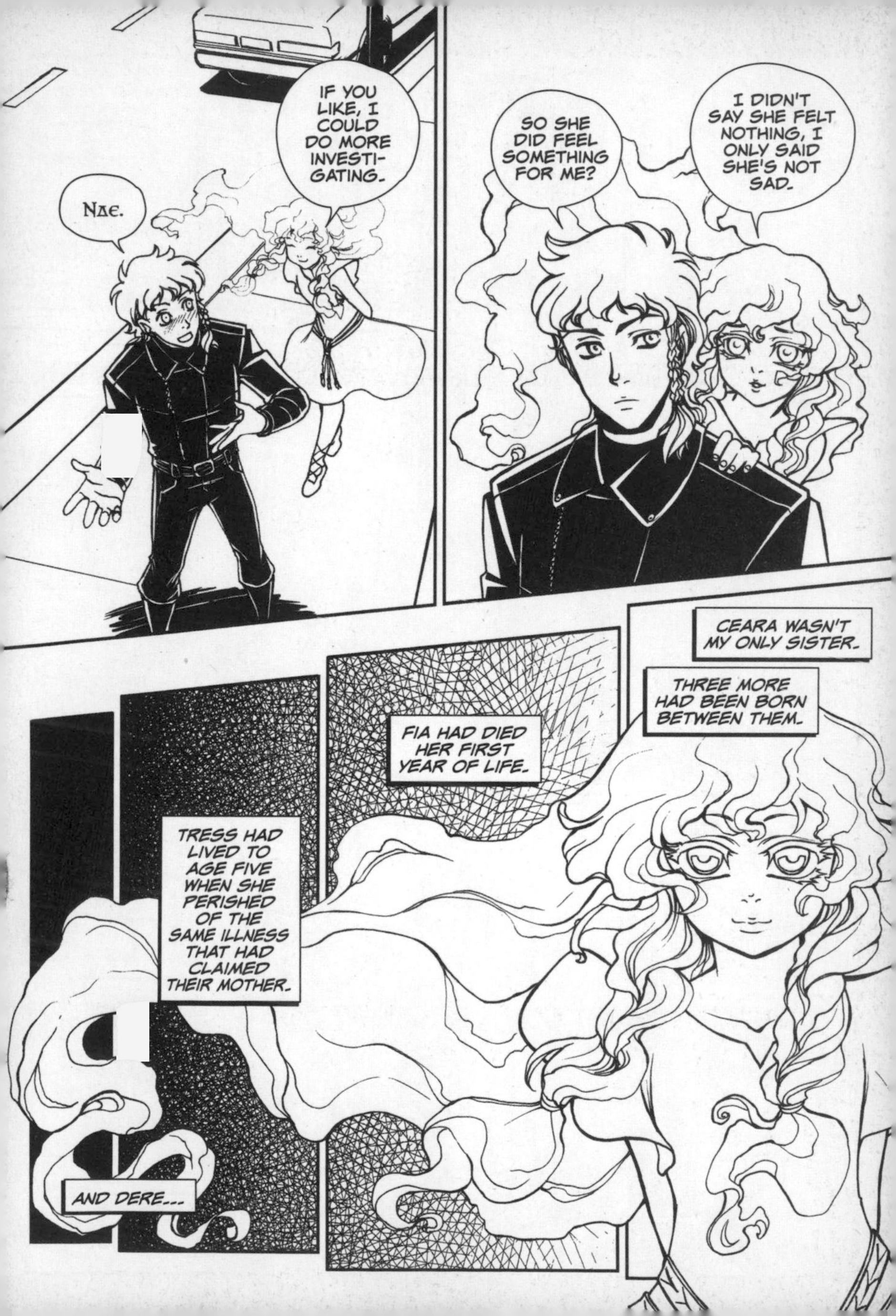
IF YOU LIKE, I COULD DO MORE INVESTI-GATING.
NAE.
SO SHE DID FEEL SOMETHING FOR ME?
I DIDN'T SAY SHE FELT NOTHING, I ONLY SAID SHE'S NOT SAD.
CEARA WASN'T MY ONLY SISTER.
THREE MORE HAD BEEN BORN BETWEEN THEM.
FIA HAD DIED HER FIRST YEAR OF LIFE.
TRESS HAD LIVED TO AGE FIVE WHEN SHE PERISHED OF THE SAME ILLNESS THAT HAD CLAIMED THEIR MOTHER.
AND DERE...

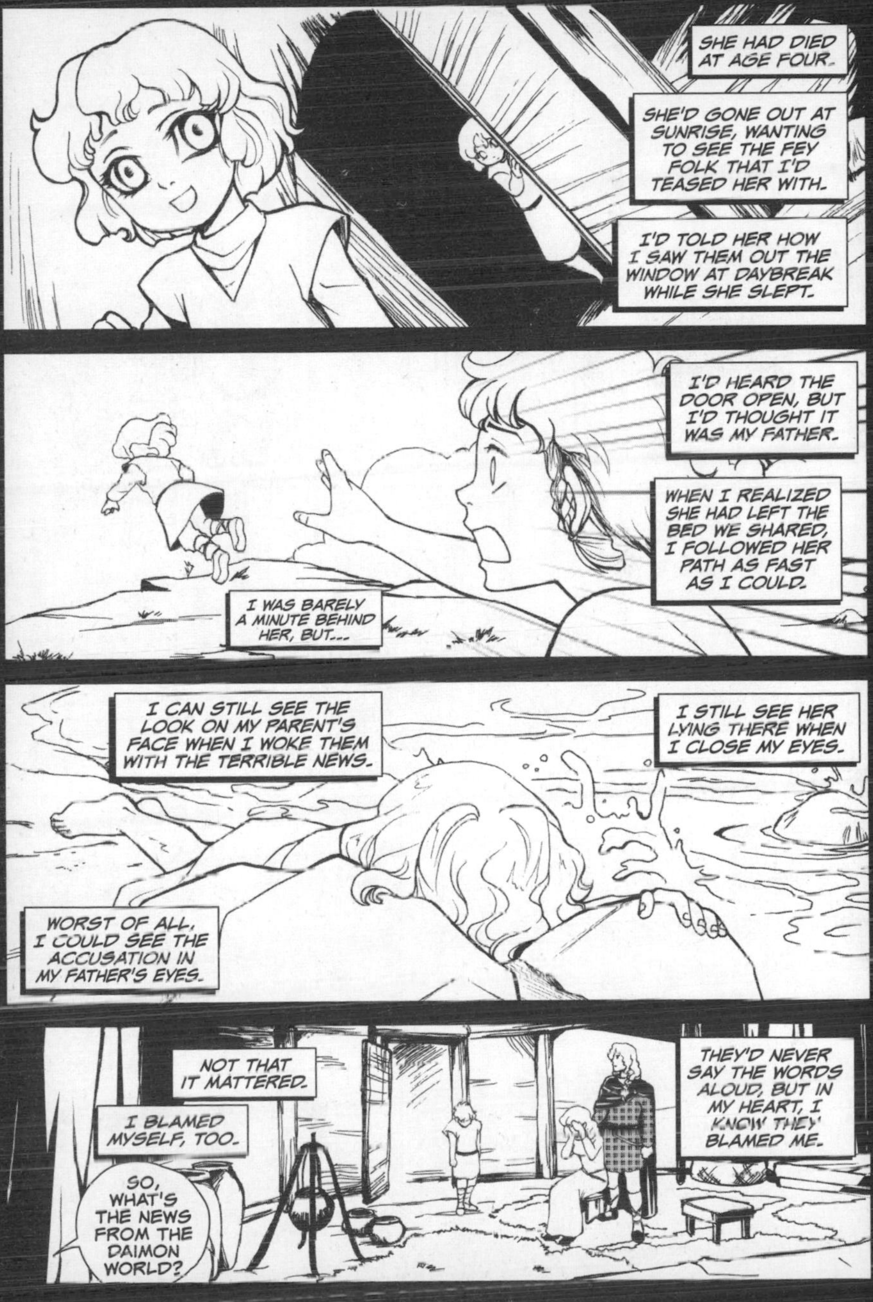

SHE HAD DIED AT AGE FOUR.
SHE'D GONE OUT AT SUNRISE, WANTING TO SEE THE FEY FOLK THAT I'D TEASED HER WITH.
I'D TOLD HER HOW I SAW THEM OUT THE WINDOW AT DAYBREAK WHILE SHE SLEPT.
I'D HEARD THE DOOR OPEN, BUT I'D THOUGHT IT WAS MY FATHER.
WHEN I REALIZED SHE HAD LEFT THE BED WE SHARED, I FOLLOWED HER PATH AS FAST AS I COULD.
I WAS BARELY A MINUTE BEHIND HER, BUT...
I CAN STILL SEE THE LOOK ON MY PARENT'S FACE WHEN I WOKE THEM WITH THE TERRIBLE NEWS.
I STILL SEE HER LYING THERE WHEN I CLOSE MY EYES.
WORST OF ALL, I COULD SEE THE ACCUSATION IN MY FATHER'S EYES.
NOT THAT IT MATTERED.
I BLAMED MYSELF, TOO.
THEY'D NEVER SAY THE WORDS ALOUD, BUT IN MY HEART, I KNOW THEY BLAMED ME.
SO, WHAT'S THE NEWS FROM THE DAIMON WORLD?

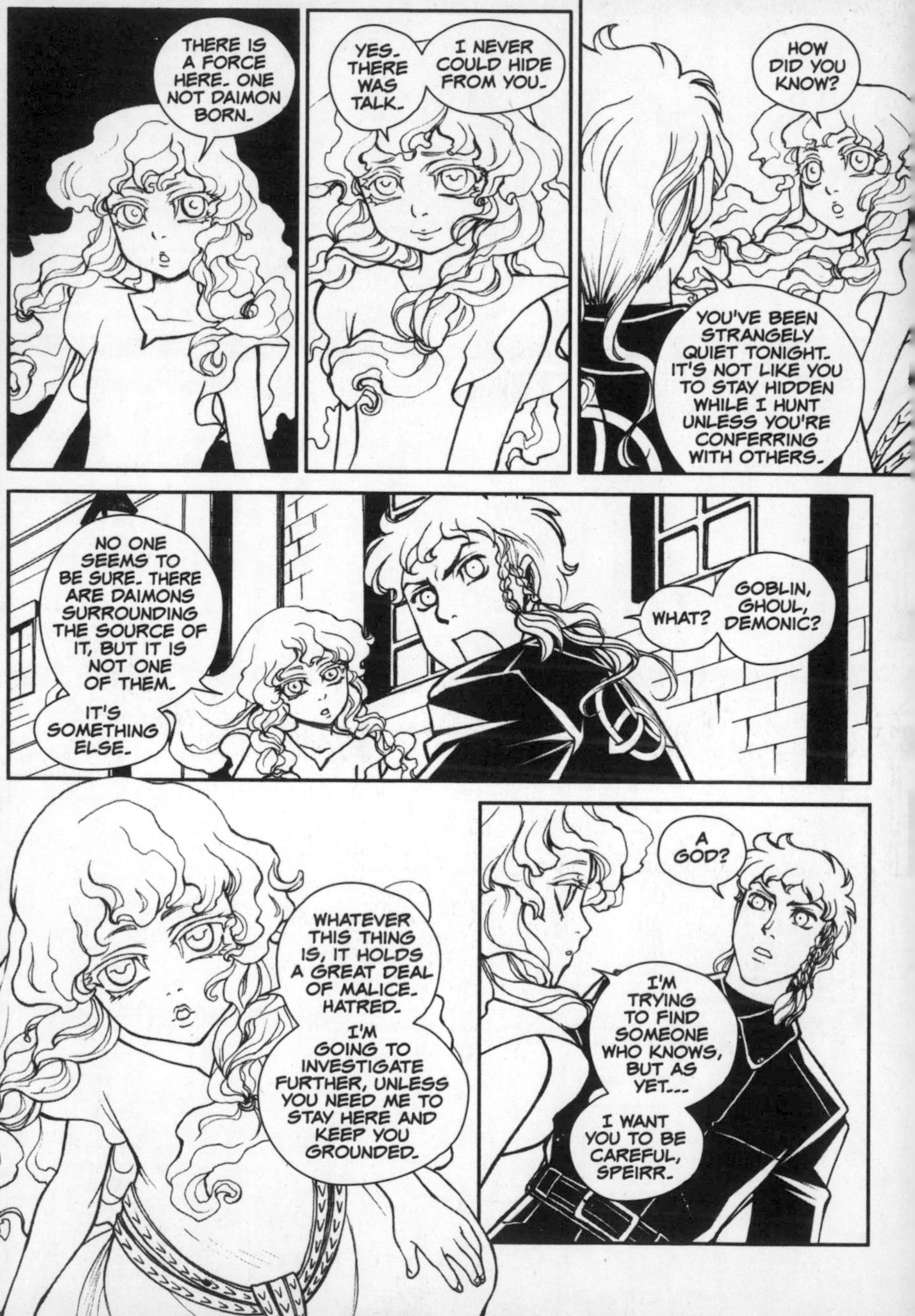
THERE IS A FORCE HERE. ONE NOT DAIMON BORN.
YES. THERE WAS TALK.
I NEVER COULD HIDE FROM YOU.
HOW DID YOU KNOW?
YOU'VE BEEN STRANGELY QUIET TONIGHT. IT'S NOT LIKE YOU TO STAY HIDDEN WHILE I HUNT UNLESS YOU'RE CONFERRING WITH OTHERS.
NO ONE SEEMS TO BE SURE. THERE ARE DAIMONS SURROUNDING THE SOURCE OF IT, BUT IT IS NOT ONE OF THEM.
IT'S SOMETHING ELSE.
WHAT?
GOBLIN, GHOUL, DEMONIC?
WHATEVER THIS THING IS, IT HOLDS A GREAT DEAL OF MALICE. HATRED.
I'M GOING TO INVESTIGATE FURTHER, UNLESS YOU NEED ME TO STAY HERE AND KEEP YOU GROUNDED.
A GOD?
I'M TRYING TO FIND SOMEONE WHO KNOWS, BUT AS YET...
I WANT YOU TO BE CAREFUL, SPEIRR.

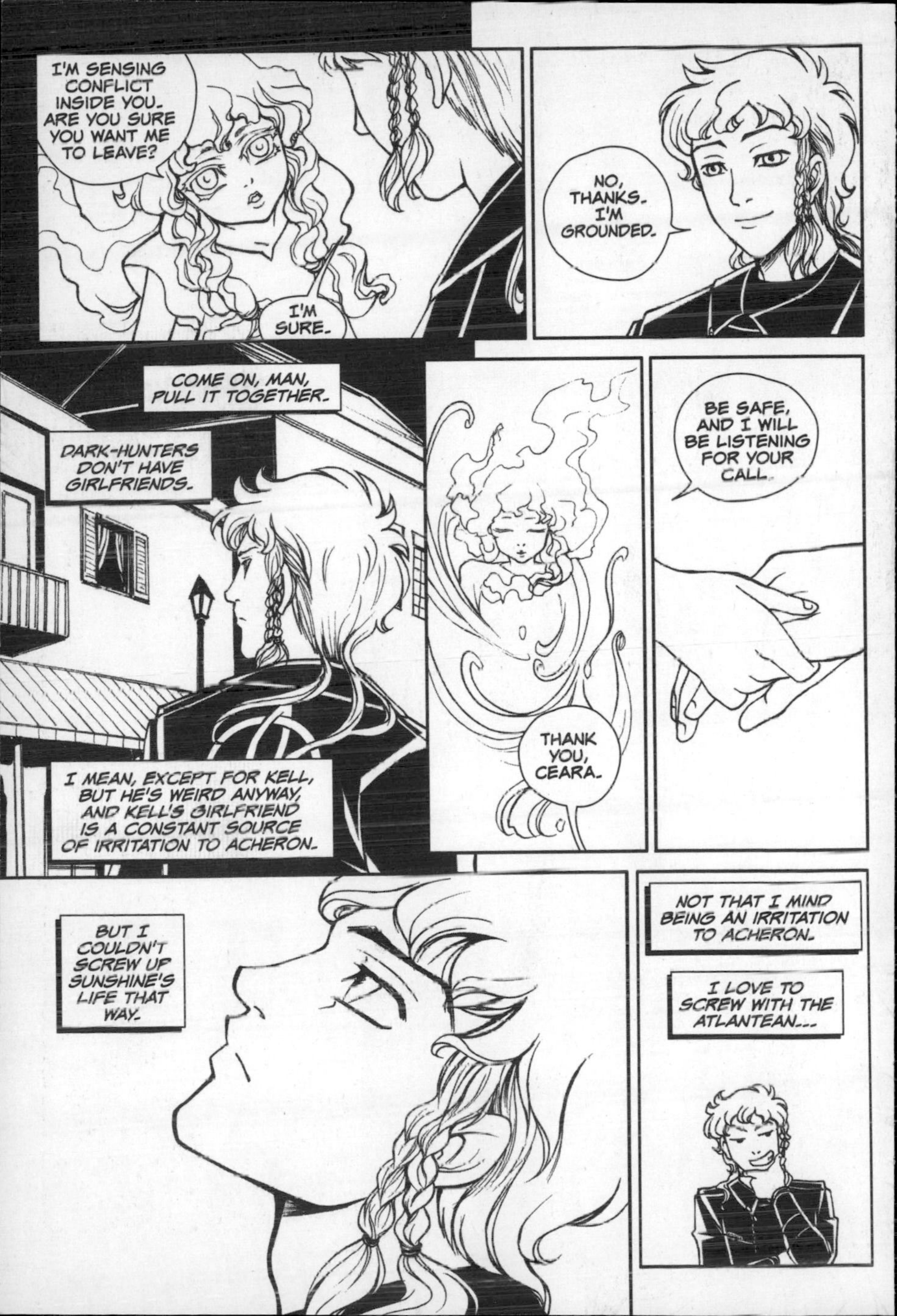
I'M SENSING CONFLICT INSIDE YOU. ARE YOU SURE YOU WANT ME TO LEAVE?
I'M SURE.
NO, THANKS. I'M GROUNDED.
COME ON, MAN, PULL IT TOGETHER.
DARK-HUNTERS DON'T HAVE GIRLFRIENDS.
I MEAN, EXCEPT FOR KELL, BUT HE'S WEIRD ANYWAY, AND KELL'S GIRLFRIEND IS A CONSTANT SOURCE OF IRRITATION TO ACHERON.
THANK YOU, CEARA.
BE SAFE, AND I WILL BE LISTENING FOR YOUR CALL.
BUT I COULDN'T SCREW UP SUNSHINE'S LIFE THAT WAY.
NOT THAT I MIND BEING AN IRRITATION TO ACHERON.
I LOVE TO SCREW WITH THE ATLANTEAN...

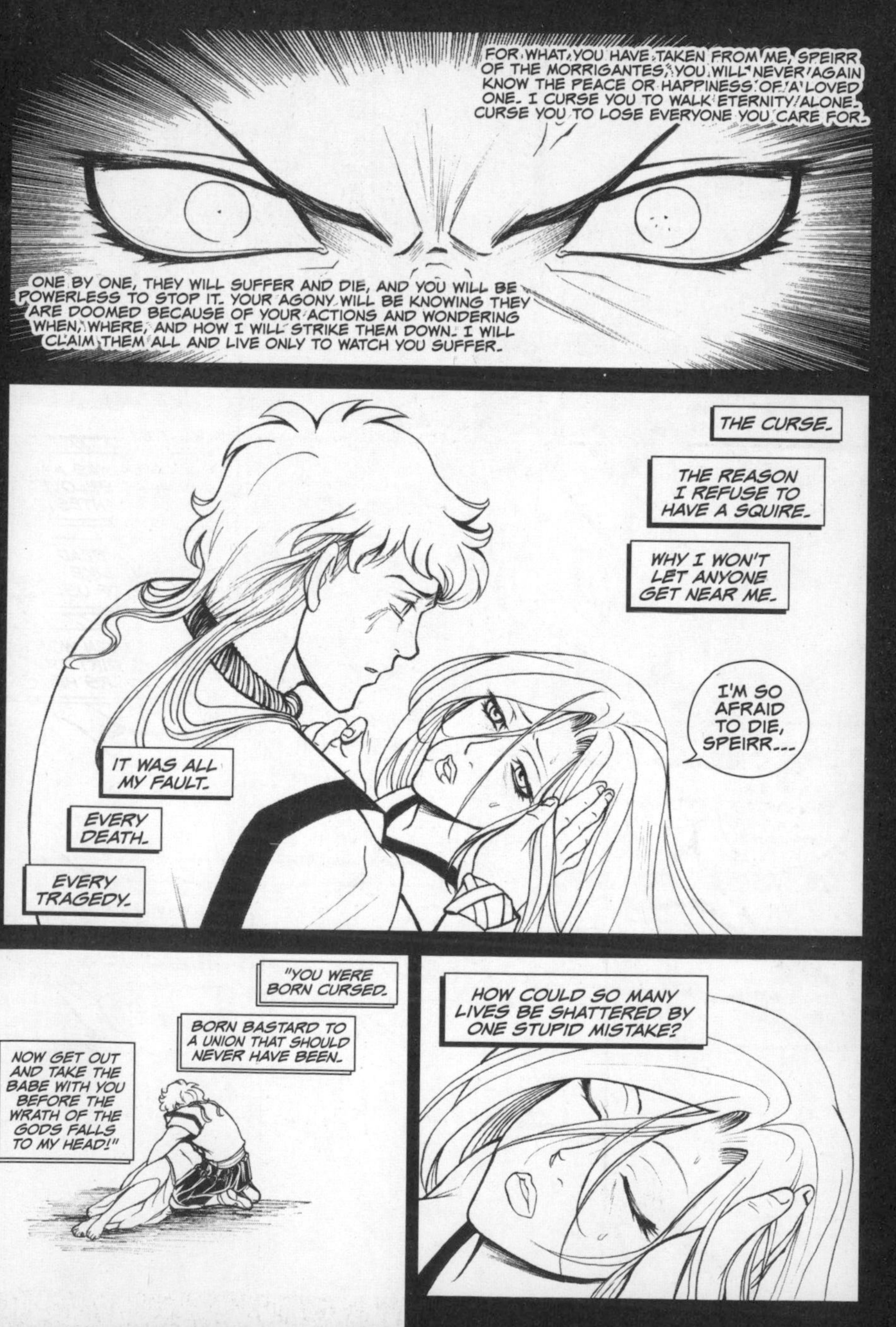
FOR WHAT YOU HAVE TAKEN FROM ME, SPEIRR OF THE MORRIGANTES, YOU WILL NEVER AGAIN KNOW THE PEACE OR HAPPINESS OF A LOVED ONE. I CURSE YOU TO WALK ETERNITY ALONE. CURSE YOU TO LOSE EVERYONE YOU CARE FOR.
ONE BY ONE, THEY WILL SUFFER AND DIE, AND YOU WILL BE POWERLESS TO STOP IT. YOUR AGONY WILL BE KNOWING THEY ARE DOOMED BECAUSE OF YOUR ACTIONS AND WONDERING WHEN, WHERE, AND HOW I WILL STRIKE THEM DOWN. I WILL CLAIM THEM ALL AND LIVE ONLY TO WATCH YOU SUFFER.
THE CURSE.
THE REASON I REFUSE TO HAVE A SQUIRE.
WHY I WON'T LET ANYONE GET NEAR ME.
I'M SO AFRAID TO DIE, SPEIRR...
IT WAS ALL MY FAULT.
EVERY DEATH.
EVERY TRAGEDY.
"YOU WERE BORN CURSED.
BORN BASTARD TO A UNION THAT SHOULD NEVER HAVE BEEN.
NOW GET OUT AND TAKE THE BABE WITH YOU BEFORE THE WRATH OF THE GODS FALLS TO MY HEAD!"
HOW COULD SO MANY LIVES BE SHATTERED BY ONE STUPID MISTAKE?

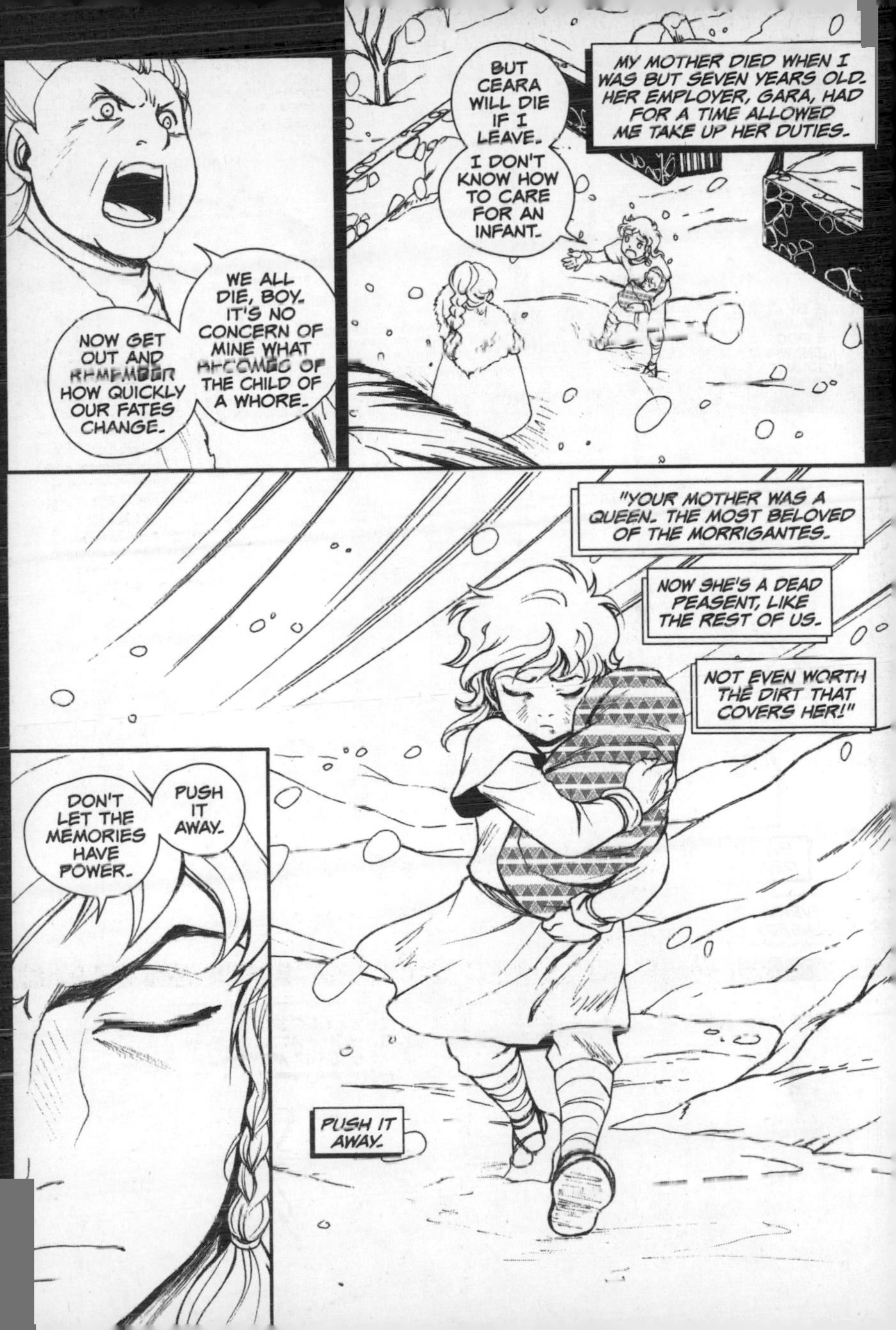

WE ALL DIE, BOY. IT'S NO CONCERN OF MINE WHAT BECOMES OF THE CHILD OF A WHORE.
NOW GET OUT AND REMEMBER HOW QUICKLY OUR FATES CHANGE.
MY MOTHER DIED WHEN I WAS BUT SEVEN YEARS OLD. HER EMPLOYER, GARA, HAD FOR A TIME ALLOWED ME TAKE UP HER DUTIES.
BUT CEARA WILL DIE IF I LEAVE.
I DON'T KNOW HOW TO CARE FOR AN INFANT.
"YOUR MOTHER WAS A QUEEN. THE MOST BELOVED OF THE MORRIGANTES.
NOW SHE'S A DEAD PEASENT, LIKE THE REST OF US.
NOT EVEN WORTH THE DIRT THAT COVERS HER!"
DON'T LET THE MEMORIES HAVE POWER.
PUSH IT AWAY.
PUSH IT AWAY.

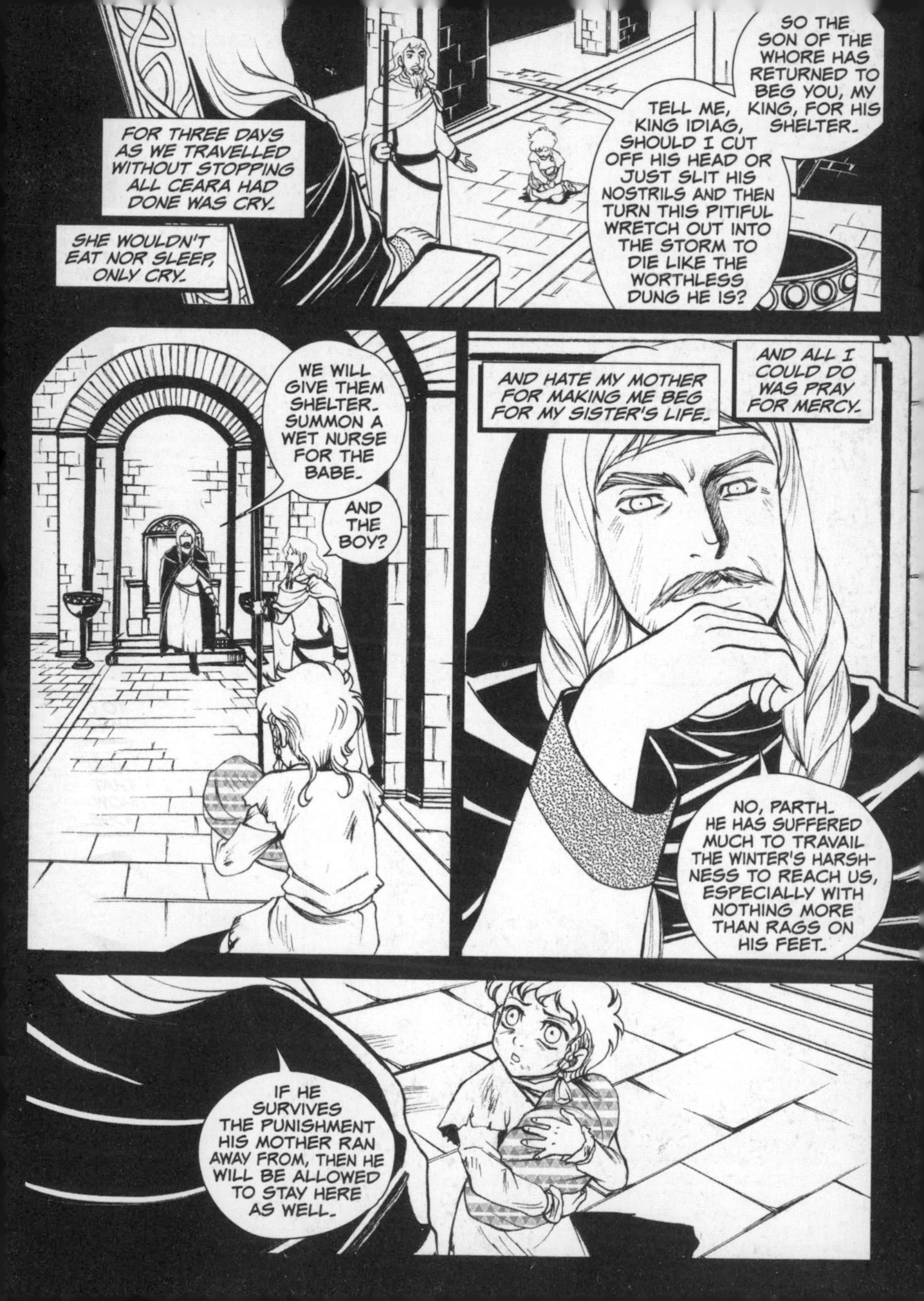
FOR THREE DAYS AS WE TRAVELLED WITHOUT STOPPING ALL CEARA HAD DONE WAS CRY.
SHE WOULDN'T EAT NOR SLEEP, ONLY CRY.
SO THE SON OF THE WHORE HAS RETURNED TO BEG YOU, MY KING, FOR HIS SHELTER.
TELL ME, KING IDIAG, SHOULD I CUT OFF HIS HEAD OR JUST SLIT HIS NOSTRILS AND THEN TURN THIS PITIFUL WRETCH OUT INTO THE STORM TO DIE LIKE THE WORTHLESS DUNG HE IS?
WE WILL GIVE THEM SHELTER. SUMMON A WET NURSE FOR THE BABE.
AND THE BOY?
AND HATE MY MOTHER FOR MAKING ME BEG FOR MY SISTER'S LIFE.
AND ALL I COULD DO WAS PRAY FOR MERCY.
NO, PARTH. HE HAS SUFFERED MUCH TO TRAVAIL THE WINTER'S HARSHNESS TO REACH US, ESPECIALLY WITH NOTHING MORE THAN RAGS ON HIS FEET.
IF HE SURVIVES THE PUNISHMENT HIS MOTHER RAN AWAY FROM, THEN HE WILL BE ALLOWED TO STAY HERE AS WELL.

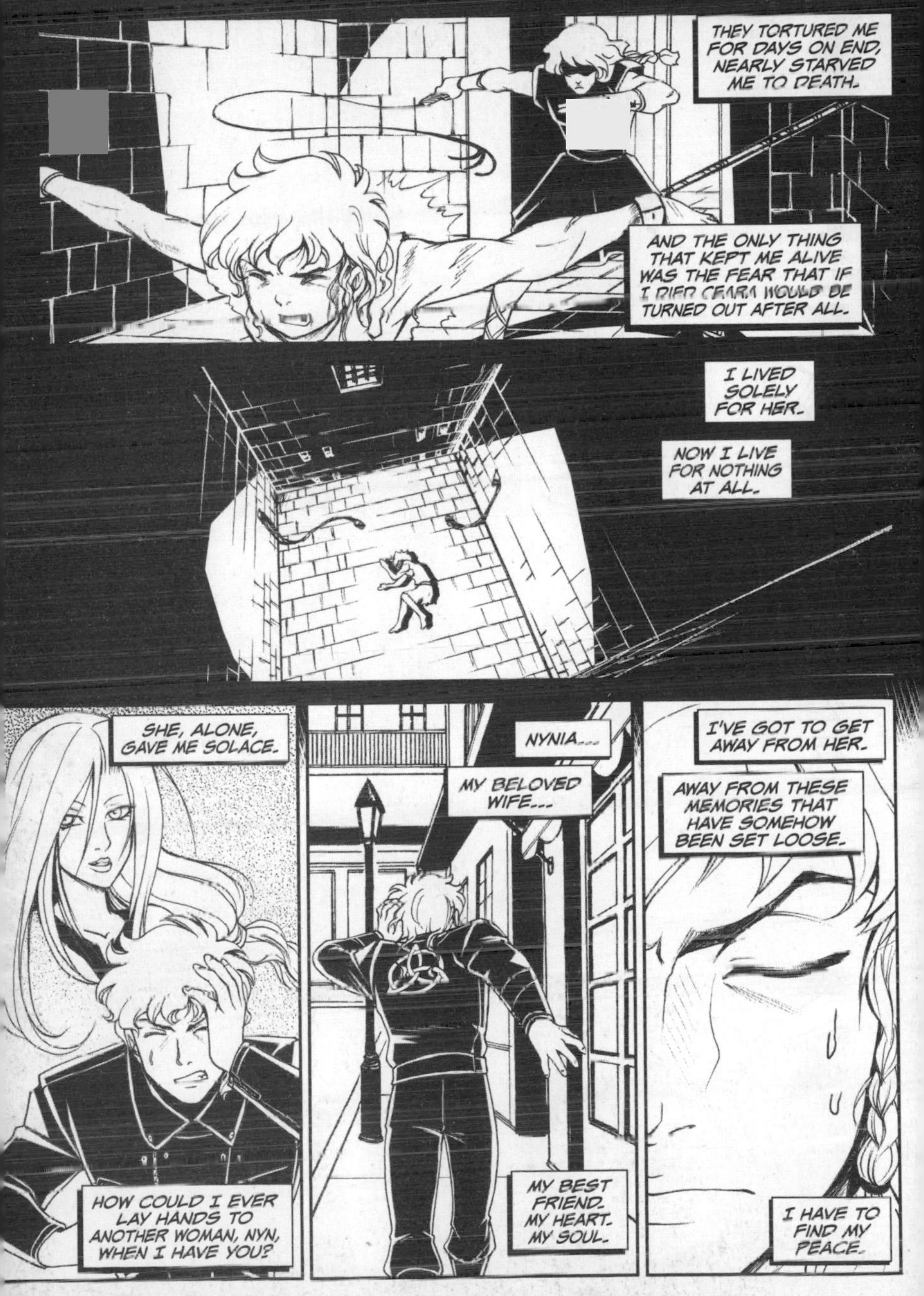
THEY TORTURED ME FOR DAYS ON END, NEARLY STARVED ME TO DEATH.
AND THE ONLY THING THAT KEPT ME ALIVE WAS THE FEAR THAT IF I DIED CEARA WOULD BE TURNED OUT AFTER ALL.
I LIVED SOLELY FOR HER.
NOW I LIVE FOR NOTHING AT ALL.
SHE, ALONE, GAVE ME SOLACE.
HOW COULD I EVER LAY HANDS TO ANOTHER WOMAN, NYN, WHEN I HAVE YOU?
NYNIA...
MY BELOVED WIFE...
MY BEST FRIEND. MY HEART. MY SOUL.
I'VE GOT TO GET AWAY FROM HER.
AWAY FROM THESE MEMORIES THAT HAVE SOMEHOW BEEN SET LOOSE.
I HAVE TO FIND MY PEACE.

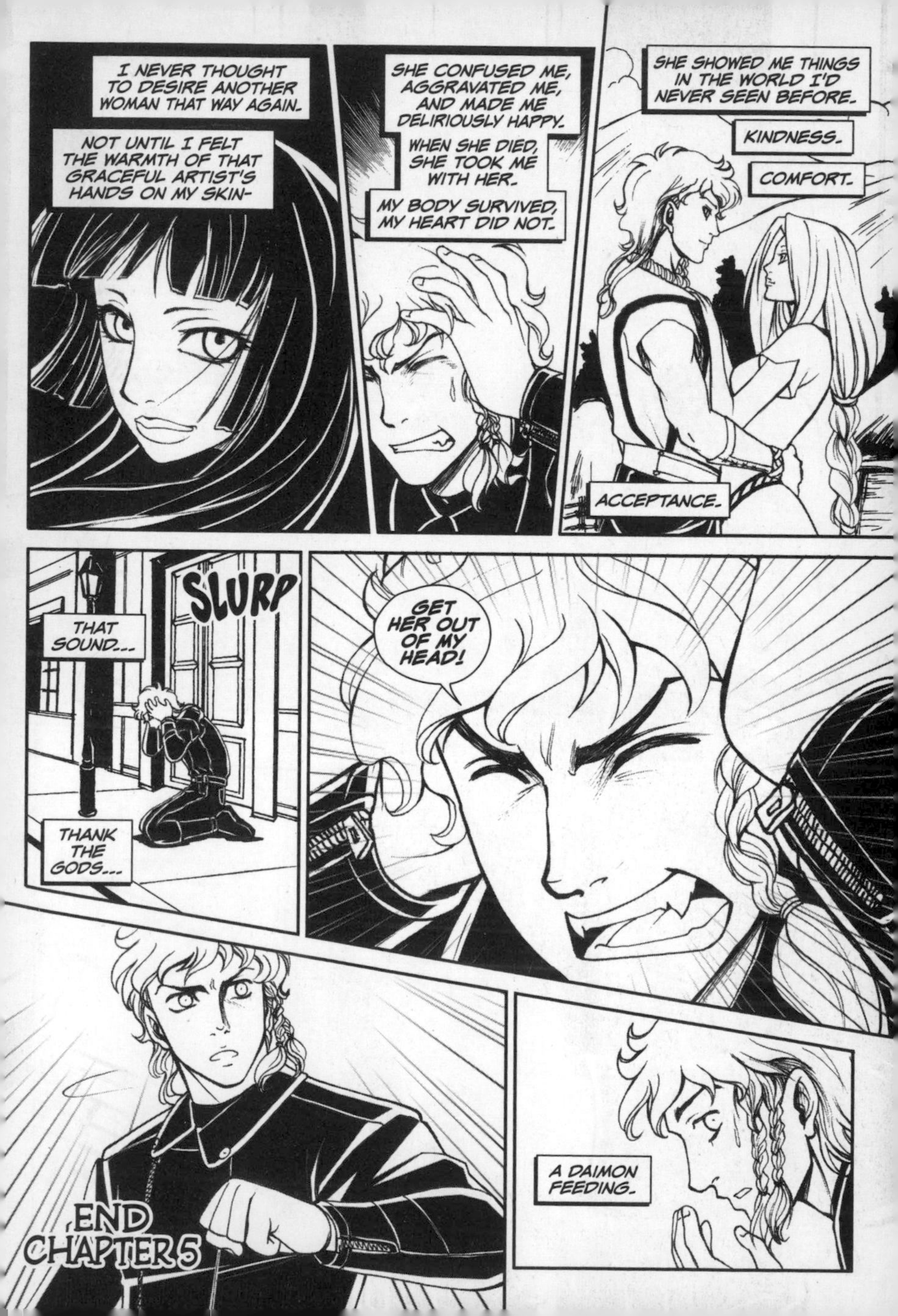

I NEVER THOUGHT TO DESIRE ANOTHER WOMAN THAT WAY AGAIN.
NOT UNTIL I FELT THE WARMTH OF THAT GRACEFUL ARTIST'S HANDS ON MY SKIN-
SHE CONFUSED ME, AGGRAVATED ME, AND MADE ME DELIRIOUSLY HAPPY.
WHEN SHE DIED, SHE TOOK ME WITH HER.
MY BODY SURVIVED, MY HEART DID NOT.
SHE SHOWED ME THINGS IN THE WORLD I'D NEVER SEEN BEFORE.
KINDNESS.
COMFORT.
ACCEPTANCE.
SLURP
THAT SOUND...
THANK THE GODS...
GET HER OUT OF MY HEAD!
A DAIMON FEEDING.
END CHAPTER 5

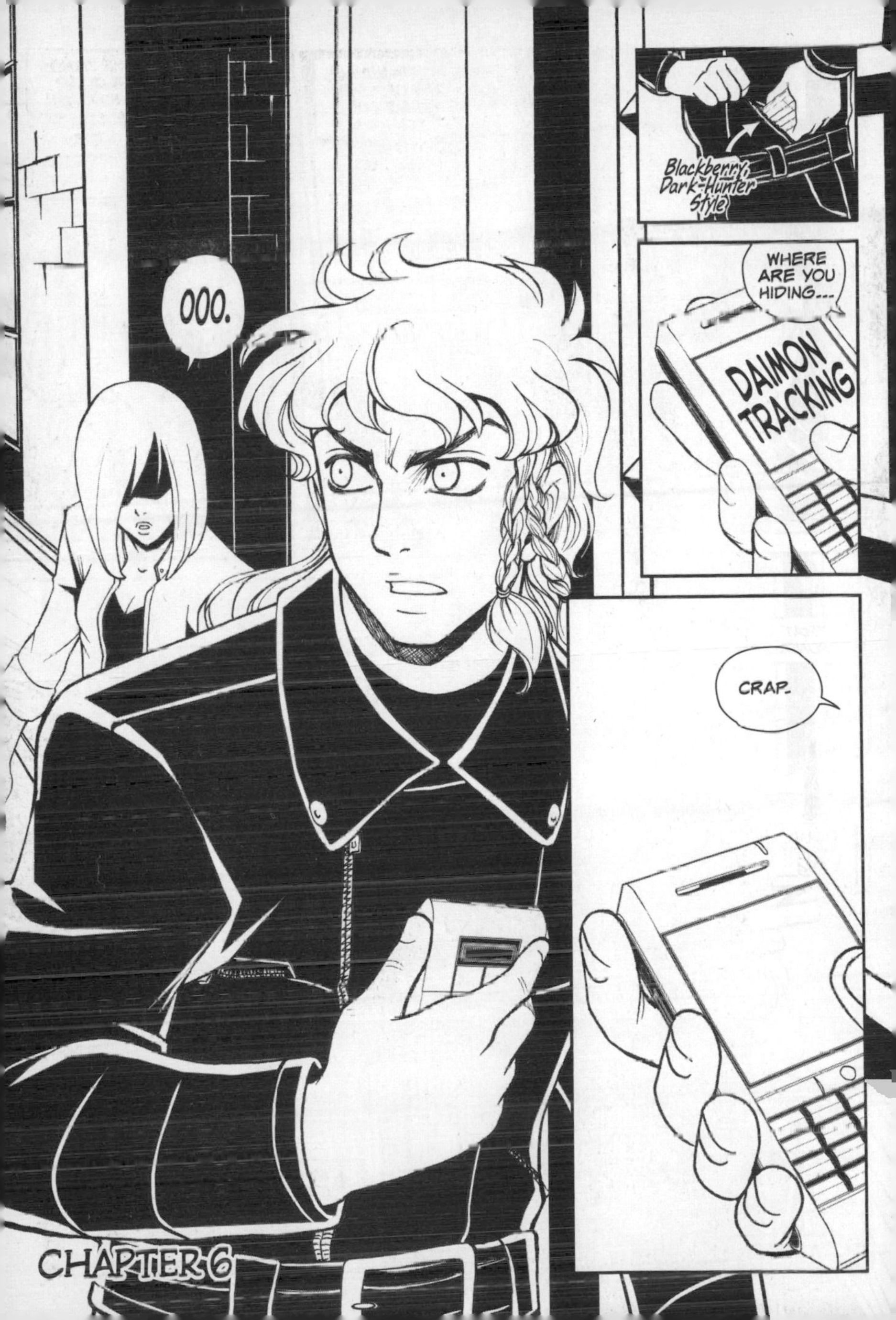
Blackberry, Dark-Hunter Style
OOO.
WHERE ARE YOU HIDING...
DAIMON TRACKING
CRAP.
CHAPTER 6

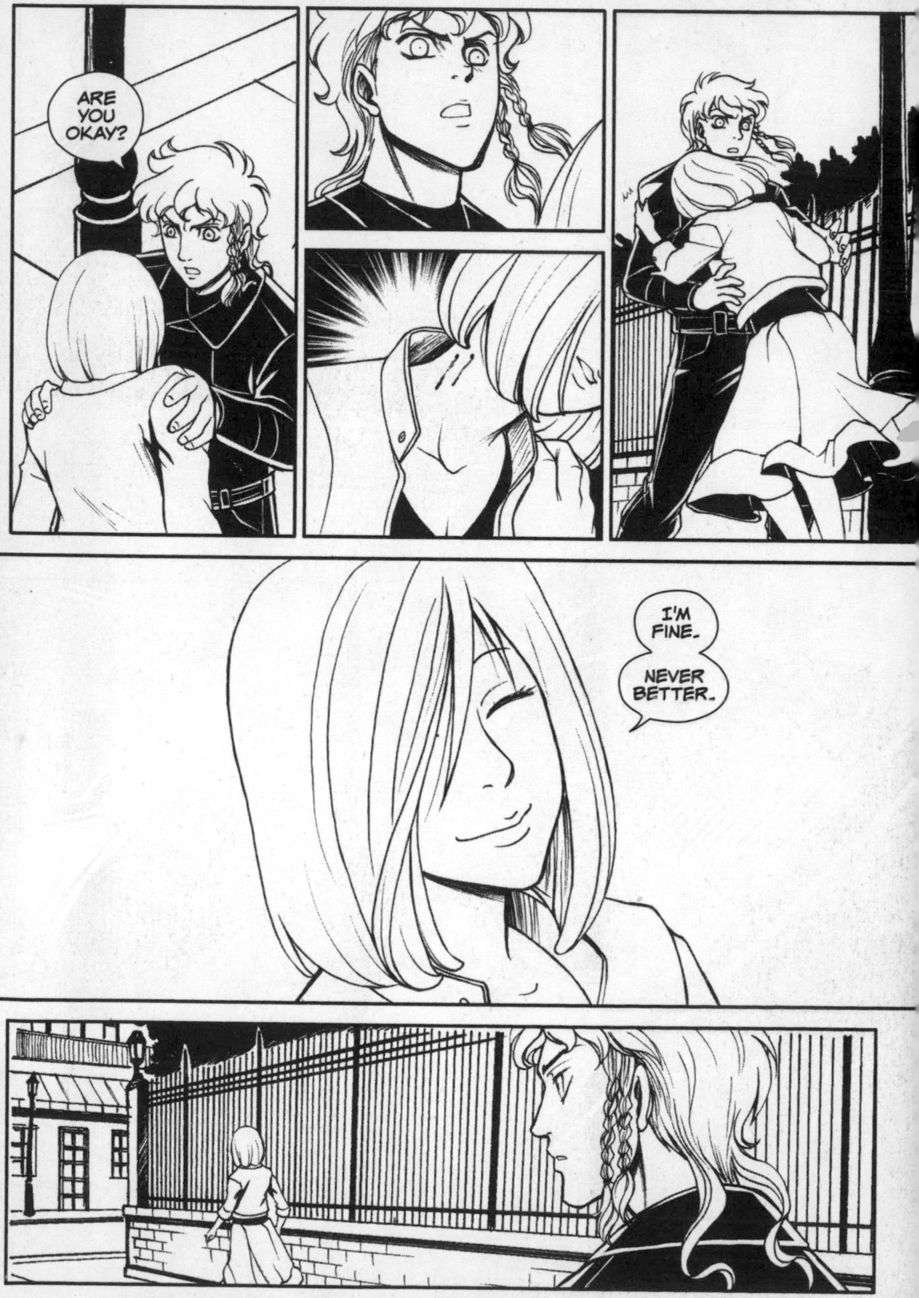
ARE YOU OKAY?
I'M FINE.
NEVER BETTER.

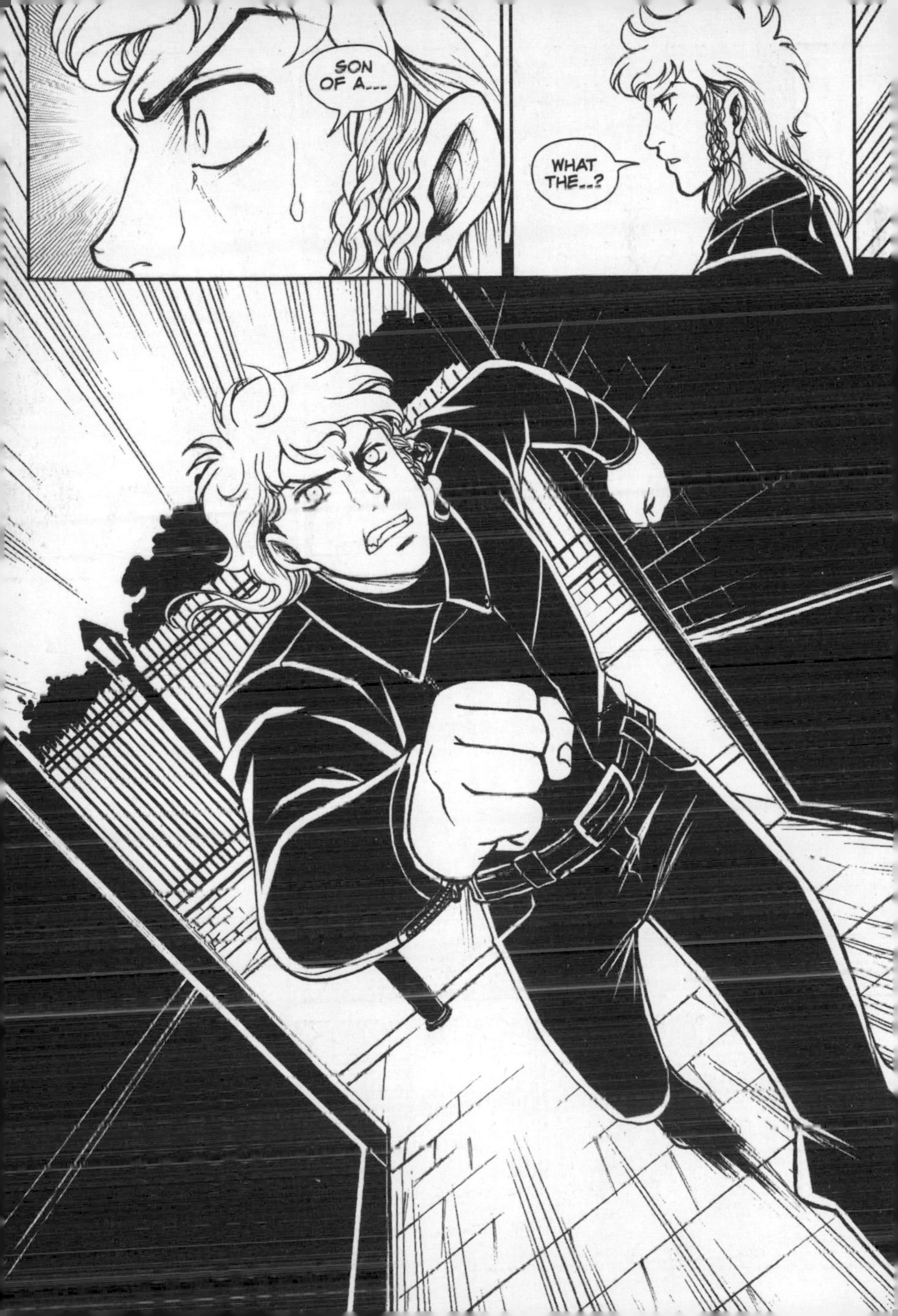
SON OF A...
WHAT THE..?

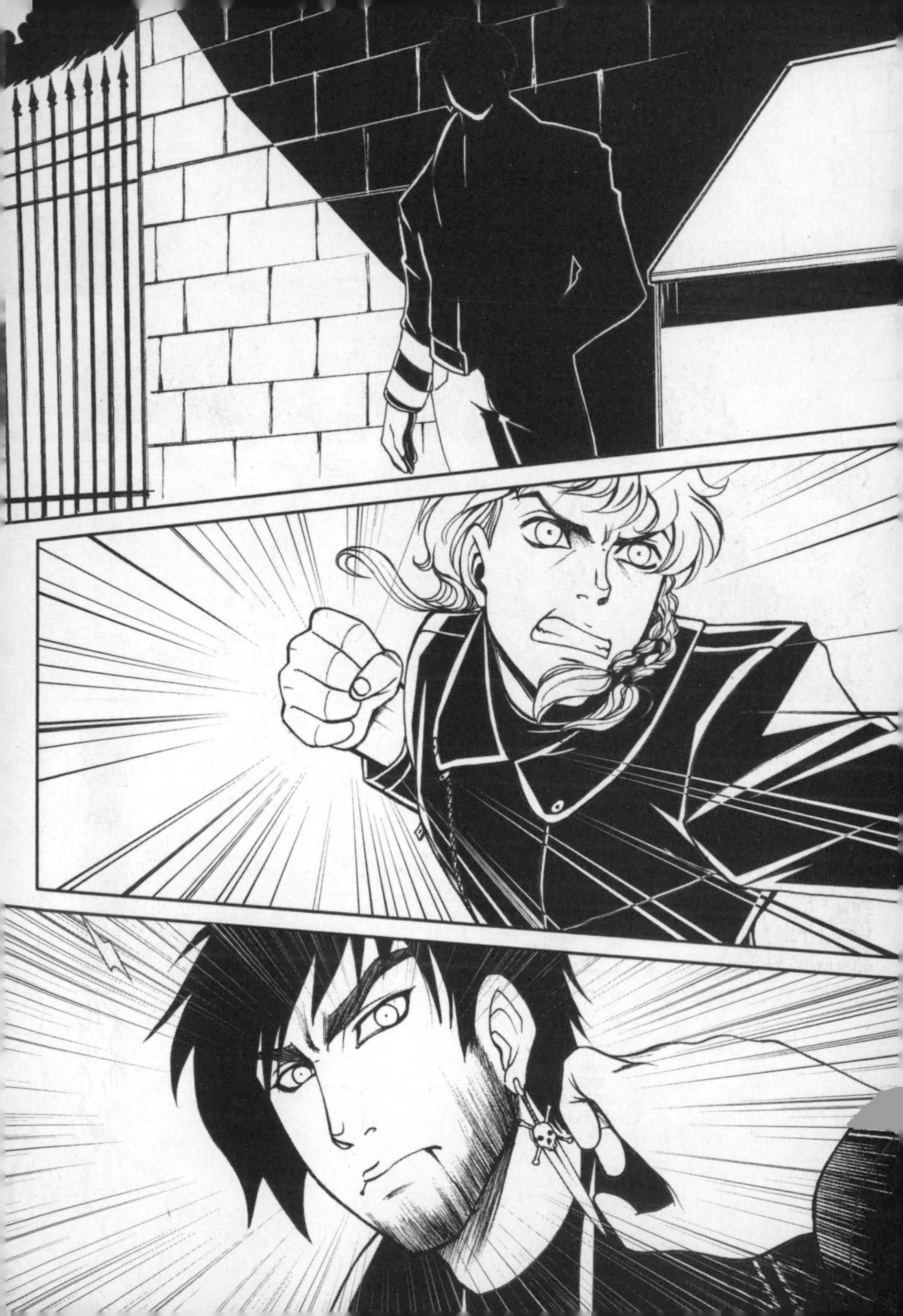

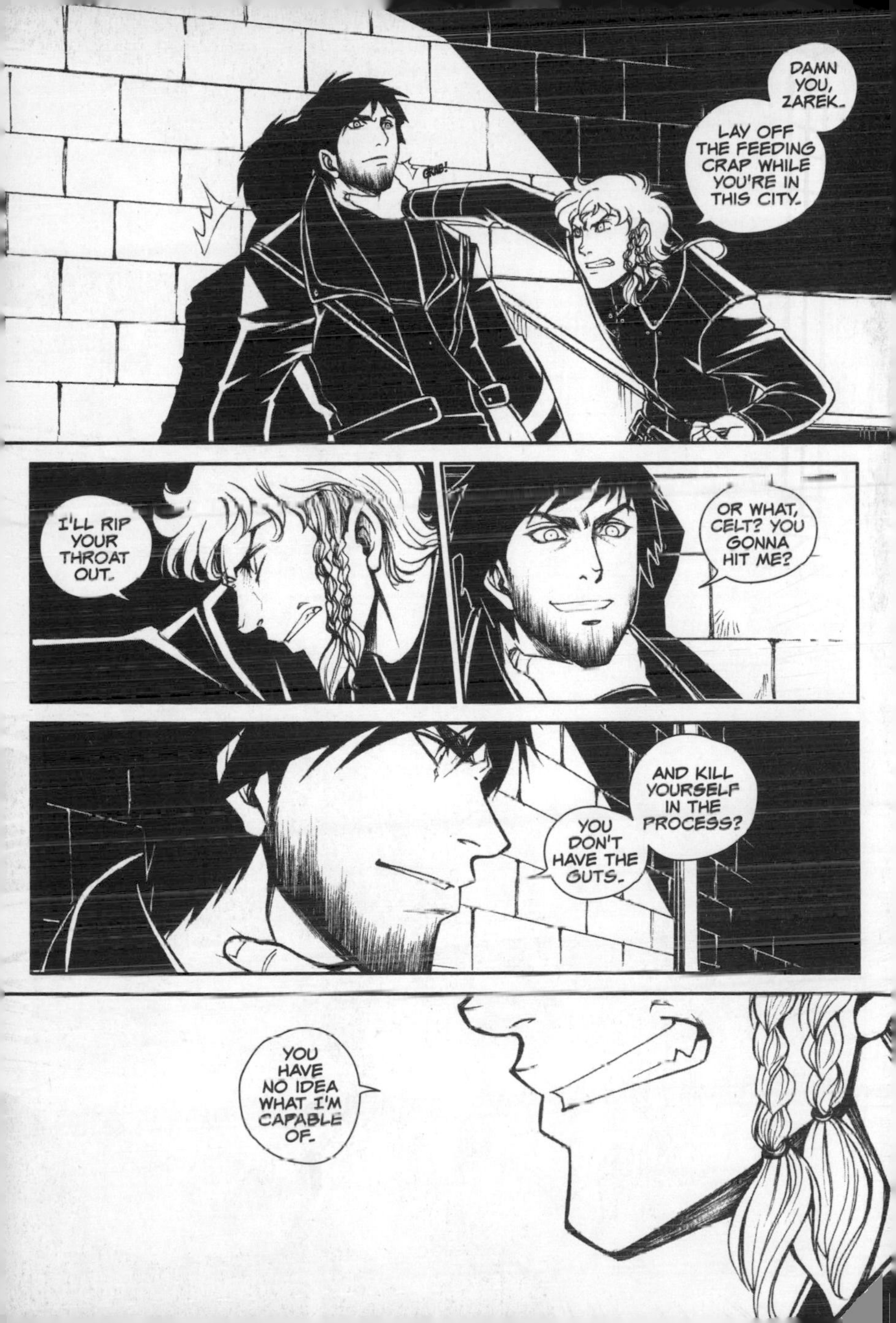
DAMN YOU, ZAREK.
LAY OFF THE FEEDING CRAP WHILE YOU'RE IN THIS CITY.
I'LL RIP YOUR THROAT OUT.
OR WHAT, CELT? YOU GONNA HIT ME?
AND KILL YOURSELF IN THE PROCESS?
YOU DON'T HAVE THE GUTS.
YOU HAVE NO IDEA WHAT I'M CAPABLE OF.

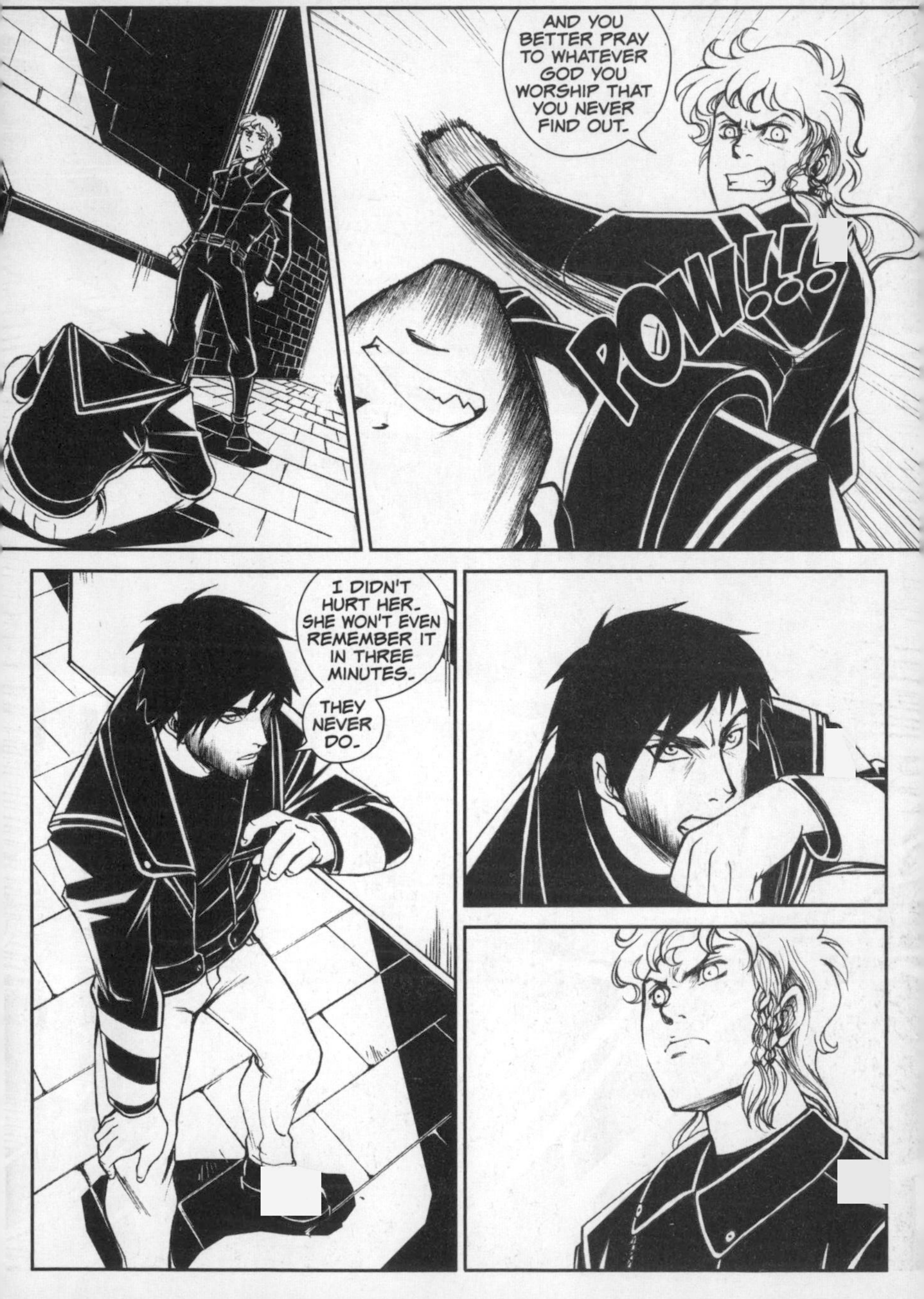
AND YOU BETTER PRAY TO WHATEVER GOD YOU WORSHIP THAT YOU NEVER FIND OUT.
POW!!!
I DIDN'T HURT HER. SHE WON'T EVEN REMEMBER IT IN THREE MINUTES.
THEY NEVER DO.

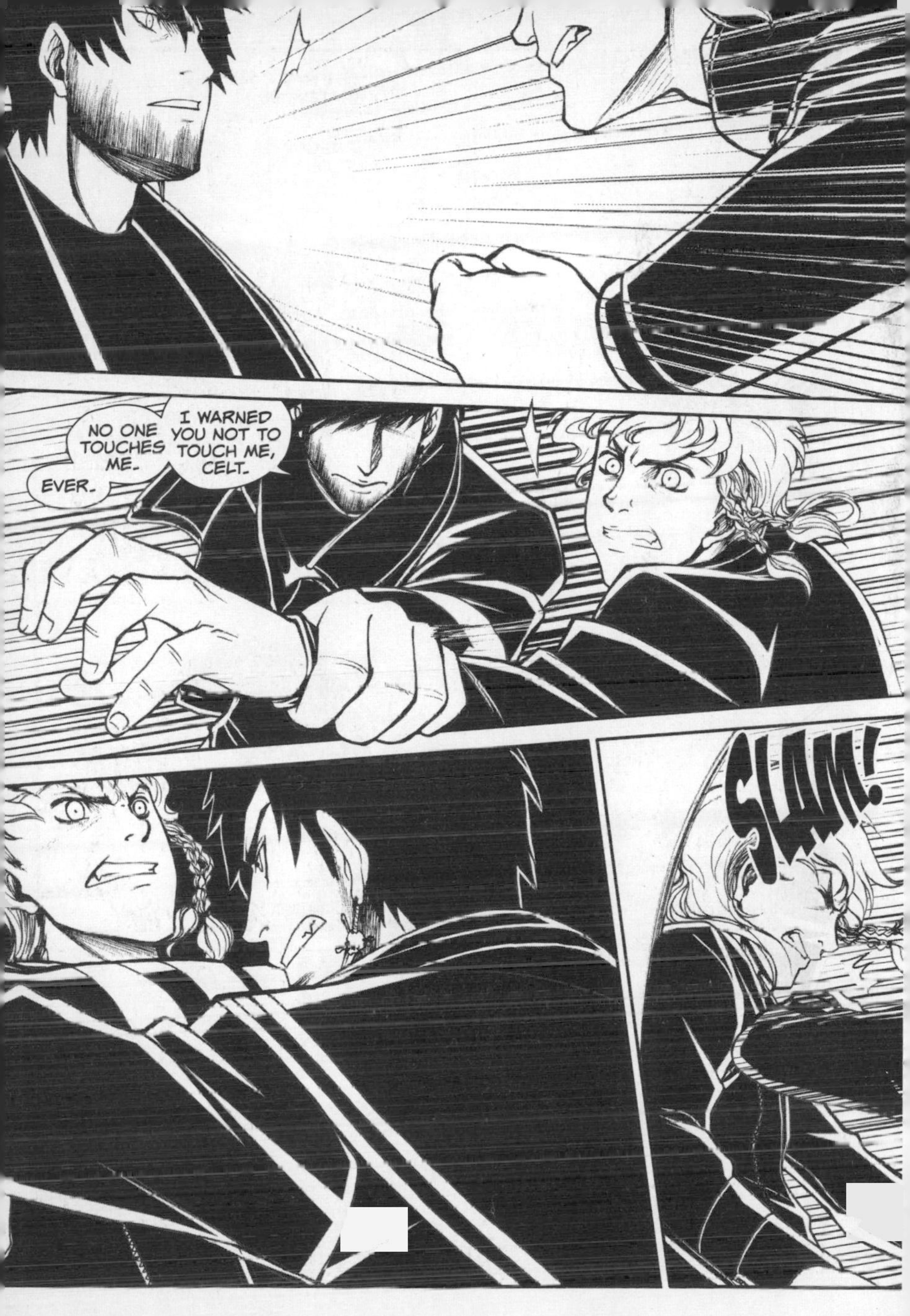
I WARNED YOU NOT TO TOUCH ME, CELT.
NO ONE TOUCHES ME.
EVER.
SLAM!

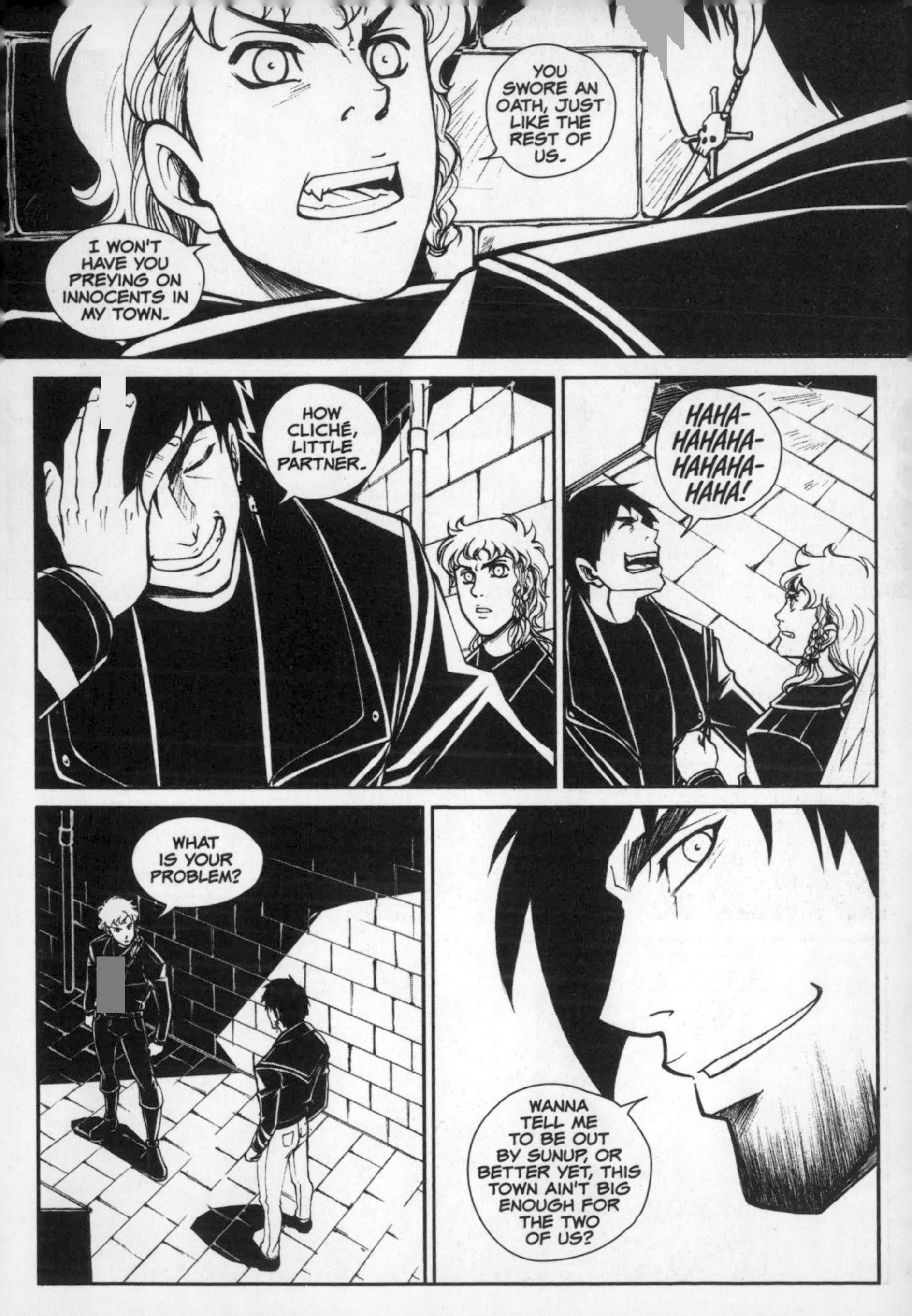

YOU SWORE AN OATH, JUST LIKE THE REST OF US...
I WON'T HAVE YOU PREYING ON INNOCENTS IN MY TOWN...
HOW CLICHÉ, LITTLE PARTNER...
HAHA-HAHAHA-HAHAHA-HAHA!
WHAT IS YOUR PROBLEM?
WANNA TELL ME TO BE OUT BY SUNUP, OR BETTER YET, THIS TOWN AIN'T BIG ENOUGH FOR THE TWO OF US?

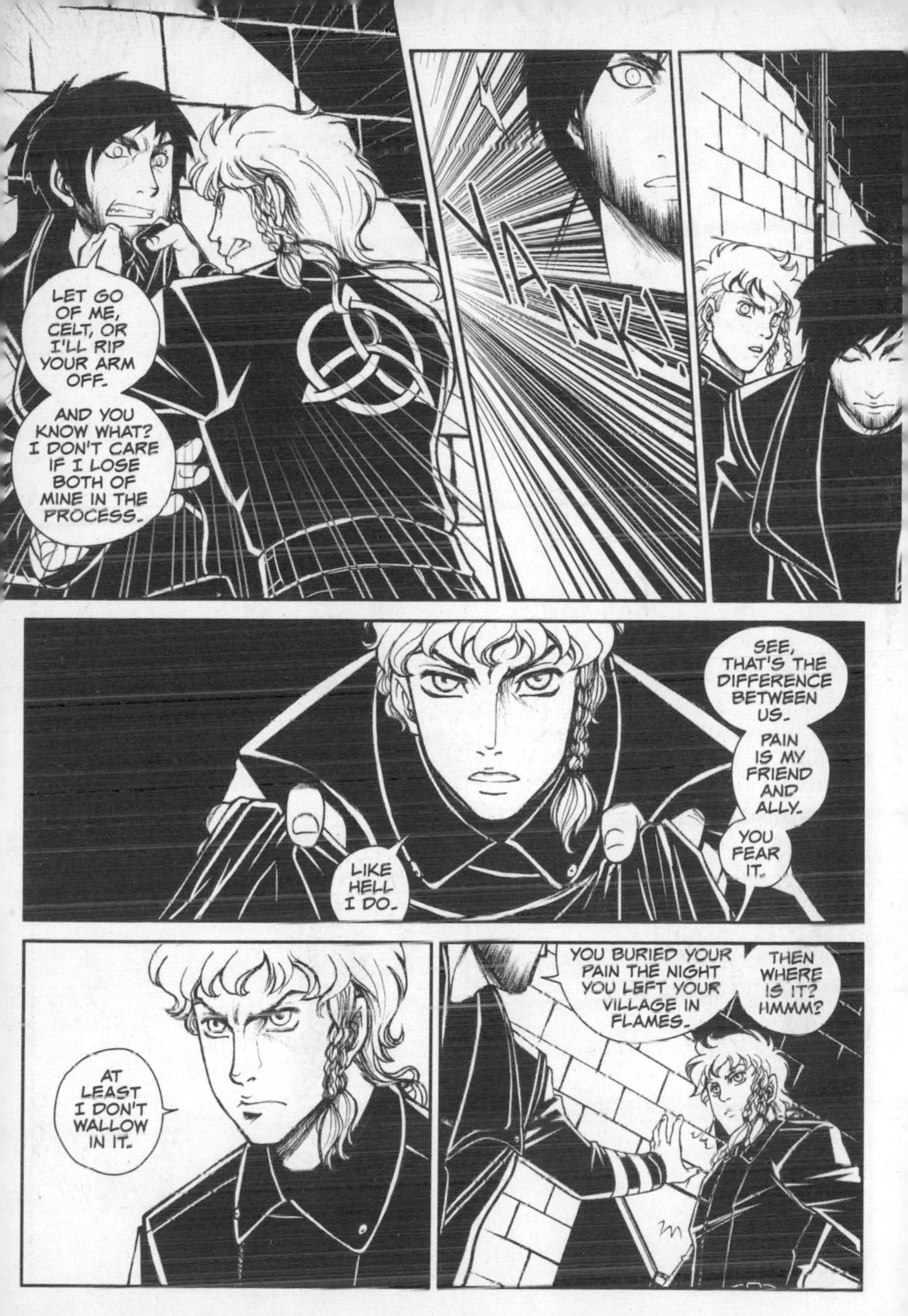

LET GO OF ME, CELT, OR I'LL RIP YOUR ARM OFF.
AND YOU KNOW WHAT? I DON'T CARE IF I LOSE BOTH OF MINE IN THE PROCESS.
YANK!!
SEE, THAT'S THE DIFFERENCE BETWEEN US.
PAIN IS MY FRIEND AND ALLY.
YOU FEAR IT.
LIKE HELL I DO.
AT LEAST I DON'T WALLOW IN IT.
YOU BURIED YOUR PAIN THE NIGHT YOU LEFT YOUR VILLAGE IN FLAMES.
THEN WHERE IS IT? HMMM?

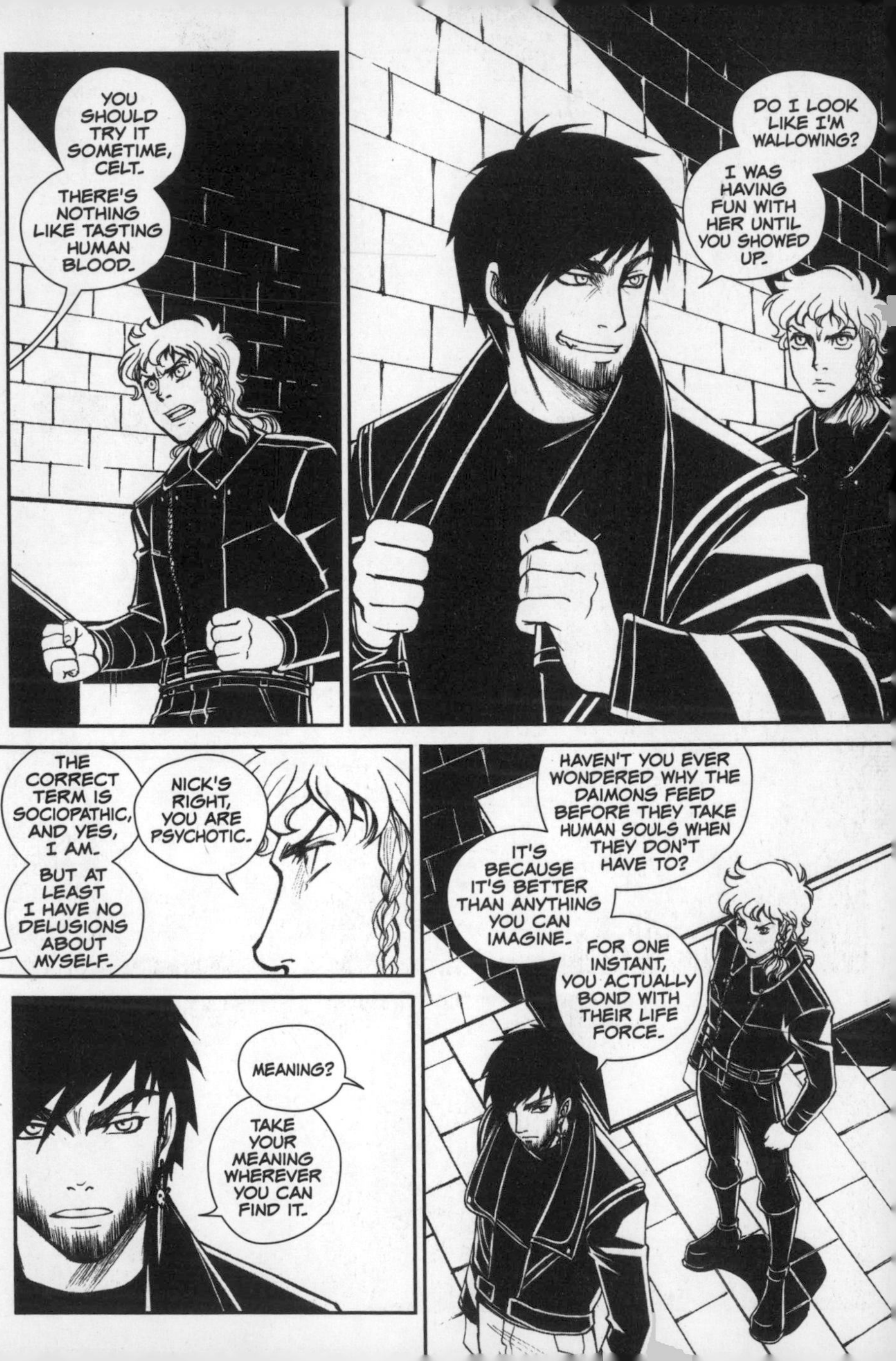
YOU SHOULD TRY IT SOMETIME, CELT.
THERE'S NOTHING LIKE TASTING HUMAN BLOOD.
DO I LOOK LIKE I'M WALLOWING?
I WAS HAVING FUN WITH HER UNTIL YOU SHOWED UP.
NICK'S RIGHT, YOU ARE PSYCHOTIC.
THE CORRECT TERM IS SOCIOPATHIC, AND YES, I AM.
BUT AT LEAST I HAVE NO DELUSIONS ABOUT MYSELF.
MEANING?
TAKE YOUR MEANING WHEREVER YOU CAN FIND IT.
HAVEN'T YOU EVER WONDERED WHY THE DAIMONS FEED BEFORE THEY TAKE HUMAN SOULS WHEN THEY DON'T HAVE TO?
IT'S BECAUSE IT'S BETTER THAN ANYTHING YOU CAN IMAGINE.
FOR ONE INSTANT, YOU ACTUALLY BOND WITH THEIR LIFE FORCE.

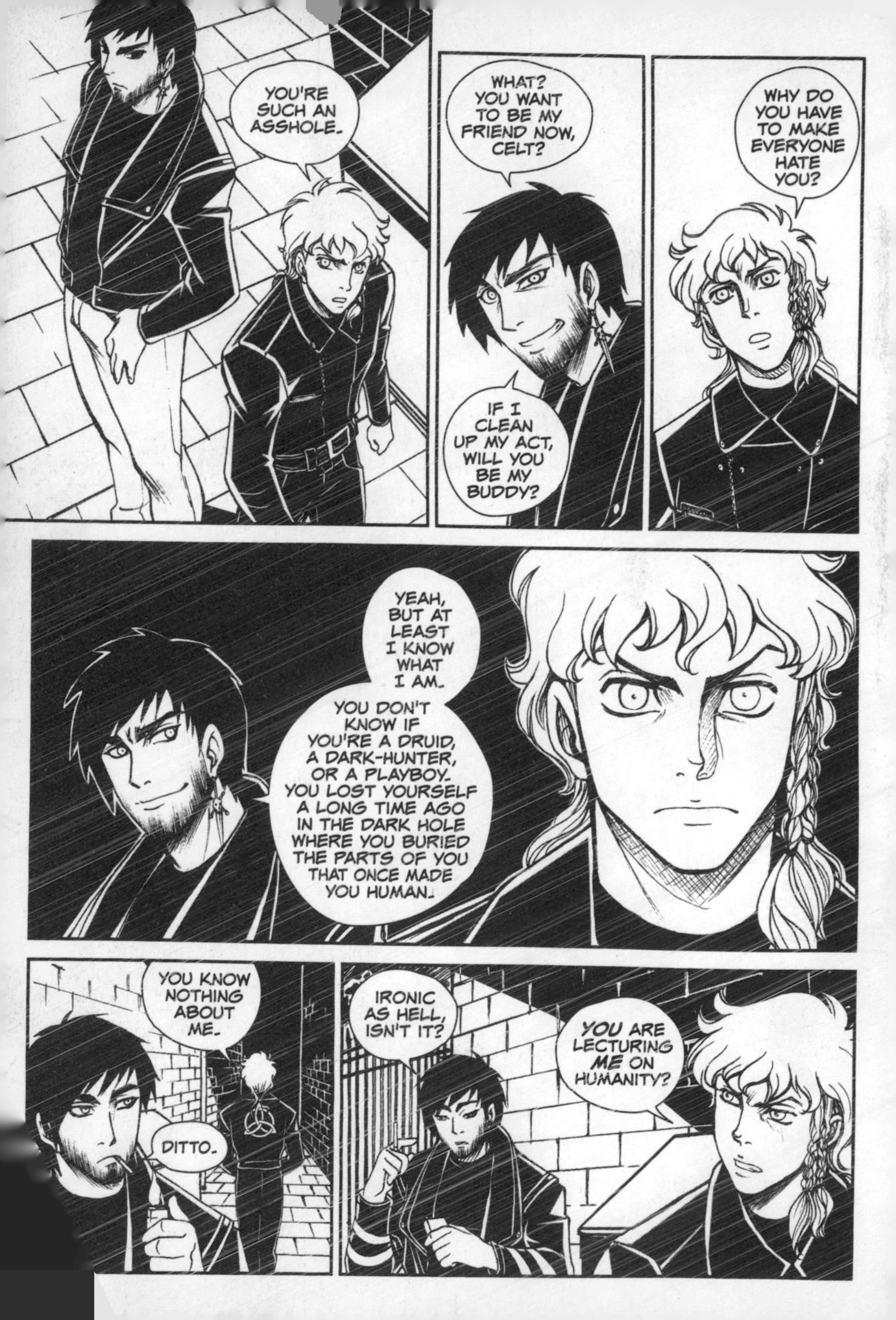
YOU'RE SUCH AN ASSHOLE.
WHAT? YOU WANT TO BE MY FRIEND NOW, CELT?
IF I CLEAN UP MY ACT, WILL YOU BE MY BUDDY?
WHY DO YOU HAVE TO MAKE EVERYONE HATE YOU?
YEAH, BUT AT LEAST I KNOW WHAT I AM.
YOU DON'T KNOW IF YOU'RE A DRUID, A DARK-HUNTER, OR A PLAYBOY. YOU LOST YOURSELF A LONG TIME AGO IN THE DARK HOLE WHERE YOU BURIED THE PARTS OF YOU THAT ONCE MADE YOU HUMAN.
YOU KNOW NOTHING ABOUT ME.
DITTO.
IRONIC AS HELL, ISN'T IT?
YOU ARE LECTURING *ME* ON HUMANITY?

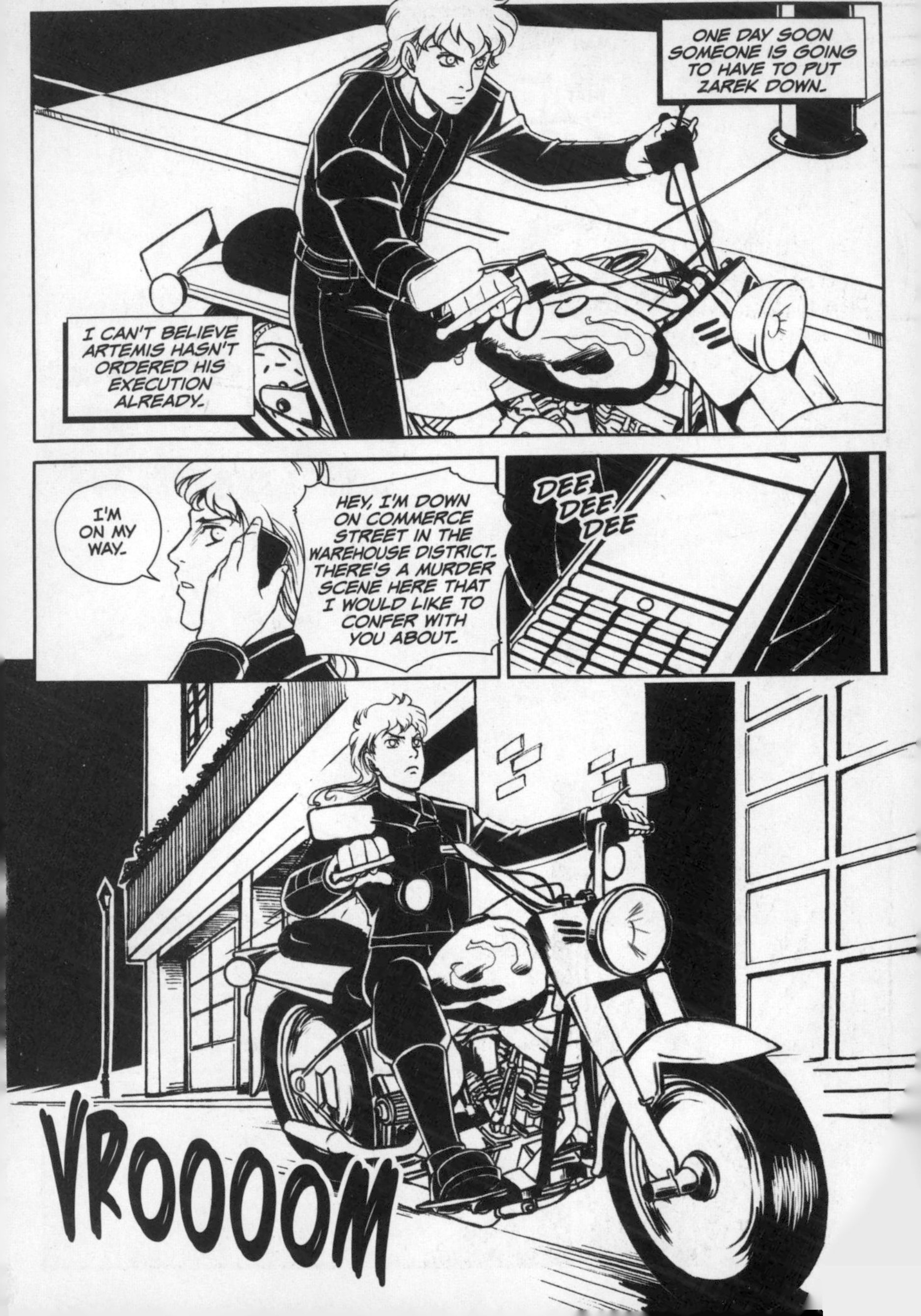
ONE DAY SOON SOMEONE IS GOING TO HAVE TO PUT ZAREK DOWN.
I CAN'T BELIEVE ARTEMIS HASN'T ORDERED HIS EXECUTION ALREADY.
DEE DEE DEE
HEY, I'M DOWN ON COMMERCE STREET IN THE WAREHOUSE DISTRICT. THERE'S A MURDER SCENE HERE THAT I WOULD LIKE TO CONFER WITH YOU ABOUT.
I'M ON MY WAY.
VROOOOM

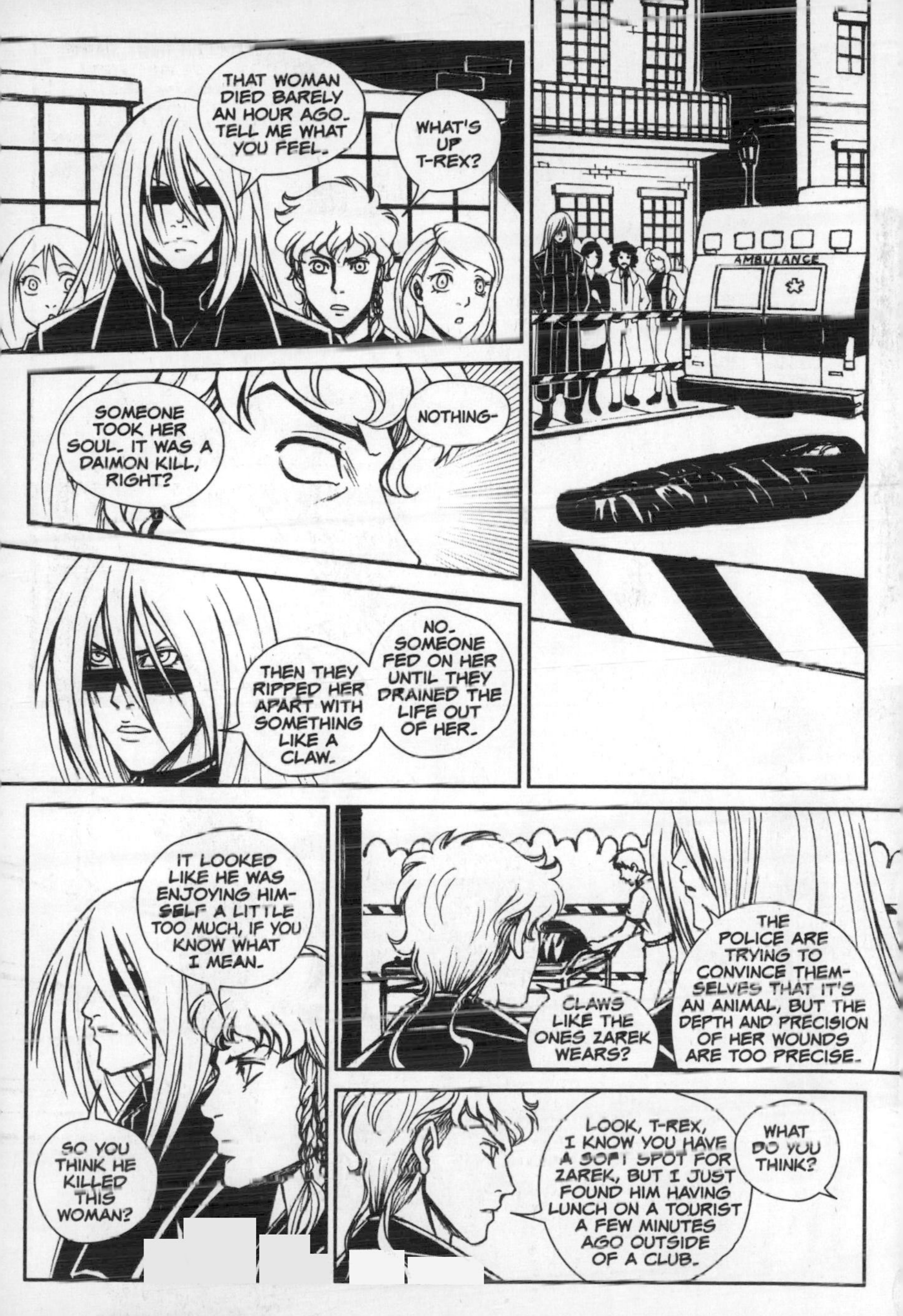
THAT WOMAN DIED BARELY AN HOUR AGO. TELL ME WHAT YOU FEEL.
WHAT'S UP T-REX?
AMBULANCE
SOMEONE TOOK HER SOUL. IT WAS A DAIMON KILL, RIGHT?
NOTHING.
NO. SOMEONE FED ON HER UNTIL THEY DRAINED THE LIFE OUT OF HER.
THEN THEY RIPPED HER APART WITH SOMETHING LIKE A CLAW.
IT LOOKED LIKE HE WAS ENJOYING HIM-SELF A LITTLE TOO MUCH, IF YOU KNOW WHAT I MEAN.
THE POLICE ARE TRYING TO CONVINCE THEM-SELVES THAT IT'S AN ANIMAL, BUT THE DEPTH AND PRECISION OF HER WOUNDS ARE TOO PRECISE.
CLAWS LIKE THE ONES ZAREK WEARS?
LOOK, T-REX, I KNOW YOU HAVE A SOFT SPOT FOR ZAREK, BUT I JUST FOUND HIM HAVING LUNCH ON A TOURIST A FEW MINUTES AGO OUTSIDE OF A CLUB.
WHAT DO YOU THINK?
SO YOU THINK HE KILLED THIS WOMAN?

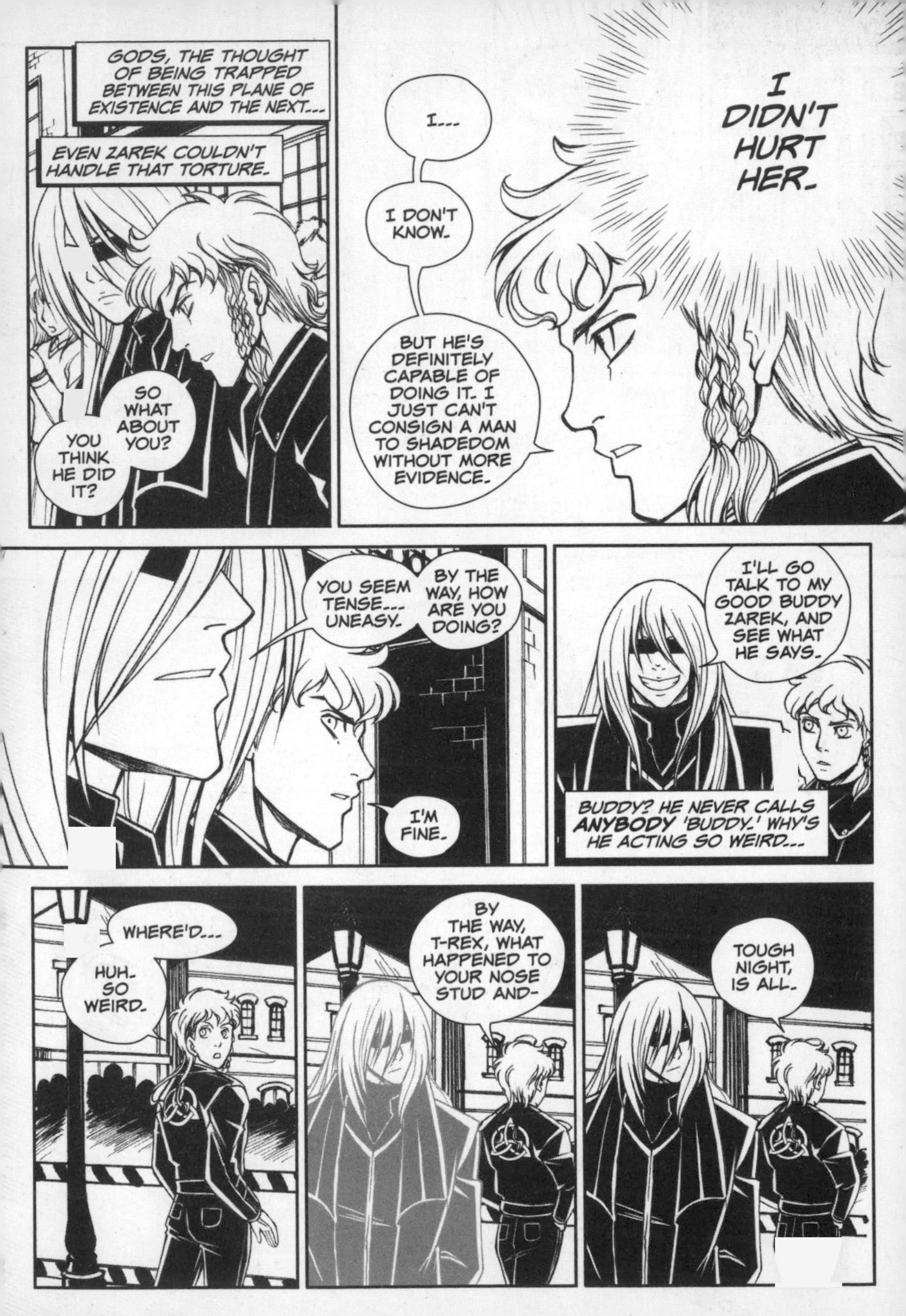
GODS, THE THOUGHT OF BEING TRAPPED BETWEEN THIS PLANE OF EXISTENCE AND THE NEXT...
EVEN ZAREK COULDN'T HANDLE THAT TORTURE.
SO WHAT ABOUT YOU?
YOU THINK HE DID IT?
I...
I DON'T KNOW.
BUT HE'S DEFINITELY CAPABLE OF DOING IT. I JUST CAN'T CONSIGN A MAN TO SHADEDOM WITHOUT MORE EVIDENCE.
I DIDN'T HURT HER.
YOU SEEM TENSE... UNEASY.
BY THE WAY, HOW ARE YOU DOING?
I'M FINE.
I'LL GO TALK TO MY GOOD BUDDY ZAREK, AND SEE WHAT HE SAYS.
BUDDY? HE NEVER CALLS **ANYBODY** 'BUDDY.' WHY'S HE ACTING SO WEIRD...
WHERE'D...
HUH. SO WEIRD.
BY THE WAY, T-REX, WHAT HAPPENED TO YOUR NOSE STUD AND-
TOUGH NIGHT, IS ALL.

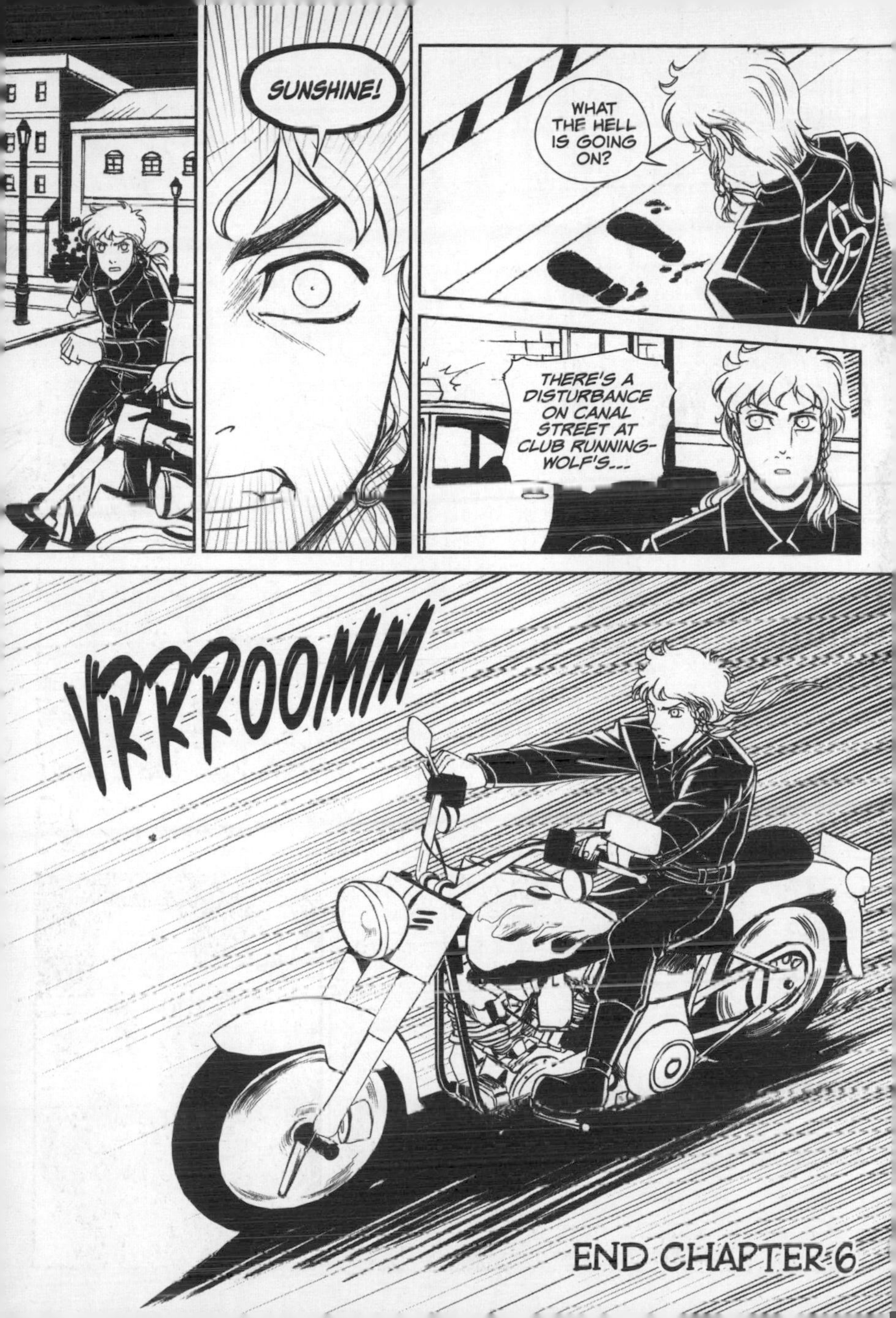
SUNSHINE!
WHAT THE HELL IS GOING ON?
THERE'S A DISTURBANCE ON CANAL STREET AT CLUB RUNNING-WOLF'S...
VRRROOMM
END CHAPTER 6

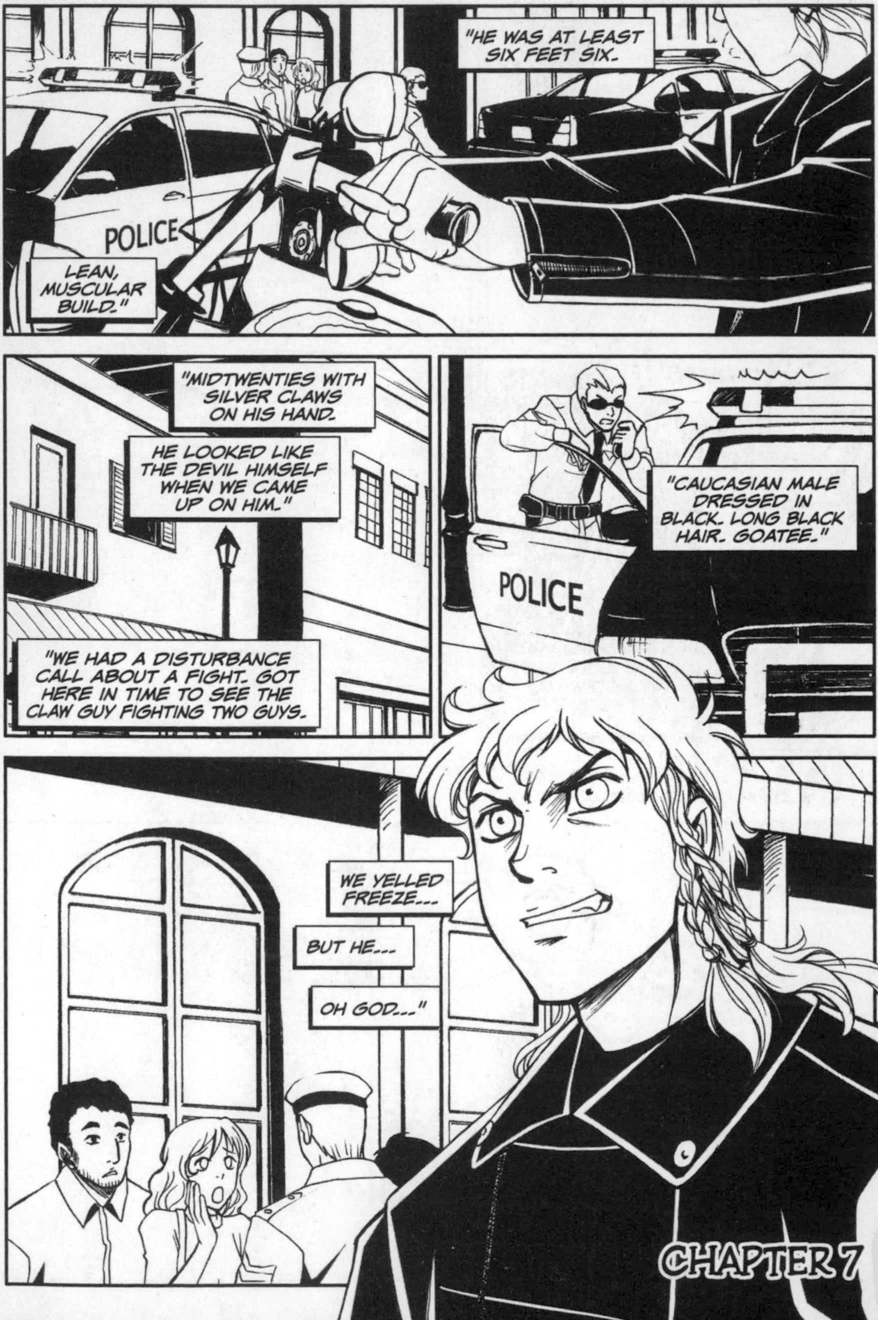
"HE WAS AT LEAST SIX FEET SIX.
POLICE
LEAN, MUSCULAR BUILD."
"MIDTWENTIES WITH SILVER CLAWS ON HIS HAND.
HE LOOKED LIKE THE DEVIL HIMSELF WHEN WE CAME UP ON HIM."
"WE HAD A DISTURBANCE CALL ABOUT A FIGHT. GOT HERE IN TIME TO SEE THE CLAW GUY FIGHTING TWO GUYS.
POLICE
"CAUCASIAN MALE DRESSED IN BLACK. LONG BLACK HAIR. GOATEE."
WE YELLED FREEZE...
BUT HE...
OH GOD..."
CHAPTER 7

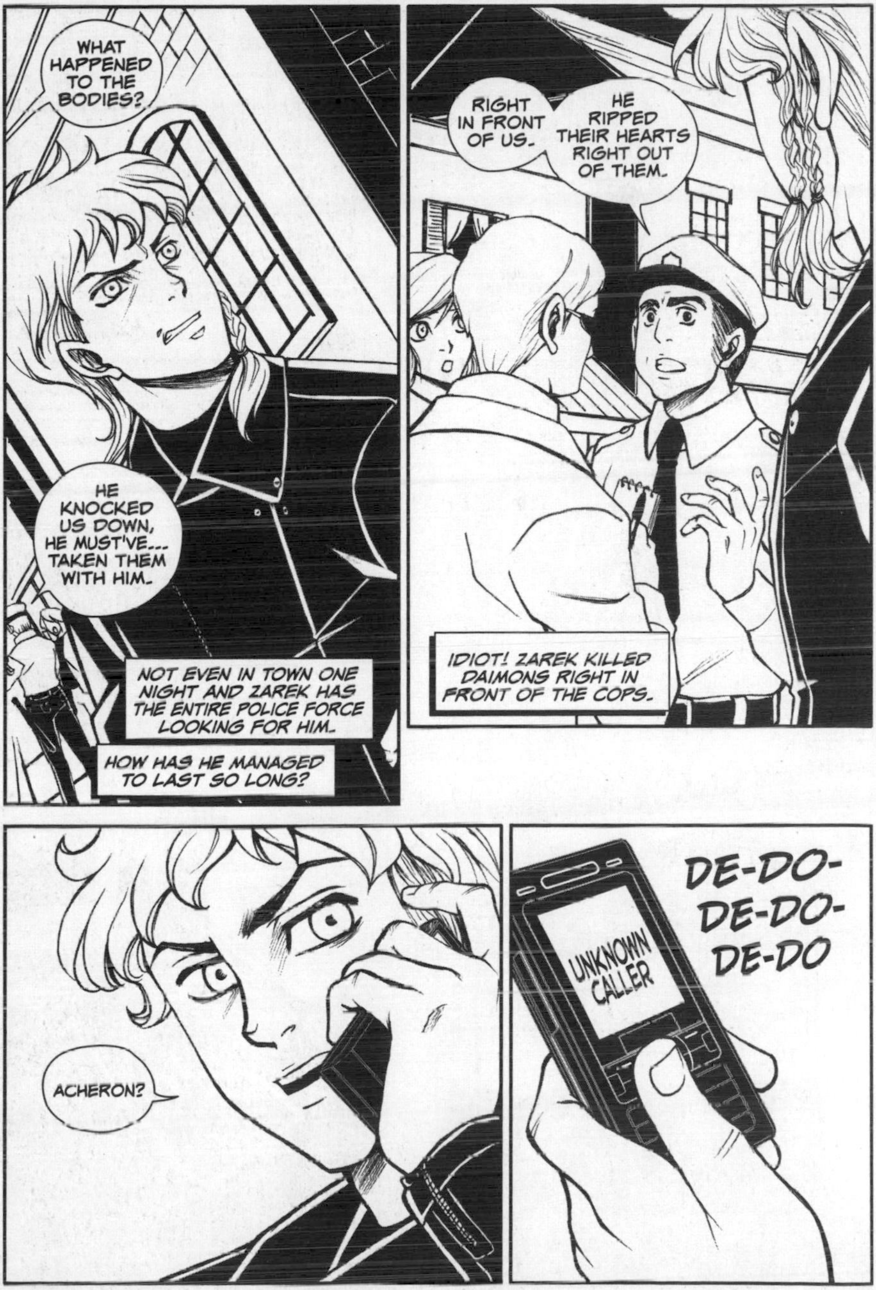
WHAT HAPPENED TO THE BODIES?
HE KNOCKED US DOWN, HE MUST'VE... TAKEN THEM WITH HIM.
NOT EVEN IN TOWN ONE NIGHT AND ZAREK HAS THE ENTIRE POLICE FORCE LOOKING FOR HIM.
HOW HAS HE MANAGED TO LAST SO LONG?
RIGHT IN FRONT OF US.
HE RIPPED THEIR HEARTS RIGHT OUT OF THEM.
IDIOT! ZAREK KILLED DAIMONS RIGHT IN FRONT OF THE COPS.
ACHERON?
UNKNOWN CALLER
DE-DO-DE-DO-DE-DO

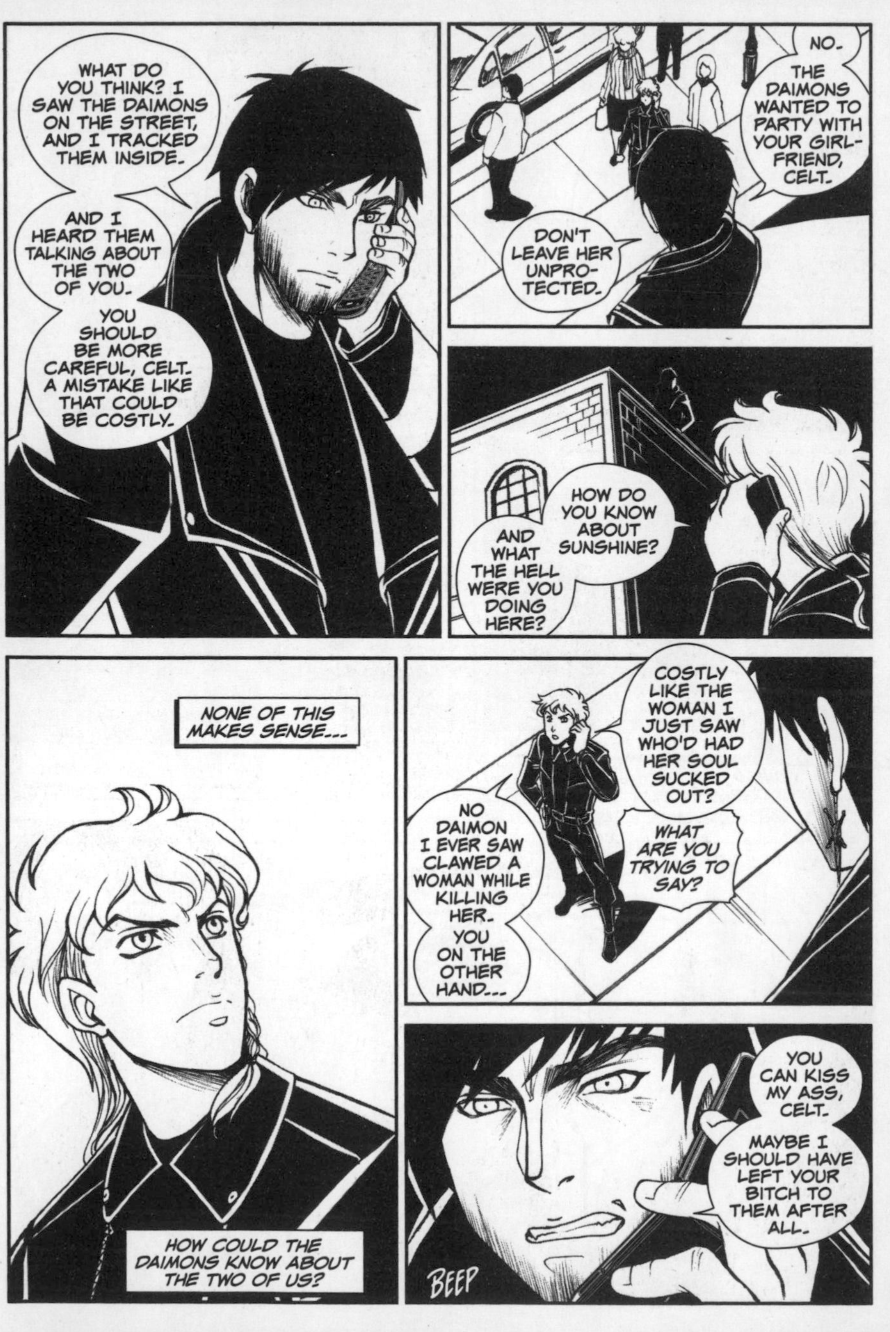
WHAT DO YOU THINK? I SAW THE DAIMONS ON THE STREET, AND I TRACKED THEM INSIDE.
AND I HEARD THEM TALKING ABOUT THE TWO OF YOU.
YOU SHOULD BE MORE CAREFUL, CELT. A MISTAKE LIKE THAT COULD BE COSTLY.
NO.
THE DAIMONS WANTED TO PARTY WITH YOUR GIRL-FRIEND, CELT.
DON'T LEAVE HER UNPRO-TECTED.
HOW DO YOU KNOW ABOUT SUNSHINE?
AND WHAT THE HELL WERE YOU DOING HERE?
NONE OF THIS MAKES SENSE...
HOW COULD THE DAIMONS KNOW ABOUT THE TWO OF US?
COSTLY LIKE THE WOMAN I JUST SAW WHO'D HAD HER SOUL SUCKED OUT?
WHAT ARE YOU TRYING TO SAY?
NO DAIMON I EVER SAW CLAWED A WOMAN WHILE KILLING HER.
YOU ON THE OTHER HAND...
YOU CAN KISS MY ASS, CELT.
MAYBE I SHOULD HAVE LEFT YOUR BITCH TO THEM AFTER ALL.
BEEP

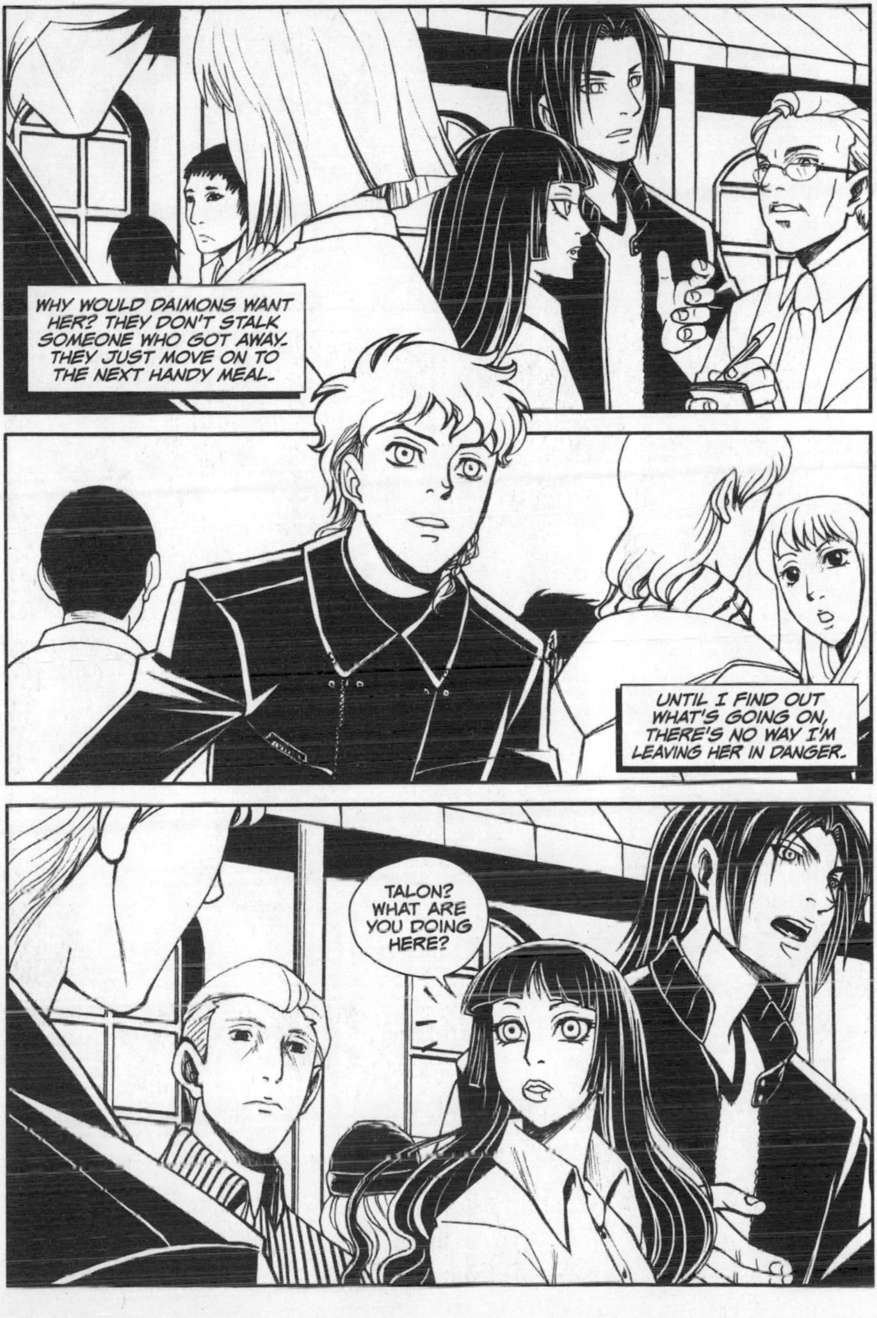
WHY WOULD DAIMONS WANT HER? THEY DON'T STALK SOMEONE WHO GOT AWAY. THEY JUST MOVE ON TO THE NEXT HANDY MEAL.
UNTIL I FIND OUT WHAT'S GOING ON, THERE'S NO WAY I'M LEAVING HER IN DANGER.
TALON? WHAT ARE YOU DOING HERE?

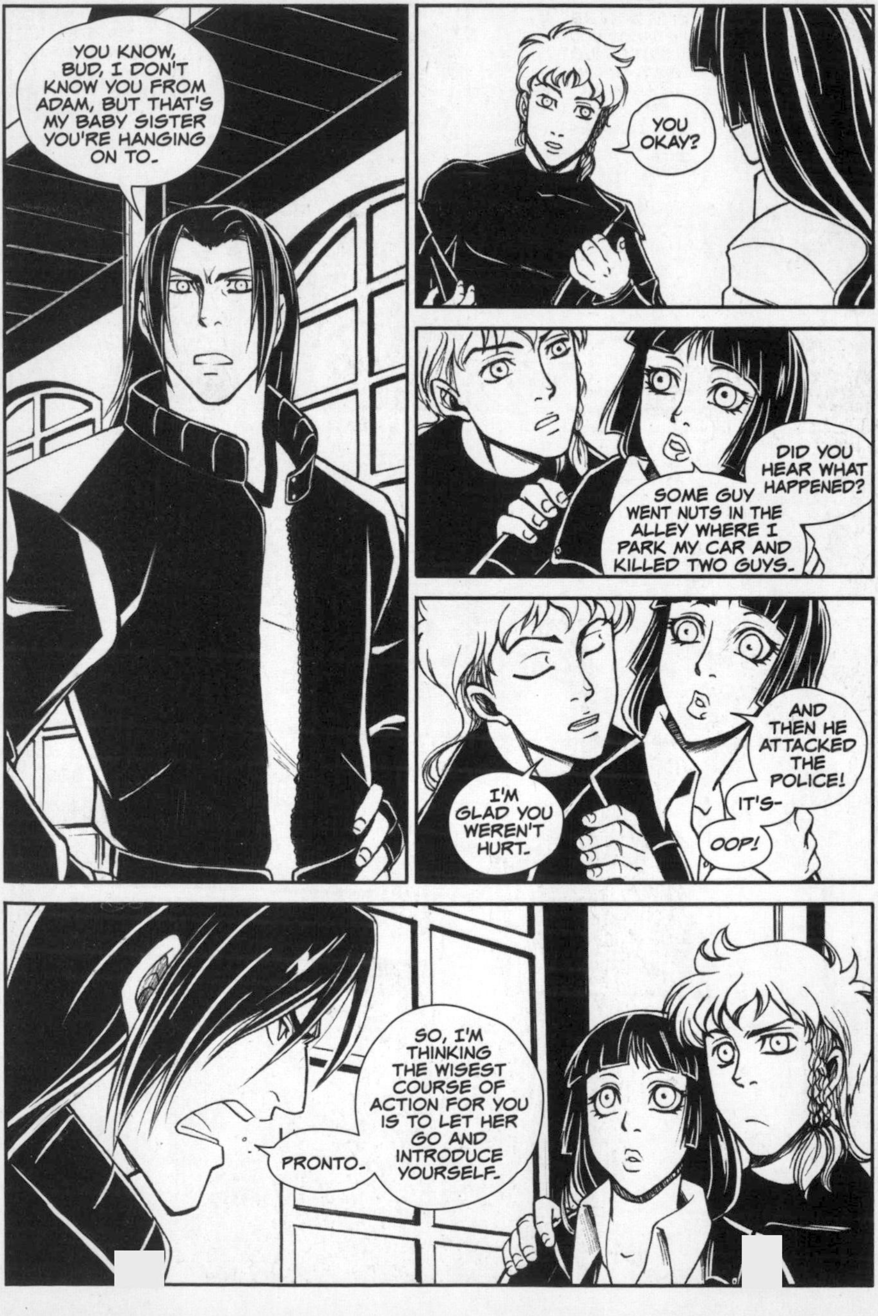
YOU KNOW, BUD, I DON'T KNOW YOU FROM ADAM, BUT THAT'S MY BABY SISTER YOU'RE HANGING ON TO.
YOU OKAY?
DID YOU HEAR WHAT HAPPENED?
SOME GUY WENT NUTS IN THE ALLEY WHERE I PARK MY CAR AND KILLED TWO GUYS.
AND THEN HE ATTACKED THE POLICE!
IT'S-
I'M GLAD YOU WEREN'T HURT.
OOP!
SO, I'M THINKING THE WISEST COURSE OF ACTION FOR YOU IS TO LET HER GO AND INTRODUCE YOURSELF.
PRONTO.

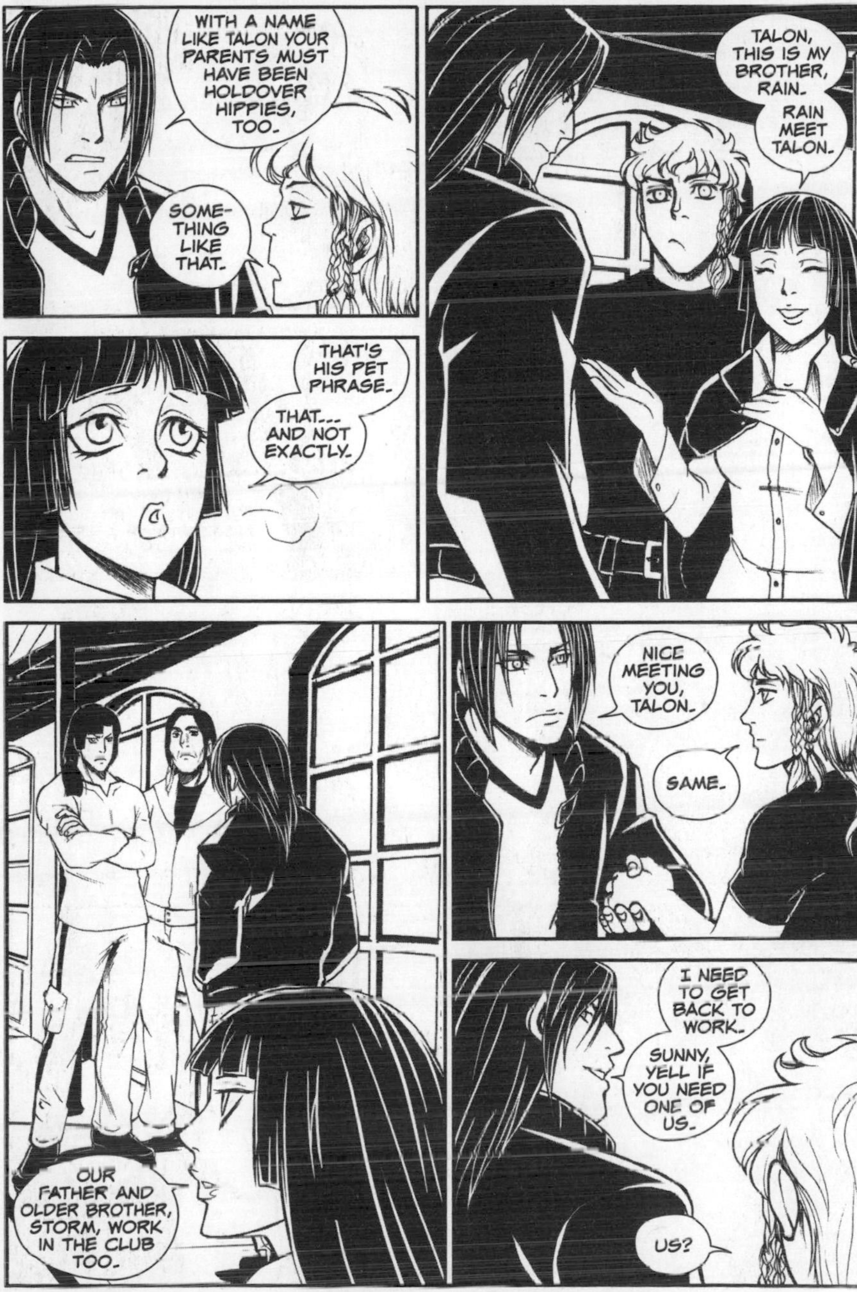
WITH A NAME LIKE TALON YOUR PARENTS MUST HAVE BEEN HOLDOVER HIPPIES, TOO.
SOME-THING LIKE THAT.
THAT'S HIS PET PHRASE.
THAT... AND NOT EXACTLY.
TALON, THIS IS MY BROTHER, RAIN.
RAIN MEET TALON.
OUR FATHER AND OLDER BROTHER, STORM, WORK IN THE CLUB TOO.
NICE MEETING YOU, TALON.
SAME.
I NEED TO GET BACK TO WORK.
SUNNY, YELL IF YOU NEED ONE OF US.
US?

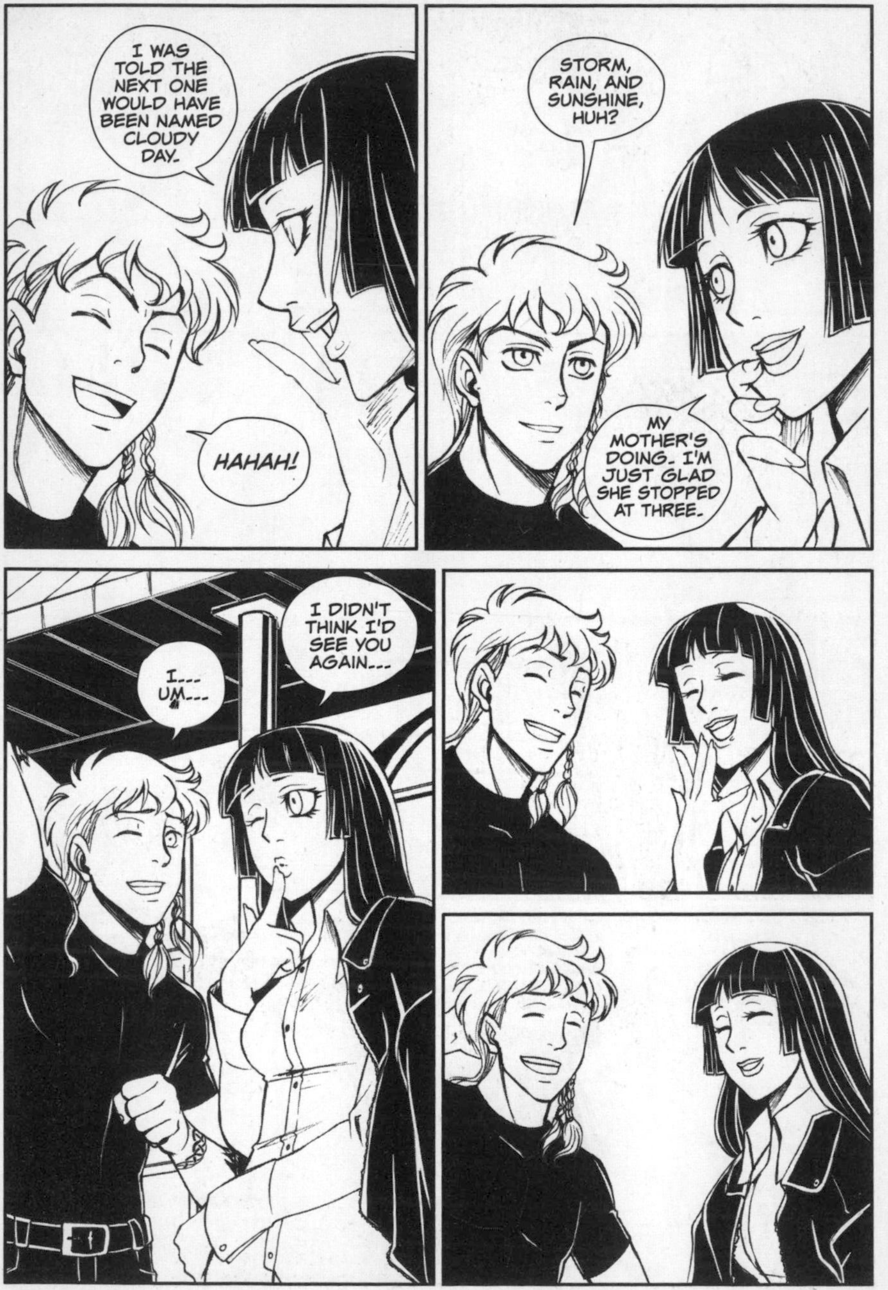
I WAS TOLD THE NEXT ONE WOULD HAVE BEEN NAMED CLOUDY DAY.
HAHAH!
STORM, RAIN, AND SUNSHINE, HUH?
MY MOTHER'S DOING. I'M JUST GLAD SHE STOPPED AT THREE.
I DIDN'T THINK I'D SEE YOU AGAIN...
I... UM...

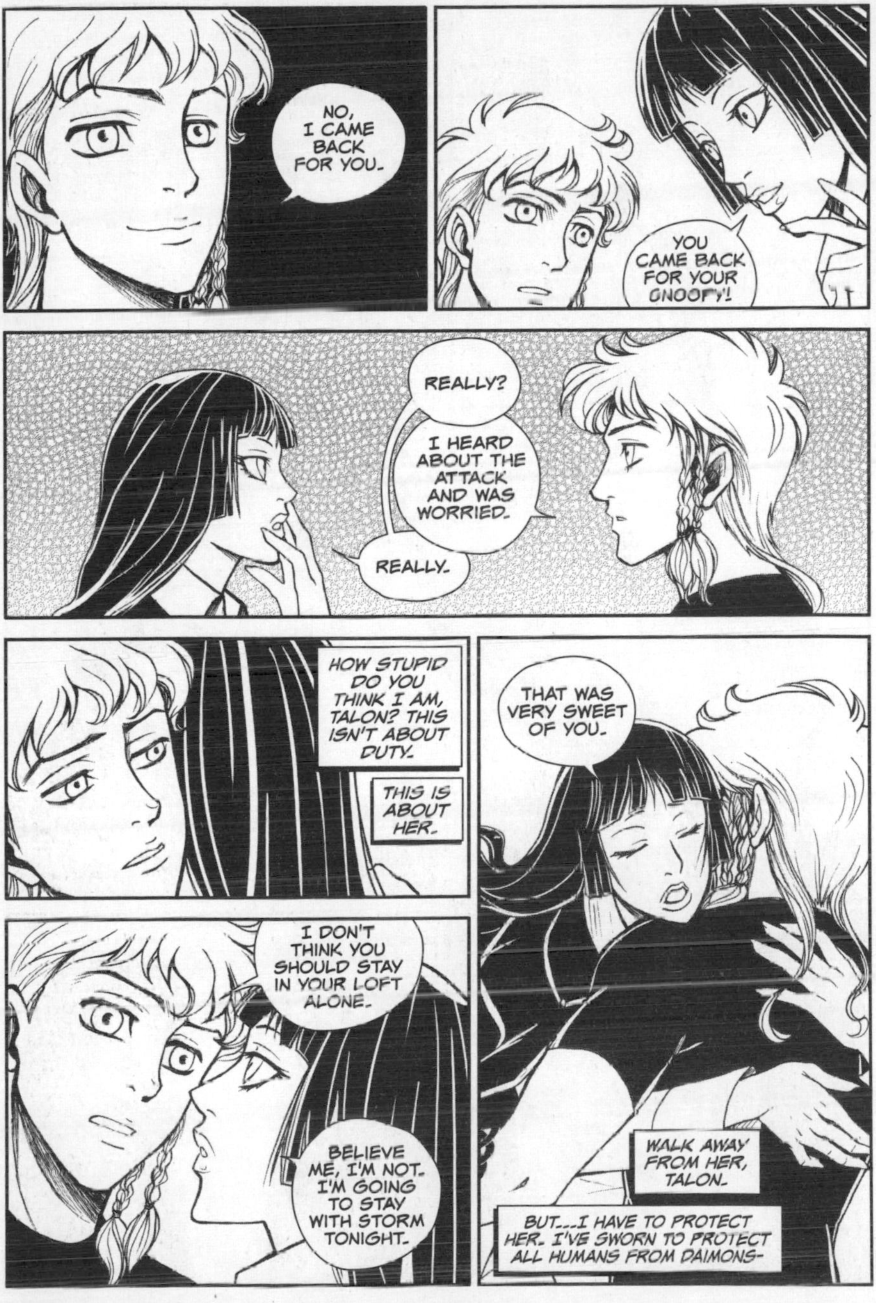
NO, I CAME BACK FOR YOU.
YOU CAME BACK FOR YOUR GNOOFY!
REALLY?
I HEARD ABOUT THE ATTACK AND WAS WORRIED.
REALLY.
HOW STUPID DO YOU THINK I AM, TALON? THIS ISN'T ABOUT DUTY.
THIS IS ABOUT HER.
I DON'T THINK YOU SHOULD STAY IN YOUR LOFT ALONE.
BELIEVE ME, I'M NOT. I'M GOING TO STAY WITH STORM TONIGHT.
THAT WAS VERY SWEET OF YOU.
WALK AWAY FROM HER, TALON.
BUT...I HAVE TO PROTECT HER. I'VE SWORN TO PROTECT ALL HUMANS FROM DAIMONS-

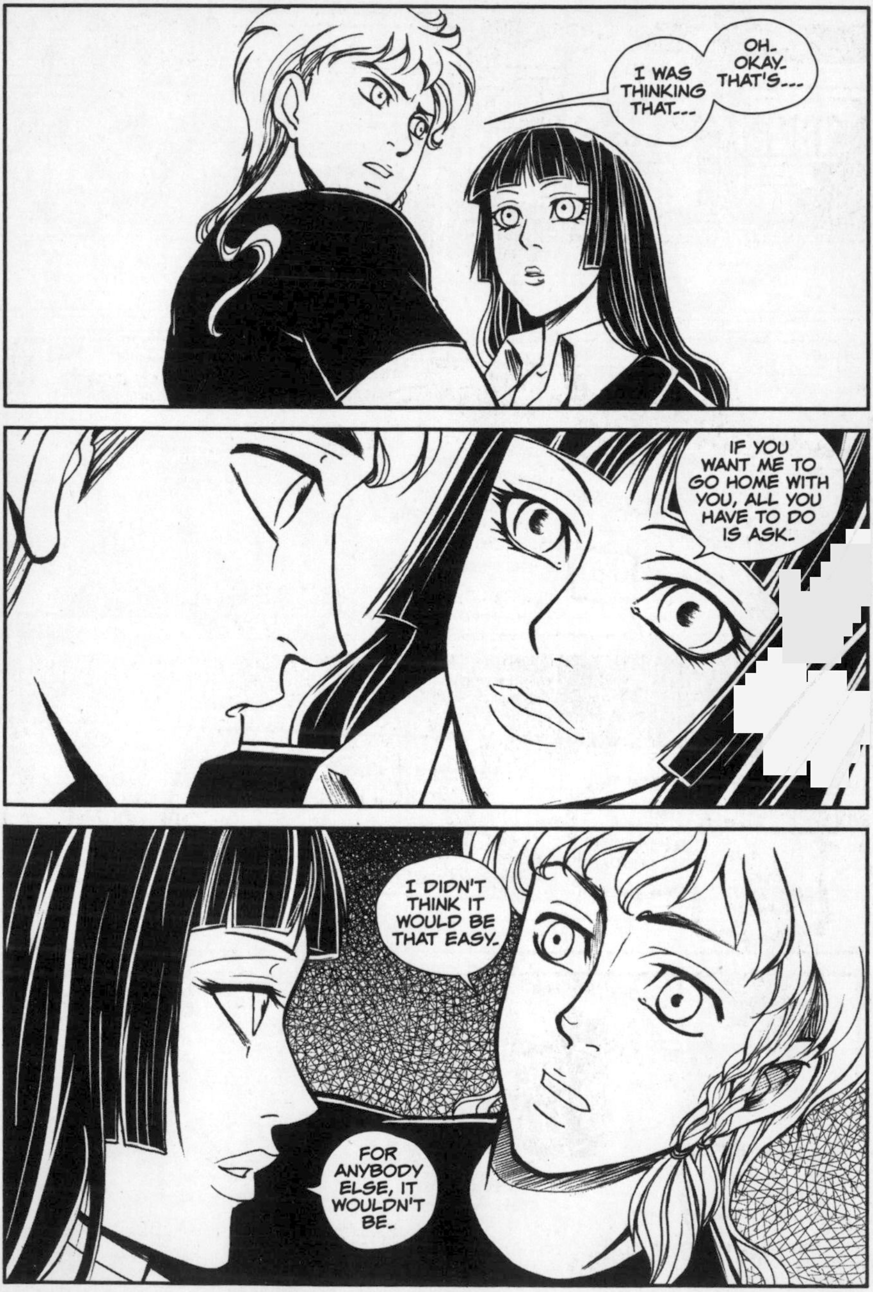
I WAS THINKING THAT...
OH. OKAY. THAT'S...
IF YOU WANT ME TO GO HOME WITH YOU, ALL YOU HAVE TO DO IS ASK.
I DIDN'T THINK IT WOULD BE THAT EASY.
FOR ANYBODY ELSE, IT WOULDN'T BE.

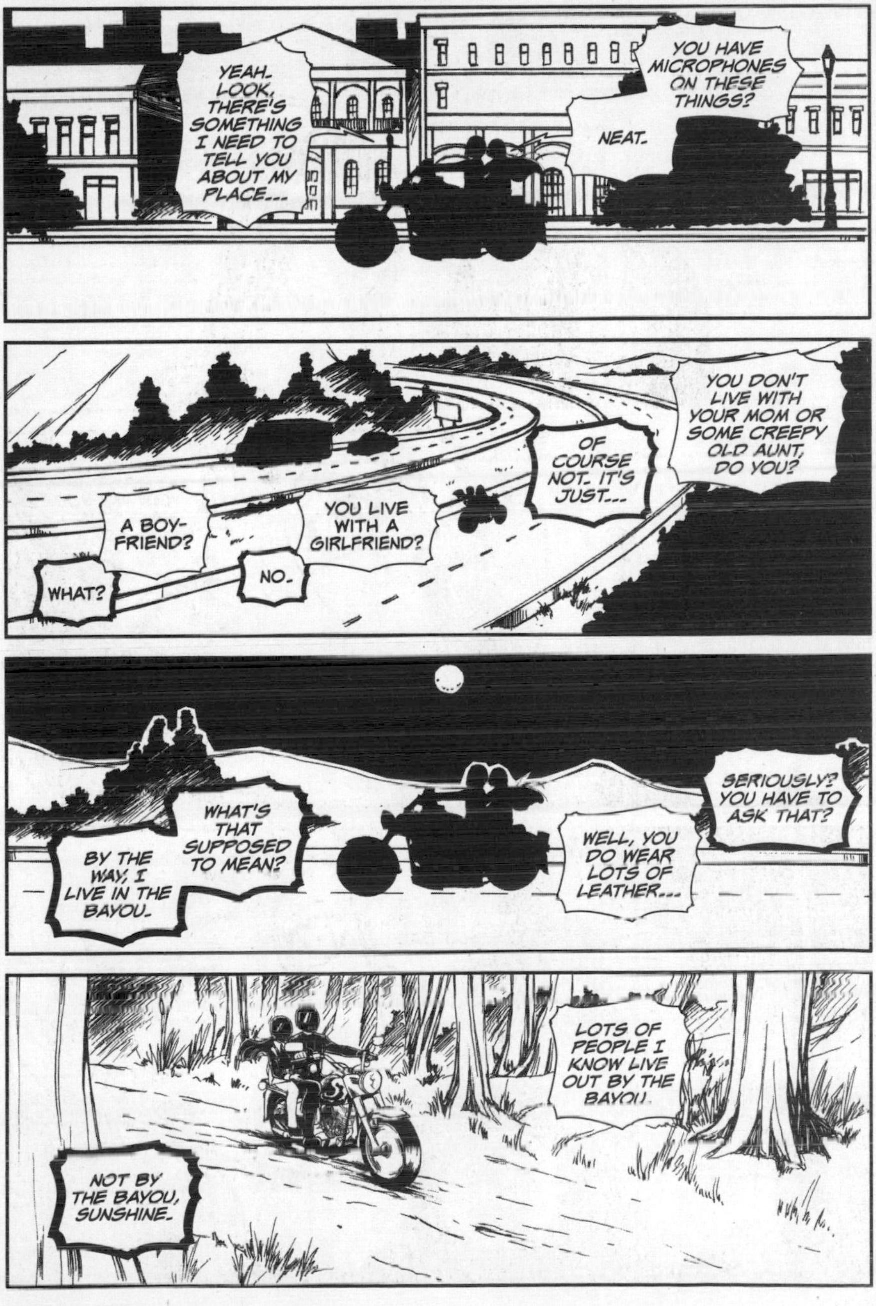
YEAH. LOOK, THERE'S SOMETHING I NEED TO TELL YOU ABOUT MY PLACE...
YOU HAVE MICROPHONES ON THESE THINGS?
NEAT.
YOU DON'T LIVE WITH YOUR MOM OR SOME CREEPY OLD AUNT, DO YOU?
OF COURSE NOT. IT'S JUST...
YOU LIVE WITH A GIRLFRIEND?
NO.
A BOY-FRIEND?
WHAT?
SERIOUSLY? YOU HAVE TO ASK THAT?
WELL, YOU DO WEAR LOTS OF LEATHER...
WHAT'S THAT SUPPOSED TO MEAN?
BY THE WAY, I LIVE IN THE BAYOU.
LOTS OF PEOPLE I KNOW LIVE OUT BY THE BAYOU.
NOT BY THE BAYOU, SUNSHINE.

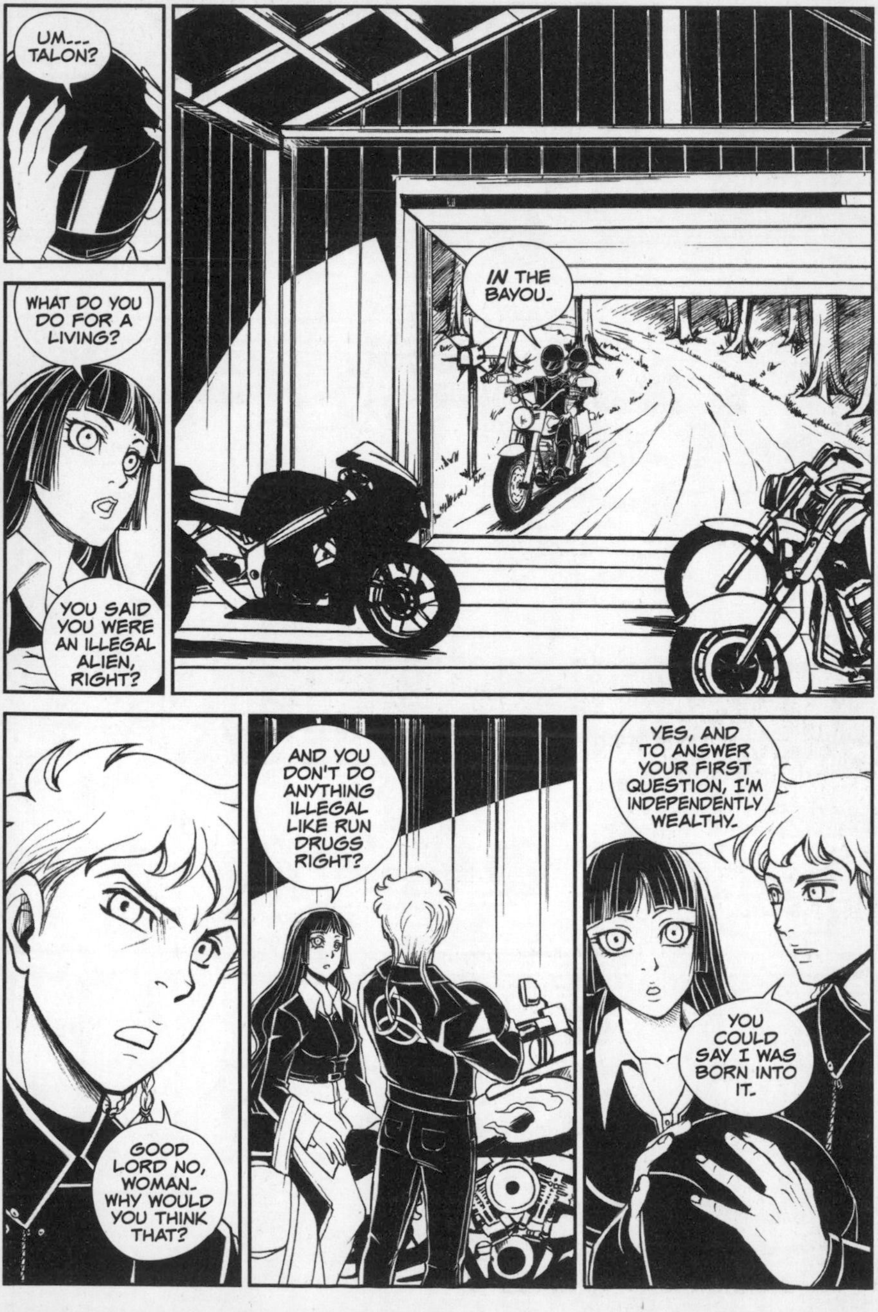
UM... TALON?
WHAT DO YOU DO FOR A LIVING?
IN THE BAYOU.
YOU SAID YOU WERE AN ILLEGAL ALIEN, RIGHT?
GOOD LORD NO, WOMAN. WHY WOULD YOU THINK THAT?
AND YOU DON'T DO ANYTHING ILLEGAL LIKE RUN DRUGS RIGHT?
YES, AND TO ANSWER YOUR FIRST QUESTION, I'M INDEPENDENTLY WEALTHY.
YOU COULD SAY I WAS BORN INTO IT.

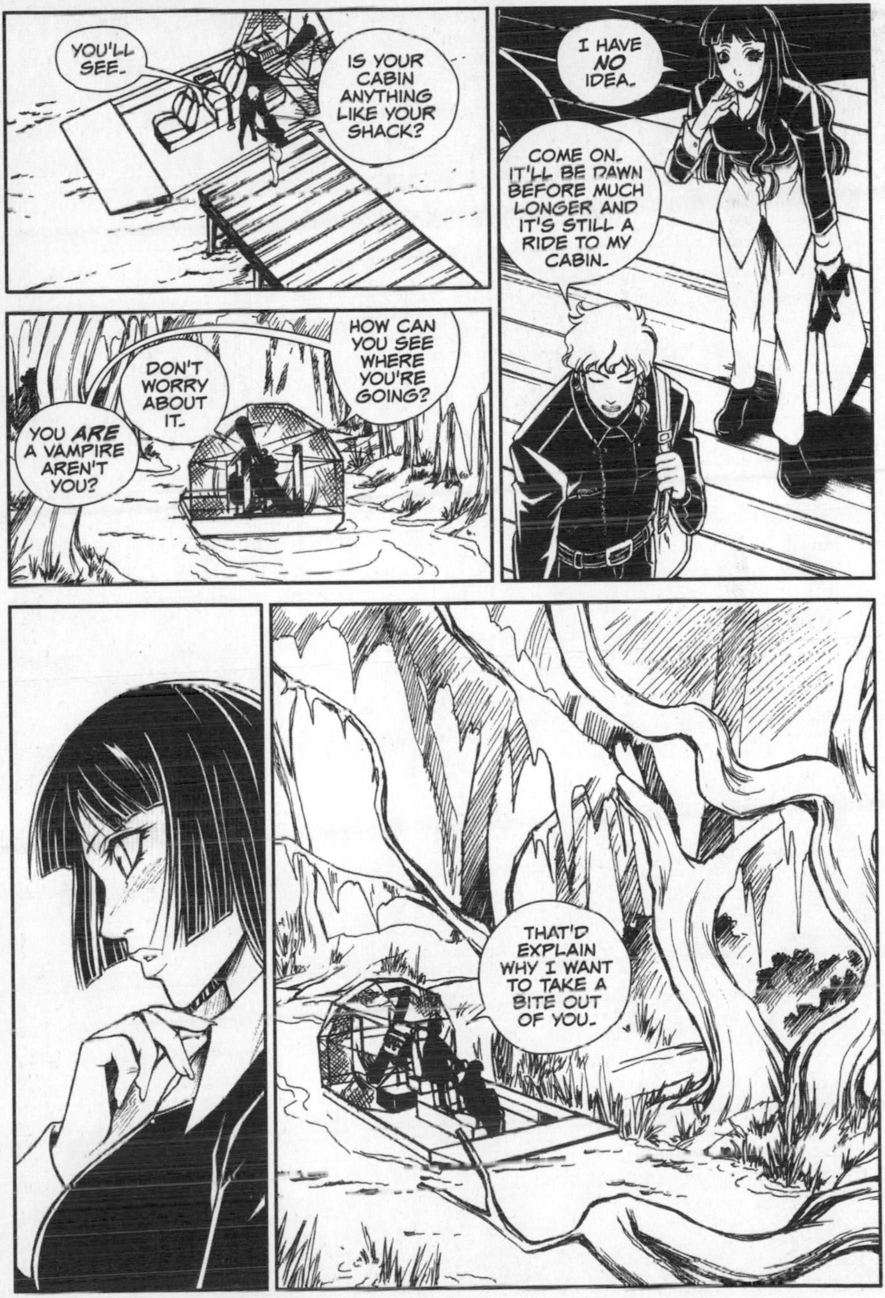
YOU'LL SEE.
IS YOUR CABIN ANYTHING LIKE YOUR SHACK?
I HAVE NO IDEA.
COME ON. IT'LL BE DAWN BEFORE MUCH LONGER AND IT'S STILL A RIDE TO MY CABIN.
HOW CAN YOU SEE WHERE YOU'RE GOING?
DON'T WORRY ABOUT IT.
YOU ARE A VAMPIRE AREN'T YOU?
THAT'D EXPLAIN WHY I WANT TO TAKE A BITE OUT OF YOU.

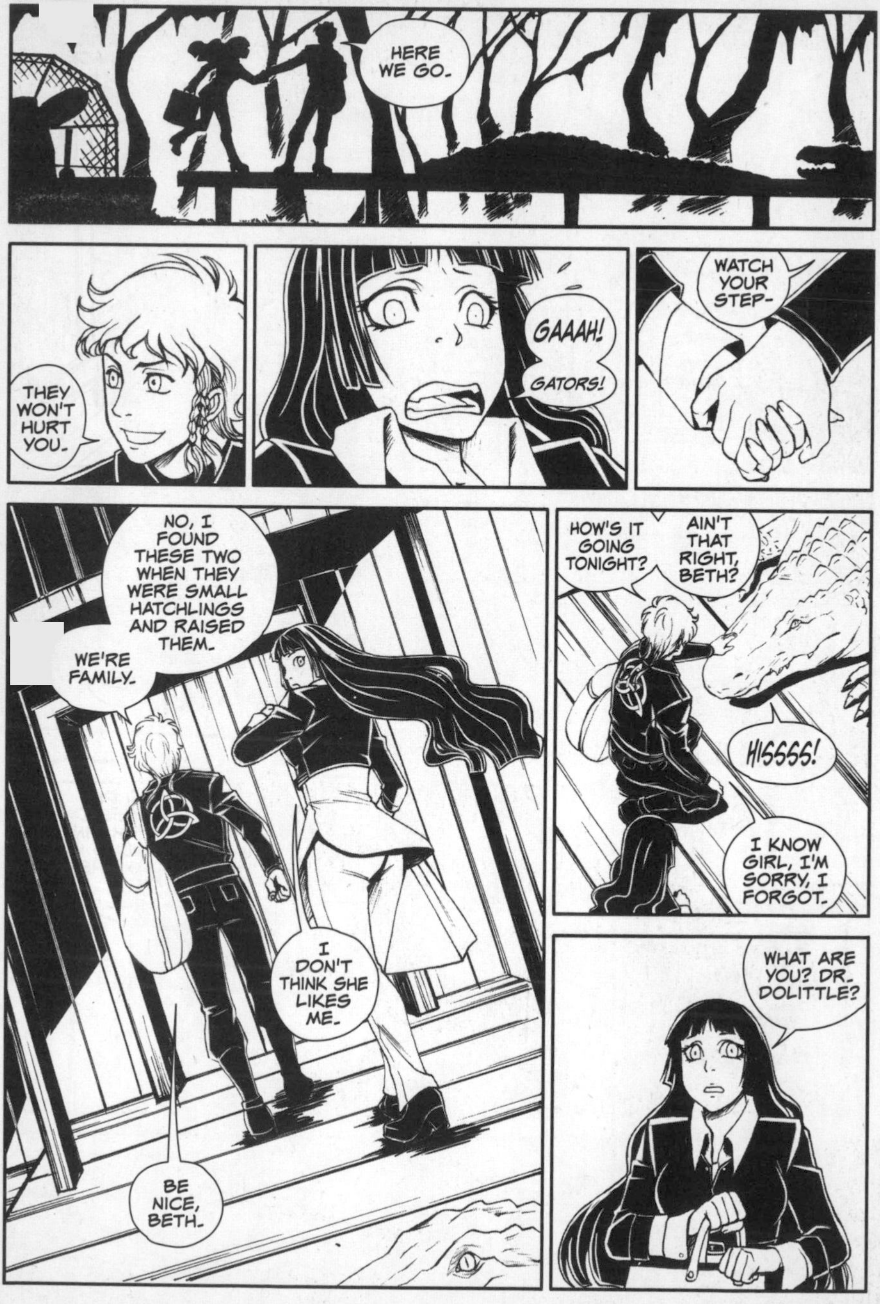

HERE WE GO.
THEY WON'T HURT YOU.
GAAAH!
GATORS!
WATCH YOUR STEP.
NO, I FOUND THESE TWO WHEN THEY WERE SMALL HATCHLINGS AND RAISED THEM.
WE'RE FAMILY.
I DON'T THINK SHE LIKES ME.
BE NICE, BETH.
HOW'S IT GOING TONIGHT?
AIN'T THAT RIGHT, BETH?
HISSSS!
I KNOW GIRL, I'M SORRY, I FORGOT.
WHAT ARE YOU? DR. DOLITTLE?

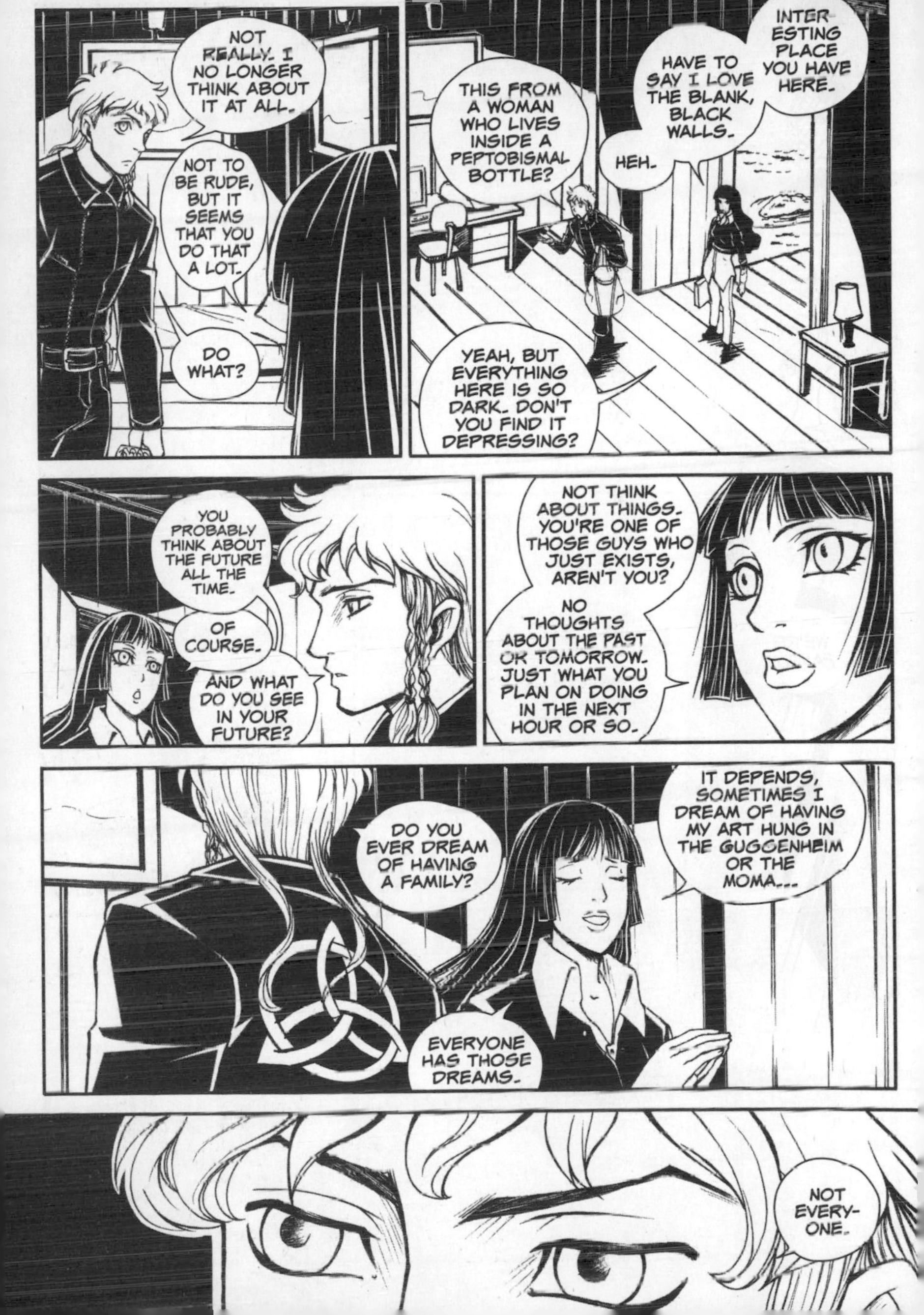
NOT REALLY. I NO LONGER THINK ABOUT IT AT ALL.
NOT TO BE RUDE, BUT IT SEEMS THAT YOU DO THAT A LOT.
DO WHAT?
INTER-ESTING PLACE YOU HAVE HERE.
HAVE TO SAY I LOVE THE BLANK, BLACK WALLS.
HEH.
THIS FROM A WOMAN WHO LIVES INSIDE A PEPTOBISMAL BOTTLE?
YEAH, BUT EVERYTHING HERE IS SO DARK. DON'T YOU FIND IT DEPRESSING?
YOU PROBABLY THINK ABOUT THE FUTURE ALL THE TIME.
OF COURSE.
AND WHAT DO YOU SEE IN YOUR FUTURE?
NOT THINK ABOUT THINGS. YOU'RE ONE OF THOSE GUYS WHO JUST EXISTS, AREN'T YOU?
NO THOUGHTS ABOUT THE PAST OR TOMORROW. JUST WHAT YOU PLAN ON DOING IN THE NEXT HOUR OR SO.
DO YOU EVER DREAM OF HAVING A FAMILY?
IT DEPENDS, SOMETIMES I DREAM OF HAVING MY ART HUNG IN THE GUGGENHEIM OR THE MOMA...
EVERYONE HAS THOSE DREAMS.
NOT EVERY-ONE.

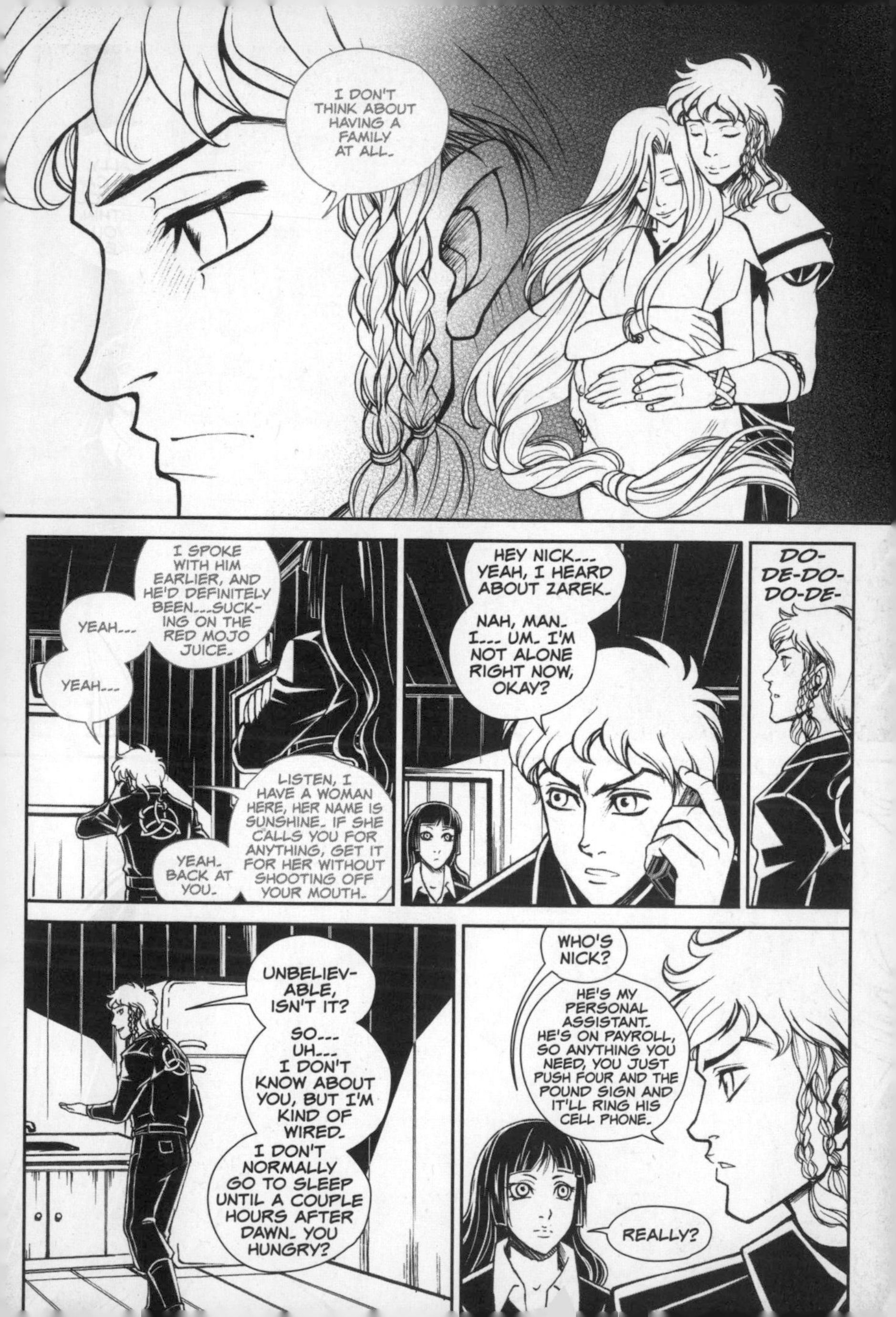
I DON'T THINK ABOUT HAVING A FAMILY AT ALL.
I SPOKE WITH HIM EARLIER, AND HE'D DEFINITELY BEEN...SUCK-ING ON THE RED MOJO JUICE.
YEAH...
YEAH...
LISTEN, I HAVE A WOMAN HERE, HER NAME IS SUNSHINE. IF SHE CALLS YOU FOR ANYTHING, GET IT FOR HER WITHOUT SHOOTING OFF YOUR MOUTH.
YEAH. BACK AT YOU.
HEY NICK... YEAH, I HEARD ABOUT ZAREK.
NAH, MAN. I... UM. I'M NOT ALONE RIGHT NOW, OKAY?
DO-DE-DO-DO-DE-
UNBELIEV-ABLE, ISN'T IT?
SO... UH... I DON'T KNOW ABOUT YOU, BUT I'M KIND OF WIRED.
I DON'T NORMALLY GO TO SLEEP UNTIL A COUPLE HOURS AFTER DAWN. YOU HUNGRY?
WHO'S NICK?
HE'S MY PERSONAL ASSISTANT. HE'S ON PAYROLL, SO ANYTHING YOU NEED, YOU JUST PUSH FOUR AND THE POUND SIGN AND IT'LL RING HIS CELL PHONE.
REALLY?

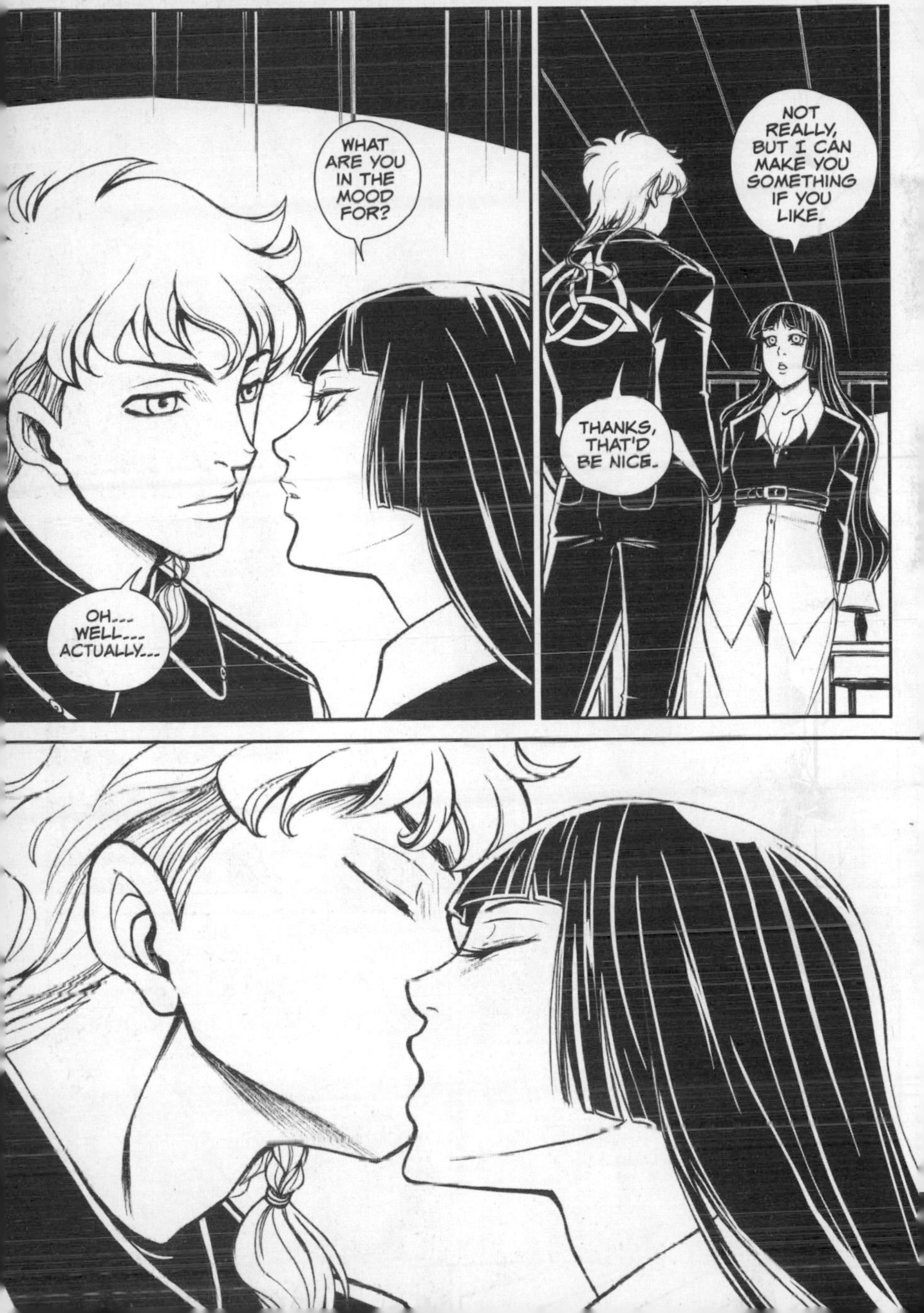

WHAT ARE YOU IN THE MOOD FOR?
OH... WELL... ACTUALLY...
NOT REALLY, BUT I CAN MAKE YOU SOMETHING IF YOU LIKE.
THANKS, THAT'D BE NICE.

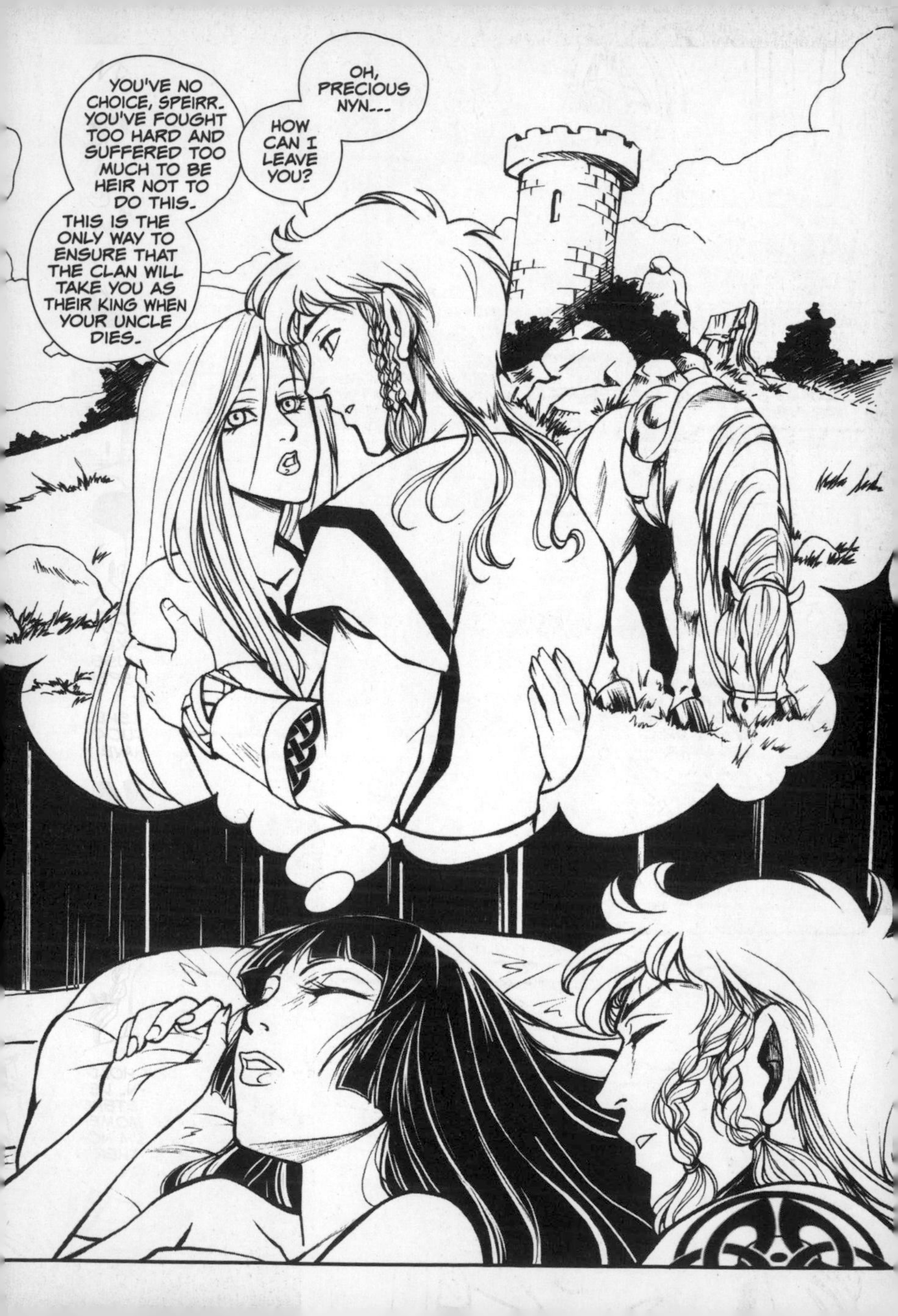

OH, PRECIOUS NYN...
HOW CAN I LEAVE YOU?
YOU'VE NO CHOICE, SPEIRR. YOU'VE FOUGHT TOO HARD AND SUFFERED TOO MUCH TO BE HEIR NOT TO DO THIS.
THIS IS THE ONLY WAY TO ENSURE THAT THE CLAN WILL TAKE YOU AS THEIR KING WHEN YOUR UNCLE DIES.

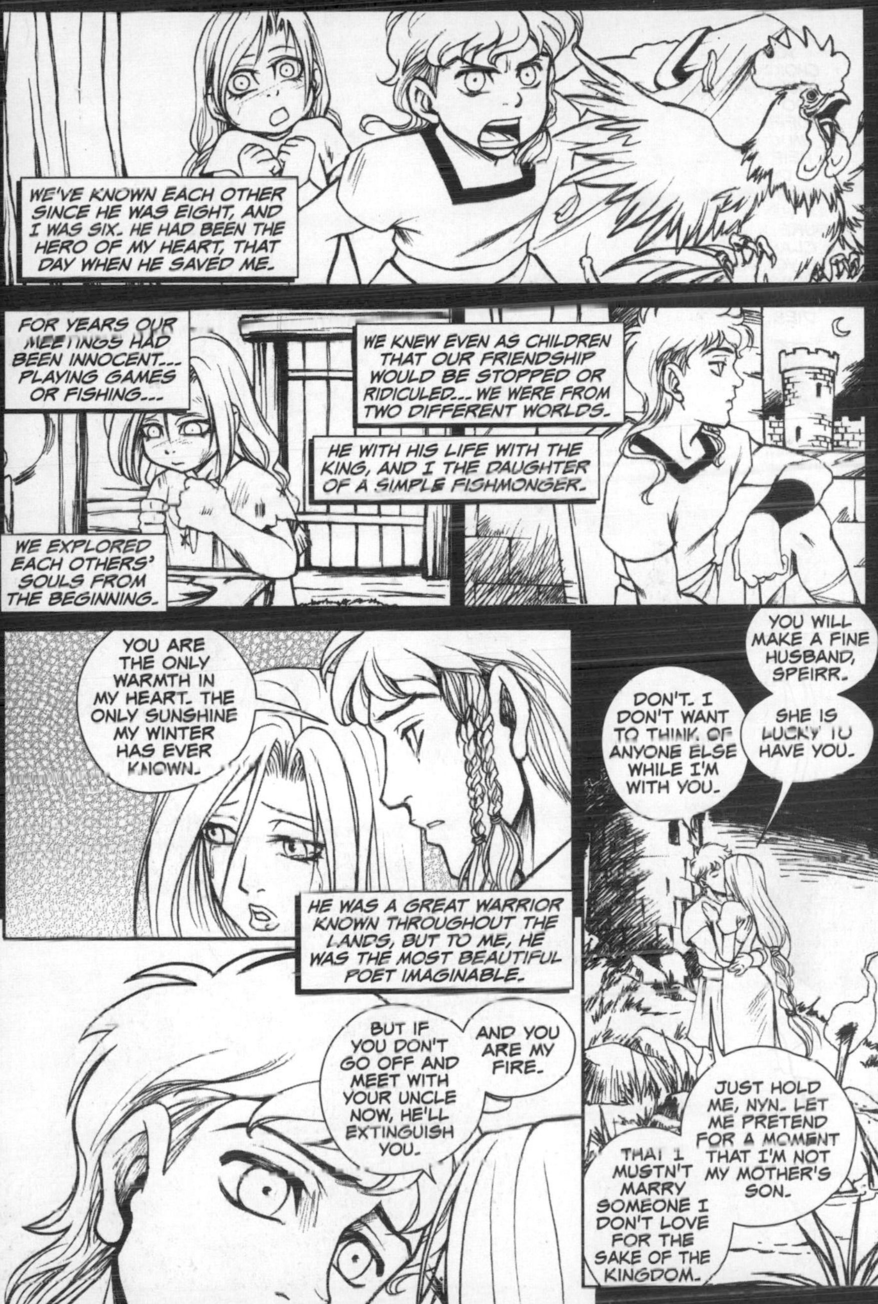

WE'VE KNOWN EACH OTHER SINCE HE WAS EIGHT, AND I WAS SIX. HE HAD BEEN THE HERO OF MY HEART, THAT DAY WHEN HE SAVED ME.
FOR YEARS OUR MEETINGS HAD BEEN INNOCENT... PLAYING GAMES OR FISHING...
WE EXPLORED EACH OTHERS' SOULS FROM THE BEGINNING.
WE KNEW EVEN AS CHILDREN THAT OUR FRIENDSHIP WOULD BE STOPPED OR RIDICULED... WE WERE FROM TWO DIFFERENT WORLDS.
HE WITH HIS LIFE WITH THE KING, AND I THE DAUGHTER OF A SIMPLE FISHMONGER.
YOU ARE THE ONLY WARMTH IN MY HEART. THE ONLY SUNSHINE MY WINTER HAS EVER KNOWN.
HE WAS A GREAT WARRIOR KNOWN THROUGHOUT THE LANDS, BUT TO ME, HE WAS THE MOST BEAUTIFUL POET IMAGINABLE.
YOU WILL MAKE A FINE HUSBAND, SPEIRR.
SHE IS LUCKY TO HAVE YOU.
DON'T. I DON'T WANT TO THINK OF ANYONE ELSE WHILE I'M WITH YOU.
AND YOU ARE MY FIRE.
BUT IF YOU DON'T GO OFF AND MEET WITH YOUR UNCLE NOW, HE'LL EXTINGUISH YOU.
JUST HOLD ME, NYN. LET ME PRETEND FOR A MOMENT THAT I'M NOT MY MOTHER'S SON.
THAT I MUSTN'T MARRY SOMEONE I DON'T LOVE FOR THE SAKE OF THE KINGDOM.

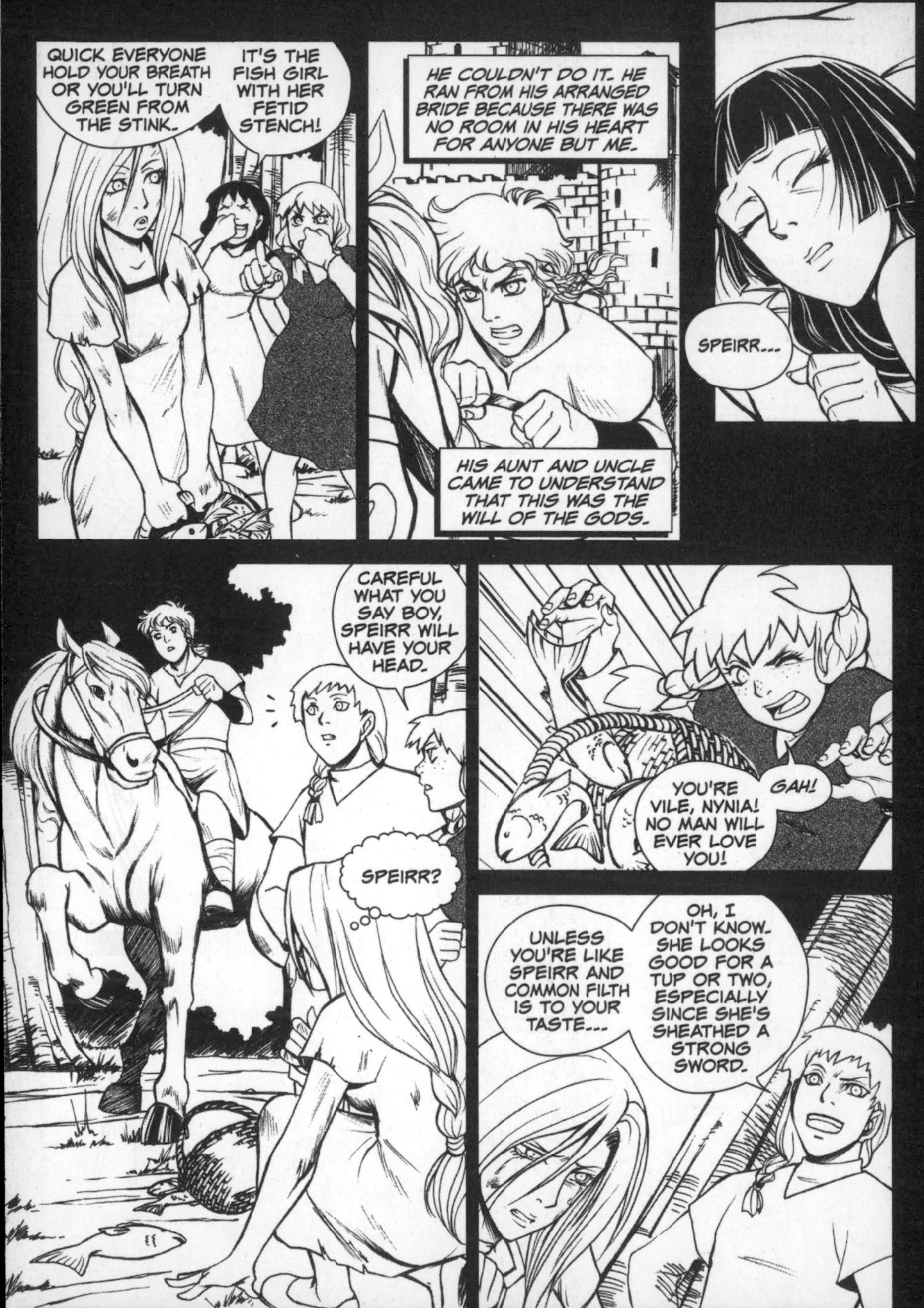

QUICK EVERYONE HOLD YOUR BREATH OR YOU'LL TURN GREEN FROM THE STINK.
IT'S THE FISH GIRL WITH HER FETID STENCH!
HE COULDN'T DO IT. HE RAN FROM HIS ARRANGED BRIDE BECAUSE THERE WAS NO ROOM IN HIS HEART FOR ANYONE BUT ME.
HIS AUNT AND UNCLE CAME TO UNDERSTAND THAT THIS WAS THE WILL OF THE GODS.
SPEIRR...
CAREFUL WHAT YOU SAY BOY, SPEIRR WILL HAVE YOUR HEAD.
SPEIRR?
GAH!
YOU'RE VILE, NYNIA! NO MAN WILL EVER LOVE YOU!
UNLESS YOU'RE LIKE SPEIRR AND COMMON FILTH IS TO YOUR TASTE...
OH, I DON'T KNOW. SHE LOOKS GOOD FOR A TUP OR TWO, ESPECIALLY SINCE SHE'S SHEATHED A STRONG SWORD.

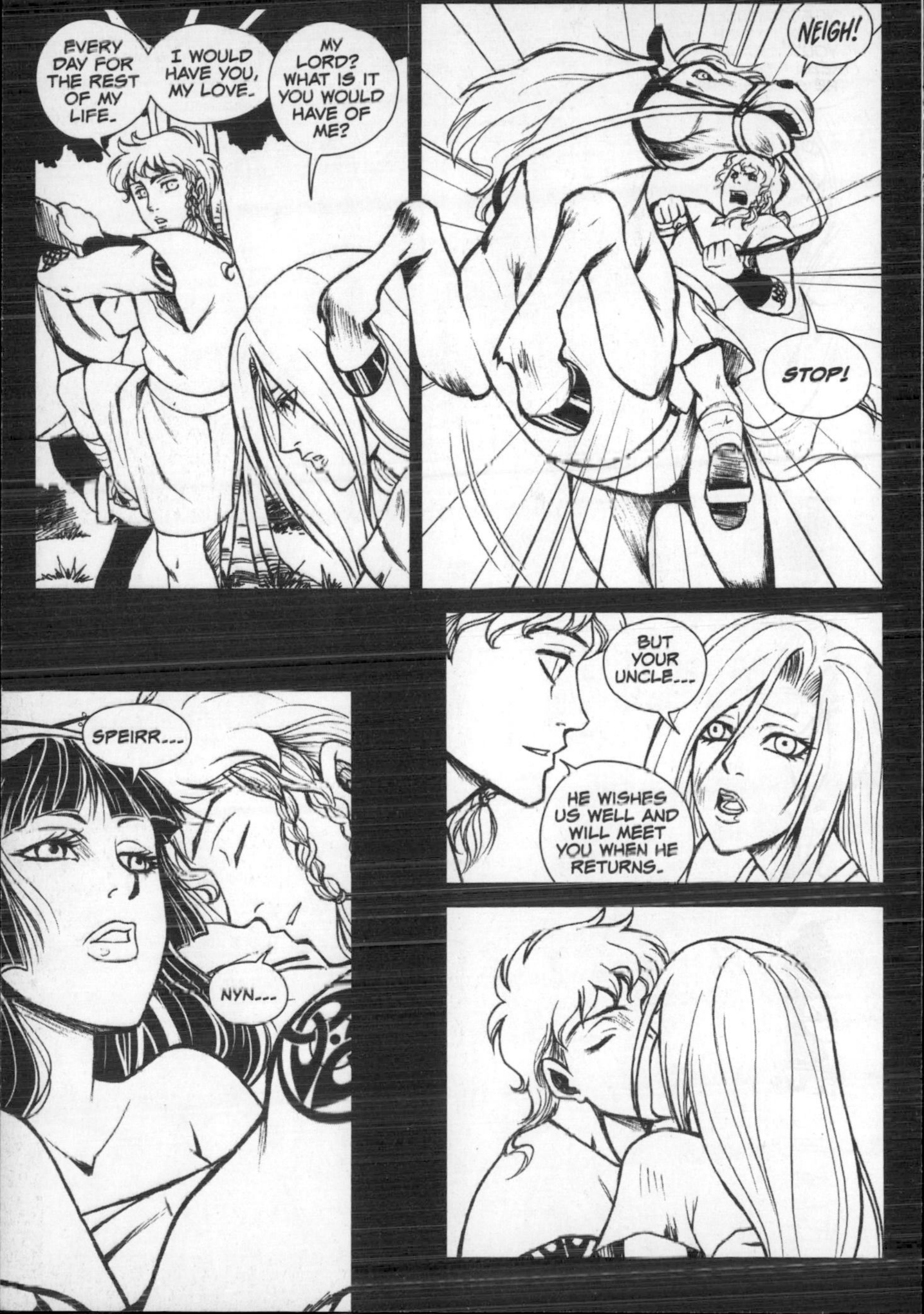
EVERY DAY FOR THE REST OF MY LIFE.
I WOULD HAVE YOU, MY LOVE.
MY LORD? WHAT IS IT YOU WOULD HAVE OF ME?
NEIGH!
STOP!
BUT YOUR UNCLE...
HE WISHES US WELL AND WILL MEET YOU WHEN HE RETURNS.
SPEIRR...
NYN...

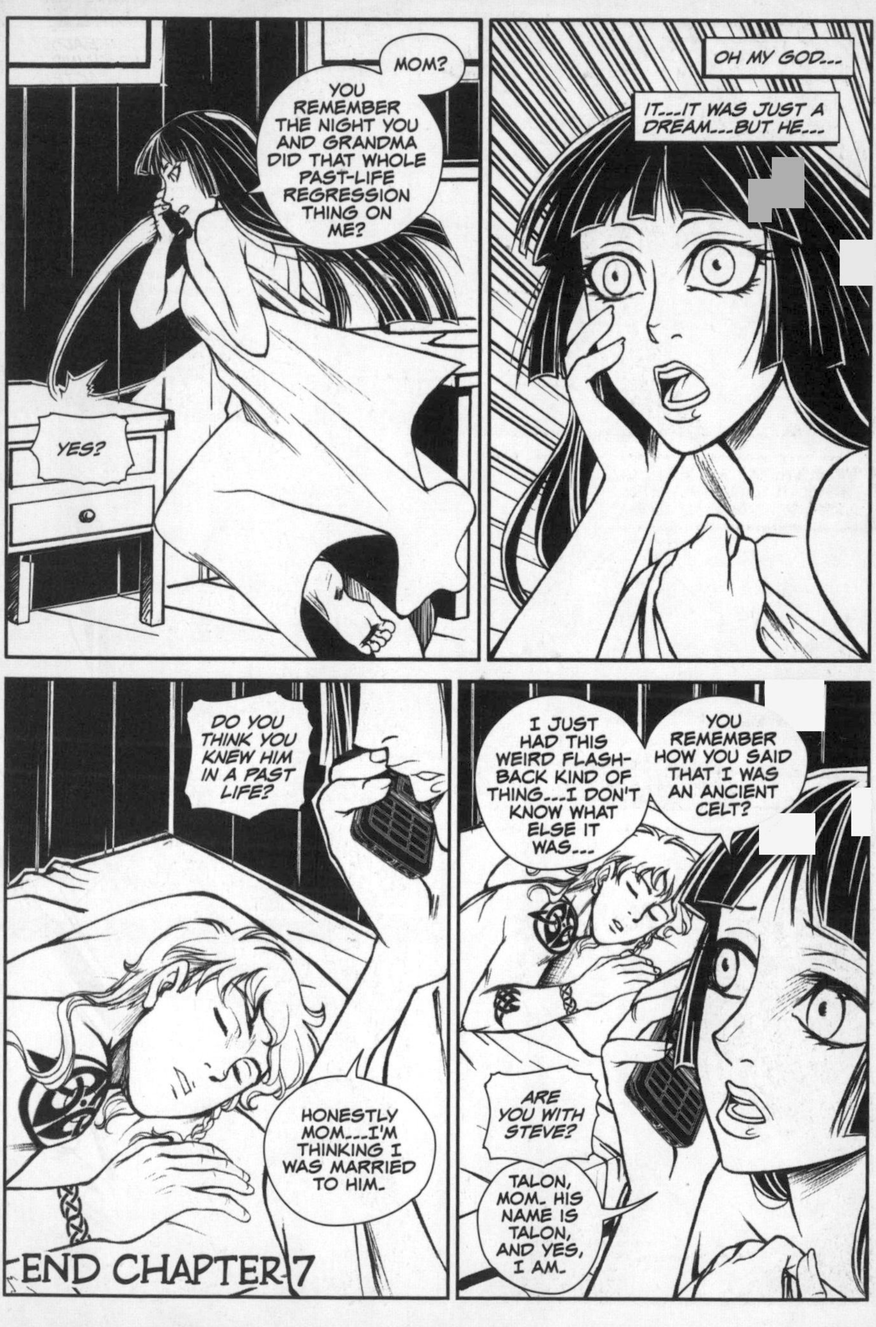
MOM?
YOU REMEMBER THE NIGHT YOU AND GRANDMA DID THAT WHOLE PAST-LIFE REGRESSION THING ON ME?
YES?
OH MY GOD...
IT...IT WAS JUST A DREAM...BUT HE...
DO YOU THINK YOU KNEW HIM IN A PAST LIFE?
HONESTLY MOM...I'M THINKING I WAS MARRIED TO HIM.
END CHAPTER 7
YOU REMEMBER HOW YOU SAID THAT I WAS AN ANCIENT CELT?
I JUST HAD THIS WEIRD FLASH-BACK KIND OF THING...I DON'T KNOW WHAT ELSE IT WAS...
ARE YOU WITH STEVE?
TALON, MOM. HIS NAME IS TALON, AND YES, I AM.

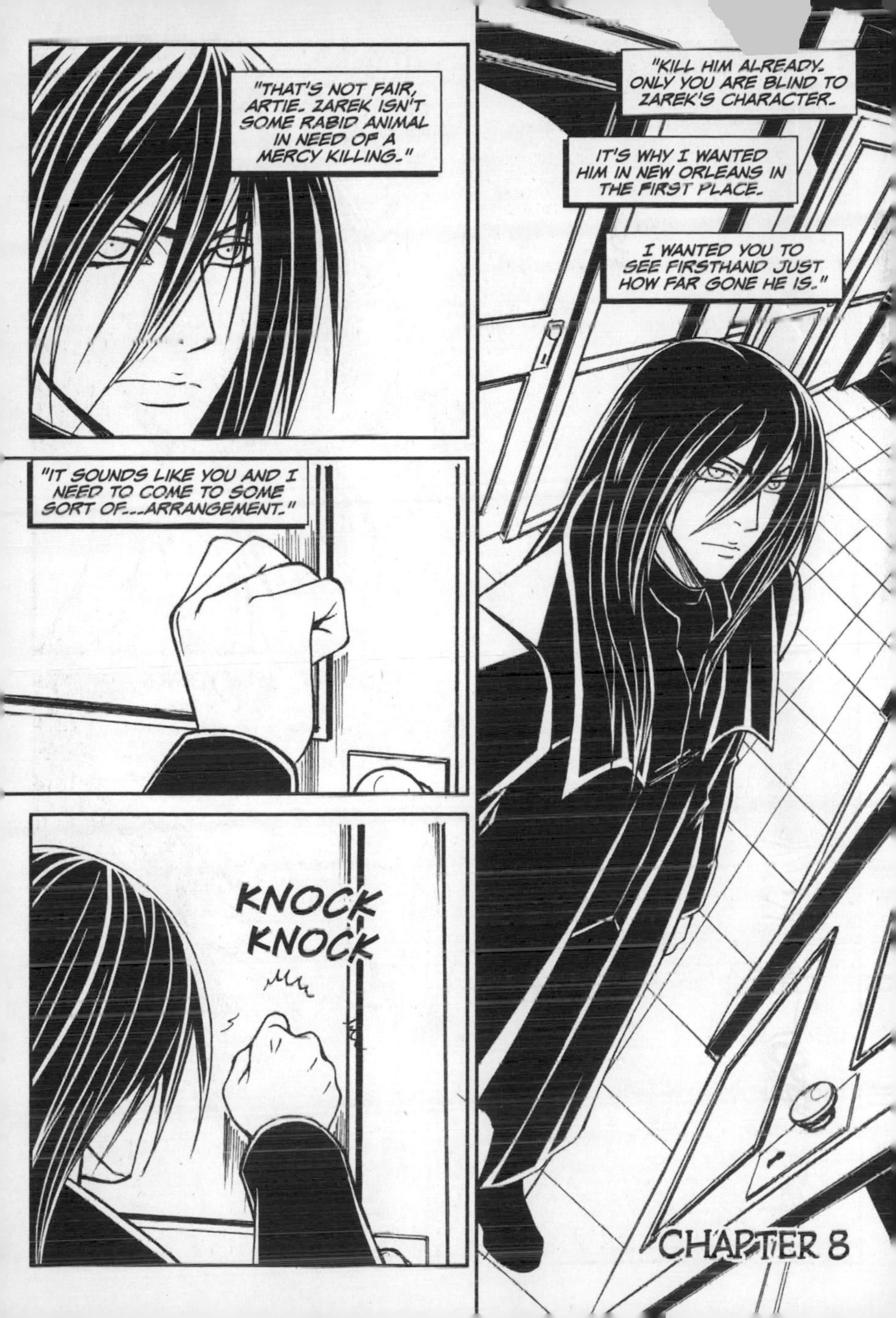
"THAT'S NOT FAIR, ARTIE. ZAREK ISN'T SOME RABID ANIMAL IN NEED OF A MERCY KILLING."
"IT SOUNDS LIKE YOU AND I NEED TO COME TO SOME SORT OF...ARRANGEMENT."
KNOCK KNOCK
"KILL HIM ALREADY. ONLY YOU ARE BLIND TO ZAREK'S CHARACTER.
IT'S WHY I WANTED HIM IN NEW ORLEANS IN THE FIRST PLACE.
I WANTED YOU TO SEE FIRSTHAND JUST HOW FAR GONE HE IS."
CHAPTER 8

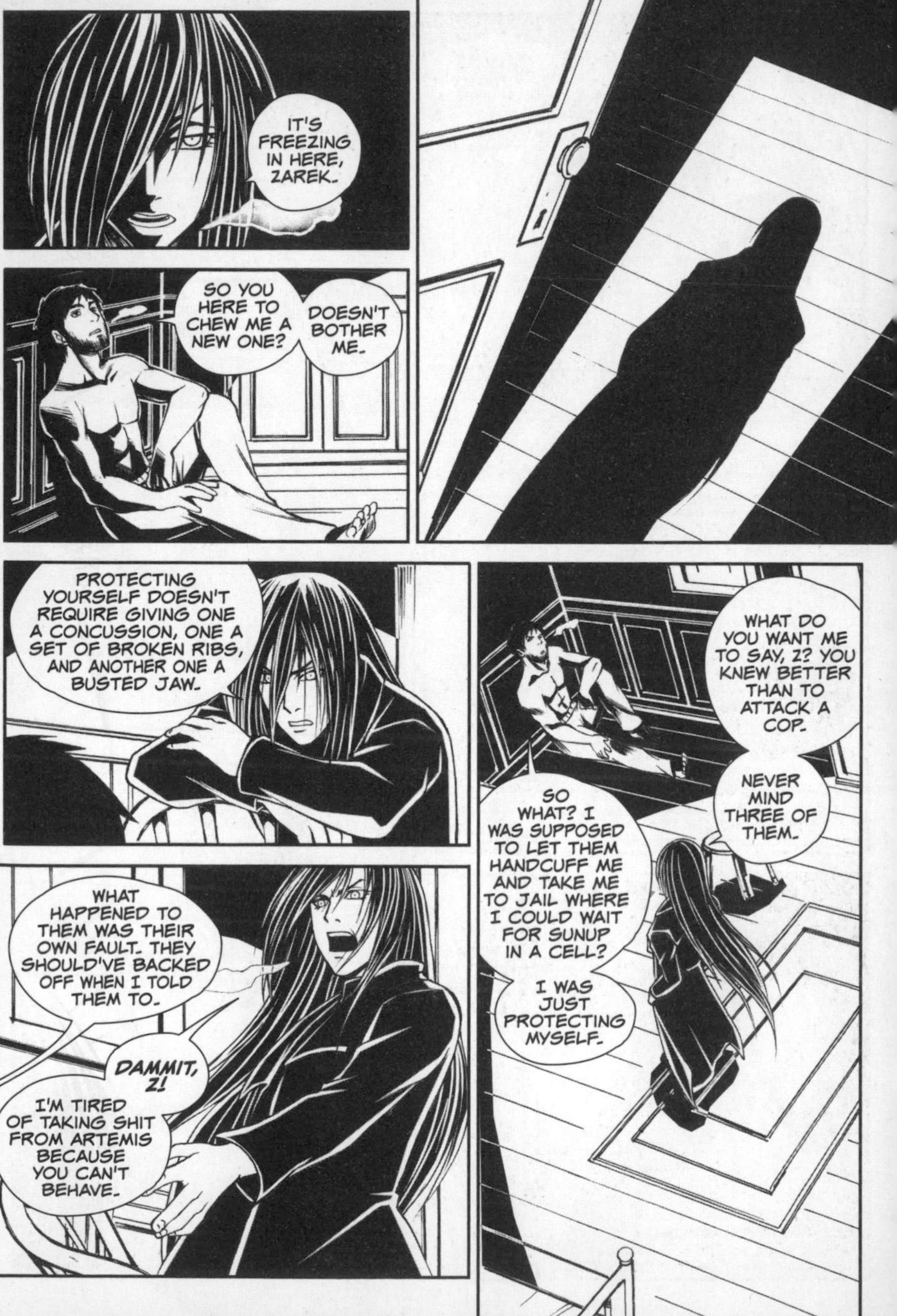
IT'S FREEZING IN HERE, ZAREK.
SO YOU HERE TO CHEW ME A NEW ONE?
DOESN'T BOTHER ME.
PROTECTING YOURSELF DOESN'T REQUIRE GIVING ONE A CONCUSSION, ONE A SET OF BROKEN RIBS, AND ANOTHER ONE A BUSTED JAW.
WHAT DO YOU WANT ME TO SAY, Z? YOU KNEW BETTER THAN TO ATTACK A COP.
NEVER MIND THREE OF THEM.
SO WHAT? I WAS SUPPOSED TO LET THEM HANDCUFF ME AND TAKE ME TO JAIL WHERE I COULD WAIT FOR SUNUP IN A CELL?
I WAS JUST PROTECTING MYSELF.
WHAT HAPPENED TO THEM WAS THEIR OWN FAULT. THEY SHOULD'VE BACKED OFF WHEN I TOLD THEM TO.
DAMMIT, Z!
I'M TIRED OF TAKING SHIT FROM ARTEMIS BECAUSE YOU CAN'T BEHAVE.

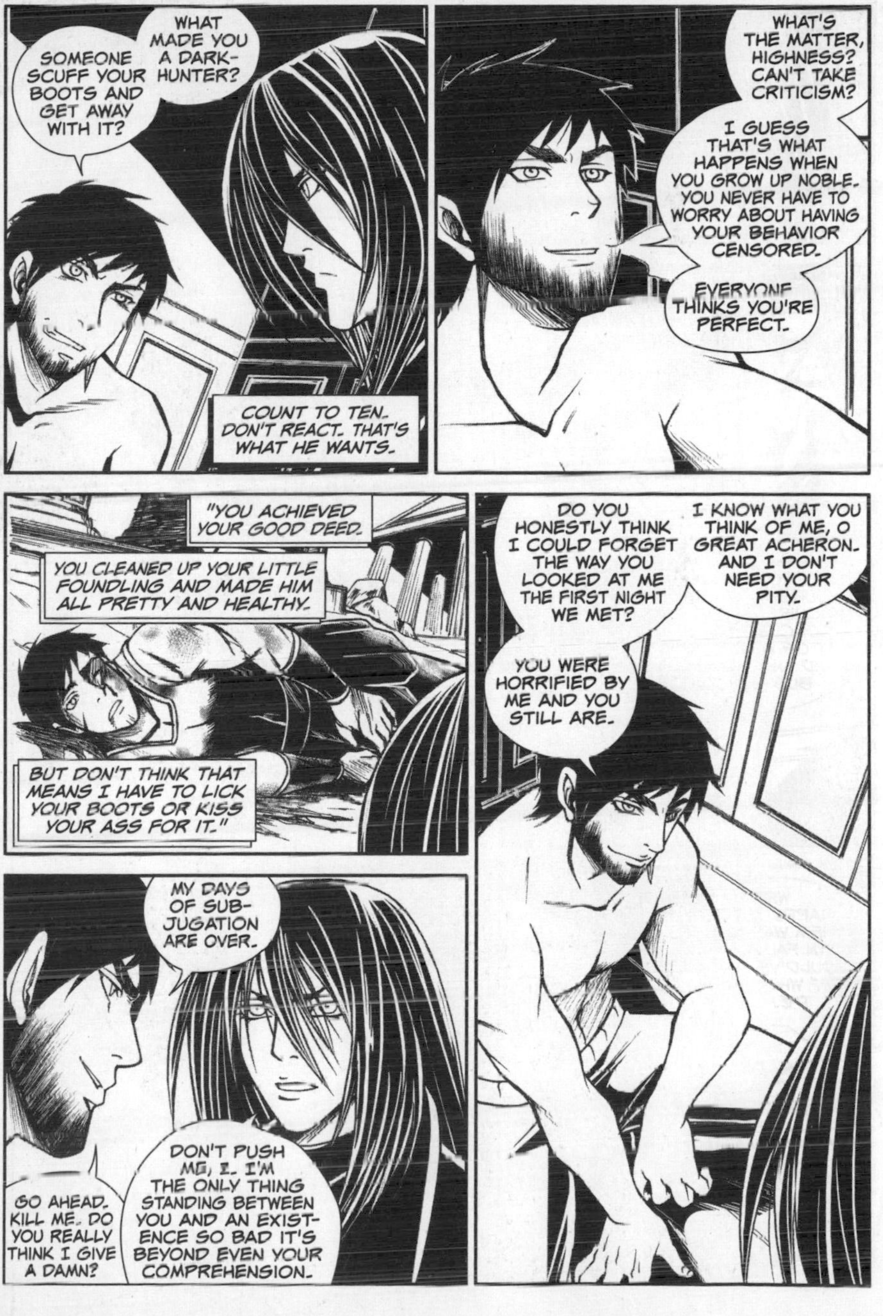

SOMEONE SCUFF YOUR BOOTS AND GET AWAY WITH IT?
WHAT MADE YOU A DARK-HUNTER?
COUNT TO TEN. DON'T REACT. THAT'S WHAT HE WANTS.
WHAT'S THE MATTER, HIGHNESS? CAN'T TAKE CRITICISM?
I GUESS THAT'S WHAT HAPPENS WHEN YOU GROW UP NOBLE. YOU NEVER HAVE TO WORRY ABOUT HAVING YOUR BEHAVIOR CENSORED.
EVERYONE THINKS YOU'RE PERFECT.
"YOU ACHIEVED YOUR GOOD DEED.
YOU CLEANED UP YOUR LITTLE FOUNDLING AND MADE HIM ALL PRETTY AND HEALTHY.
BUT DON'T THINK THAT MEANS I HAVE TO LICK YOUR BOOTS OR KISS YOUR ASS FOR IT."
DO YOU HONESTLY THINK I COULD FORGET THE WAY YOU LOOKED AT ME THE FIRST NIGHT WE MET?
I KNOW WHAT YOU THINK OF ME, O GREAT ACHERON. AND I DON'T NEED YOUR PITY.
YOU WERE HORRIFIED BY ME AND YOU STILL ARE.
MY DAYS OF SUB-JUGATION ARE OVER.
DON'T PUSH ME, Z. I'M THE ONLY THING STANDING BETWEEN YOU AND AN EXIST-ENCE SO BAD IT'S BEYOND EVEN YOUR COMPREHENSION.
GO AHEAD. KILL ME. DO YOU REALLY THINK I GIVE A DAMN?

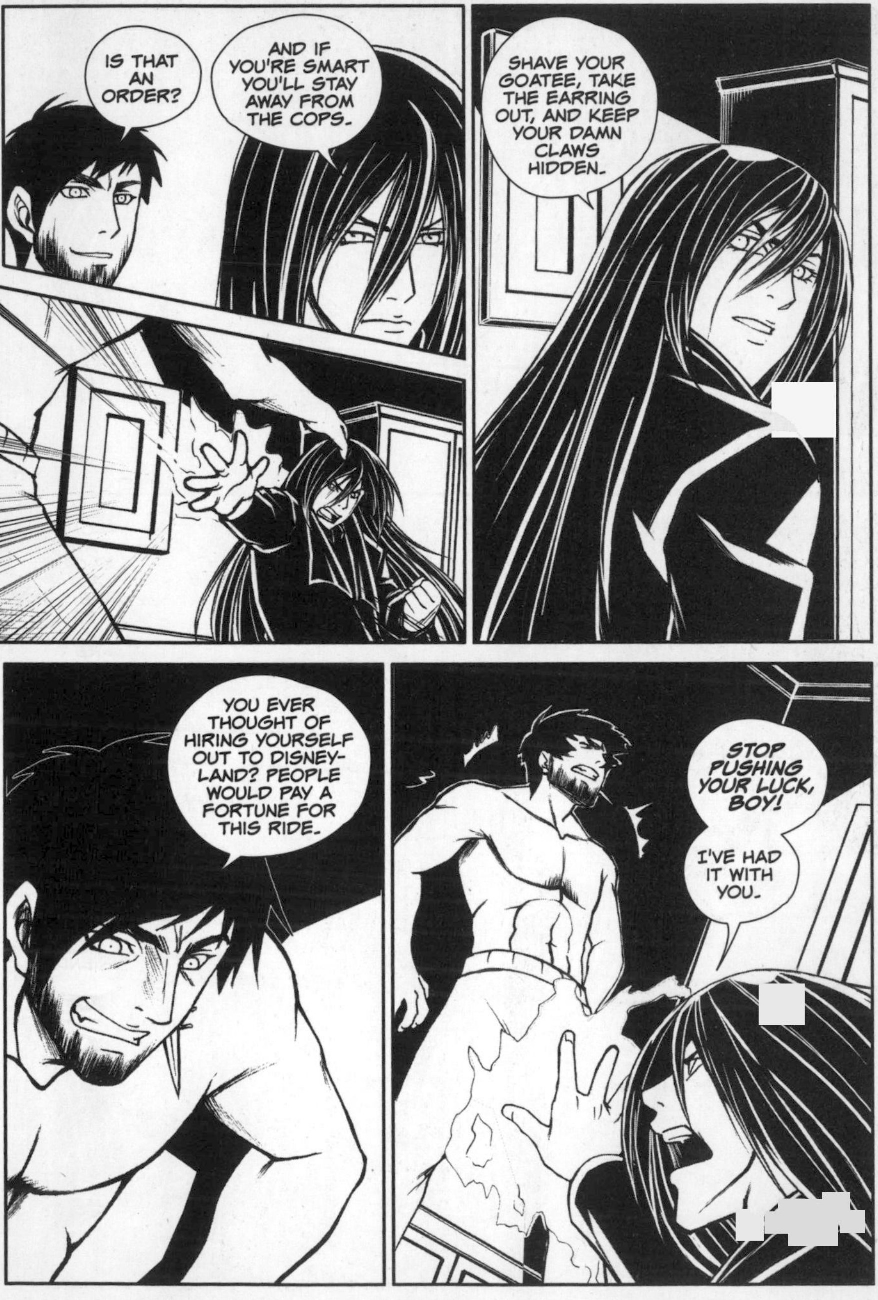
IS THAT AN ORDER?
AND IF YOU'RE SMART YOU'LL STAY AWAY FROM THE COPS.
SHAVE YOUR GOATEE, TAKE THE EARRING OUT, AND KEEP YOUR DAMN CLAWS HIDDEN.
YOU EVER THOUGHT OF HIRING YOURSELF OUT TO DISNEY-LAND? PEOPLE WOULD PAY A FORTUNE FOR THIS RIDE.
STOP PUSHING YOUR LUCK, BOY!
I'VE HAD IT WITH YOU.

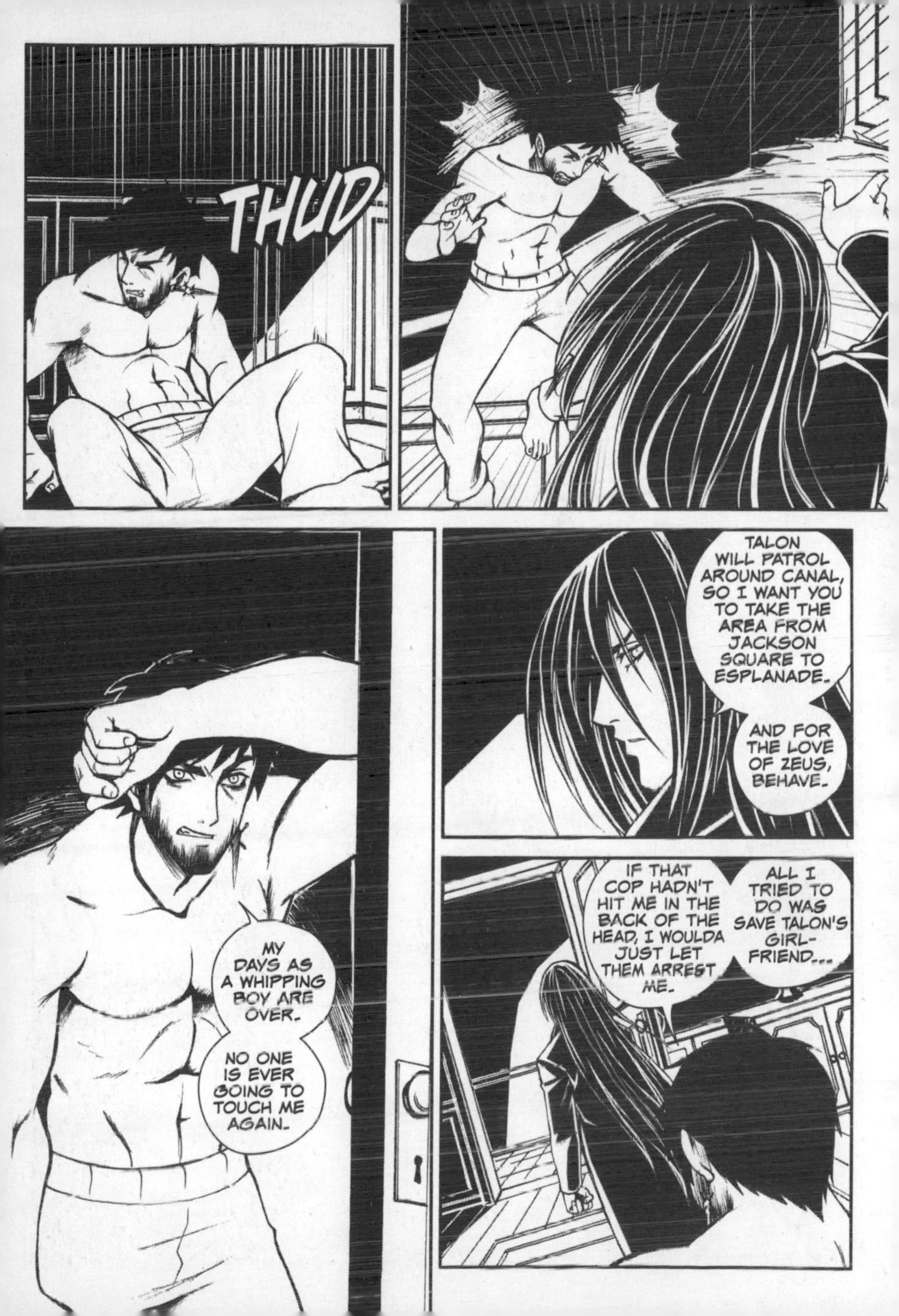
THUD
TALON WILL PATROL AROUND CANAL, SO I WANT YOU TO TAKE THE AREA FROM JACKSON SQUARE TO ESPLANADE.
AND FOR THE LOVE OF ZEUS, BEHAVE.
MY DAYS AS A WHIPPING BOY ARE OVER.
NO ONE IS EVER GOING TO TOUCH ME AGAIN.
ALL I TRIED TO DO WAS SAVE TALON'S GIRL-FRIEND...
IF THAT COP HADN'T HIT ME IN THE BACK OF THE HEAD, I WOULDA JUST LET THEM ARREST ME.

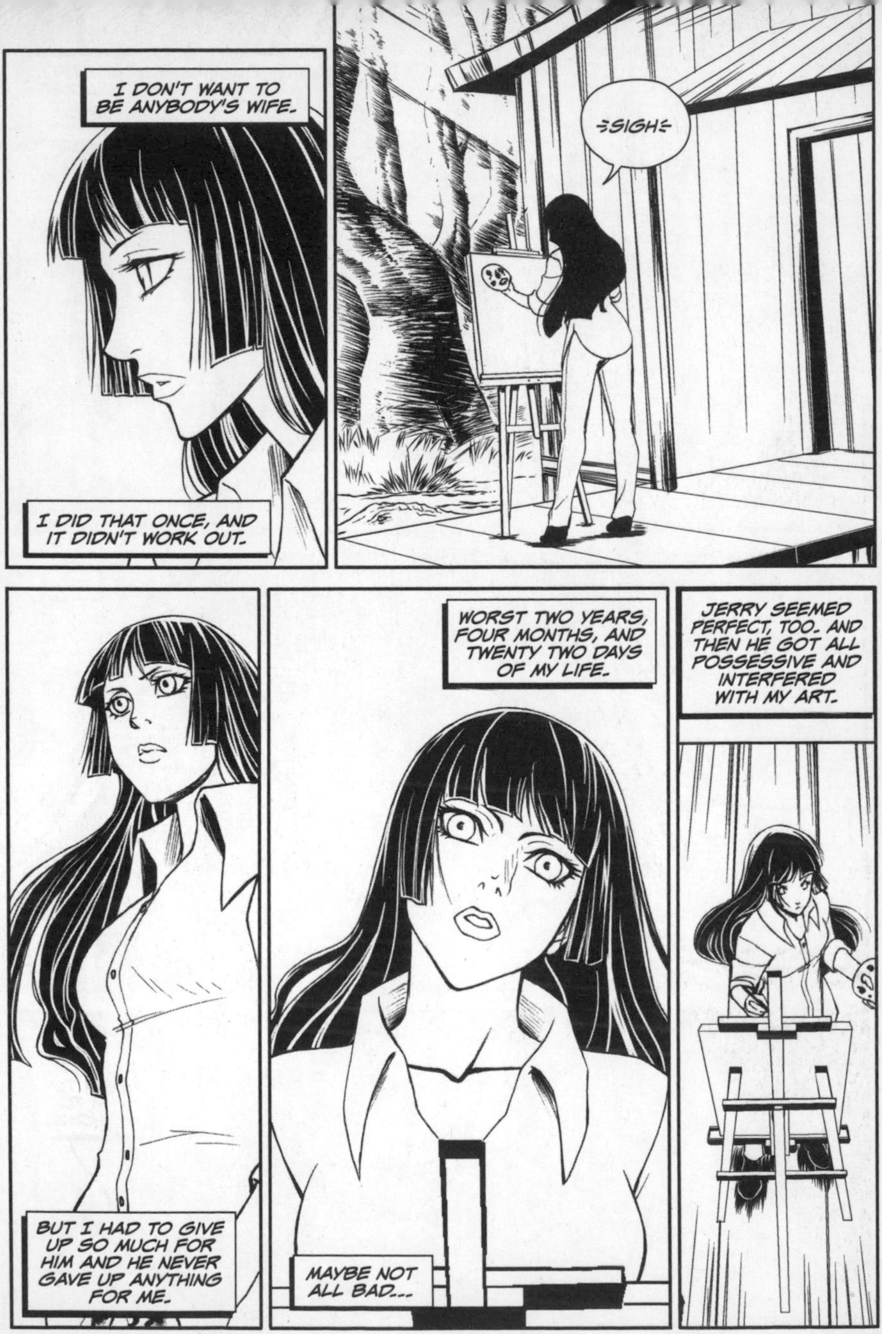
I DON'T WANT TO BE ANYBODY'S WIFE.
I DID THAT ONCE, AND IT DIDN'T WORK OUT.
SIGH
WORST TWO YEARS, FOUR MONTHS, AND TWENTY TWO DAYS OF MY LIFE.
BUT I HAD TO GIVE UP SO MUCH FOR HIM AND HE NEVER GAVE UP ANYTHING FOR ME.
MAYBE NOT ALL BAD...
JERRY SEEMED PERFECT, TOO. AND THEN HE GOT ALL POSSESSIVE AND INTERFERED WITH MY ART.

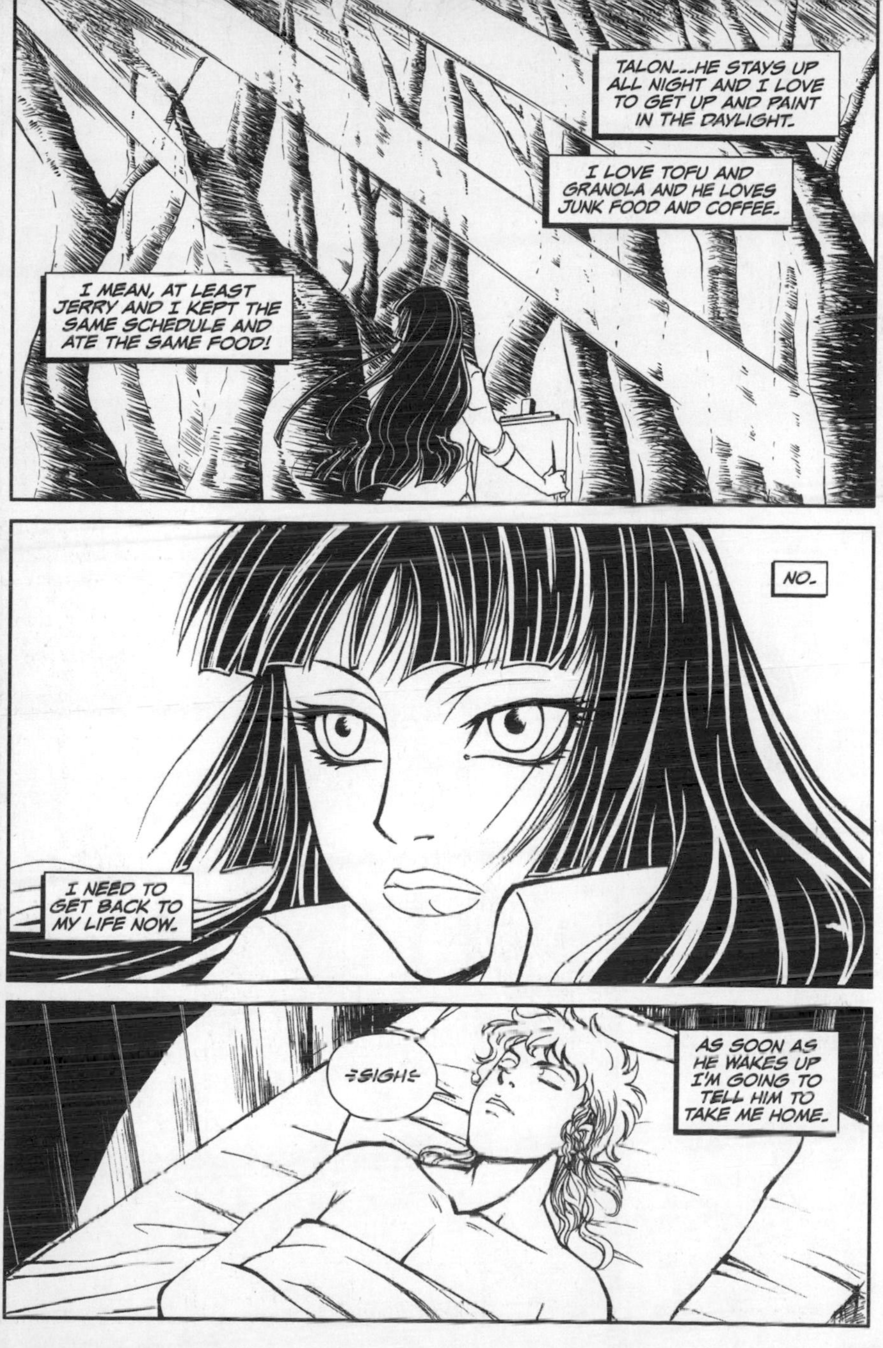
TALON...HE STAYS UP ALL NIGHT AND I LOVE TO GET UP AND PAINT IN THE DAYLIGHT.
I LOVE TOFU AND GRANOLA AND HE LOVES JUNK FOOD AND COFFEE.
I MEAN, AT LEAST JERRY AND I KEPT THE SAME SCHEDULE AND ATE THE SAME FOOD!
NO.
I NEED TO GET BACK TO MY LIFE NOW.
=SIGH=
AS SOON AS HE WAKES UP I'M GOING TO TELL HIM TO TAKE ME HOME.

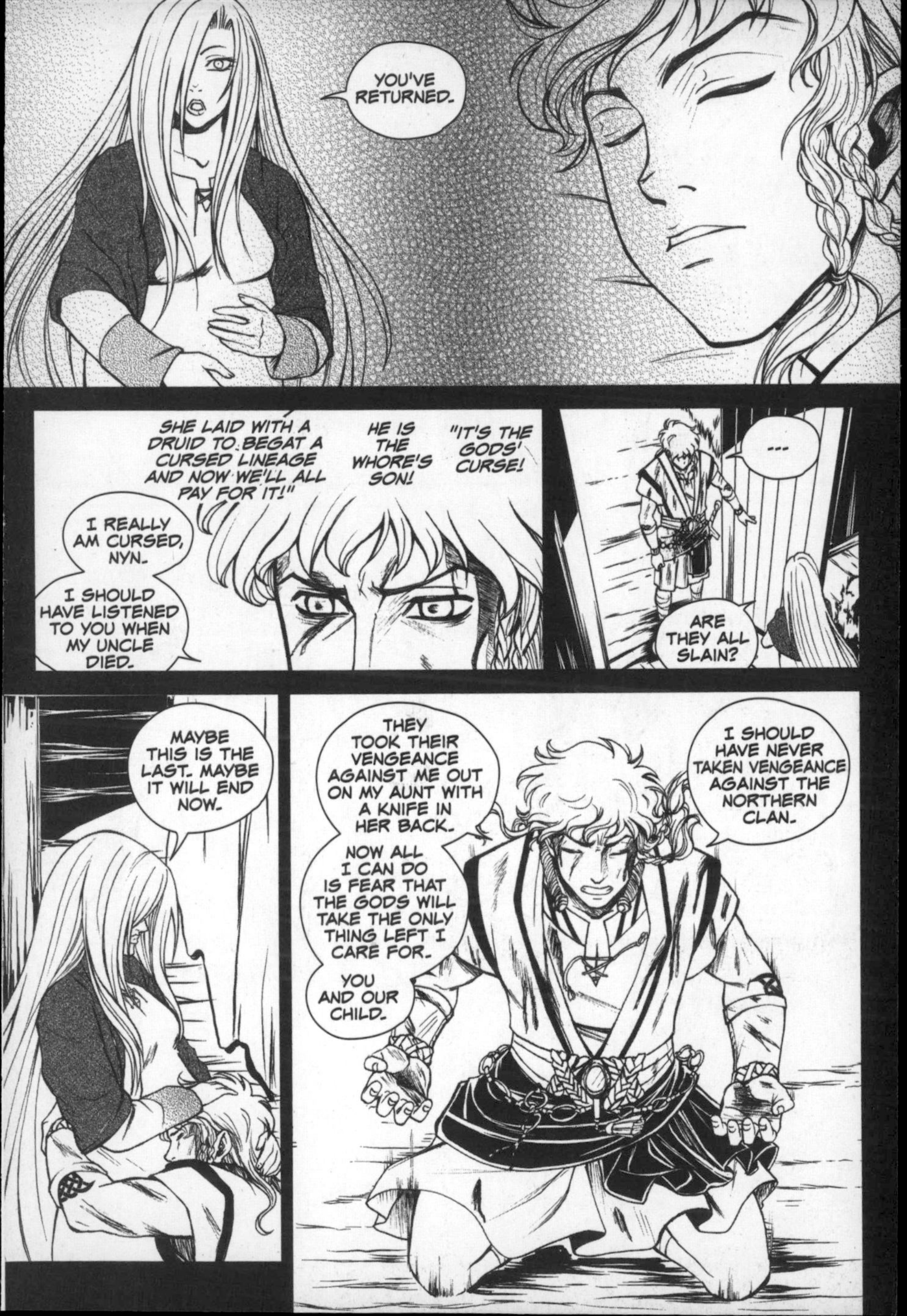
YOU'VE RETURNED.
SHE LAID WITH A DRUID TO BEGAT A CURSED LINEAGE AND NOW WE'LL ALL PAY FOR IT!"
HE IS THE WHORE'S SON!
"IT'S THE GODS' CURSE!
I REALLY AM CURSED, NYN.
I SHOULD HAVE LISTENED TO YOU WHEN MY UNCLE DIED.
...
ARE THEY ALL SLAIN?
I SHOULD HAVE NEVER TAKEN VENGEANCE AGAINST THE NORTHERN CLAN.
THEY TOOK THEIR VENGEANCE AGAINST ME OUT ON MY AUNT WITH A KNIFE IN HER BACK.
NOW ALL I CAN DO IS FEAR THAT THE GODS WILL TAKE THE ONLY THING LEFT I CARE FOR.
YOU AND OUR CHILD.
MAYBE THIS IS THE LAST. MAYBE IT WILL END NOW.

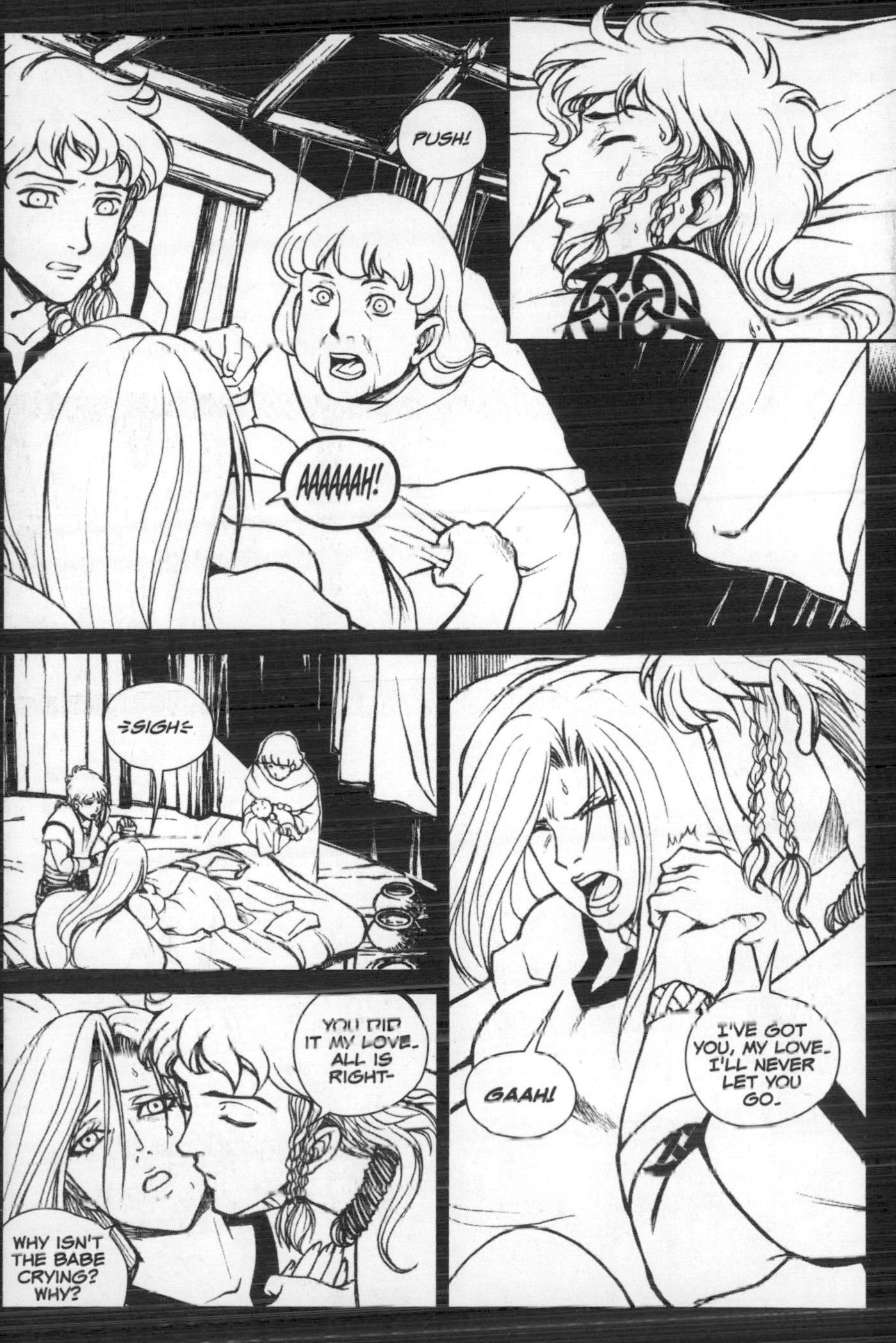
PUSH!
AAAAAAH!
~SIGH~
GAAH!
I'VE GOT YOU, MY LOVE. I'LL NEVER LET YOU GO.
YOU DID IT MY LOVE. ALL IS RIGHT.
WHY ISN'T THE BABE CRYING? WHY?

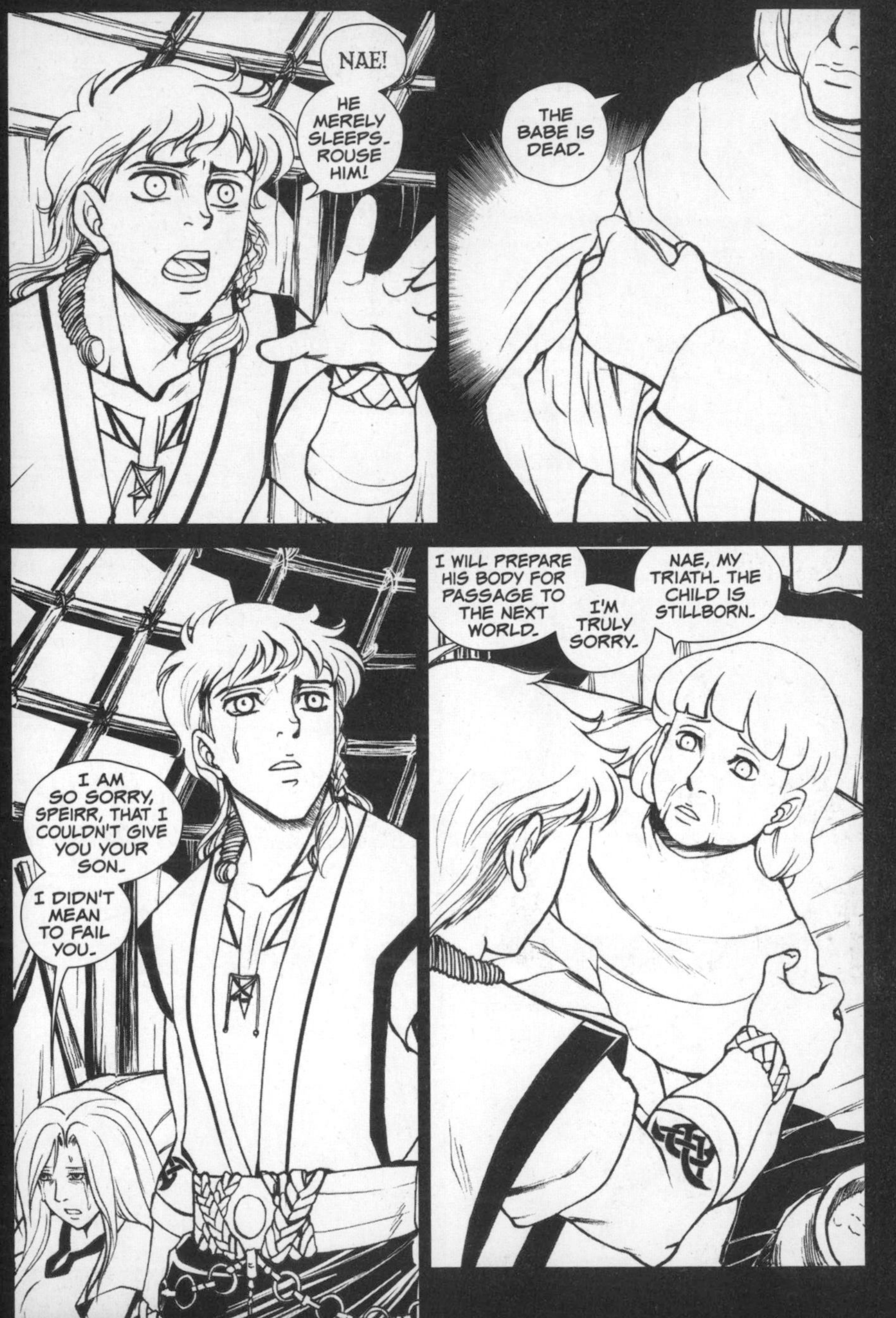
NAE!
HE MERELY SLEEPS. ROUSE HIM!
THE BABE IS DEAD.
NAE, MY TRIATH. THE CHILD IS STILLBORN.
I'M TRULY SORRY.
I WILL PREPARE HIS BODY FOR PASSAGE TO THE NEXT WORLD.
I AM SO SORRY, SPEIRR, THAT I COULDN'T GIVE YOU YOUR SON.
I DIDN'T MEAN TO FAIL YOU.

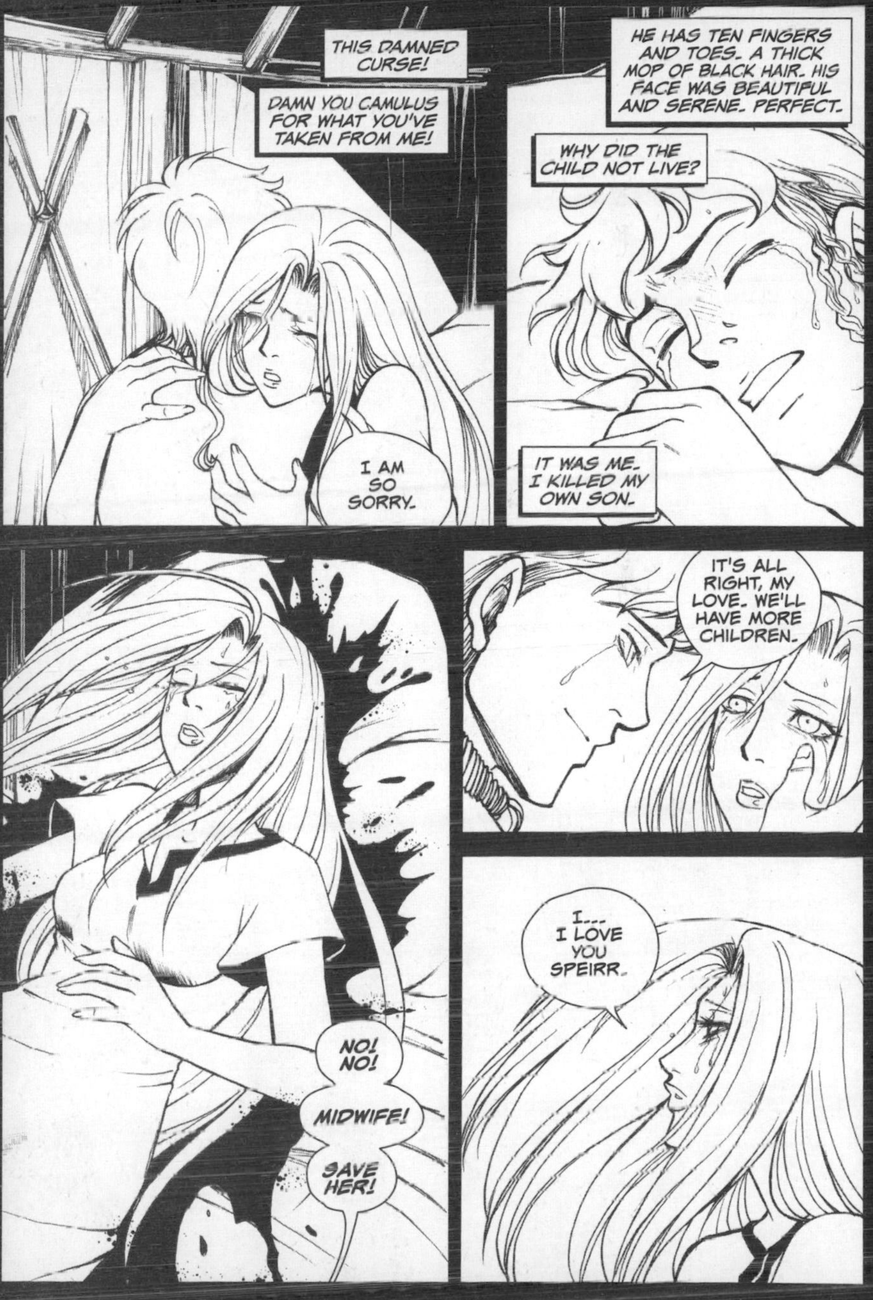

THIS DAMNED CURSE!
DAMN YOU CAMULUS FOR WHAT YOU'VE TAKEN FROM ME!
I AM SO SORRY.
HE HAS TEN FINGERS AND TOES. A THICK MOP OF BLACK HAIR. HIS FACE WAS BEAUTIFUL AND SERENE. PERFECT.
WHY DID THE CHILD NOT LIVE?
IT WAS ME. I KILLED MY OWN SON.
NO! NO!
MIDWIFE!
SAVE HER!
IT'S ALL RIGHT, MY LOVE. WE'LL HAVE MORE CHILDREN.
I... I LOVE YOU SPEIRR.

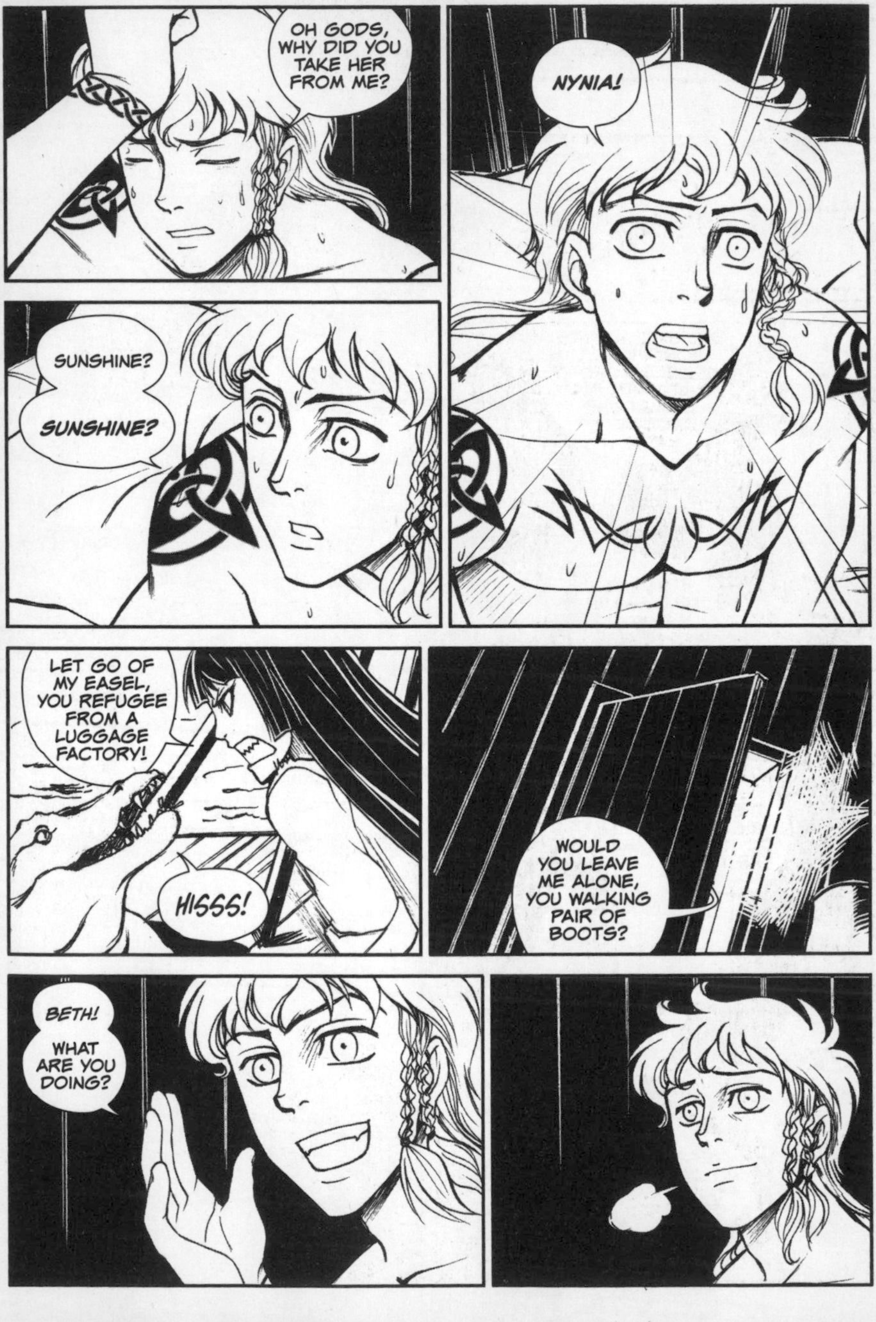
OH GODS, WHY DID YOU TAKE HER FROM ME?
NYNIA!
SUNSHINE?
SUNSHINE?
LET GO OF MY EASEL, YOU REFUGEE FROM A LUGGAGE FACTORY!
HISSS!
WOULD YOU LEAVE ME ALONE, YOU WALKING PAIR OF BOOTS?
BETH!
WHAT ARE YOU DOING?

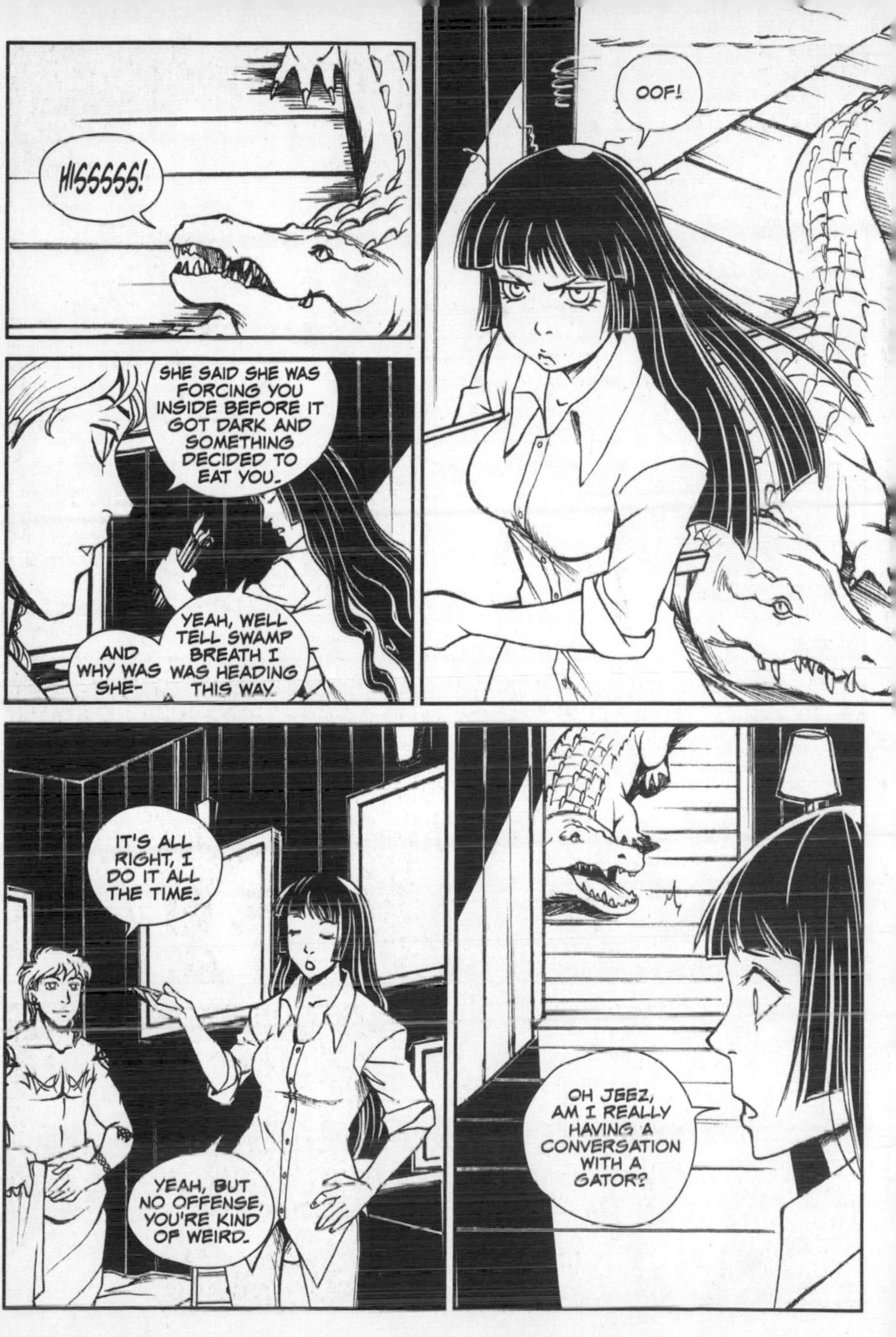
HISSSSS!
OOF!
SHE SAID SHE WAS FORCING YOU INSIDE BEFORE IT GOT DARK AND SOMETHING DECIDED TO EAT YOU.
YEAH, WELL TELL SWAMP BREATH I WAS HEADING THIS WAY.
AND WHY WAS SHE-
IT'S ALL RIGHT, I DO IT ALL THE TIME.
YEAH, BUT NO OFFENSE, YOU'RE KIND OF WEIRD.
OH JEEZ, AM I REALLY HAVING A CONVERSATION WITH A GATOR?

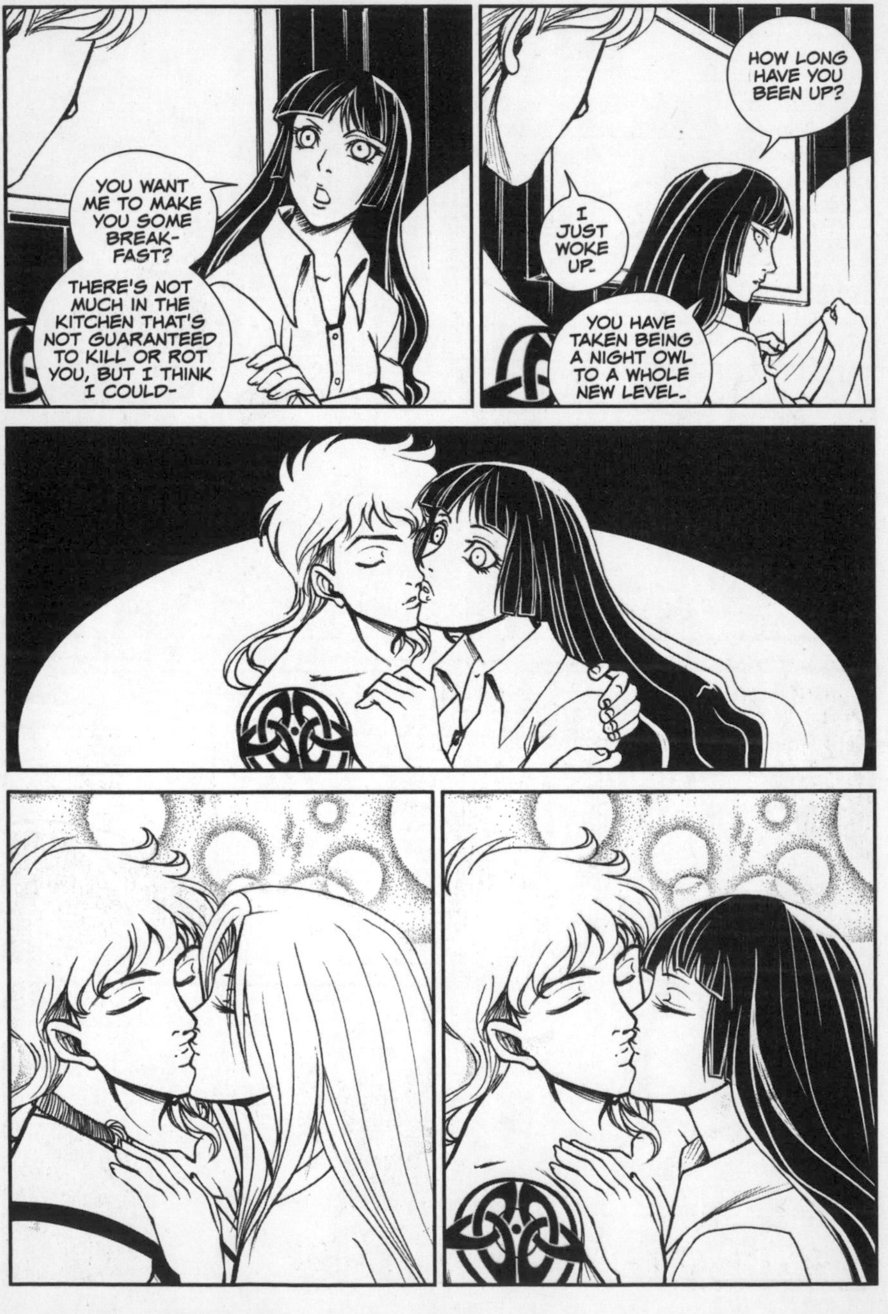
YOU WANT ME TO MAKE YOU SOME BREAK-FAST?
THERE'S NOT MUCH IN THE KITCHEN THAT'S NOT GUARANTEED TO KILL OR ROT YOU, BUT I THINK I COULD-
HOW LONG HAVE YOU BEEN UP?
I JUST WOKE UP.
YOU HAVE TAKEN BEING A NIGHT OWL TO A WHOLE NEW LEVEL.

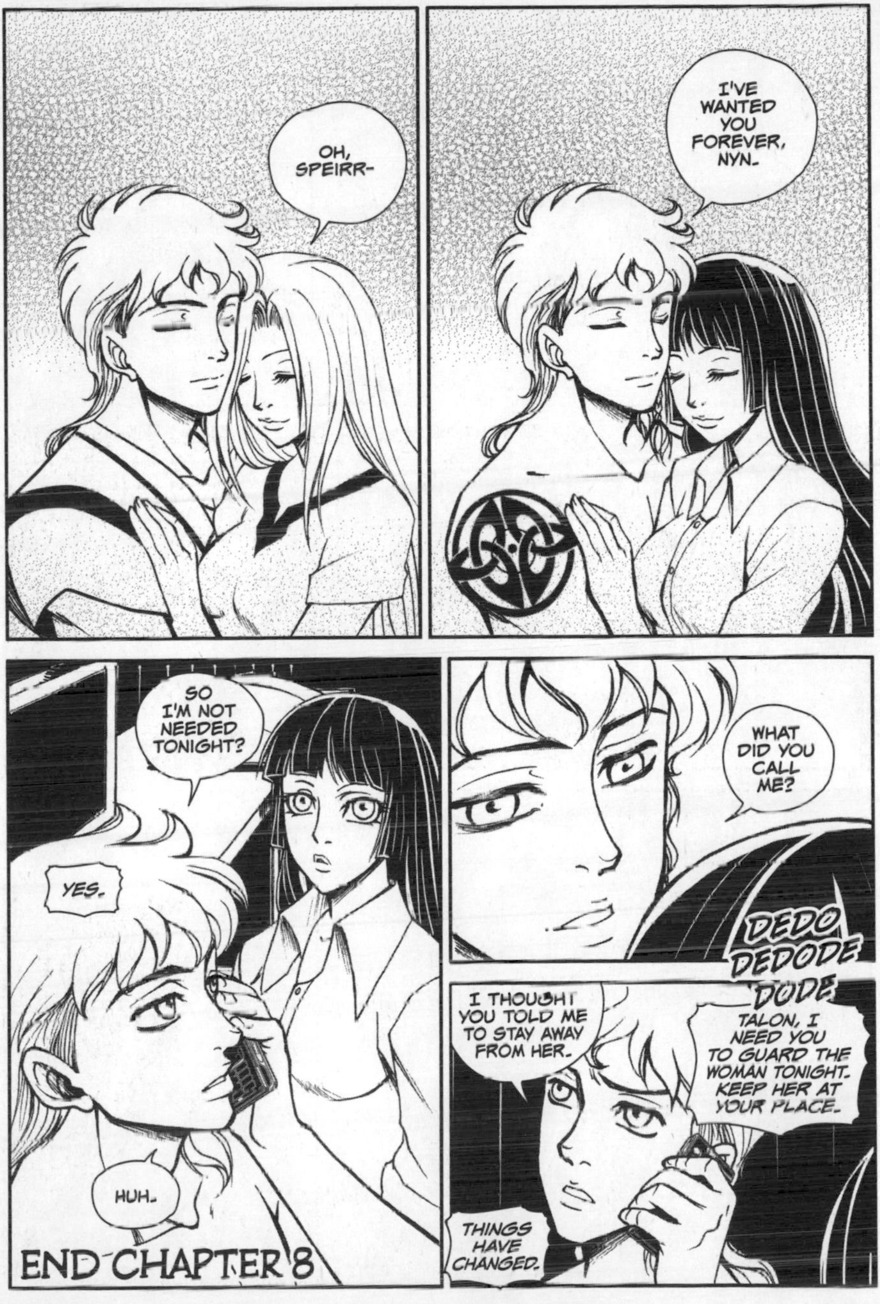
OH, SPEIRR-
I'VE WANTED YOU FOREVER, NYN.
SO I'M NOT NEEDED TONIGHT?
YES.
HUH.
WHAT DID YOU CALL ME?
DEDO DEDODE DODE
TALON, I NEED YOU TO GUARD THE WOMAN TONIGHT. KEEP HER AT YOUR PLACE.
I THOUGHT YOU TOLD ME TO STAY AWAY FROM HER.
THINGS HAVE CHANGED.
END CHAPTER 8

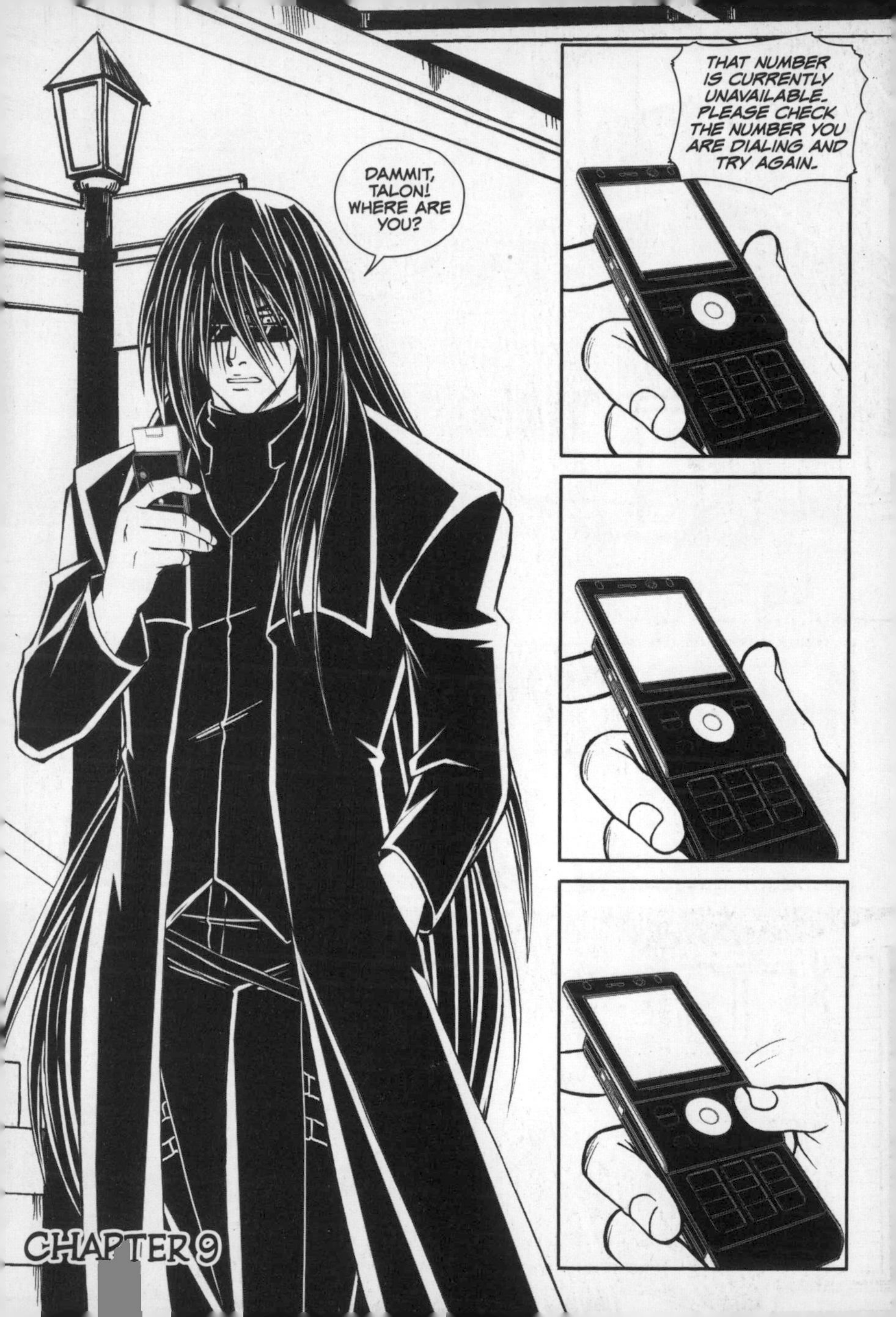
DAMMIT, TALON! WHERE ARE YOU?
THAT NUMBER IS CURRENTLY UNAVAILABLE. PLEASE CHECK THE NUMBER YOU ARE DIALING AND TRY AGAIN.
CHAPTER 9

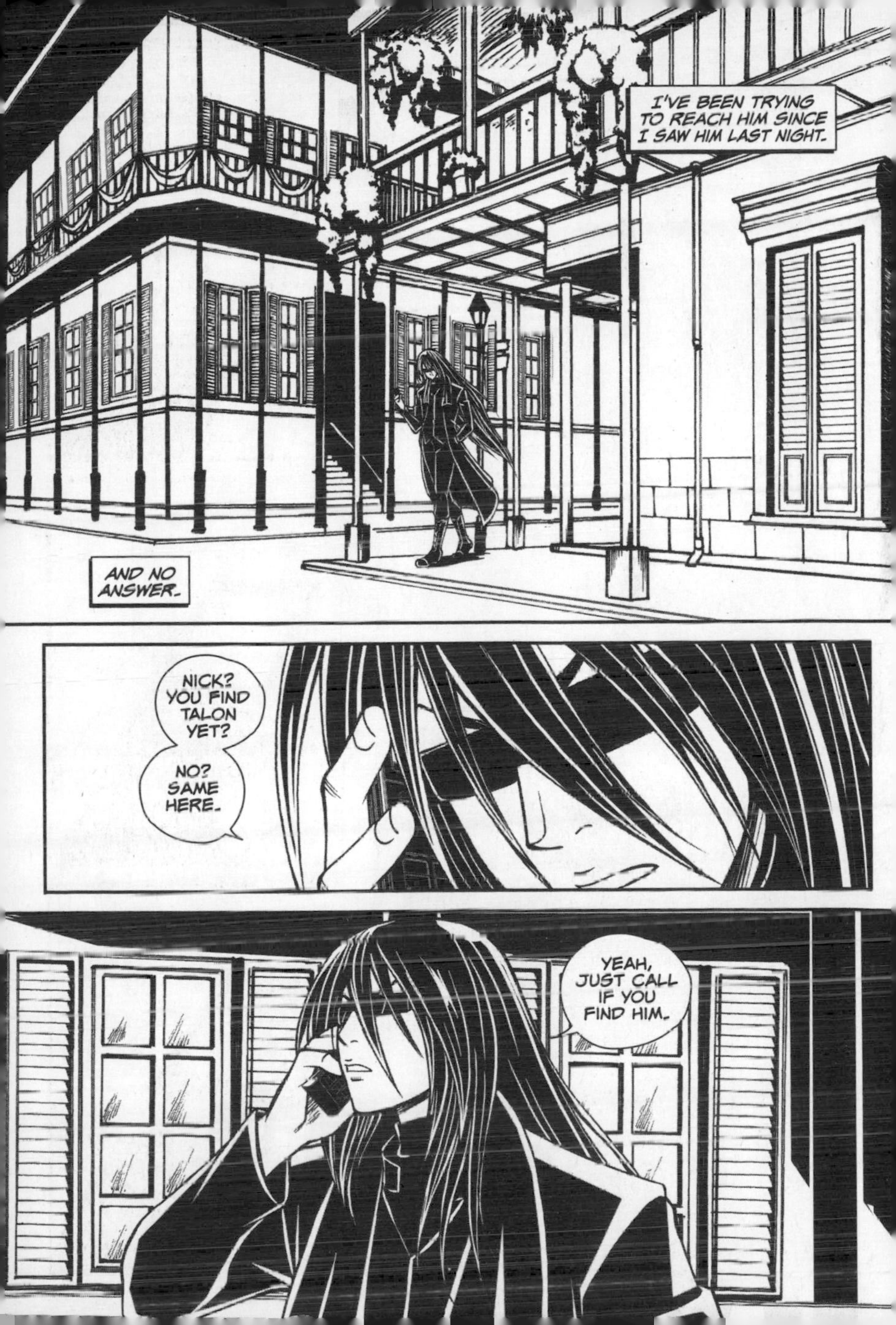
I'VE BEEN TRYING TO REACH HIM SINCE I SAW HIM LAST NIGHT...
AND NO ANSWER...
NICK? YOU FIND TALON YET?
NO? SAME HERE...
YEAH, JUST CALL IF YOU FIND HIM...

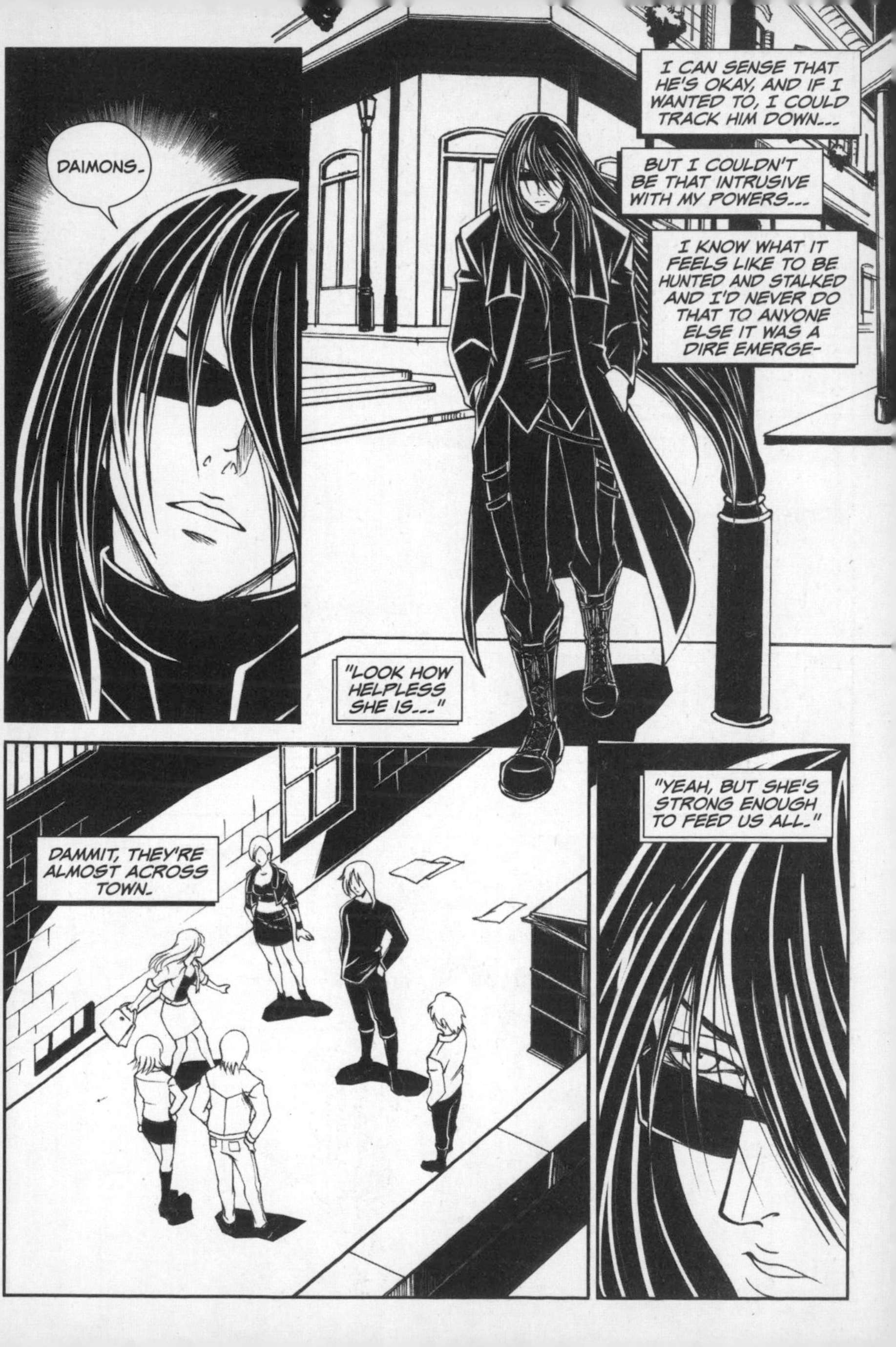
DAIMONS.
I CAN SENSE THAT HE'S OKAY, AND IF I WANTED TO, I COULD TRACK HIM DOWN...
BUT I COULDN'T BE THAT INTRUSIVE WITH MY POWERS...
I KNOW WHAT IT FEELS LIKE TO BE HUNTED AND STALKED AND I'D NEVER DO THAT TO ANYONE ELSE IT WAS A DIRE EMERGE-
"LOOK HOW HELPLESS SHE IS..."
DAMMIT, THEY'RE ALMOST ACROSS TOWN.
"YEAH, BUT SHE'S STRONG ENOUGH TO FEED US ALL."

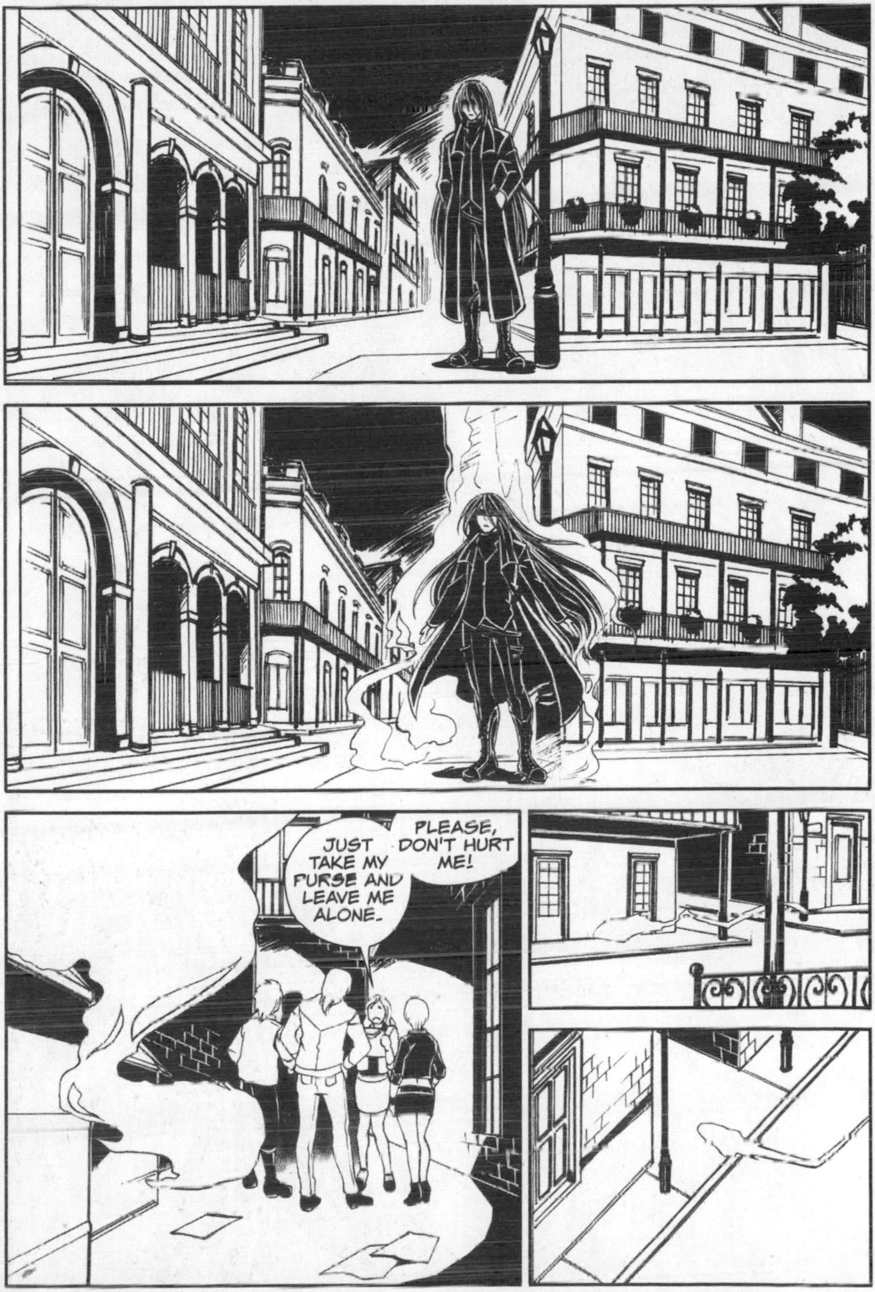
PLEASE, DON'T HURT ME!
JUST TAKE MY PURSE AND LEAVE ME ALONE.

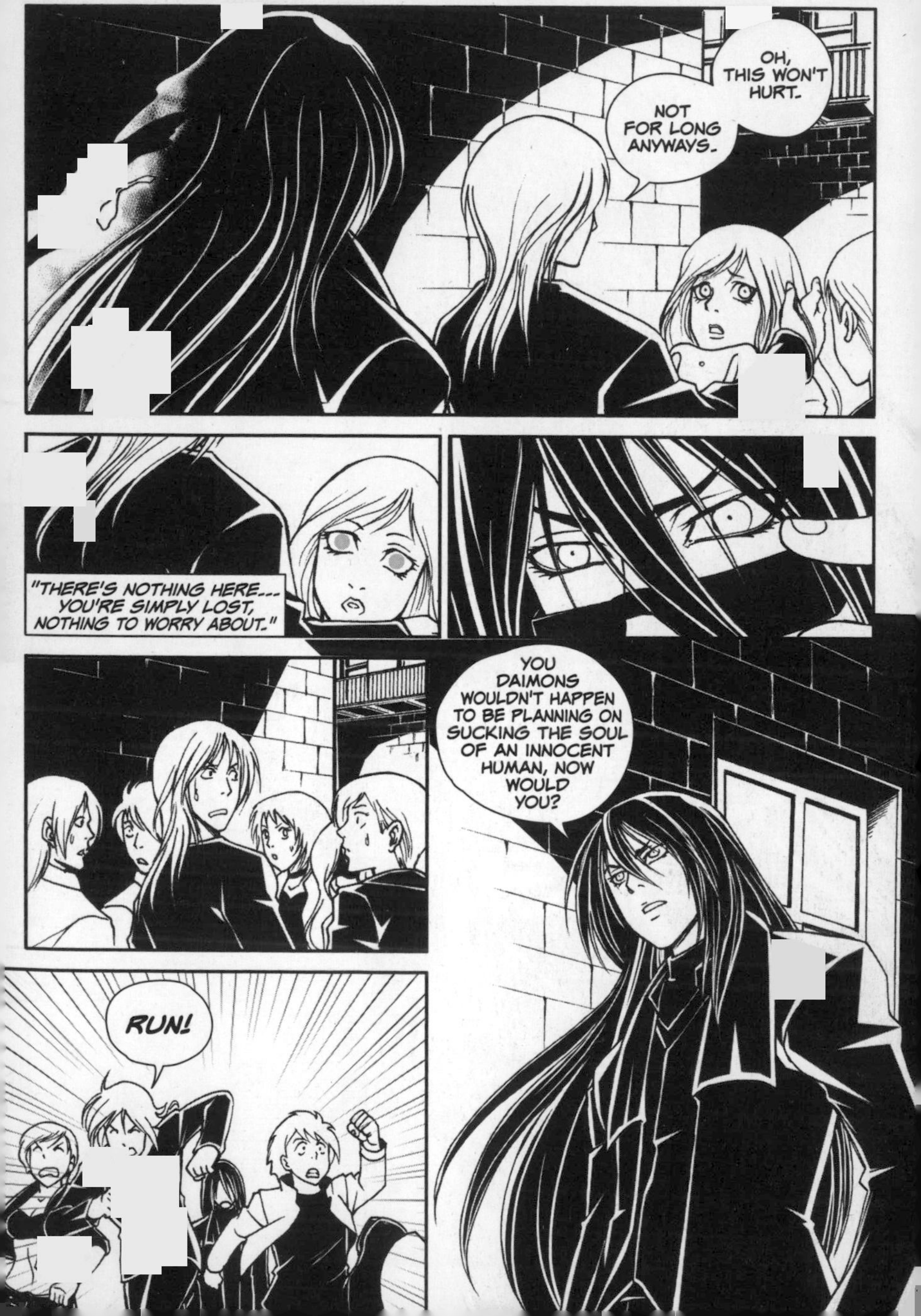

OH, THIS WON'T HURT.
NOT FOR LONG ANYWAYS.
"THERE'S NOTHING HERE... YOU'RE SIMPLY LOST, NOTHING TO WORRY ABOUT."
YOU DAIMONS WOULDN'T HAPPEN TO BE PLANNING ON SUCKING THE SOUL OF AN INNOCENT HUMAN, NOW WOULD YOU?
RUN!

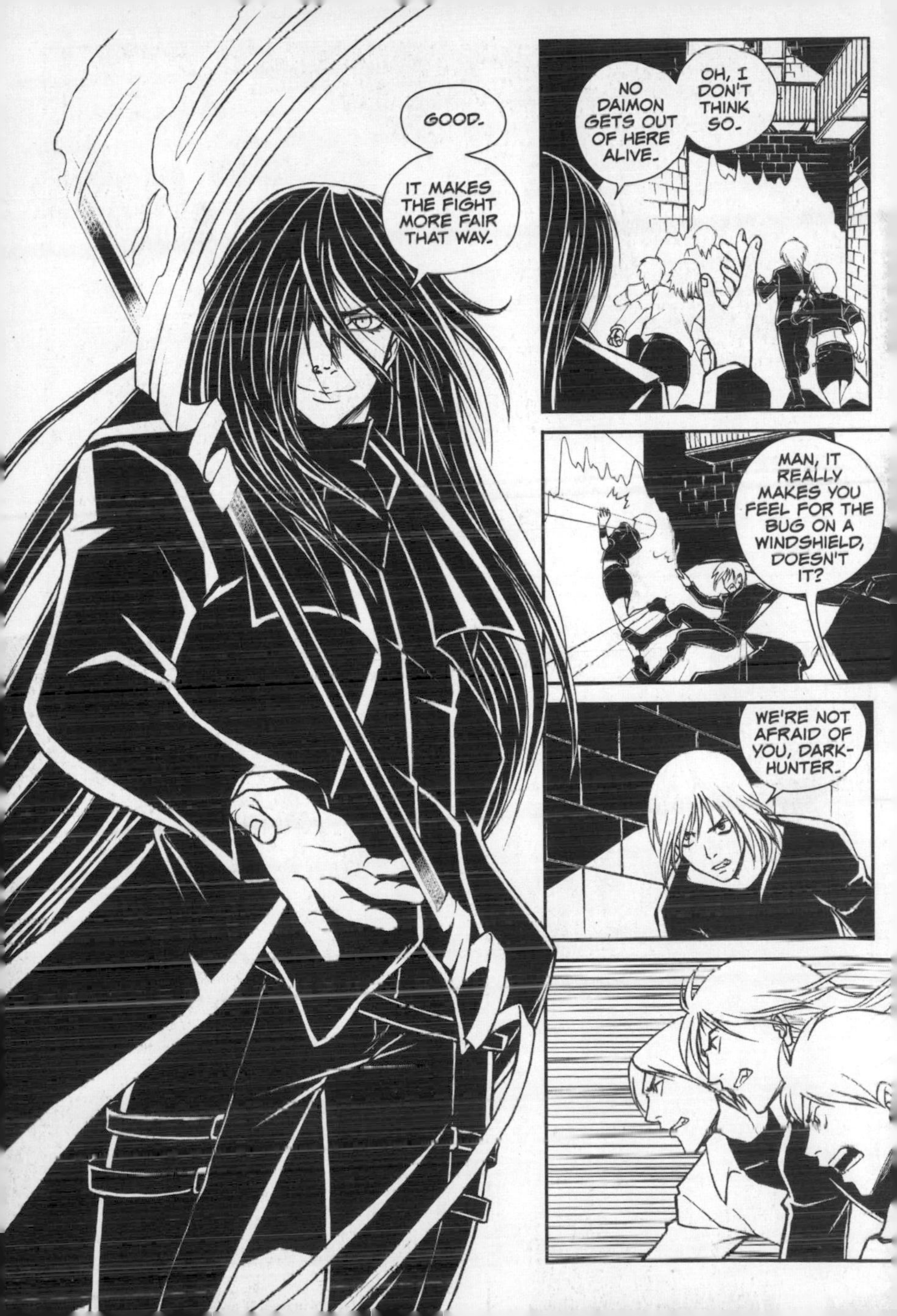
GOOD.
IT MAKES THE FIGHT MORE FAIR THAT WAY.
NO DAIMON GETS OUT OF HERE ALIVE.
OH, I DON'T THINK SO.
MAN, IT REALLY MAKES YOU FEEL FOR THE BUG ON A WINDSHIELD, DOESN'T IT?
WE'RE NOT AFRAID OF YOU, DARK-HUNTER.

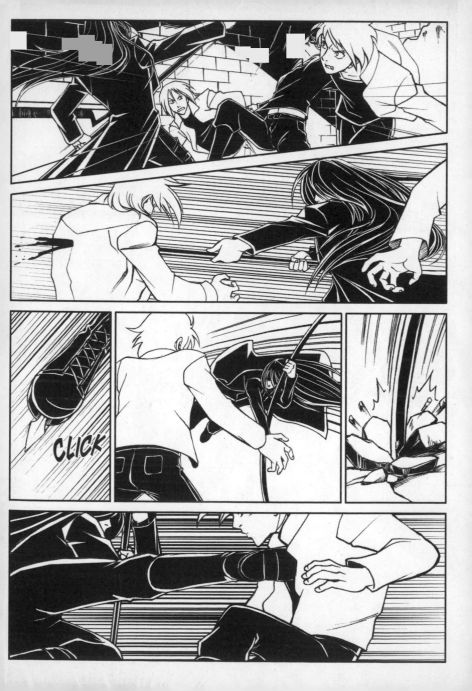

CLICK

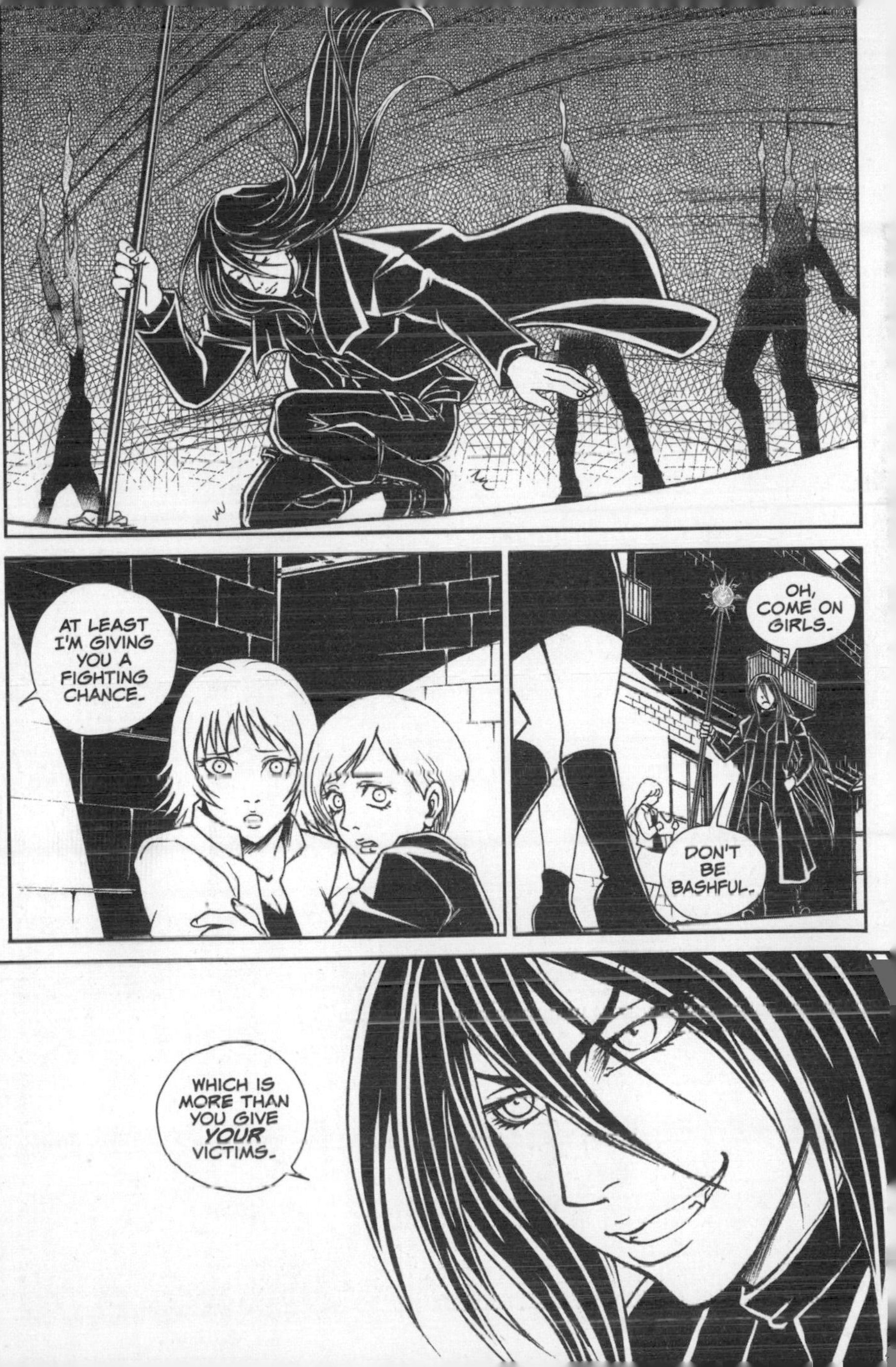
AT LEAST I'M GIVING YOU A FIGHTING CHANCE.
OH, COME ON GIRLS.
DON'T BE BASHFUL.
WHICH IS MORE THAN YOU GIVE YOUR VICTIMS.

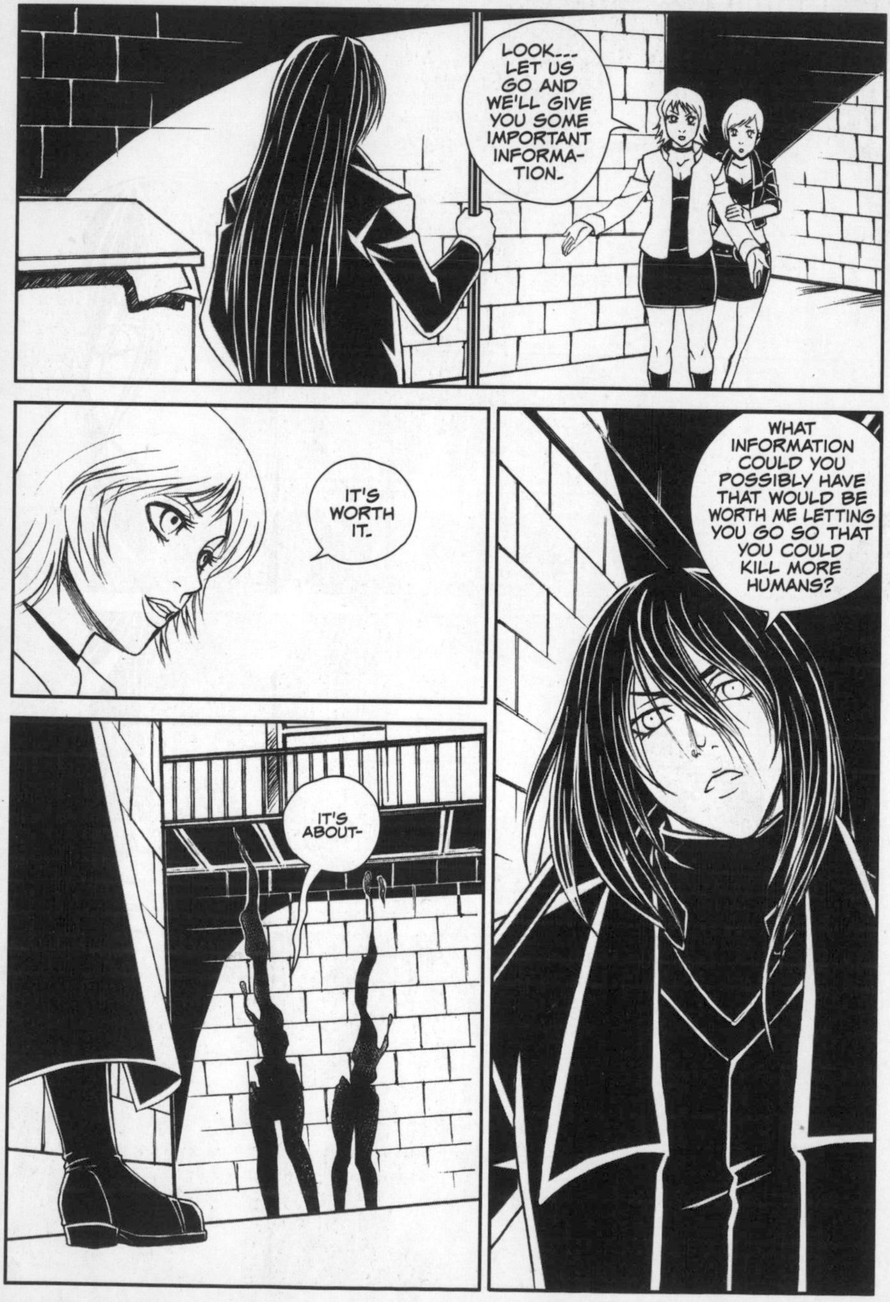
LOOK... LET US GO AND WE'LL GIVE YOU SOME IMPORTANT INFORMATION.
IT'S WORTH IT.
WHAT INFORMATION COULD YOU POSSIBLY HAVE THAT WOULD BE WORTH ME LETTING YOU GO SO THAT YOU COULD KILL MORE HUMANS?
IT'S ABOUT-

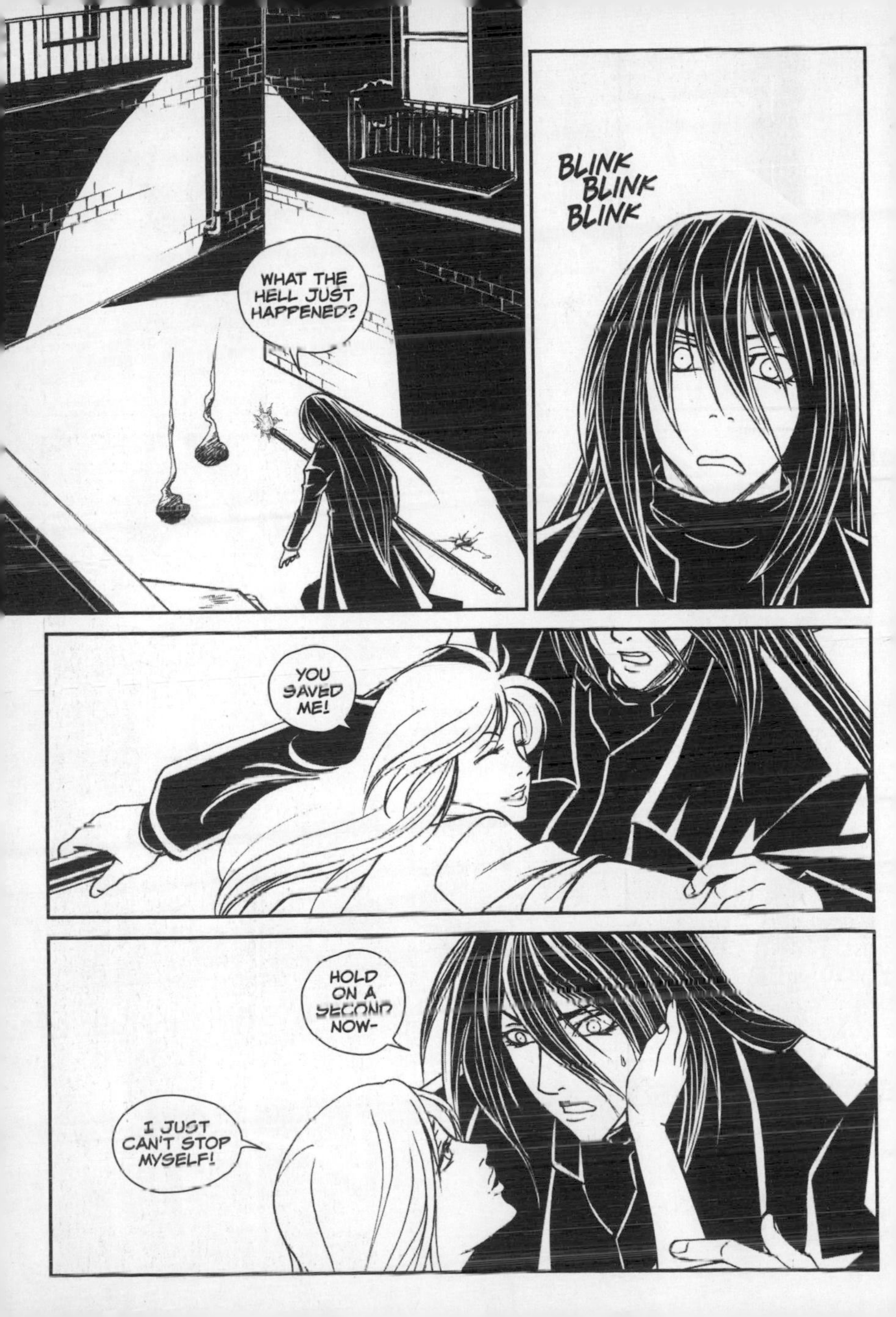
WHAT THE HELL JUST HAPPENED?
BLINK BLINK BLINK
YOU SAVED ME!
HOLD ON A SECOND NOW-
I JUST CAN'T STOP MYSELF!

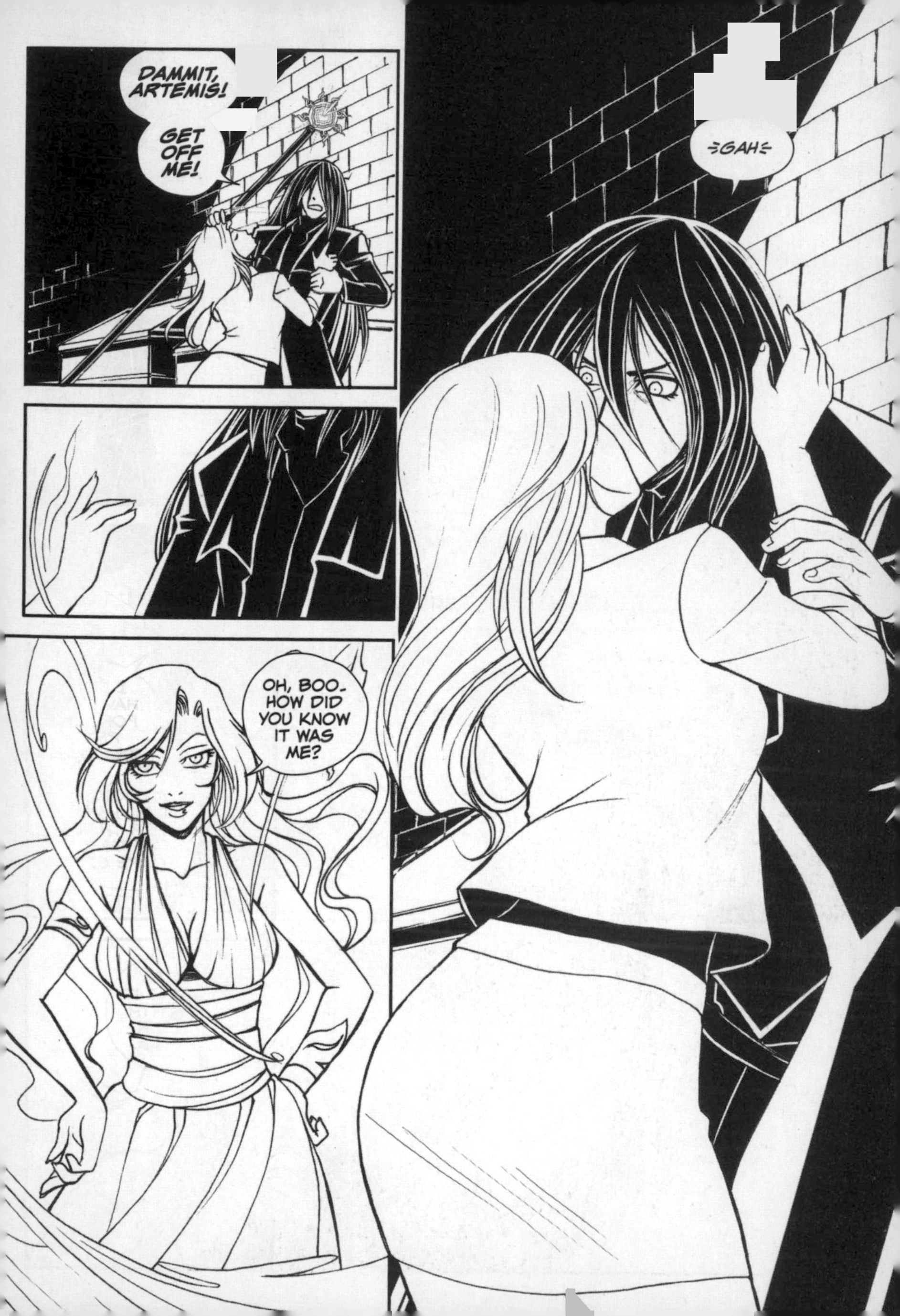
DAMMIT, ARTEMIS!
GET OFF ME!
≡GAH≡
OH, BOO-HOW DID YOU KNOW IT WAS ME?

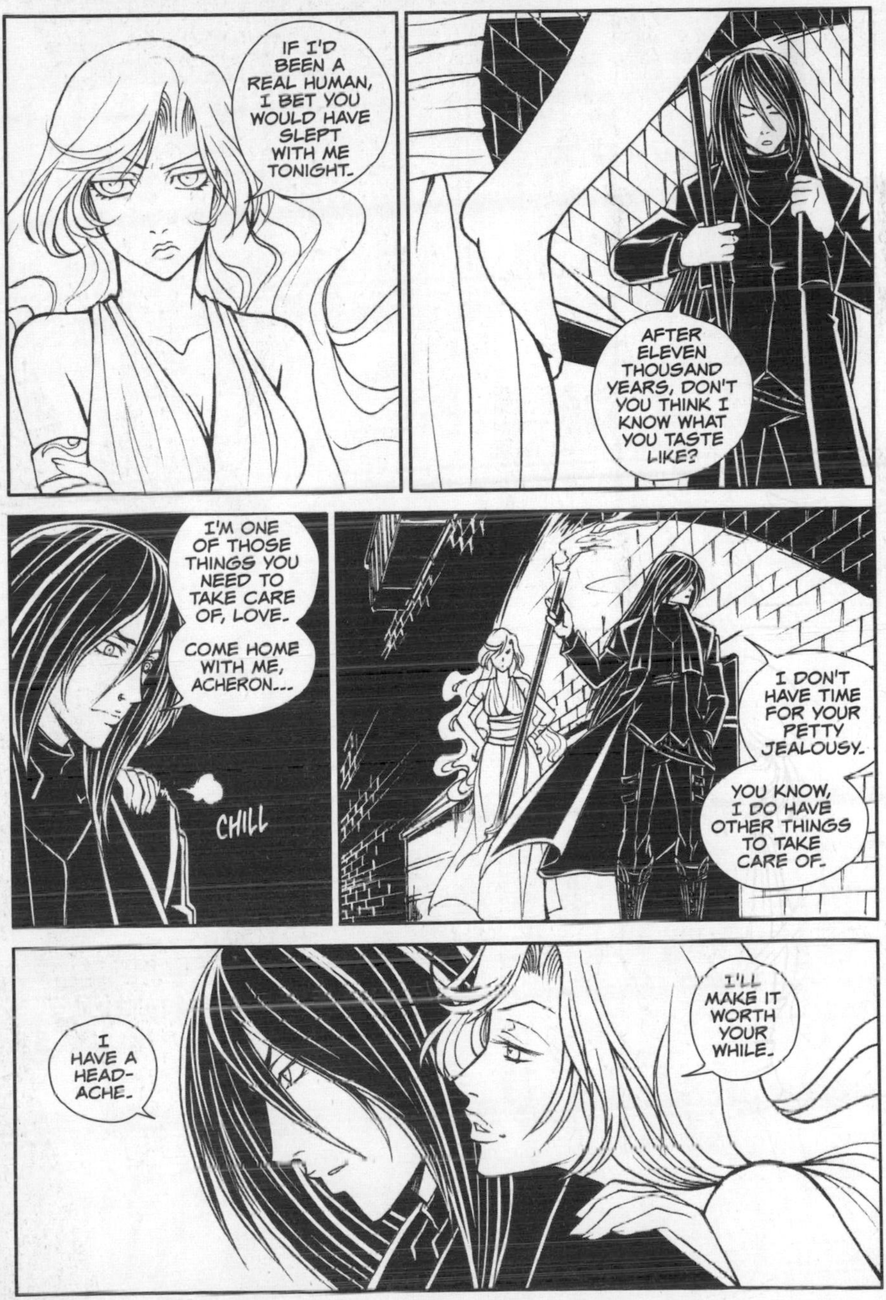
IF I'D BEEN A REAL HUMAN, I BET YOU WOULD HAVE SLEPT WITH ME TONIGHT.
AFTER ELEVEN THOUSAND YEARS, DON'T YOU THINK I KNOW WHAT YOU TASTE LIKE?
I'M ONE OF THOSE THINGS YOU NEED TO TAKE CARE OF, LOVE.
COME HOME WITH ME, ACHERON...
CHILL
I DON'T HAVE TIME FOR YOUR PETTY JEALOUSY.
YOU KNOW, I DO HAVE OTHER THINGS TO TAKE CARE OF.
I'LL MAKE IT WORTH YOUR WHILE.
I HAVE A HEAD-ACHE.

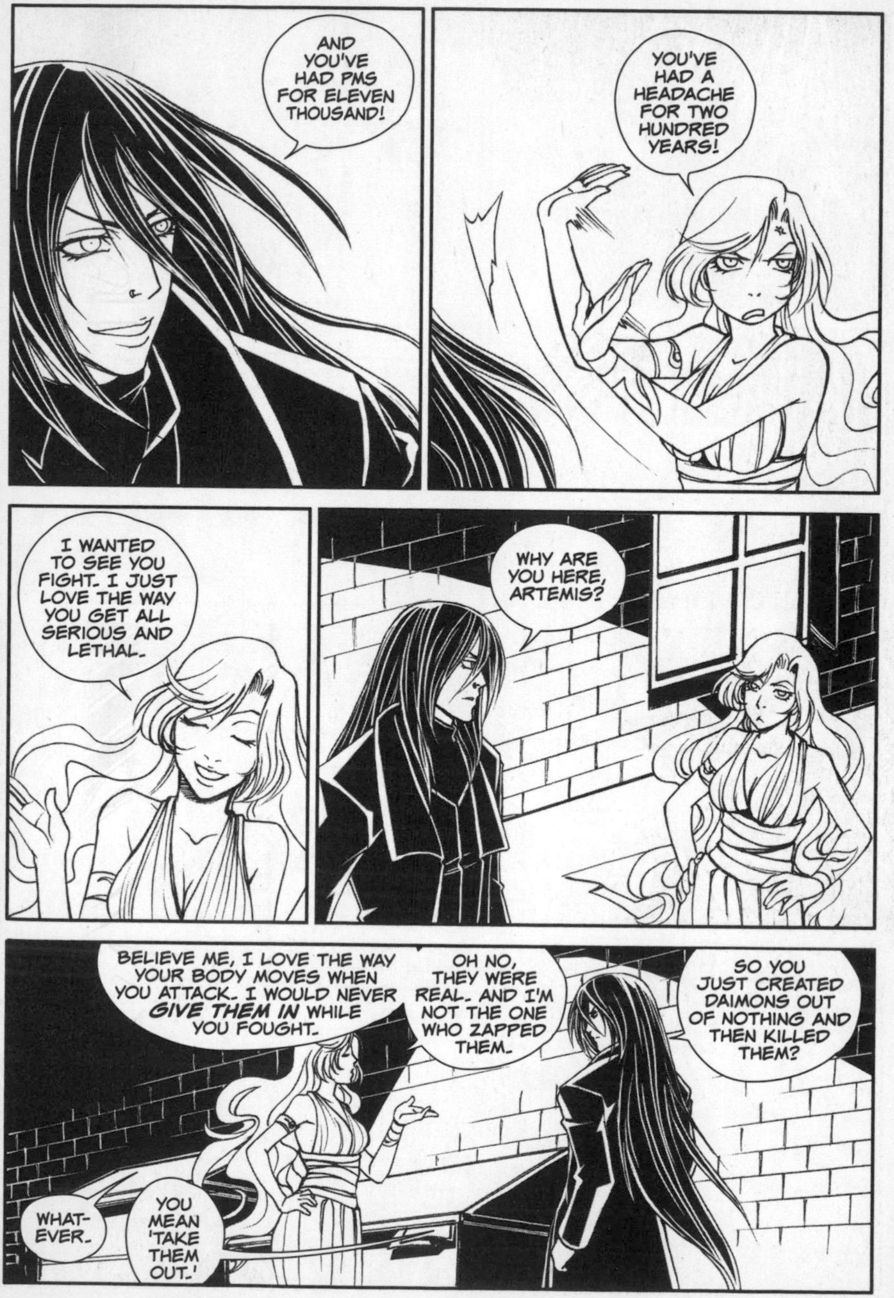
AND YOU'VE HAD PMS FOR ELEVEN THOUSAND!
YOU'VE HAD A HEADACHE FOR TWO HUNDRED YEARS!
I WANTED TO SEE YOU FIGHT. I JUST LOVE THE WAY YOU GET ALL SERIOUS AND LETHAL.
WHY ARE YOU HERE, ARTEMIS?
SO YOU JUST CREATED DAIMONS OUT OF NOTHING AND THEN KILLED THEM?
OH NO, THEY WERE REAL. AND I'M NOT THE ONE WHO ZAPPED THEM.
BELIEVE ME, I LOVE THE WAY YOUR BODY MOVES WHEN YOU ATTACK. I WOULD NEVER *GIVE THEM IN* WHILE YOU FOUGHT.
YOU MEAN 'TAKE THEM OUT.'
WHATEVER.

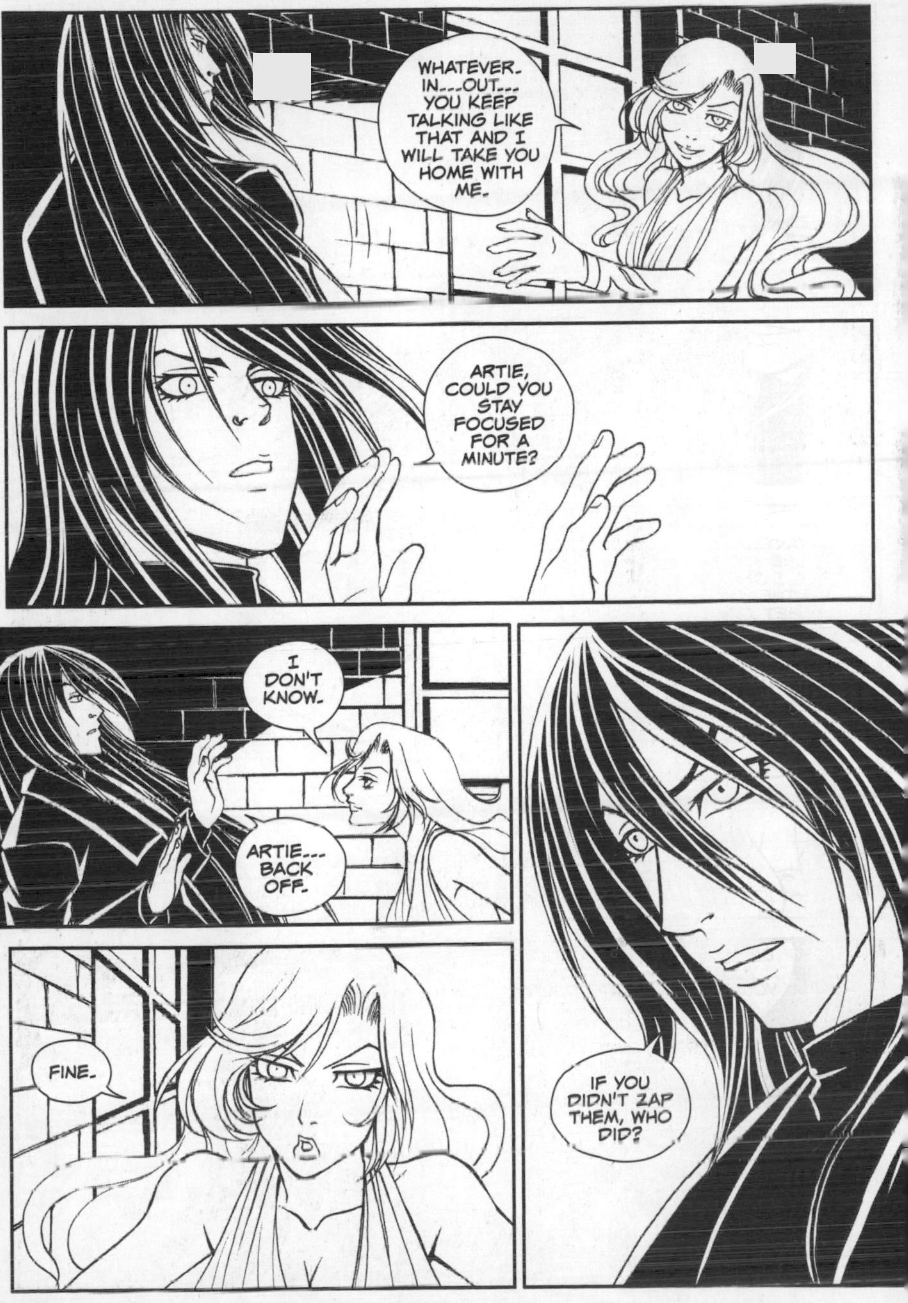
WHATEVER. IN...OUT... YOU KEEP TALKING LIKE THAT AND I WILL TAKE YOU HOME WITH ME.
ARTIE, COULD YOU STAY FOCUSED FOR A MINUTE?
I DON'T KNOW.
ARTIE... BACK OFF.
FINE.
IF YOU DIDN'T ZAP THEM, WHO DID?

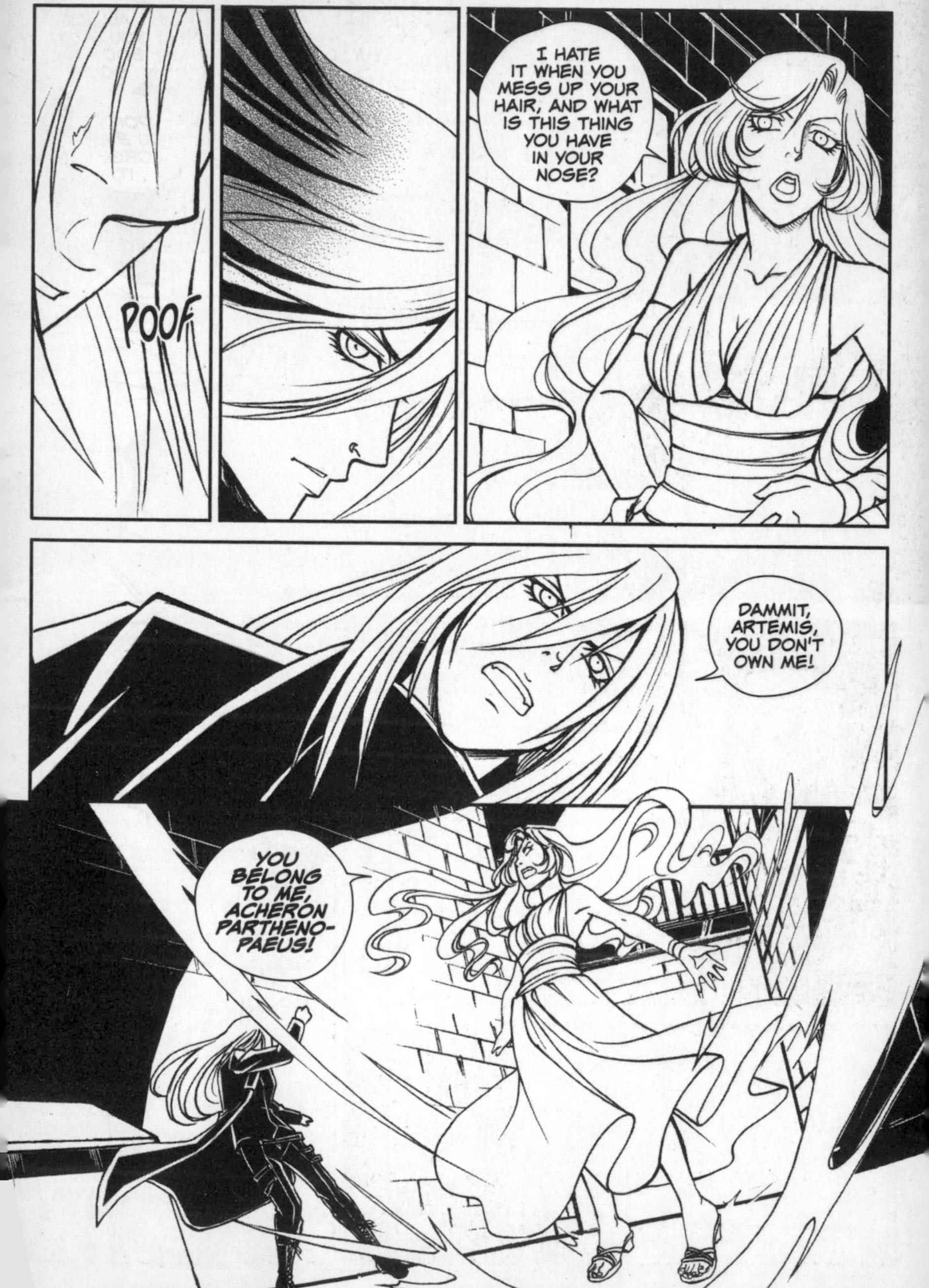
POOF
I HATE IT WHEN YOU MESS UP YOUR HAIR, AND WHAT IS THIS THING YOU HAVE IN YOUR NOSE?
DAMMIT, ARTEMIS, YOU DON'T OWN ME!
YOU BELONG TO ME, ACHERON PARTHENO-PAEUS!

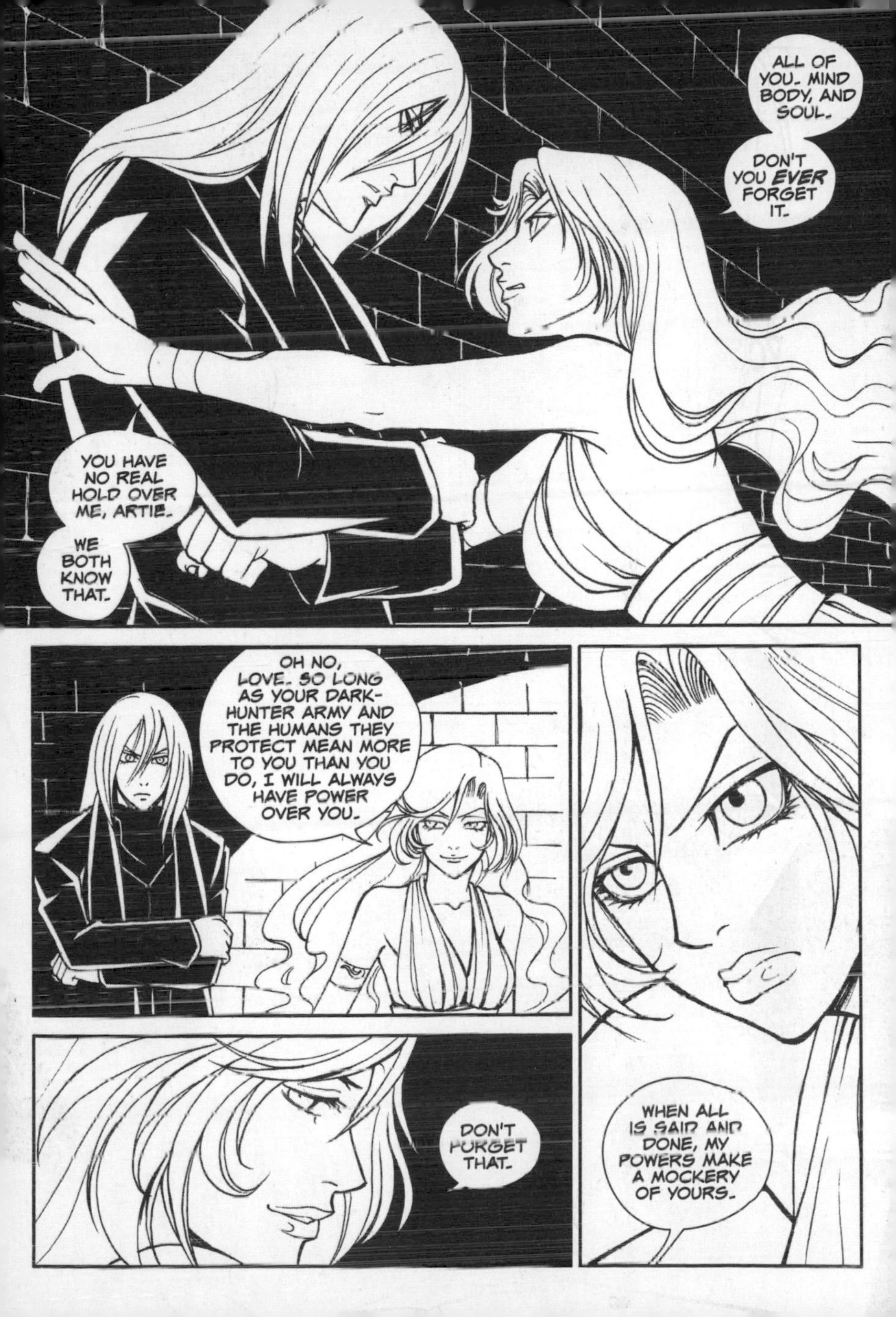
ALL OF YOU. MIND BODY, AND SOUL.
DON'T YOU EVER FORGET IT.
YOU HAVE NO REAL HOLD OVER ME, ARTIE.
WE BOTH KNOW THAT.
OH NO, LOVE. SO LONG AS YOUR DARK-HUNTER ARMY AND THE HUMANS THEY PROTECT MEAN MORE TO YOU THAN YOU DO, I WILL ALWAYS HAVE POWER OVER YOU.
WHEN ALL IS SAID AND DONE, MY POWERS MAKE A MOCKERY OF YOURS.
DON'T FORGET THAT.

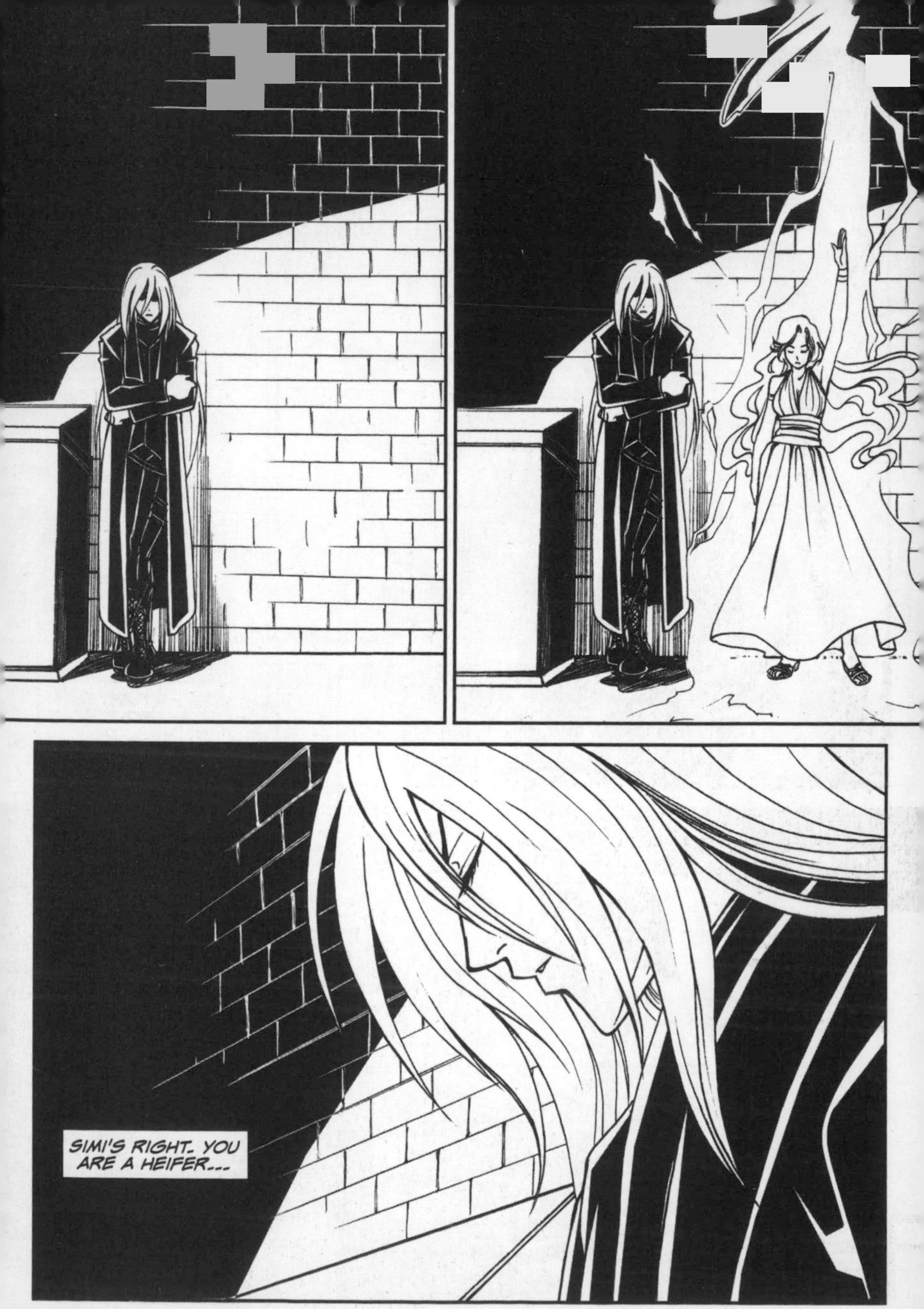
SIMI'S RIGHT. YOU ARE A HEIFER...

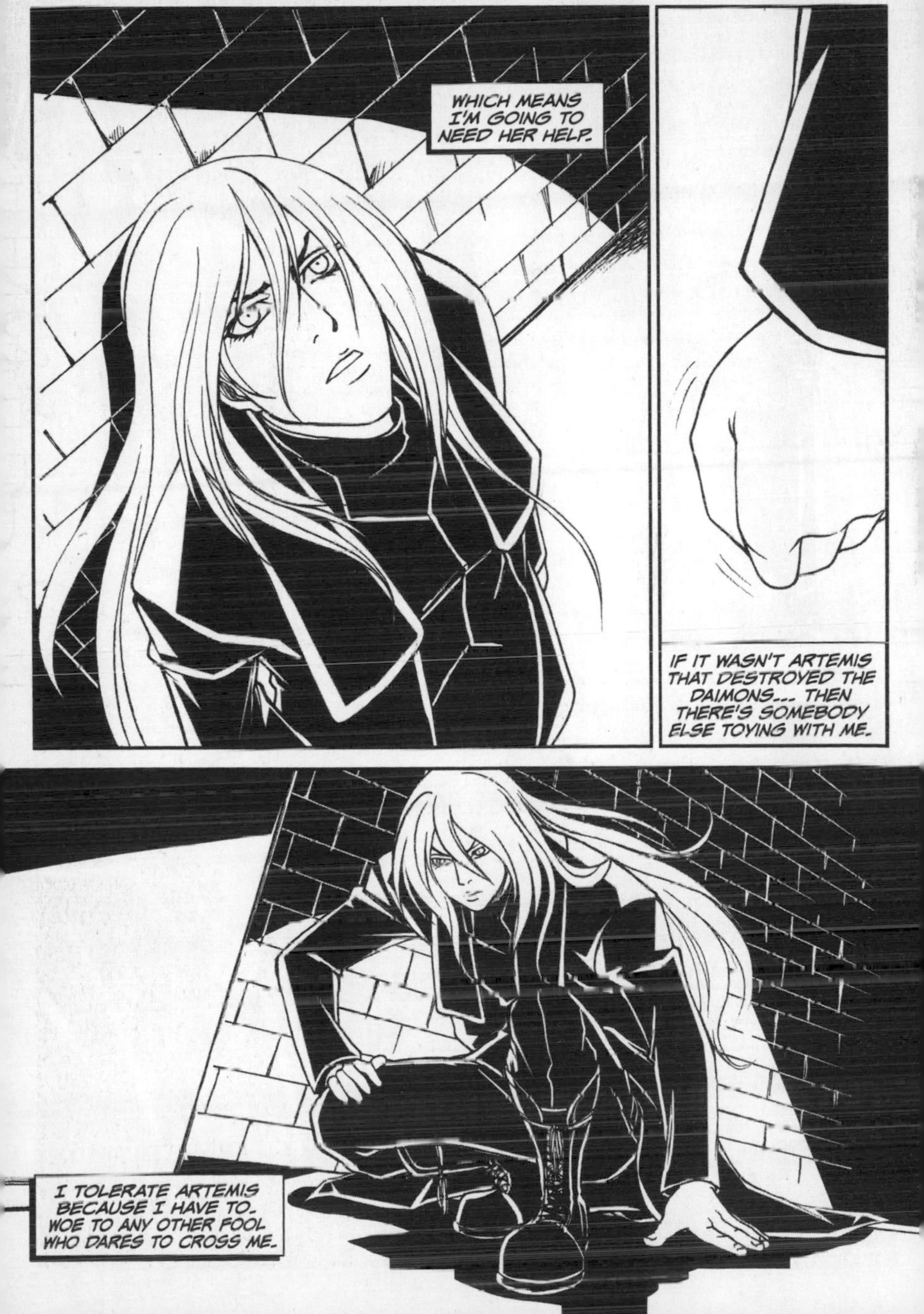
WHICH MEANS I'M GOING TO NEED HER HELP.
IF IT WASN'T ARTEMIS THAT DESTROYED THE DAIMONS... THEN THERE'S SOMEBODY ELSE TOYING WITH ME.
I TOLERATE ARTEMIS BECAUSE I HAVE TO. WOE TO ANY OTHER FOOL WHO DARES TO CROSS ME.

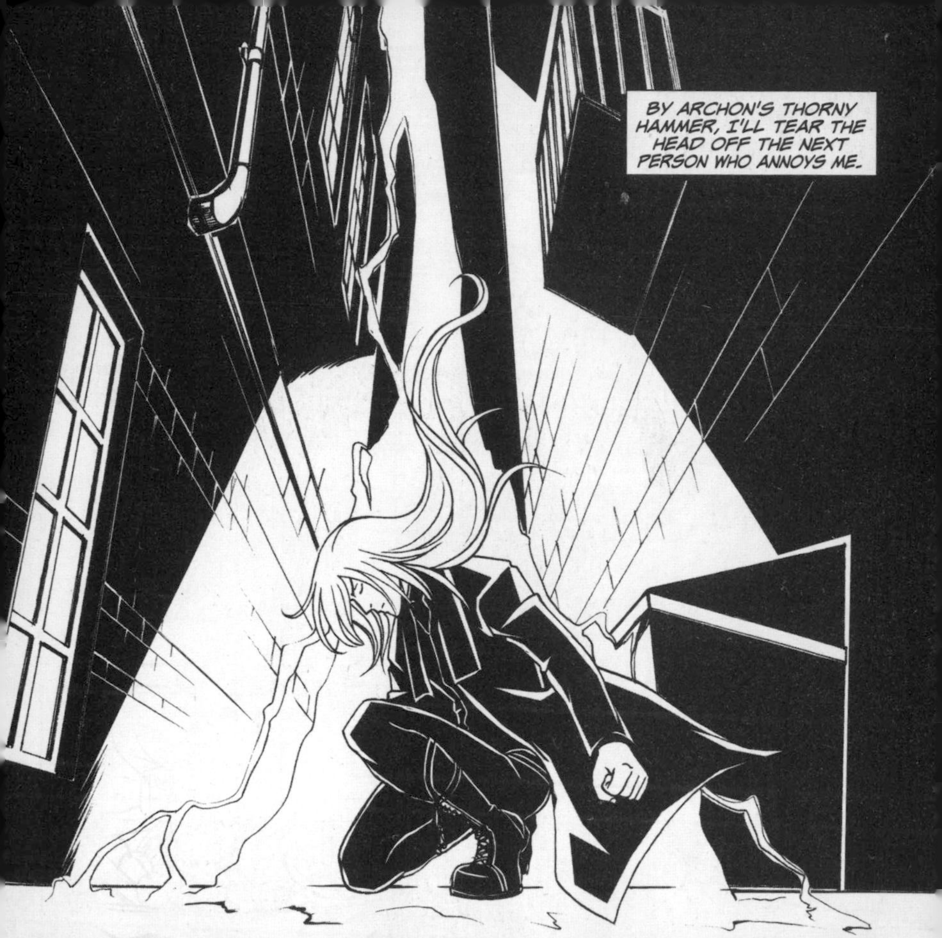
BY ARCHON'S THORNY HAMMER, I'LL TEAR THE HEAD OFF THE NEXT PERSON WHO ANNOYS ME.

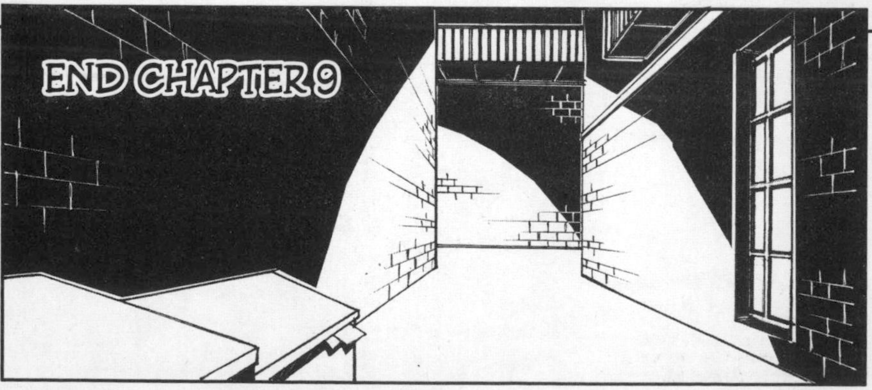
END CHAPTER 9

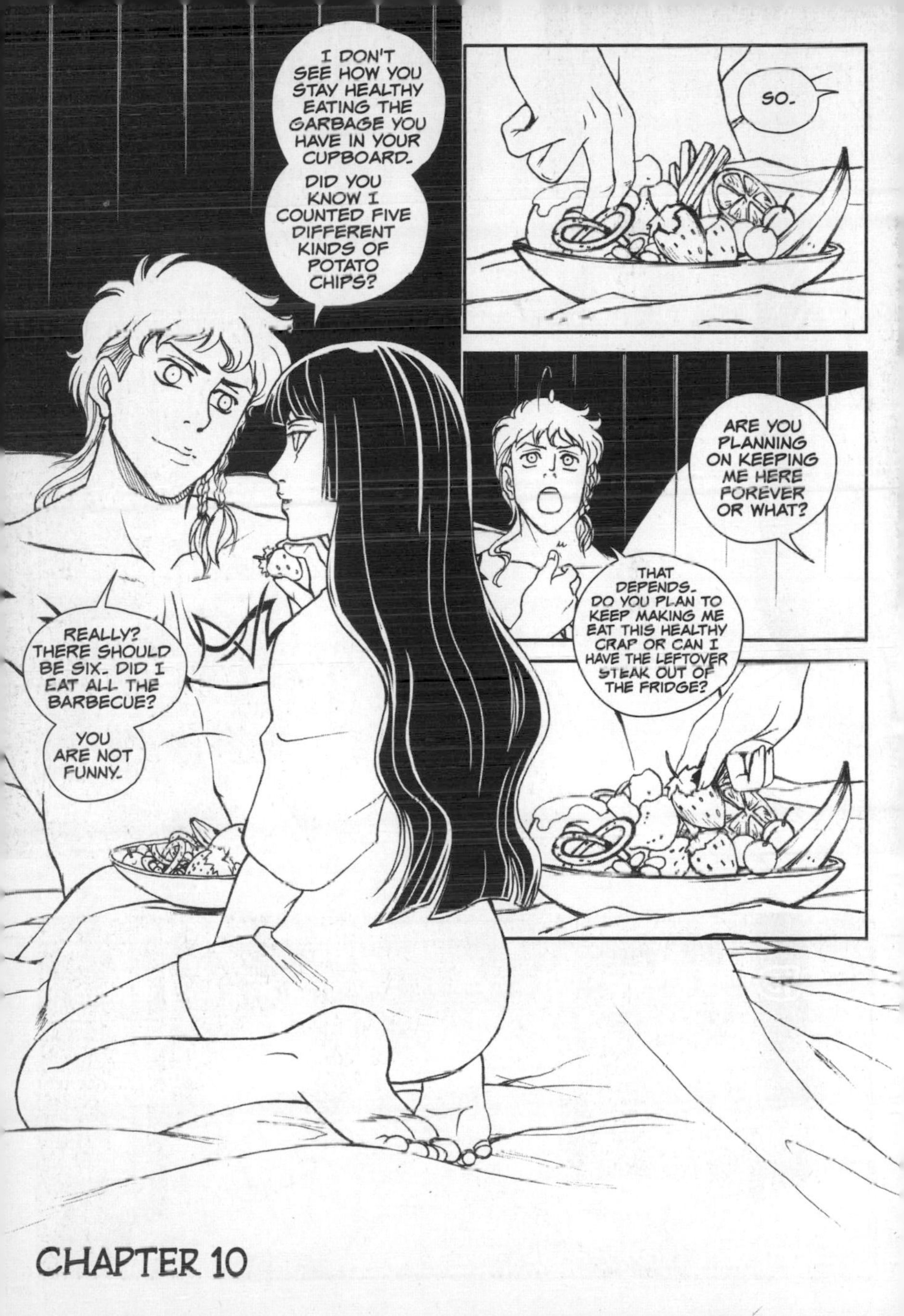
I DON'T SEE HOW YOU STAY HEALTHY EATING THE GARBAGE YOU HAVE IN YOUR CUPBOARD.
DID YOU KNOW I COUNTED FIVE DIFFERENT KINDS OF POTATO CHIPS?
REALLY? THERE SHOULD BE SIX. DID I EAT ALL THE BARBECUE?
YOU ARE NOT FUNNY.
SO.
ARE YOU PLANNING ON KEEPING ME HERE FOREVER OR WHAT?
THAT DEPENDS. DO YOU PLAN TO KEEP MAKING ME EAT THIS HEALTHY CRAP OR CAN I HAVE THE LEFTOVER STEAK OUT OF THE FRIDGE?

CHAPTER 10

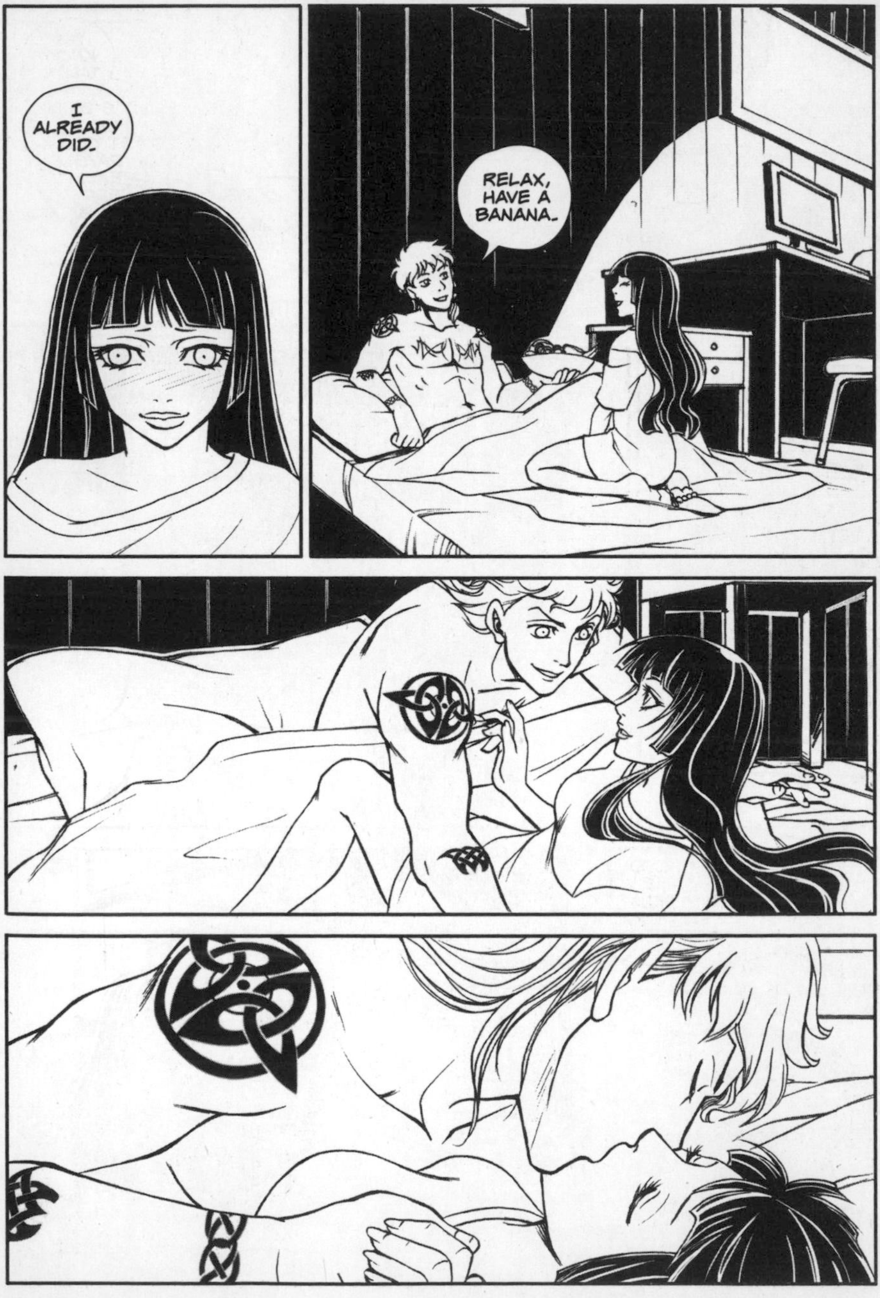
I ALREADY DID.
RELAX, HAVE A BANANA.

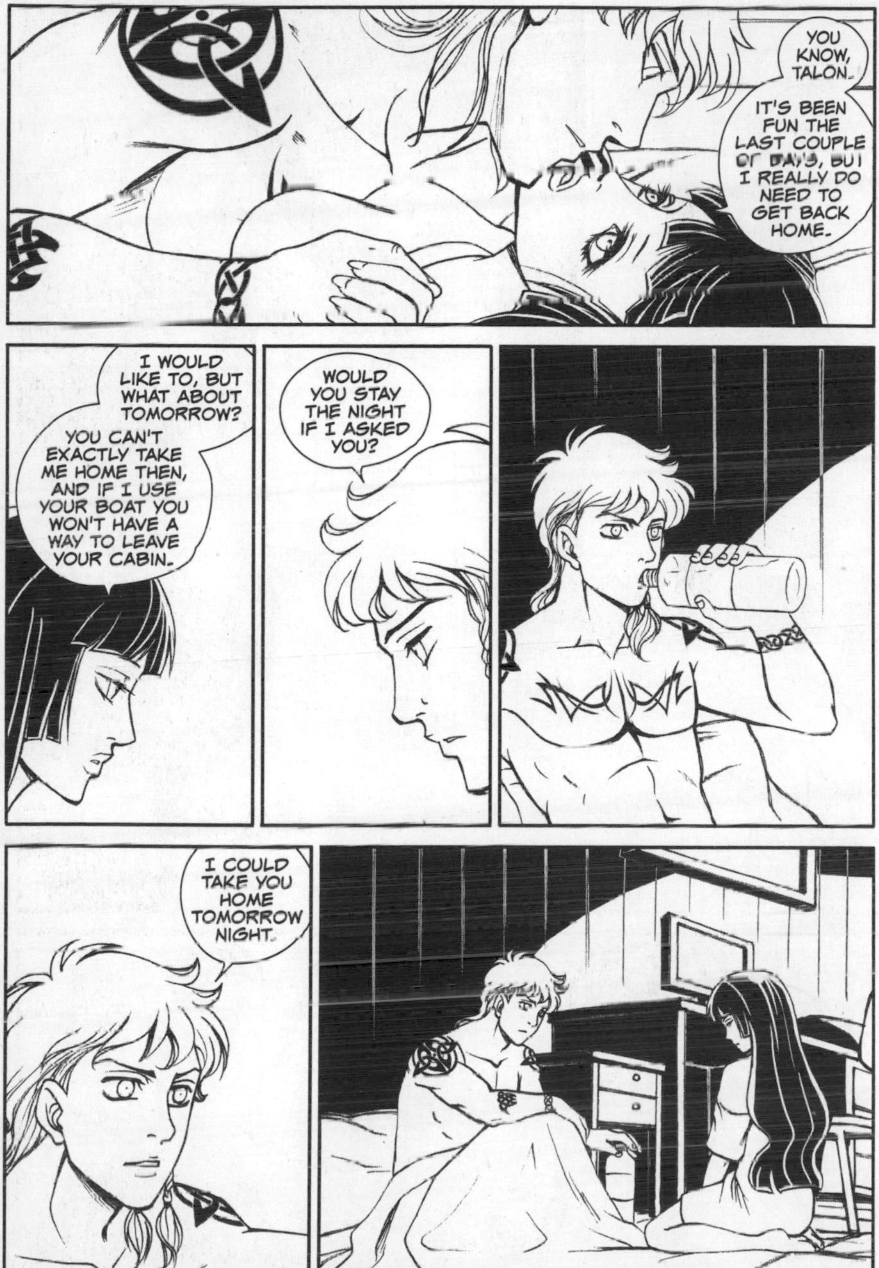
YOU KNOW, TALON...
IT'S BEEN FUN THE LAST COUPLE OF DAYS, BUT I REALLY DO NEED TO GET BACK HOME.
I WOULD LIKE TO, BUT WHAT ABOUT TOMORROW?
YOU CAN'T EXACTLY TAKE ME HOME THEN, AND IF I USE YOUR BOAT YOU WON'T HAVE A WAY TO LEAVE YOUR CABIN.
WOULD YOU STAY THE NIGHT IF I ASKED YOU?
I COULD TAKE YOU HOME TOMORROW NIGHT.

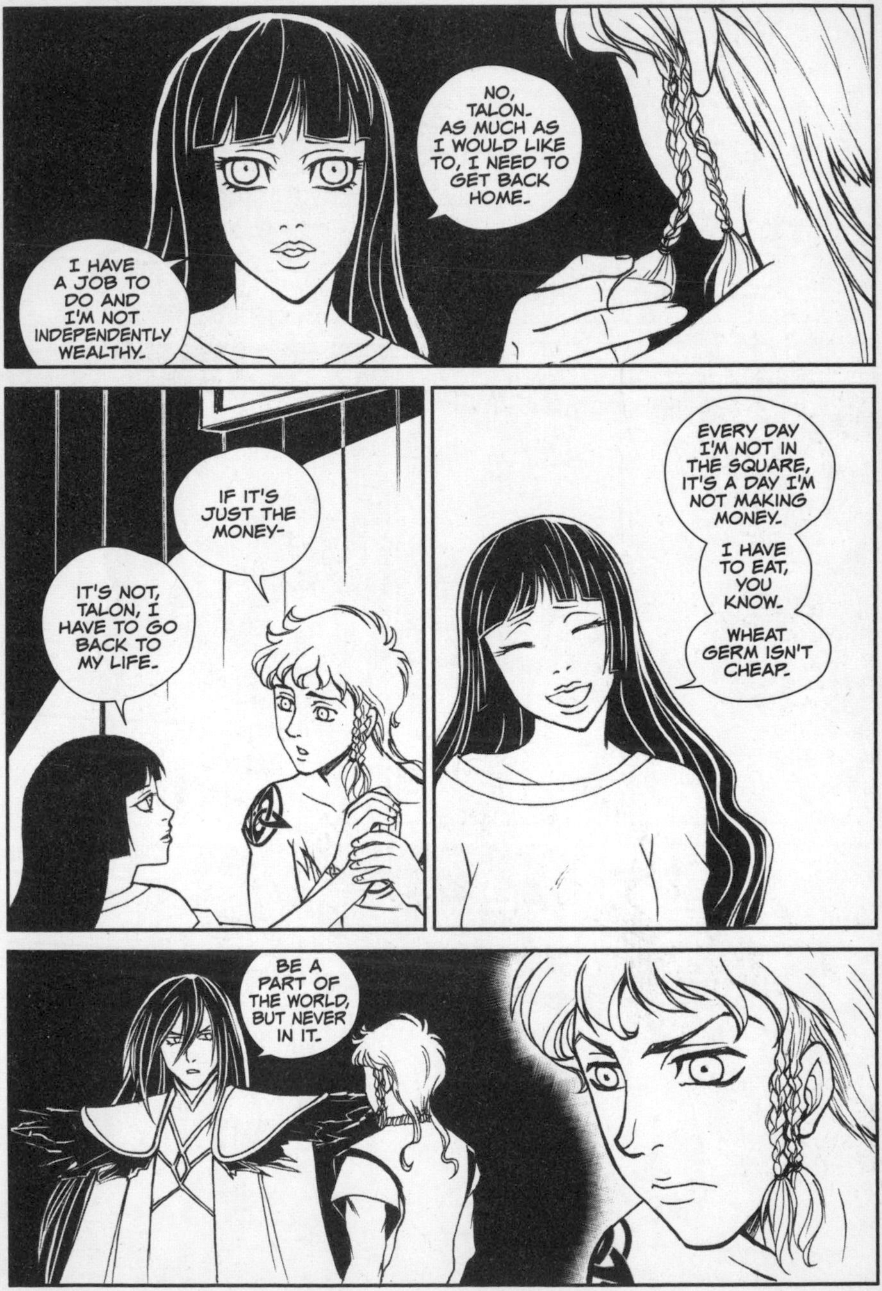
NO, TALON. AS MUCH AS I WOULD LIKE TO, I NEED TO GET BACK HOME.
I HAVE A JOB TO DO AND I'M NOT INDEPENDENTLY WEALTHY.
IF IT'S JUST THE MONEY-
IT'S NOT, TALON, I HAVE TO GO BACK TO MY LIFE.
EVERY DAY I'M NOT IN THE SQUARE, IT'S A DAY I'M NOT MAKING MONEY.
I HAVE TO EAT, YOU KNOW.
WHEAT GERM ISN'T CHEAP.
BE A PART OF THE WORLD, BUT NEVER IN IT.

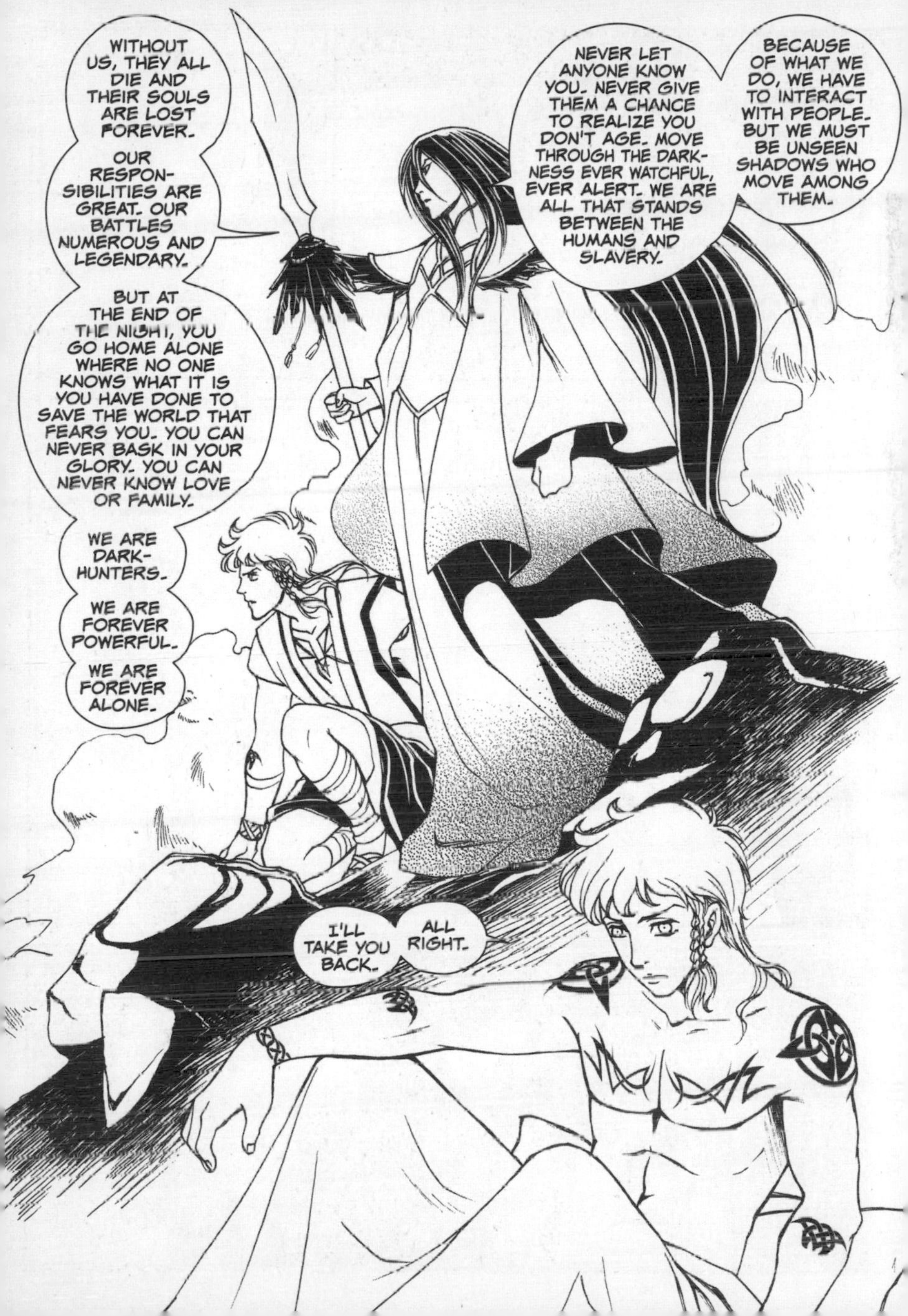
WITHOUT US, THEY ALL DIE AND THEIR SOULS ARE LOST FOREVER.
OUR RESPON-SIBILITIES ARE GREAT. OUR BATTLES NUMEROUS AND LEGENDARY.
BUT AT THE END OF THE NIGHT, YOU GO HOME ALONE WHERE NO ONE KNOWS WHAT IT IS YOU HAVE DONE TO SAVE THE WORLD THAT FEARS YOU. YOU CAN NEVER BASK IN YOUR GLORY. YOU CAN NEVER KNOW LOVE OR FAMILY.
BECAUSE OF WHAT WE DO, WE HAVE TO INTERACT WITH PEOPLE. BUT WE MUST BE UNSEEN SHADOWS WHO MOVE AMONG THEM.
NEVER LET ANYONE KNOW YOU. NEVER GIVE THEM A CHANCE TO REALIZE YOU DON'T AGE. MOVE THROUGH THE DARK-NESS EVER WATCHFUL, EVER ALERT. WE ARE ALL THAT STANDS BETWEEN THE HUMANS AND SLAVERY.
WE ARE DARK-HUNTERS.
WE ARE FOREVER POWERFUL.
WE ARE FOREVER ALONE.
ALL RIGHT.
I'LL TAKE YOU BACK.

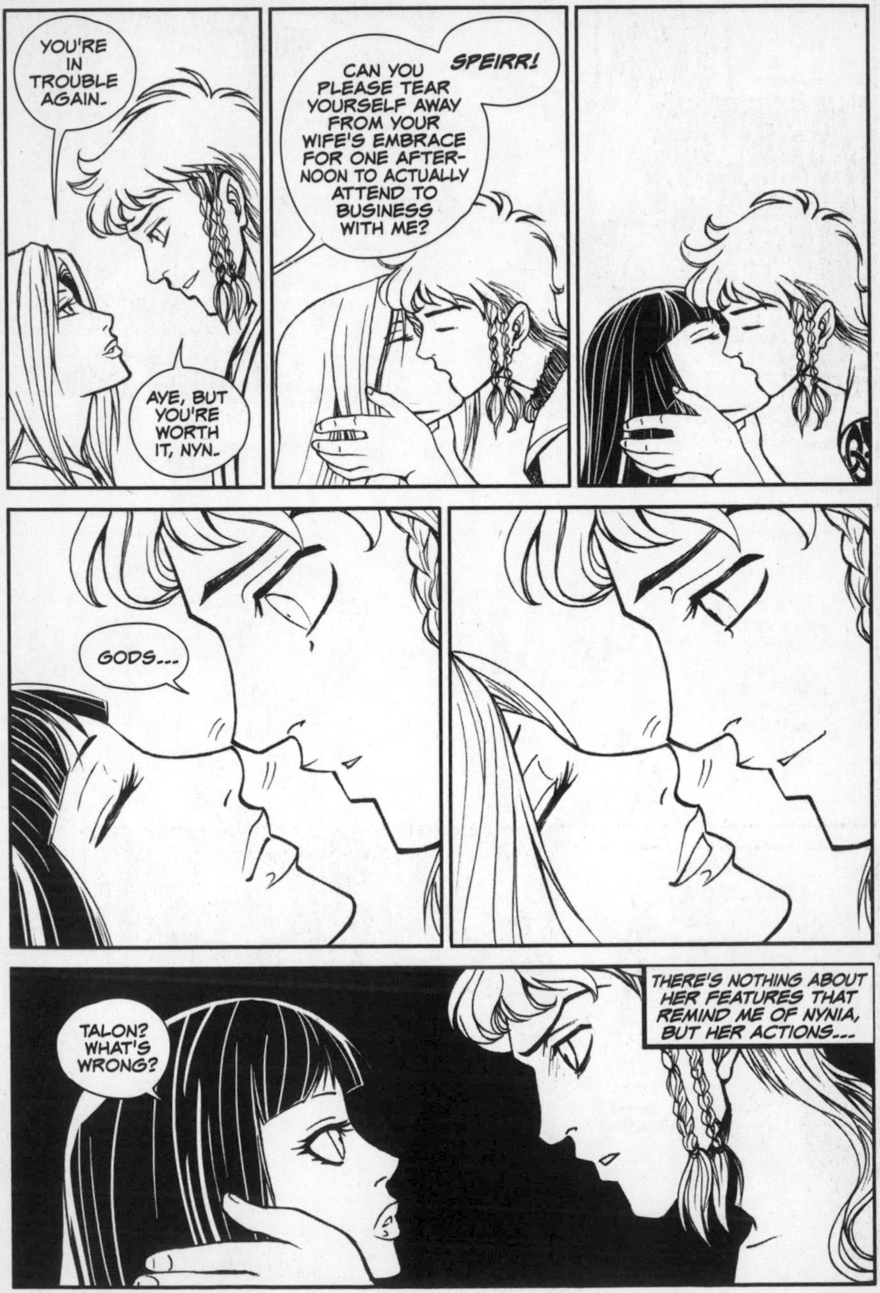
YOU'RE IN TROUBLE AGAIN.
AYE, BUT YOU'RE WORTH IT, NYN.
SPEIRR!
CAN YOU PLEASE TEAR YOURSELF AWAY FROM YOUR WIFE'S EMBRACE FOR ONE AFTER-NOON TO ACTUALLY ATTEND TO BUSINESS WITH ME?
GODS...
TALON? WHAT'S WRONG?
THERE'S NOTHING ABOUT HER FEATURES THAT REMIND ME OF NYNIA, BUT HER ACTIONS...

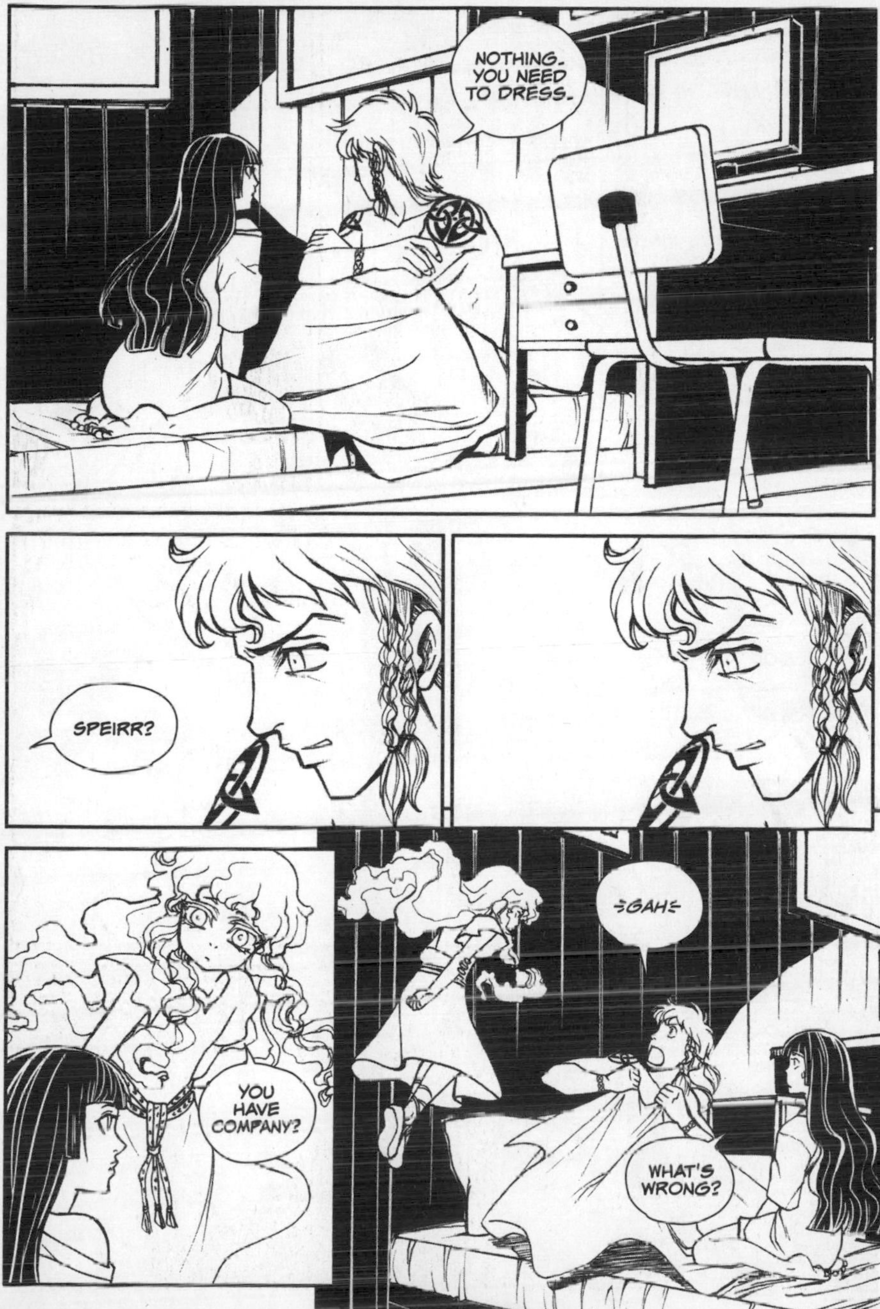
NOTHING. YOU NEED TO DRESS.
SPEIRR?
YOU HAVE COMPANY?
GAH
WHAT'S WRONG?

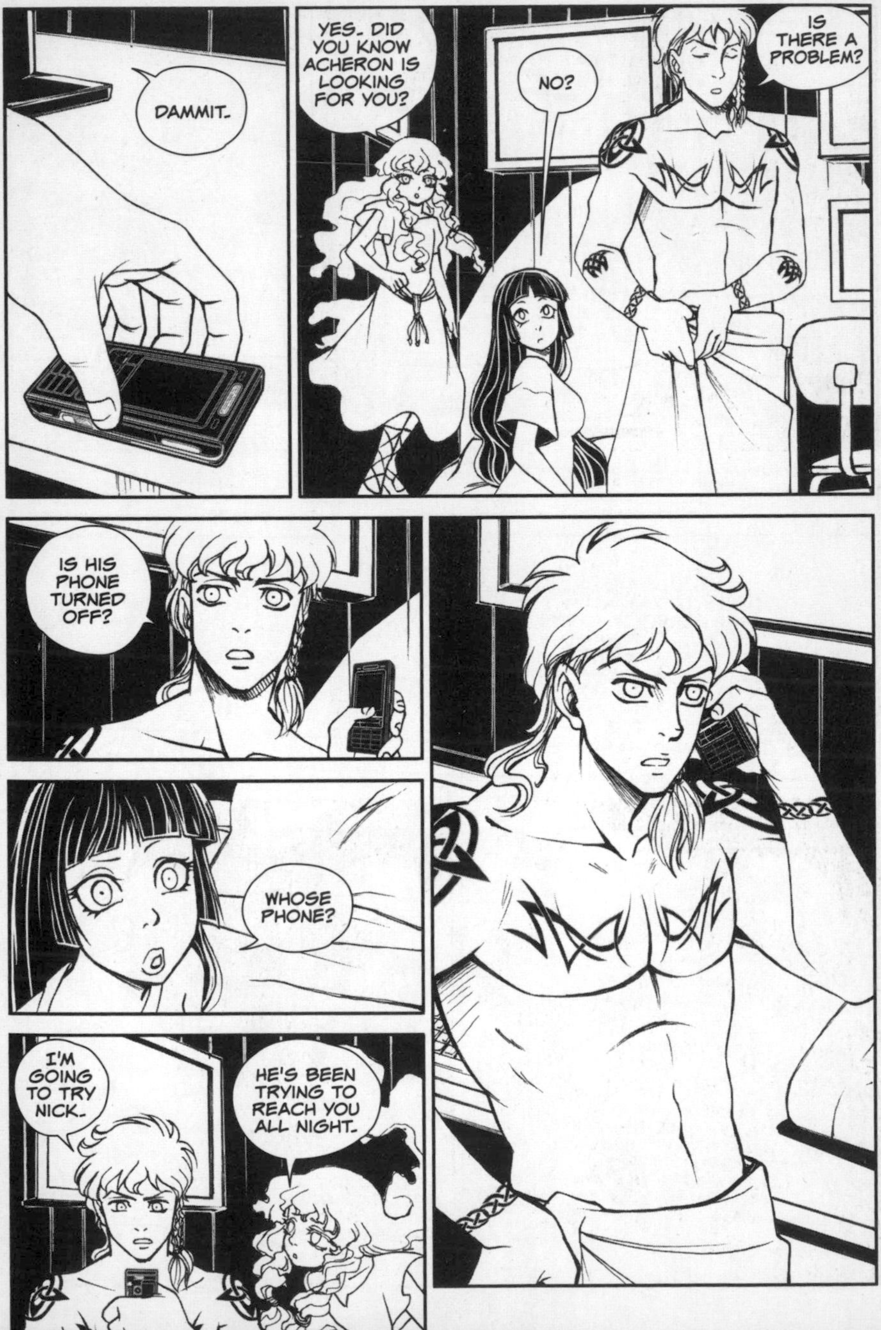
DAMMIT.
YES. DID YOU KNOW ACHERON IS LOOKING FOR YOU?
NO?
IS THERE A PROBLEM?
IS HIS PHONE TURNED OFF?
WHOSE PHONE?
I'M GOING TO TRY NICK.
HE'S BEEN TRYING TO REACH YOU ALL NIGHT.

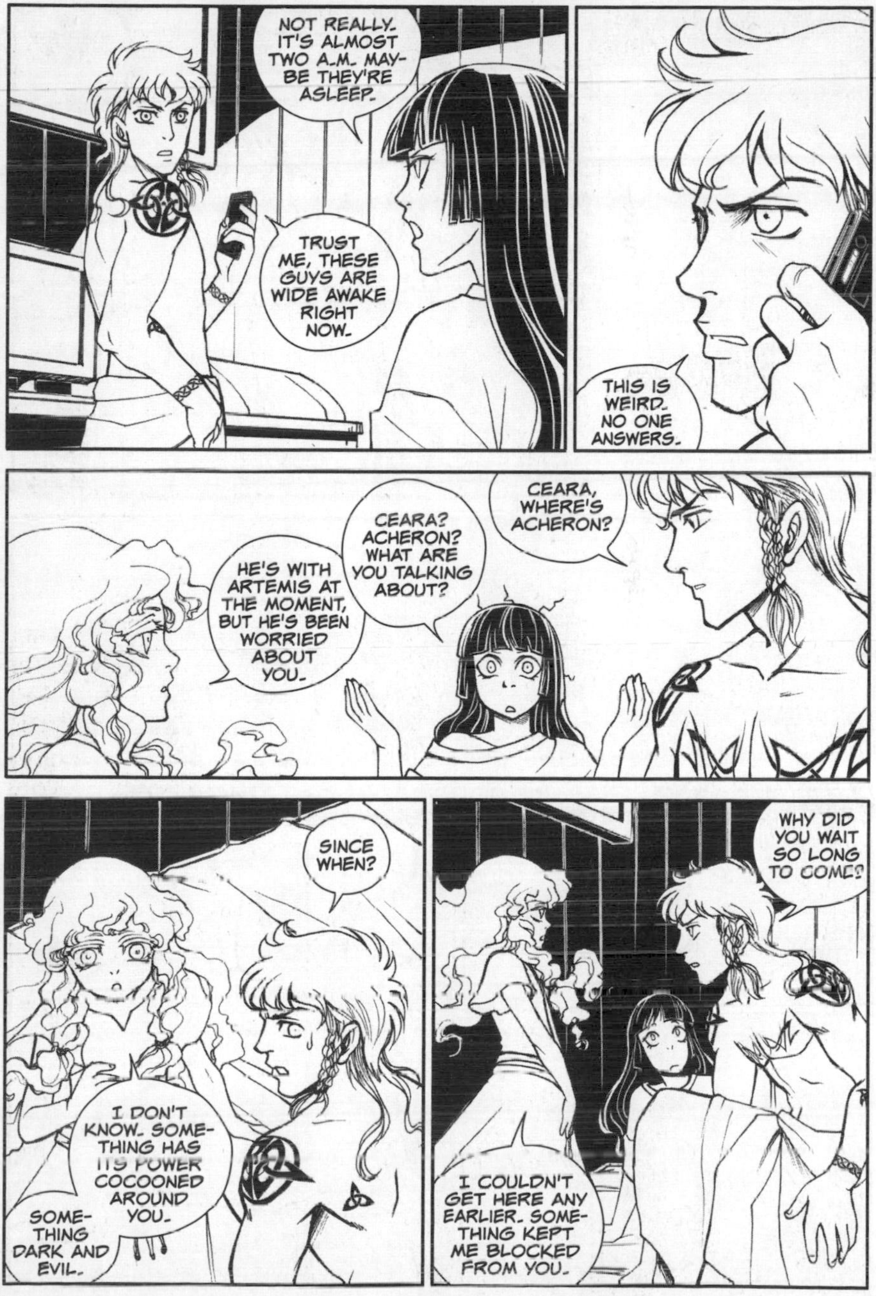
NOT REALLY. IT'S ALMOST TWO A.M. MAYBE THEY'RE ASLEEP.
TRUST ME, THESE GUYS ARE WIDE AWAKE RIGHT NOW.
THIS IS WEIRD. NO ONE ANSWERS.
CEARA, WHERE'S ACHERON?
CEARA? ACHERON? WHAT ARE YOU TALKING ABOUT?
HE'S WITH ARTEMIS AT THE MOMENT, BUT HE'S BEEN WORRIED ABOUT YOU.
SINCE WHEN?
I DON'T KNOW. SOMETHING HAS ITS POWER COCOONED AROUND YOU.
SOMETHING DARK AND EVIL.
WHY DID YOU WAIT SO LONG TO COME?
I COULDN'T GET HERE ANY EARLIER. SOMETHING KEPT ME BLOCKED FROM YOU.

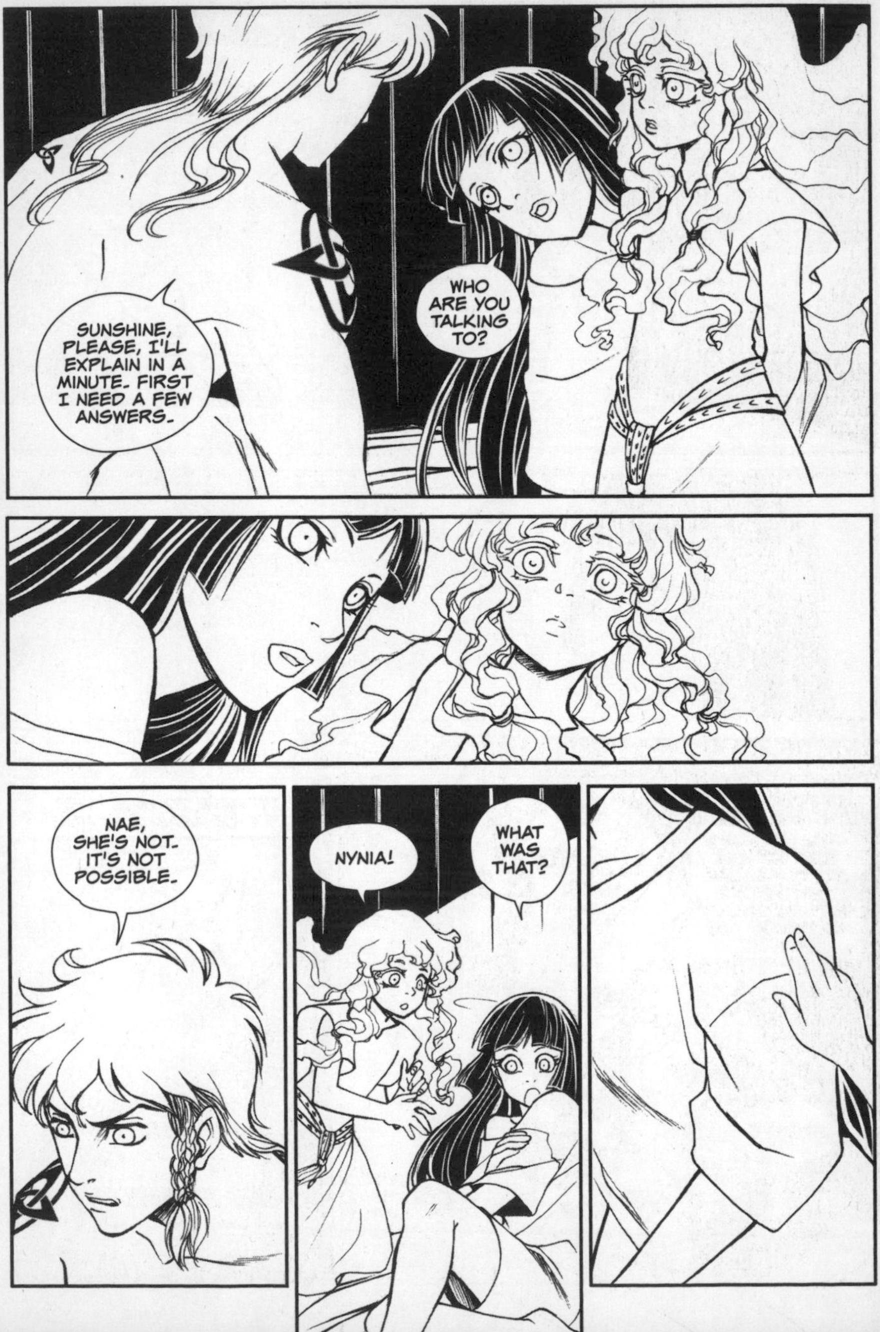
SUNSHINE, PLEASE, I'LL EXPLAIN IN A MINUTE. FIRST I NEED A FEW ANSWERS.
WHO ARE YOU TALKING TO?
NAE, SHE'S NOT. IT'S NOT POSSIBLE.
NYNIA!
WHAT WAS THAT?

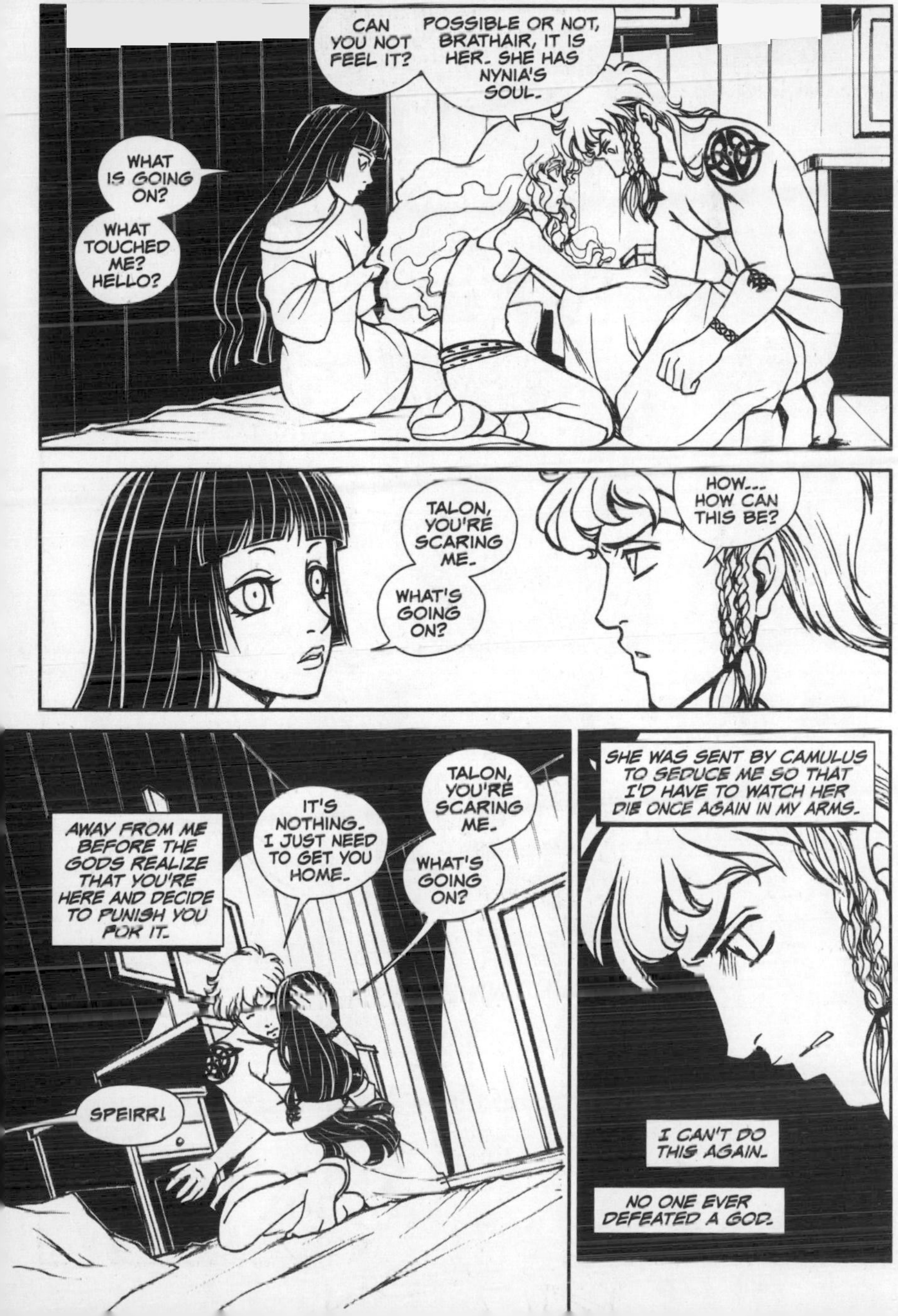
CAN YOU NOT FEEL IT?
POSSIBLE OR NOT, BRATHAIR, IT IS HER. SHE HAS NYNIA'S SOUL.
WHAT IS GOING ON?
WHAT TOUCHED ME? HELLO?
TALON, YOU'RE SCARING ME.
WHAT'S GOING ON?
HOW... HOW CAN THIS BE?
AWAY FROM ME BEFORE THE GODS REALIZE THAT YOU'RE HERE AND DECIDE TO PUNISH YOU FOR IT.
IT'S NOTHING. I JUST NEED TO GET YOU HOME.
TALON, YOU'RE SCARING ME.
WHAT'S GOING ON?
SPEIRR!
SHE WAS SENT BY CAMULUS TO SEDUCE ME SO THAT I'D HAVE TO WATCH HER DIE ONCE AGAIN IN MY ARMS.
I CAN'T DO THIS AGAIN.
NO ONE EVER DEFEATED A GOD.

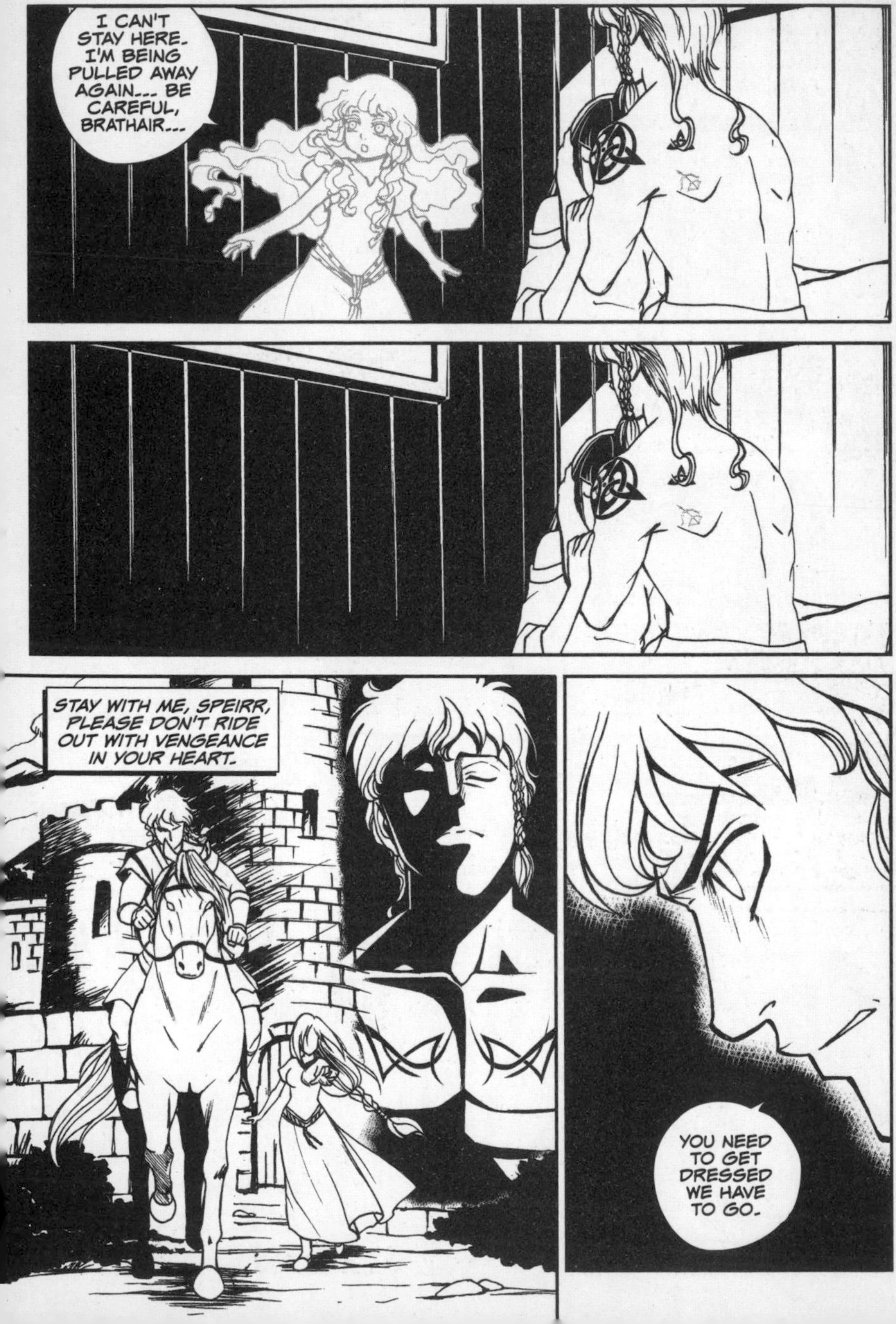
I CAN'T STAY HERE. I'M BEING PULLED AWAY AGAIN... BE CAREFUL, BRATHAIR...
STAY WITH ME, SPEIRR, PLEASE DON'T RIDE OUT WITH VENGEANCE IN YOUR HEART.
YOU NEED TO GET DRESSED WE HAVE TO GO.

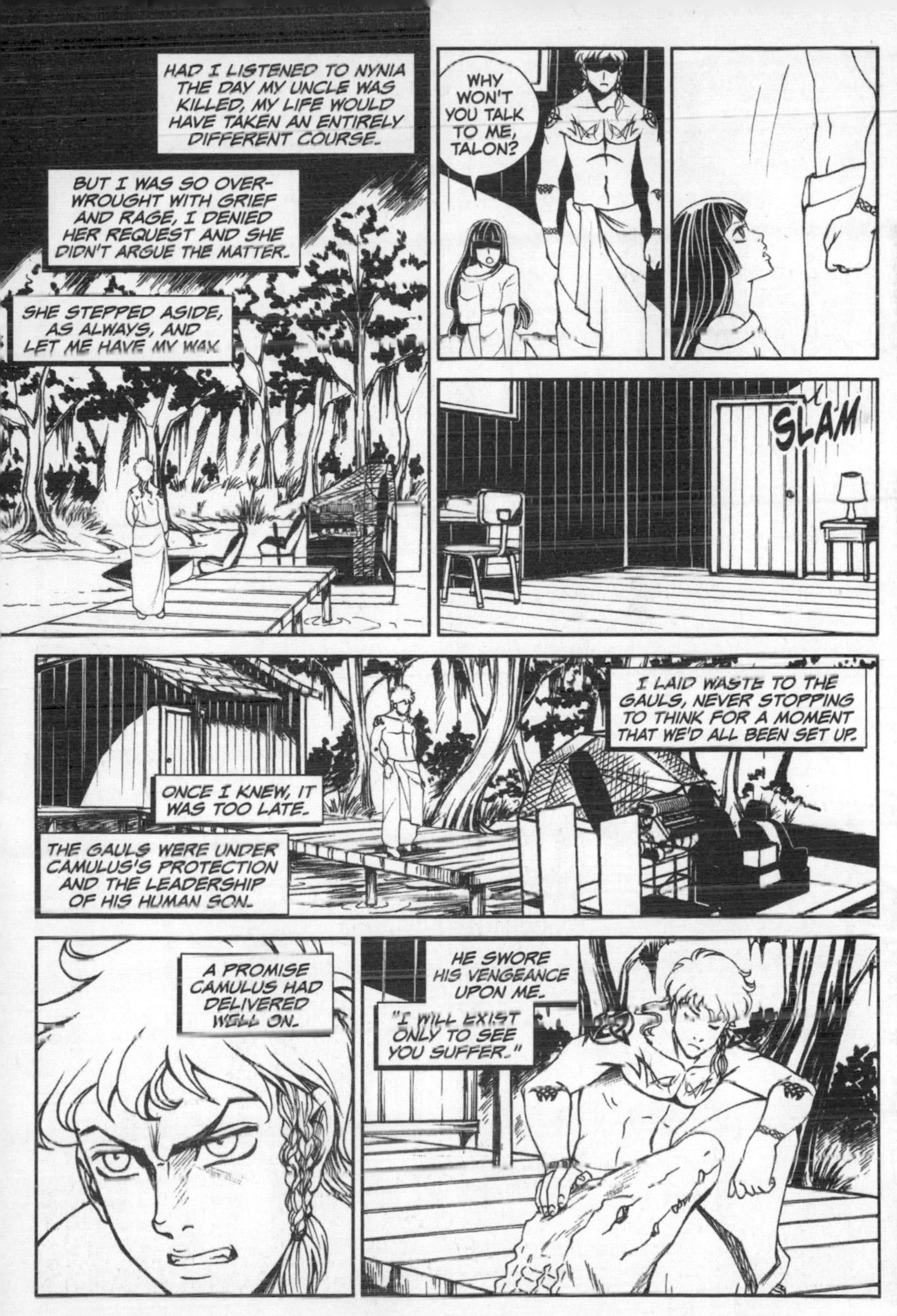
HAD I LISTENED TO NYNIA THE DAY MY UNCLE WAS KILLED, MY LIFE WOULD HAVE TAKEN AN ENTIRELY DIFFERENT COURSE.
BUT I WAS SO OVER-WROUGHT WITH GRIEF AND RAGE, I DENIED HER REQUEST AND SHE DIDN'T ARGUE THE MATTER.
SHE STEPPED ASIDE, AS ALWAYS, AND LET ME HAVE MY WAY.
WHY WON'T YOU TALK TO ME, TALON?
SLAM
I LAID WASTE TO THE GAULS, NEVER STOPPING TO THINK FOR A MOMENT THAT WE'D ALL BEEN SET UP.
ONCE I KNEW, IT WAS TOO LATE.
THE GAULS WERE UNDER CAMULUS'S PROTECTION AND THE LEADERSHIP OF HIS HUMAN SON.
A PROMISE CAMULUS HAD DELIVERED WELL ON.
HE SWORE HIS VENGEANCE UPON ME.
"I WILL EXIST ONLY TO SEE YOU SUFFER."

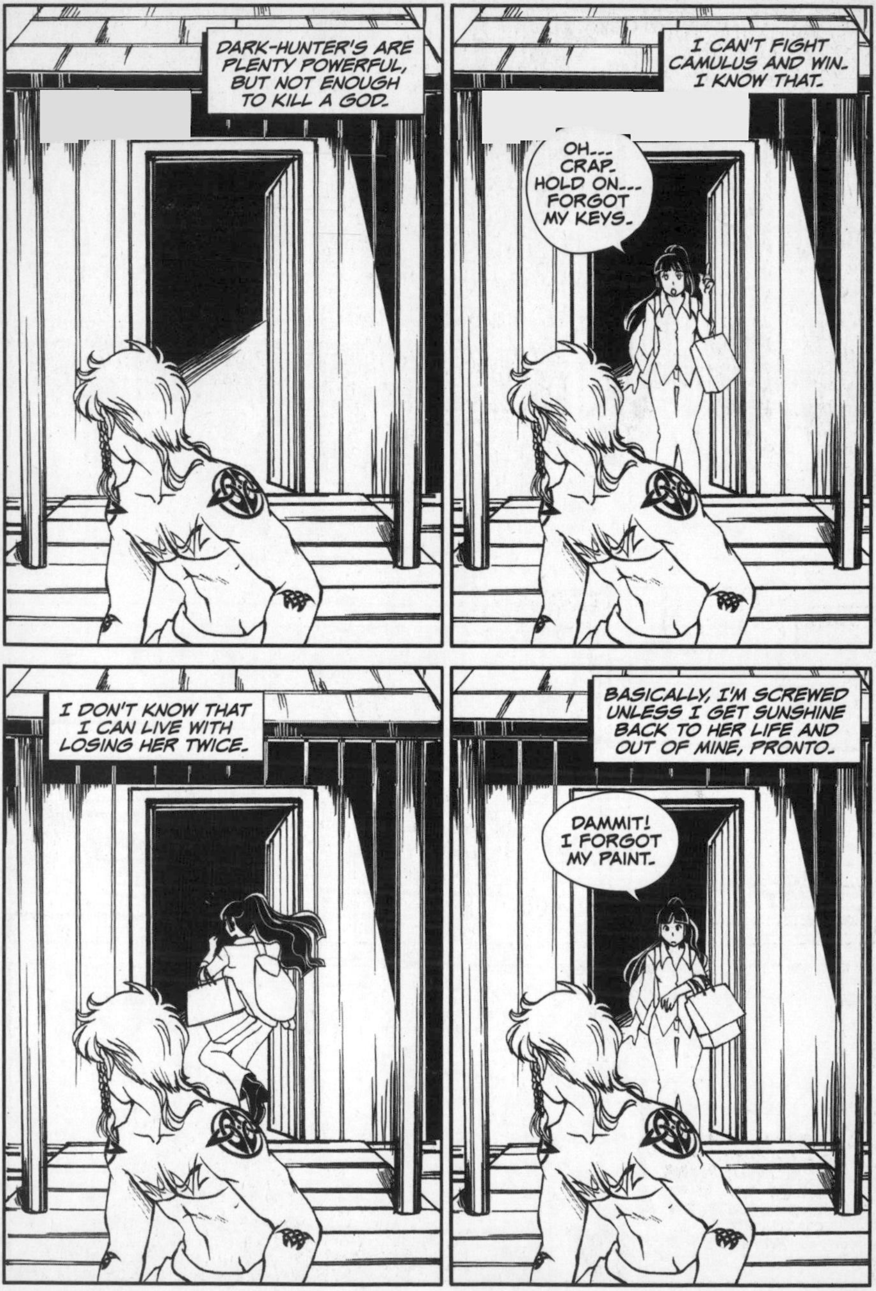
DARK-HUNTER'S ARE PLENTY POWERFUL, BUT NOT ENOUGH TO KILL A GOD.
I CAN'T FIGHT CAMULUS AND WIN. I KNOW THAT.
OH... CRAP. HOLD ON... FORGOT MY KEYS.
I DON'T KNOW THAT I CAN LIVE WITH LOSING HER TWICE.
BASICALLY, I'M SCREWED UNLESS I GET SUNSHINE BACK TO HER LIFE AND OUT OF MINE, PRONTO.
DAMMIT! I FORGOT MY PAINT.

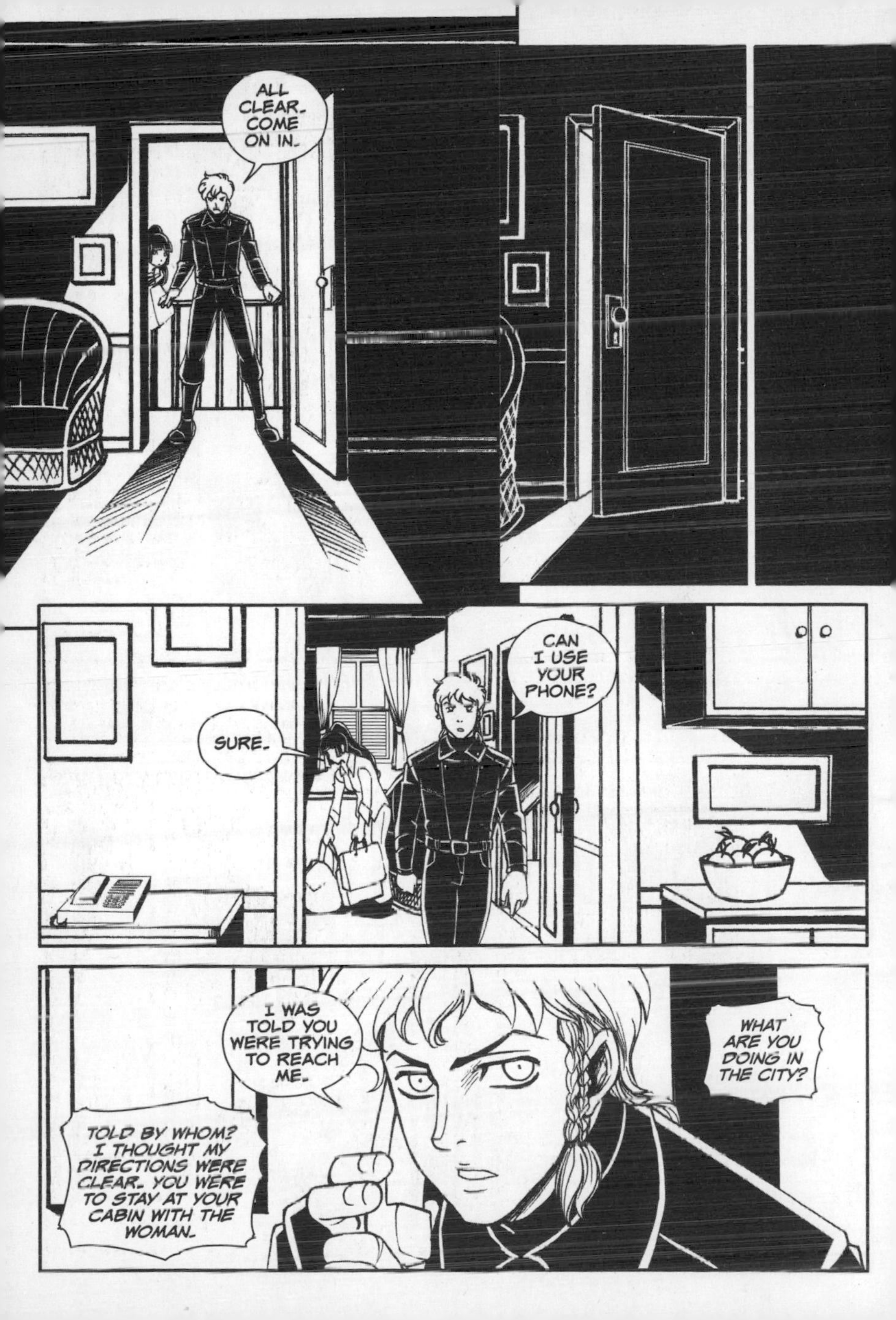
ALL CLEAR. COME ON IN.
CAN I USE YOUR PHONE?
SURE.
I WAS TOLD YOU WERE TRYING TO REACH ME.
WHAT ARE YOU DOING IN THE CITY?
TOLD BY WHOM? I THOUGHT MY DIRECTIONS WERE CLEAR. YOU WERE TO STAY AT YOUR CABIN WITH THE WOMAN.

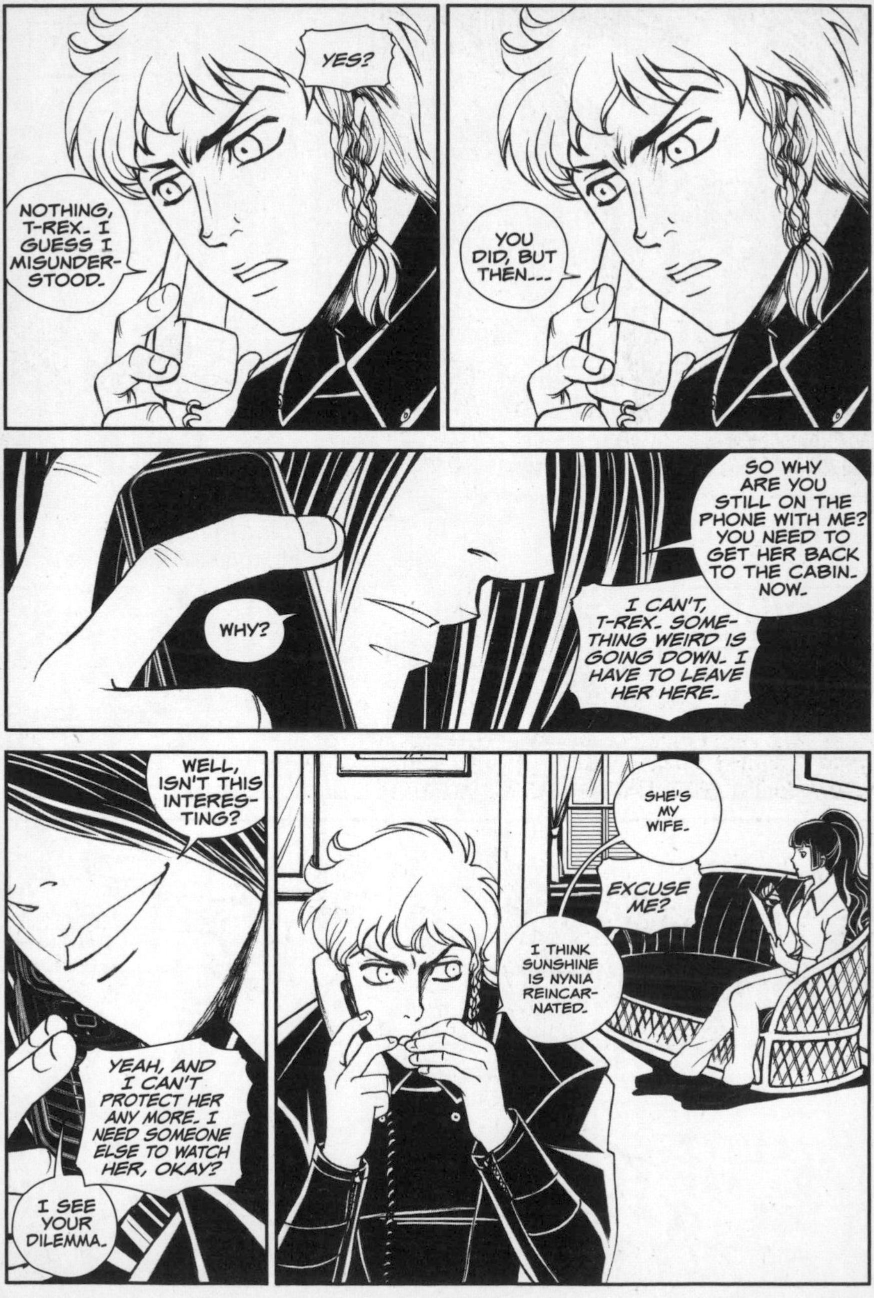
YES?
NOTHING, T-REX. I GUESS I MISUNDERSTOOD.
YOU DID, BUT THEN...
SO WHY ARE YOU STILL ON THE PHONE WITH ME? YOU NEED TO GET HER BACK TO THE CABIN. NOW.
WHY?
I CAN'T, T-REX. SOMETHING WEIRD IS GOING DOWN. I HAVE TO LEAVE HER HERE.
WELL, ISN'T THIS INTERESTING?
SHE'S MY WIFE.
EXCUSE ME?
I THINK SUNSHINE IS NYNIA REINCARNATED.
YEAH, AND I CAN'T PROTECT HER ANY MORE. I NEED SOMEONE ELSE TO WATCH HER, OKAY?
I SEE YOUR DILEMMA.

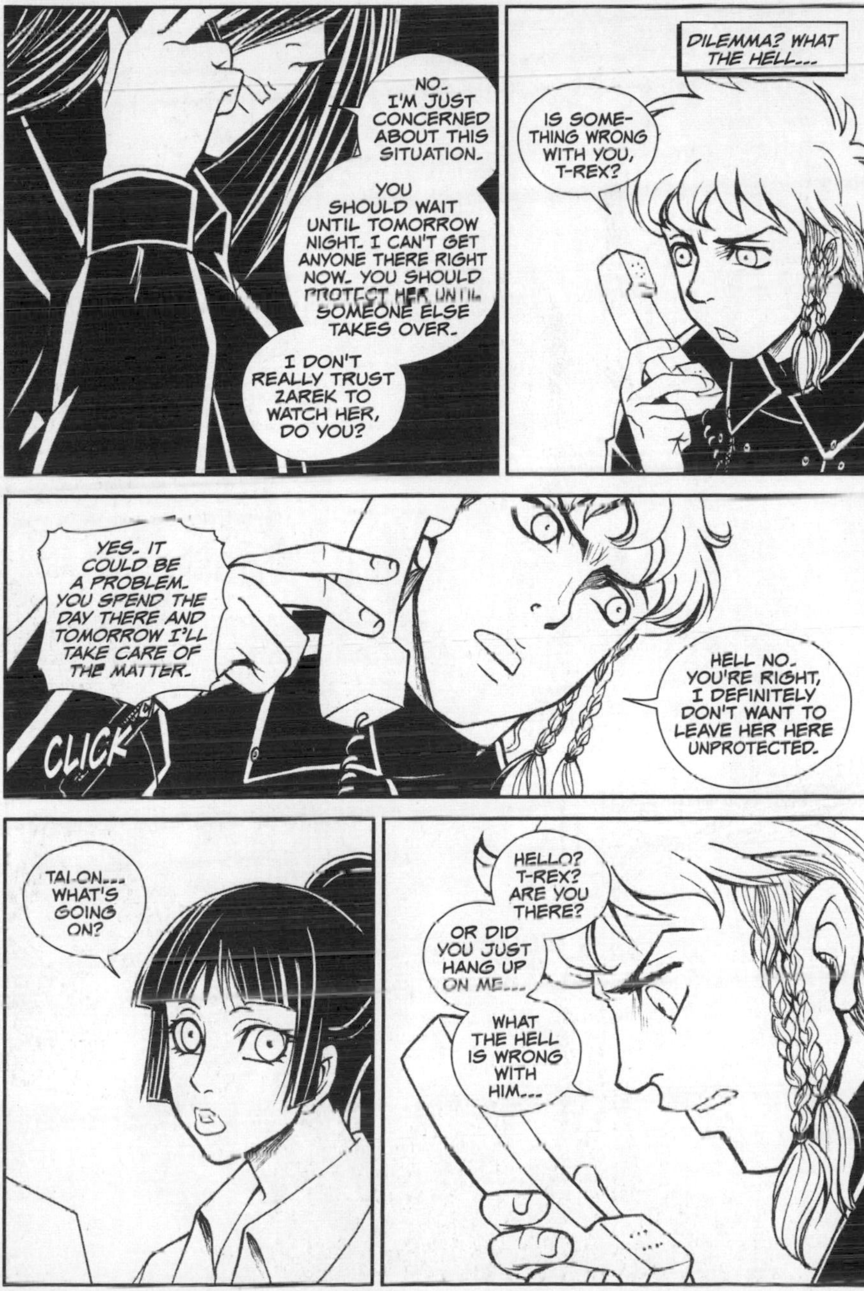
NO. I'M JUST CONCERNED ABOUT THIS SITUATION.
YOU SHOULD WAIT UNTIL TOMORROW NIGHT. I CAN'T GET ANYONE THERE RIGHT NOW. YOU SHOULD PROTECT HER UNTIL SOMEONE ELSE TAKES OVER.
I DON'T REALLY TRUST ZAREK TO WATCH HER, DO YOU?
DILEMMA? WHAT THE HELL...
IS SOMETHING WRONG WITH YOU, T-REX?
YES. IT COULD BE A PROBLEM. YOU SPEND THE DAY THERE AND TOMORROW I'LL TAKE CARE OF THE MATTER.
HELL NO. YOU'RE RIGHT, I DEFINITELY DON'T WANT TO LEAVE HER HERE UNPROTECTED.
CLICK
TAI-ON... WHAT'S GOING ON?
HELLO? T-REX? ARE YOU THERE?
OR DID YOU JUST HANG UP ON ME...
WHAT THE HELL IS WRONG WITH HIM...

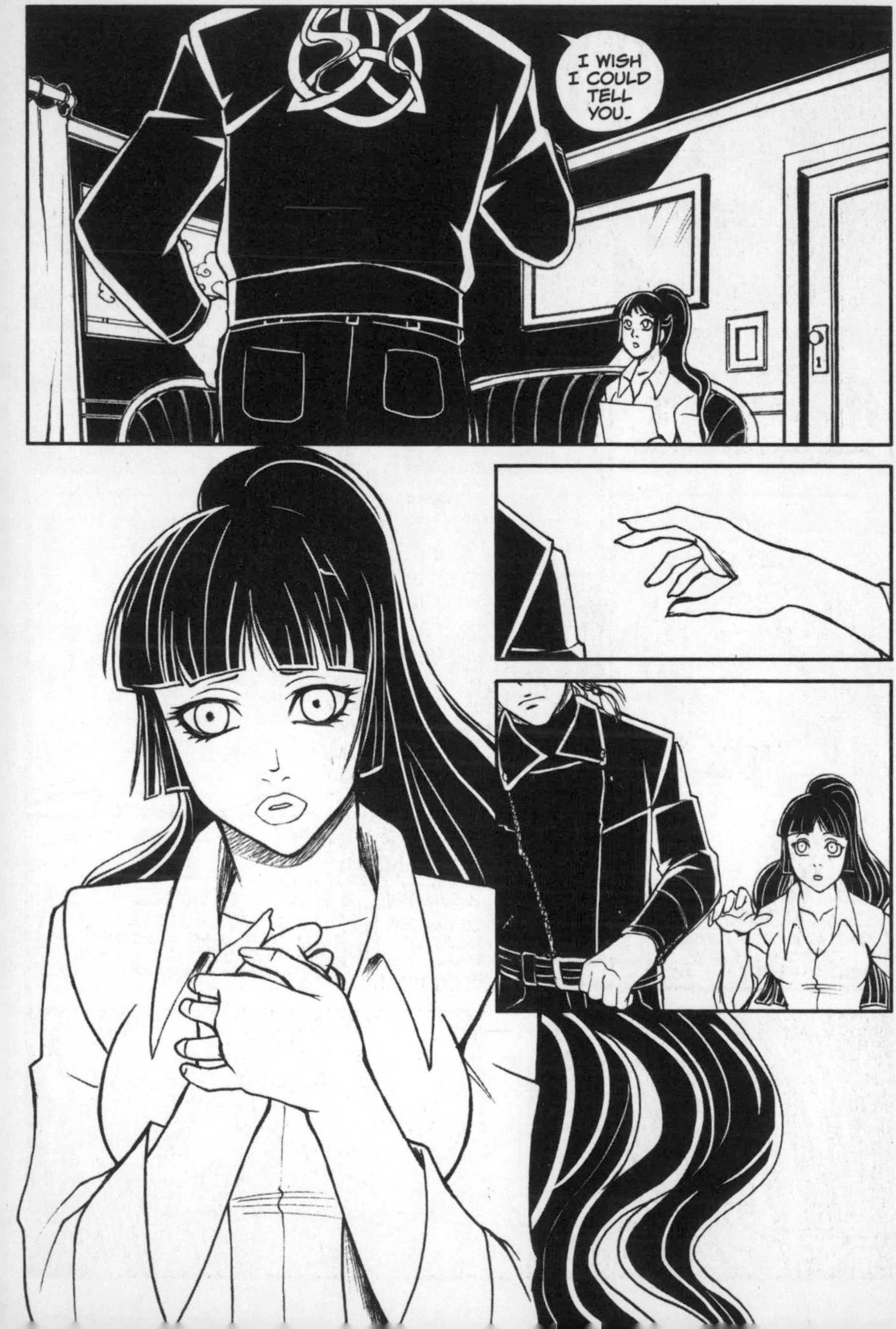
I WISH I COULD TELL YOU_

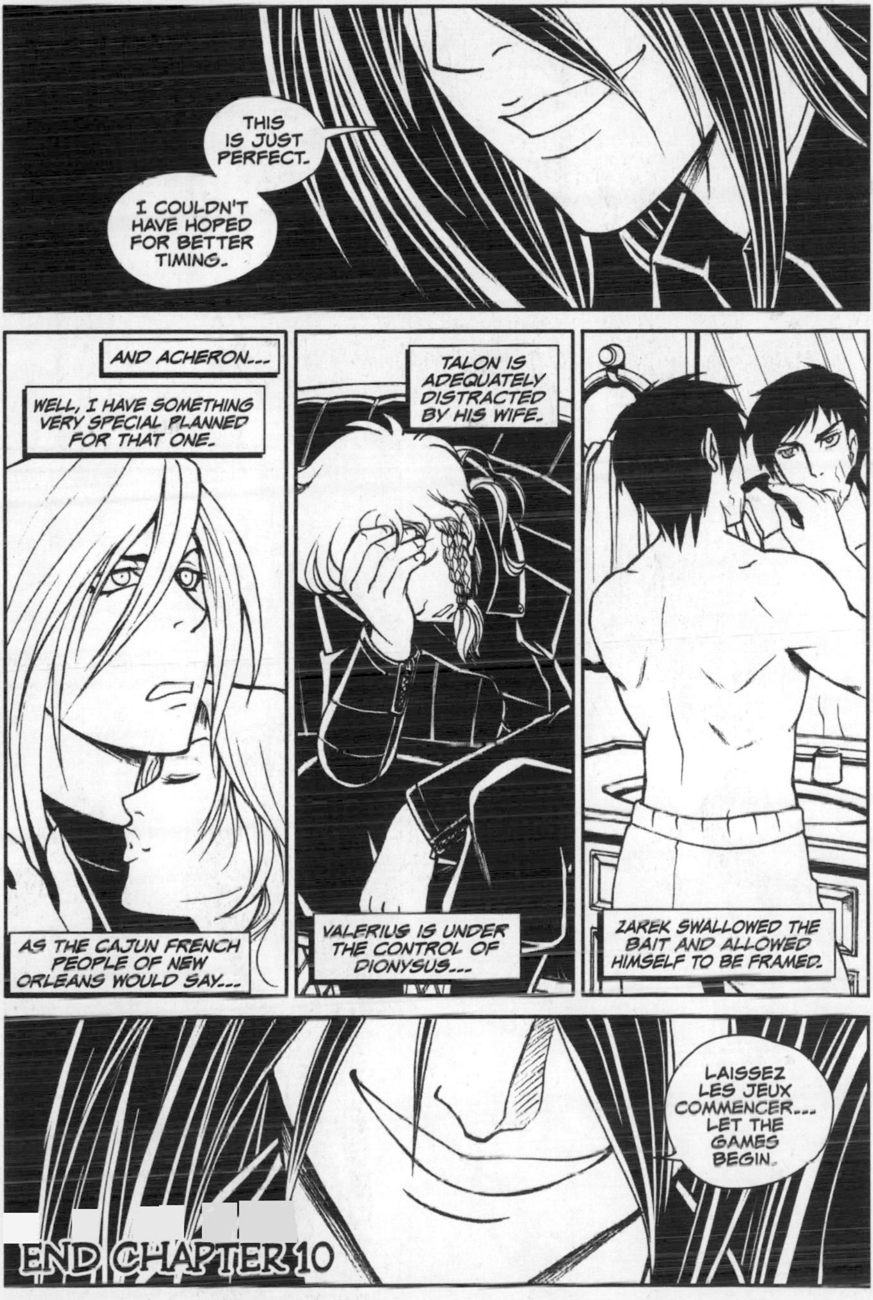
THIS IS JUST PERFECT.
I COULDN'T HAVE HOPED FOR BETTER TIMING.
AND ACHERON...
WELL, I HAVE SOMETHING VERY SPECIAL PLANNED FOR THAT ONE.
AS THE CAJUN FRENCH PEOPLE OF NEW ORLEANS WOULD SAY...
TALON IS ADEQUATELY DISTRACTED BY HIS WIFE.
VALERIUS IS UNDER THE CONTROL OF DIONYSUS...
ZAREK SWALLOWED THE BAIT AND ALLOWED HIMSELF TO BE FRAMED.
LAISSEZ LES JEUX COMMENCER... LET THE GAMES BEGIN.
END CHAPTER 10

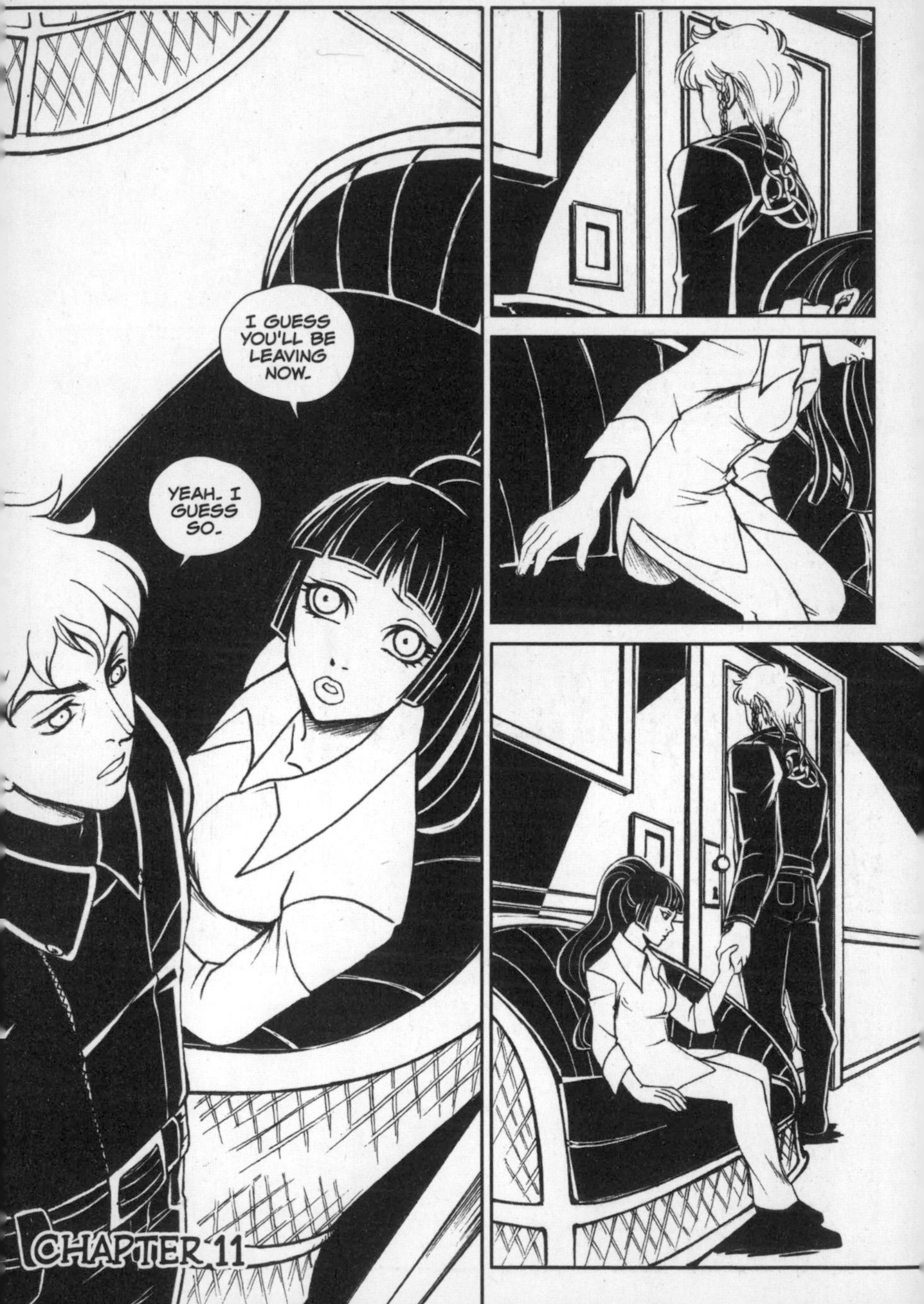

I GUESS YOU'LL BE LEAVING NOW.
YEAH. I GUESS SO.
CHAPTER 11

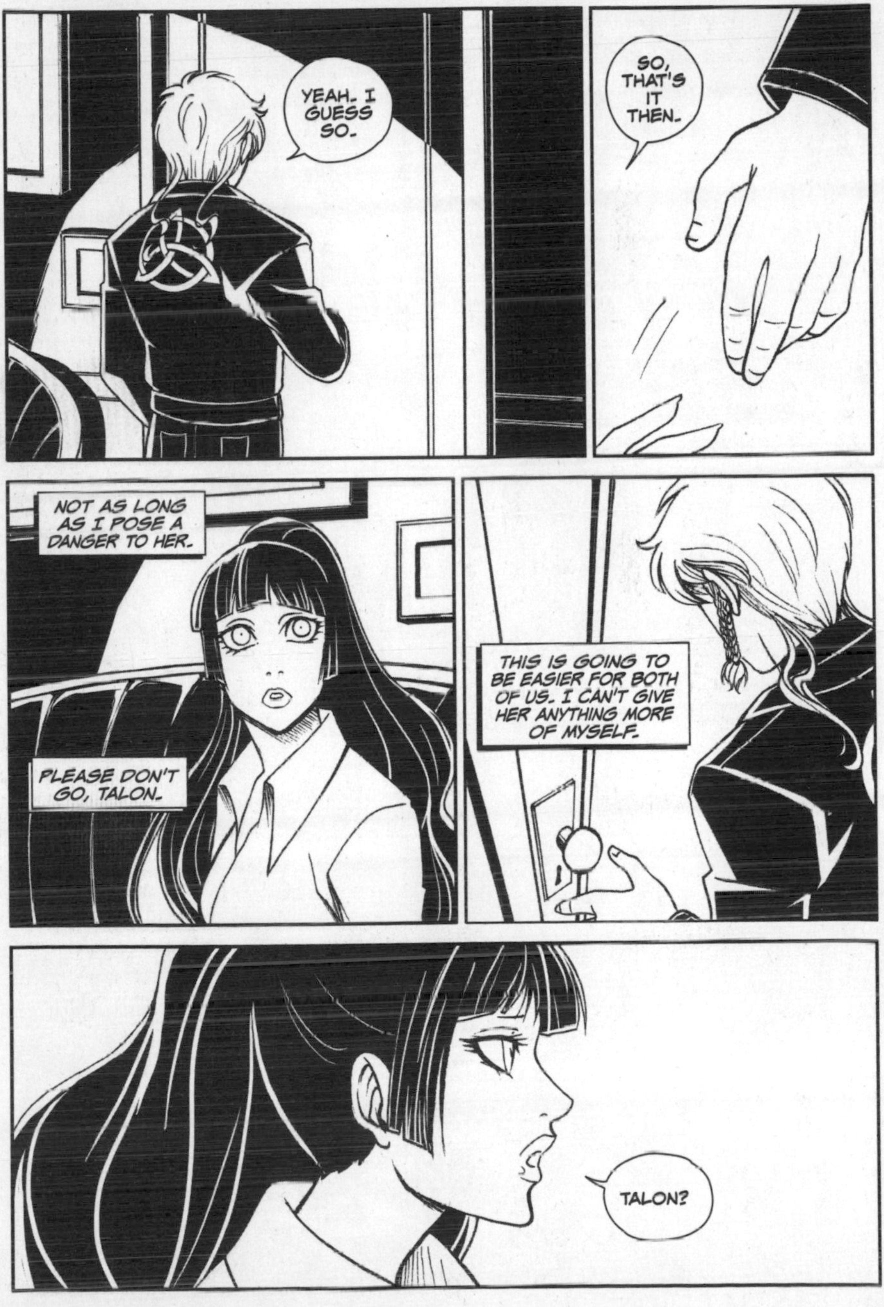

YEAH. I GUESS SO.
SO, THAT'S IT THEN.
NOT AS LONG AS I POSE A DANGER TO HER.
PLEASE DON'T GO, TALON.
THIS IS GOING TO BE EASIER FOR BOTH OF US. I CAN'T GIVE HER ANYTHING MORE OF MYSELF.
TALON?

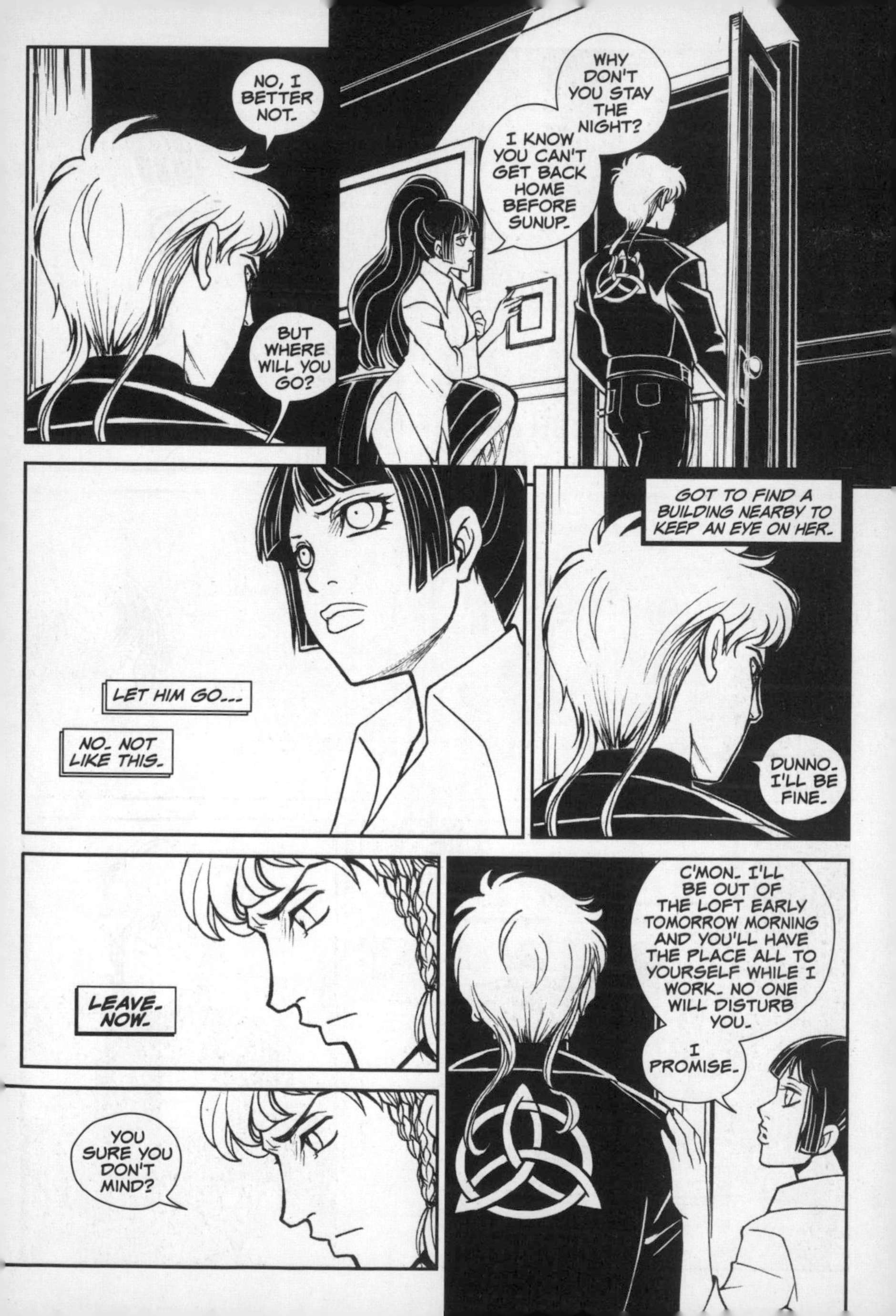
NO, I BETTER NOT.
BUT WHERE WILL YOU GO?
WHY DON'T YOU STAY THE NIGHT?
I KNOW YOU CAN'T GET BACK HOME BEFORE SUNUP.
LET HIM GO...
NO. NOT LIKE THIS.
GOT TO FIND A BUILDING NEARBY TO KEEP AN EYE ON HER.
DUNNO. I'LL BE FINE.
LEAVE. NOW.
YOU SURE YOU DON'T MIND?
C'MON. I'LL BE OUT OF THE LOFT EARLY TOMORROW MORNING AND YOU'LL HAVE THE PLACE ALL TO YOURSELF WHILE I WORK. NO ONE WILL DISTURB YOU.
I PROMISE.

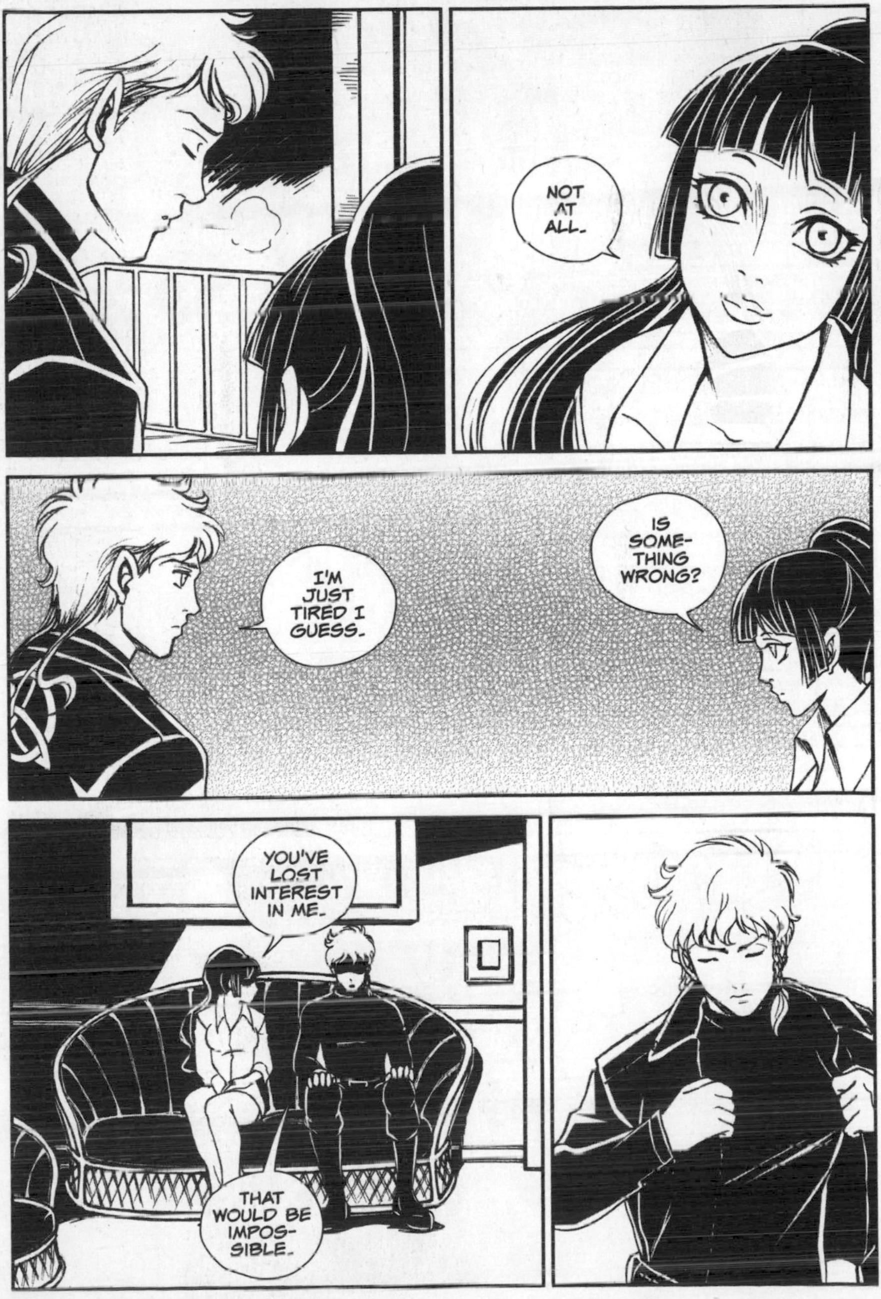

NOT AT ALL.
IS SOMETHING WRONG?
I'M JUST TIRED I GUESS.
YOU'VE LOST INTEREST IN ME.
THAT WOULD BE IMPOSSIBLE.

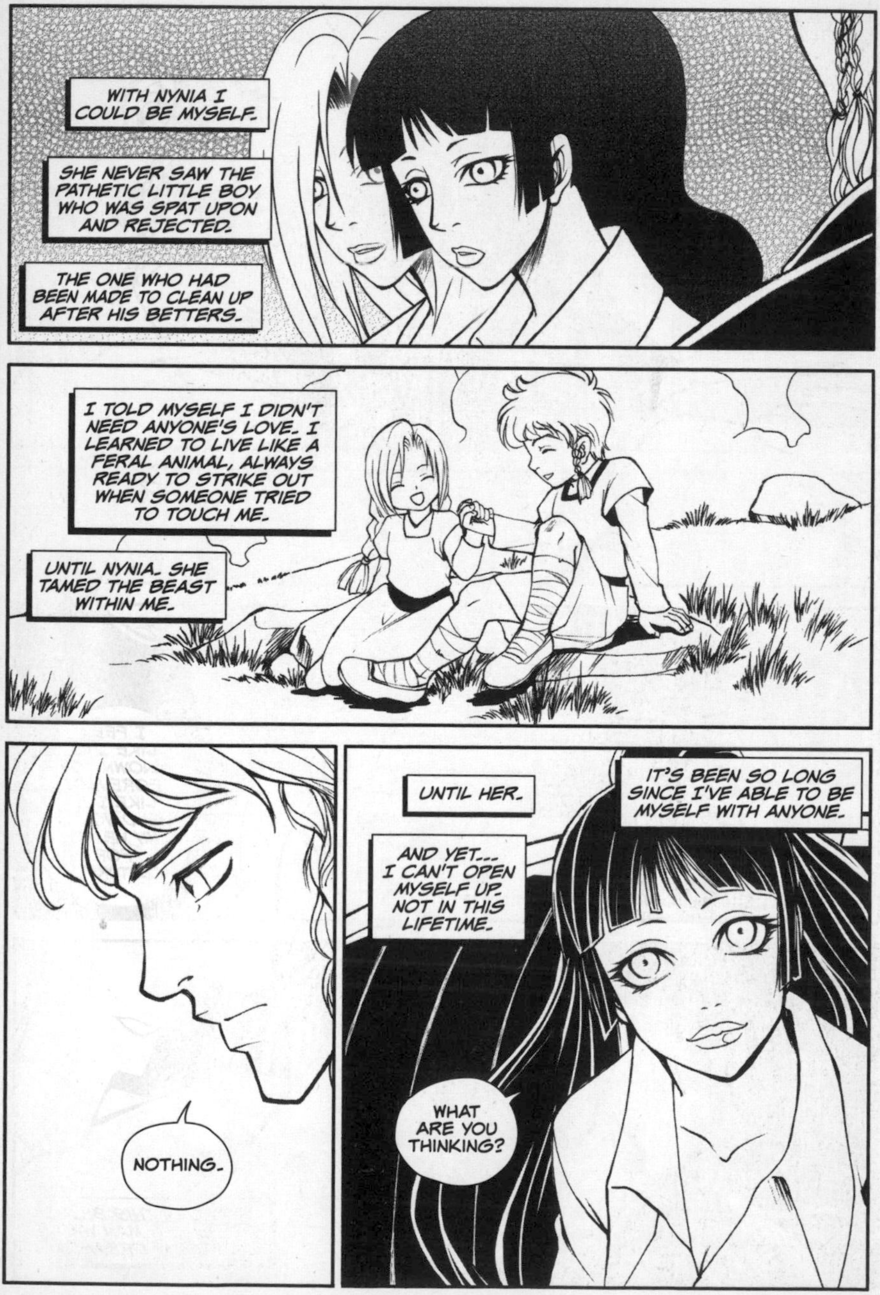
WITH NYNIA I COULD BE MYSELF.
SHE NEVER SAW THE PATHETIC LITTLE BOY WHO WAS SPAT UPON AND REJECTED.
THE ONE WHO HAD BEEN MADE TO CLEAN UP AFTER HIS BETTERS.
I TOLD MYSELF I DIDN'T NEED ANYONE'S LOVE. I LEARNED TO LIVE LIKE A FERAL ANIMAL, ALWAYS READY TO STRIKE OUT WHEN SOMEONE TRIED TO TOUCH ME.
UNTIL NYNIA. SHE TAMED THE BEAST WITHIN ME.
NOTHING.
IT'S BEEN SO LONG SINCE I'VE ABLE TO BE MYSELF WITH ANYONE.
UNTIL HER.
AND YET... I CAN'T OPEN MYSELF UP. NOT IN THIS LIFETIME.
WHAT ARE YOU THINKING?

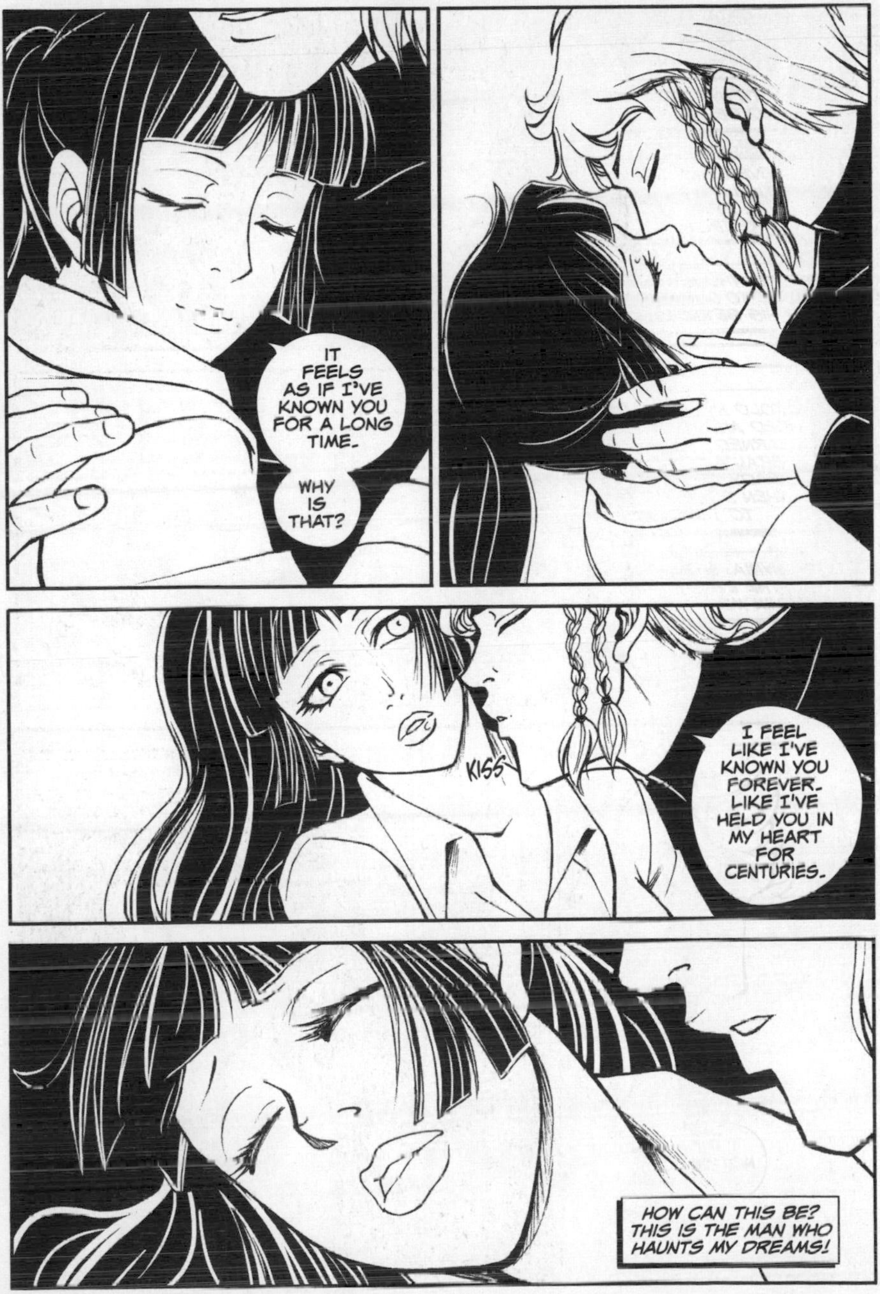
IT FEELS AS IF I'VE KNOWN YOU FOR A LONG TIME.
WHY IS THAT?
KISS
I FEEL LIKE I'VE KNOWN YOU FOREVER. LIKE I'VE HELD YOU IN MY HEART FOR CENTURIES.
HOW CAN THIS BE? THIS IS THE MAN WHO HAUNTS MY DREAMS!

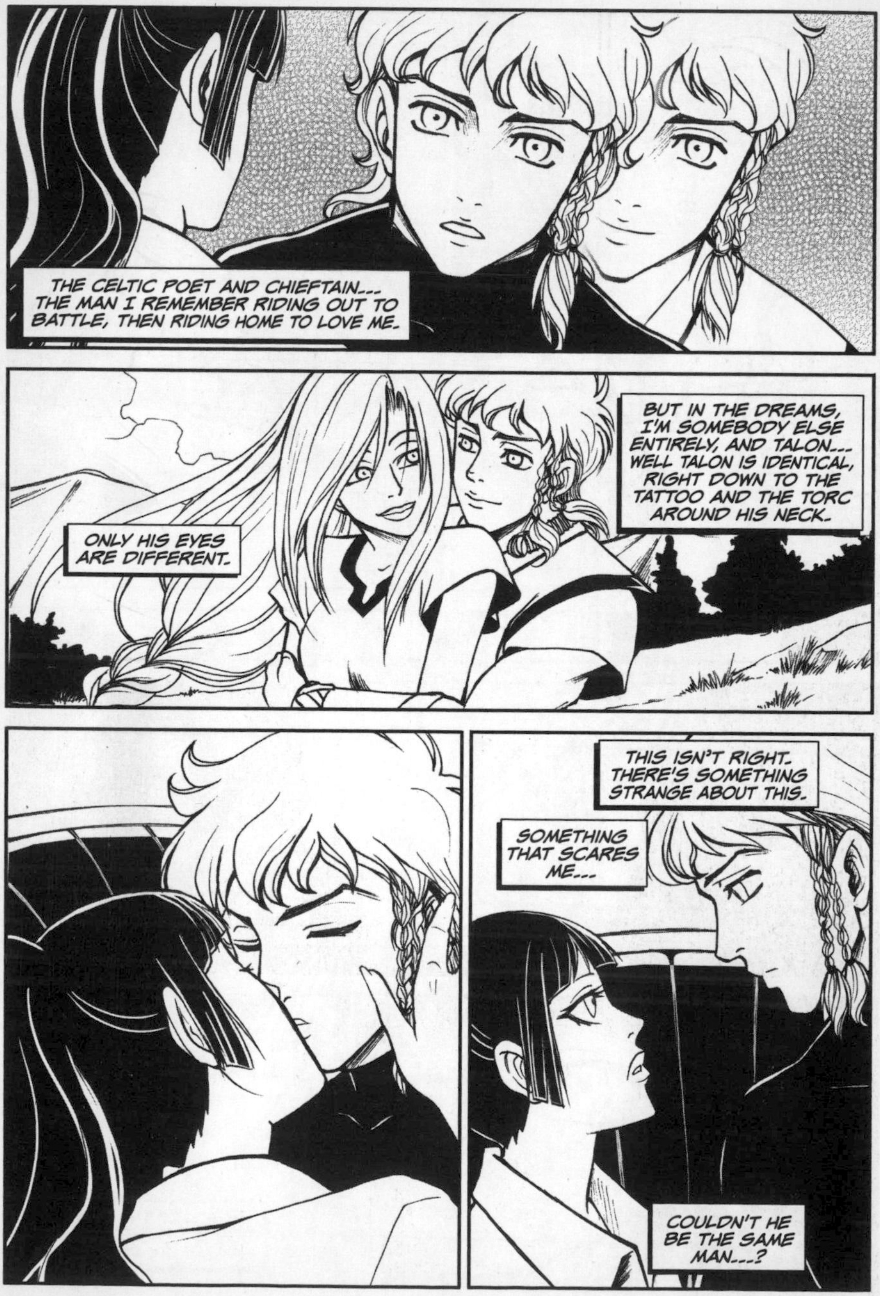
THE CELTIC POET AND CHIEFTAIN... THE MAN I REMEMBER RIDING OUT TO BATTLE, THEN RIDING HOME TO LOVE ME.
BUT IN THE DREAMS, I'M SOMEBODY ELSE ENTIRELY, AND TALON... WELL TALON IS IDENTICAL, RIGHT DOWN TO THE TATTOO AND THE TORC AROUND HIS NECK.
ONLY HIS EYES ARE DIFFERENT.
THIS ISN'T RIGHT. THERE'S SOMETHING STRANGE ABOUT THIS.
SOMETHING THAT SCARES ME...
COULDN'T HE BE THE SAME MAN...?

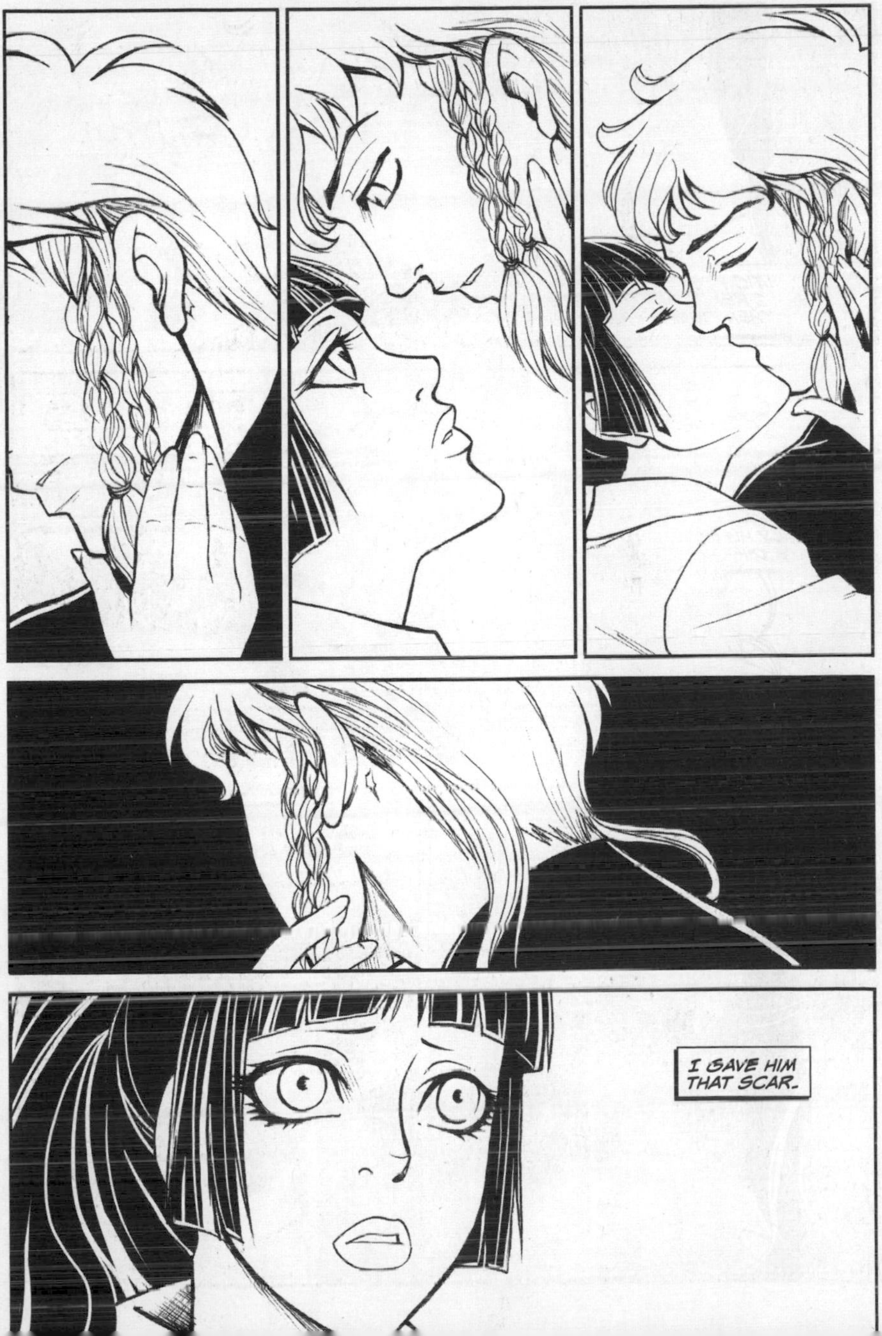
I GAVE HIM
THAT SCAR.

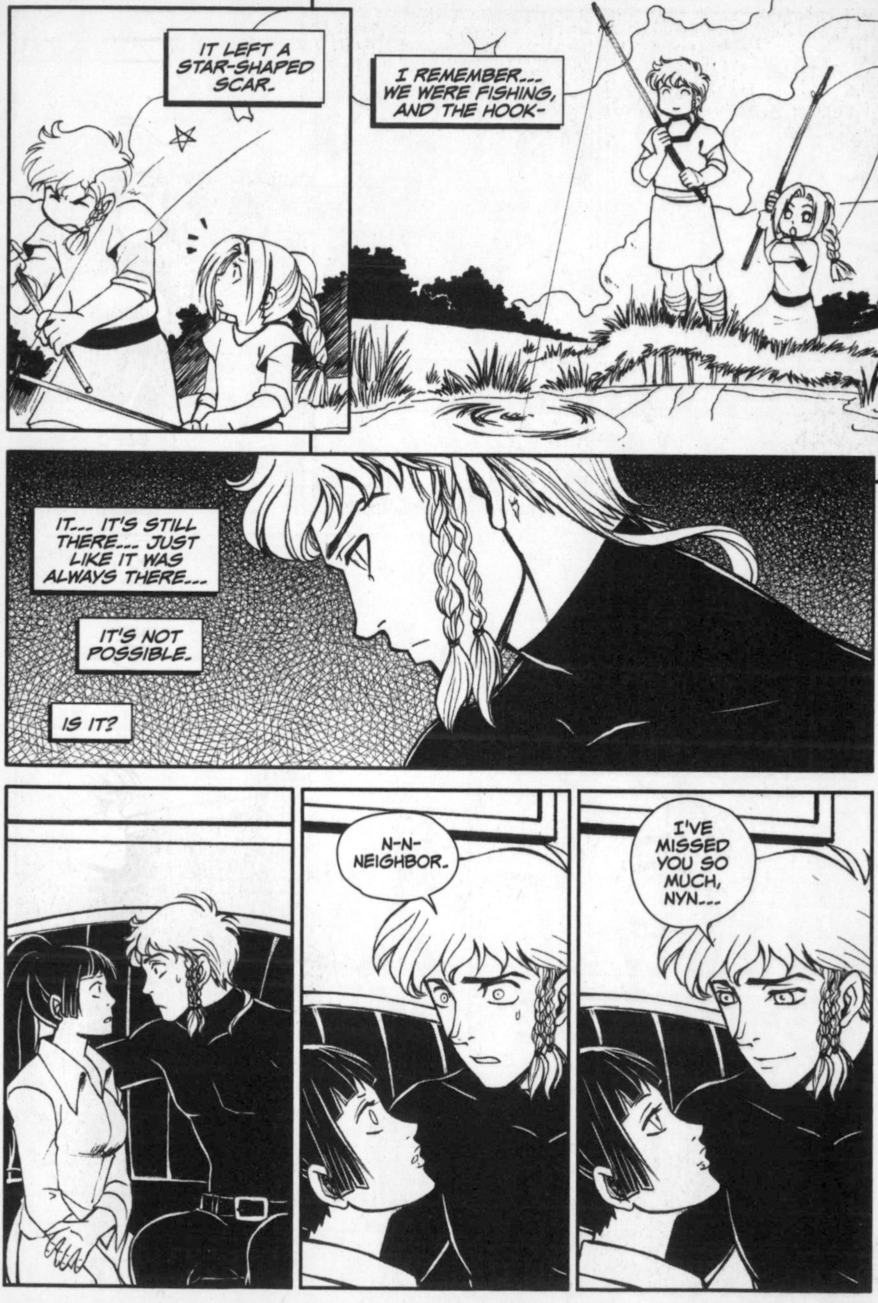

IT LEFT A STAR-SHAPED SCAR.
I REMEMBER... WE WERE FISHING, AND THE HOOK-
IT... IT'S STILL THERE... JUST LIKE IT WAS ALWAYS THERE...
IT'S NOT POSSIBLE.
IS IT?
N-N-NEIGHBOR.
I'VE MISSED YOU SO MUCH, NYN...

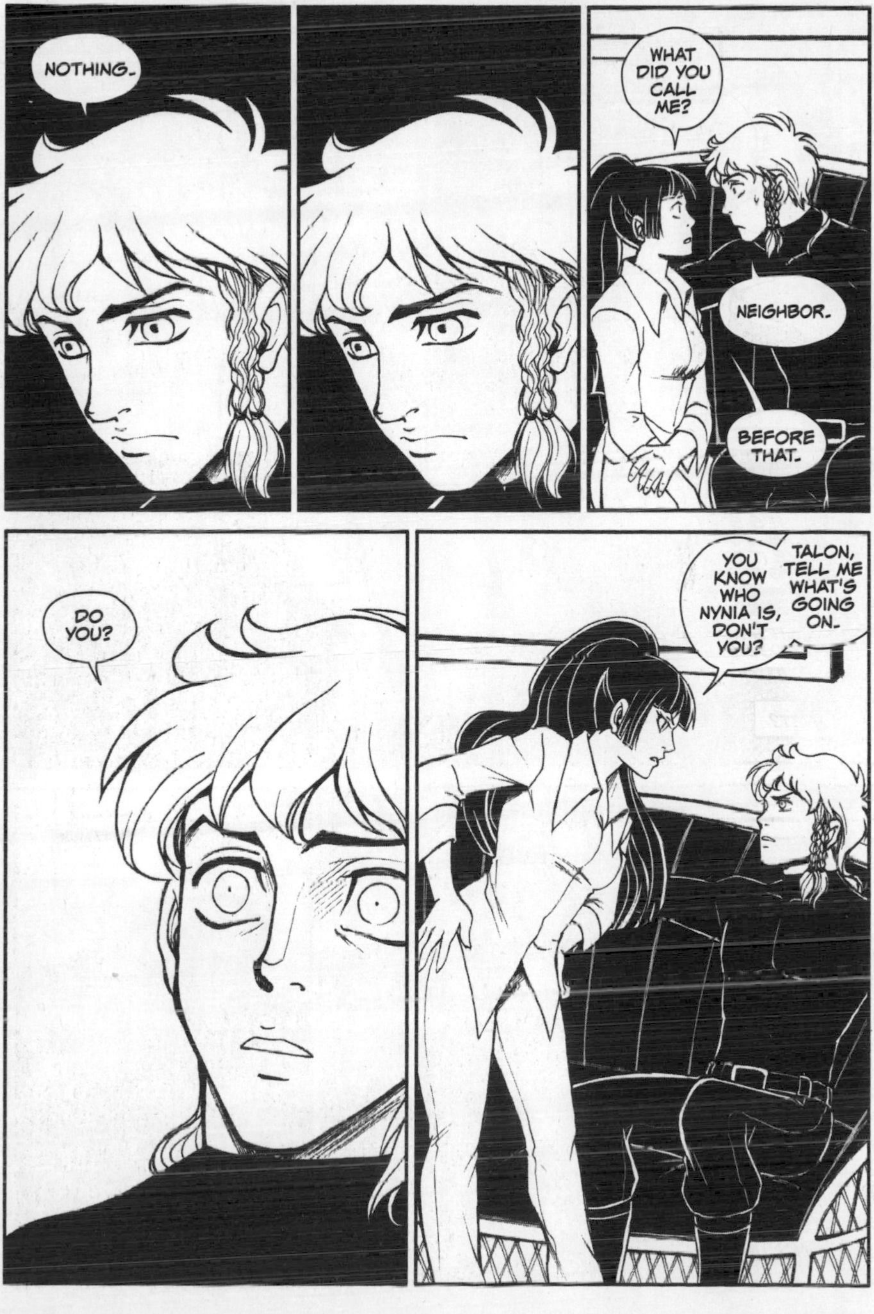
NOTHING.
WHAT DID YOU CALL ME?
NEIGHBOR.
BEFORE THAT.
DO YOU?
YOU KNOW WHO NYNIA IS, DON'T YOU?
TALON, TELL ME WHAT'S GOING ON.

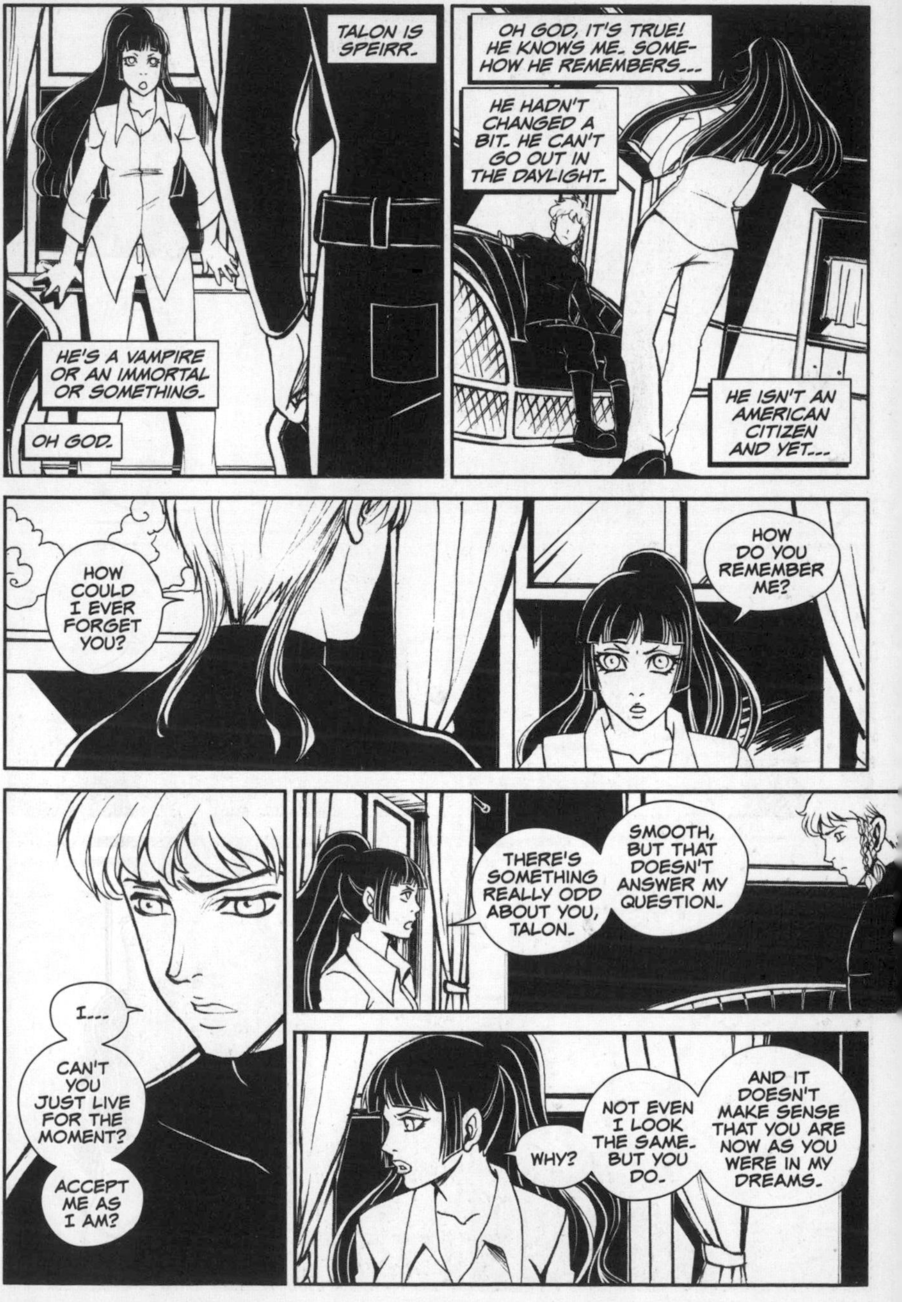

TALON IS SPEIRR.
HE'S A VAMPIRE OR AN IMMORTAL OR SOMETHING.
OH GOD.
OH GOD, IT'S TRUE! HE KNOWS ME. SOME-HOW HE REMEMBERS...
HE HADN'T CHANGED A BIT. HE CAN'T GO OUT IN THE DAYLIGHT.
HE ISN'T AN AMERICAN CITIZEN AND YET...
HOW COULD I EVER FORGET YOU?
HOW DO YOU REMEMBER ME?
THERE'S SOMETHING REALLY ODD ABOUT YOU, TALON.
SMOOTH, BUT THAT DOESN'T ANSWER MY QUESTION.
I...
CAN'T YOU JUST LIVE FOR THE MOMENT?
ACCEPT ME AS I AM?
WHY?
NOT EVEN I LOOK THE SAME. BUT YOU DO.
AND IT DOESN'T MAKE SENSE THAT YOU ARE NOW AS YOU WERE IN MY DREAMS.

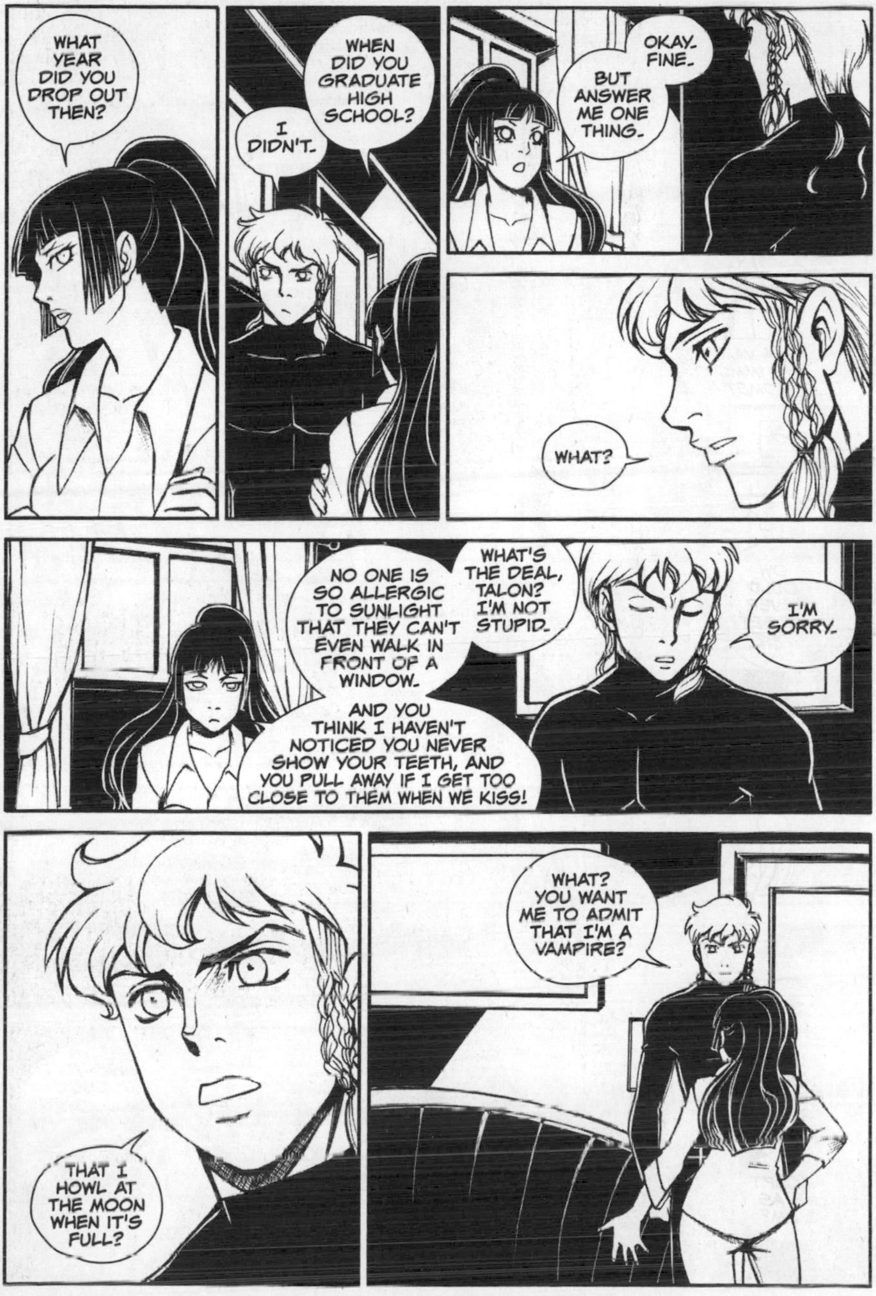
WHAT YEAR DID YOU DROP OUT THEN?
WHEN DID YOU GRADUATE HIGH SCHOOL?
I DIDN'T.
OKAY. FINE.
BUT ANSWER ME ONE THING.
WHAT?
WHAT'S THE DEAL, TALON? I'M NOT STUPID.
NO ONE IS SO ALLERGIC TO SUNLIGHT THAT THEY CAN'T EVEN WALK IN FRONT OF A WINDOW.
AND YOU THINK I HAVEN'T NOTICED YOU NEVER SHOW YOUR TEETH, AND YOU PULL AWAY IF I GET TOO CLOSE TO THEM WHEN WE KISS!
I'M SORRY.
WHAT? YOU WANT ME TO ADMIT THAT I'M A VAMPIRE?
THAT I HOWL AT THE MOON WHEN IT'S FULL?

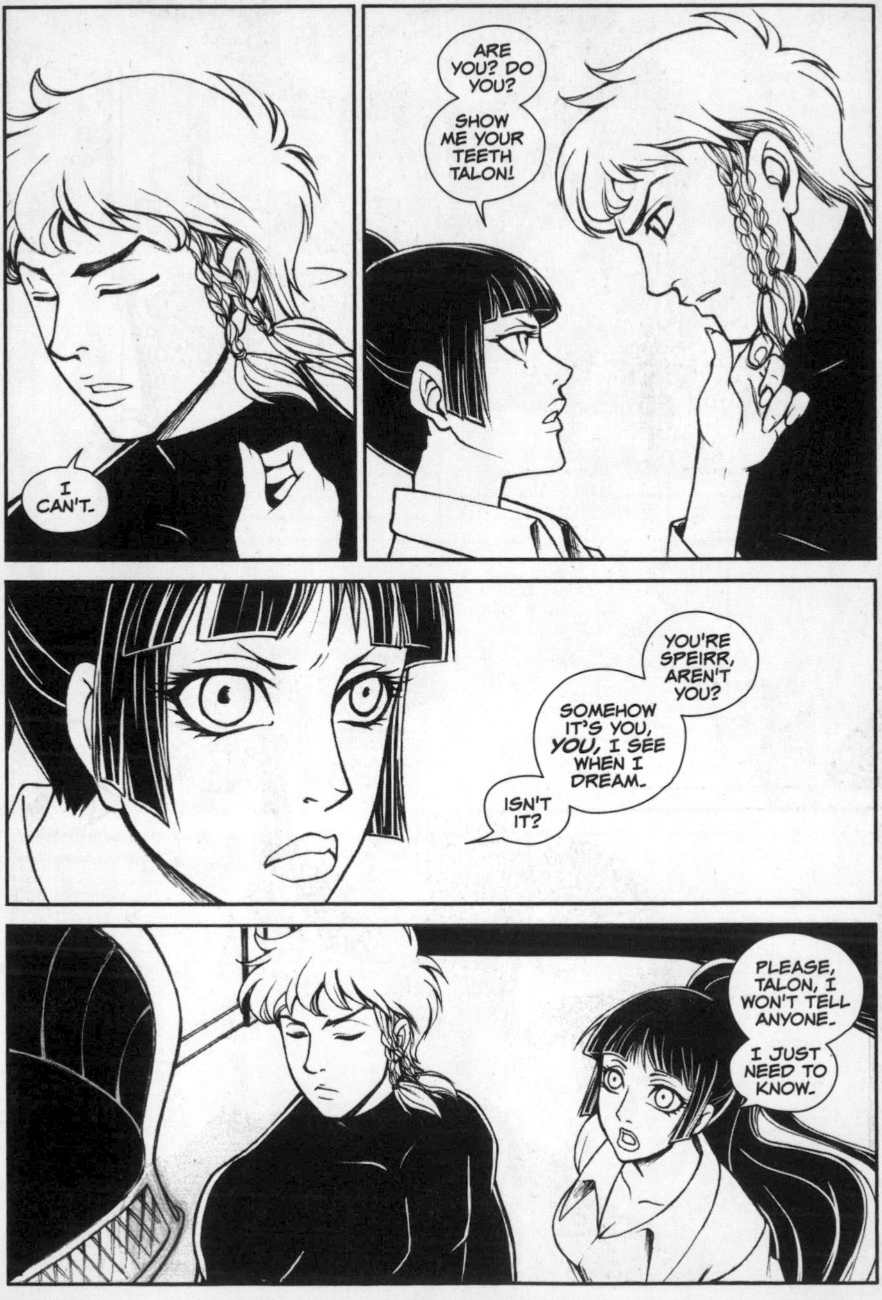
I CAN'T.
ARE YOU? DO YOU?
SHOW ME YOUR TEETH TALON!
YOU'RE SPEIRR, AREN'T YOU?
SOMEHOW IT'S YOU, *YOU,* I SEE WHEN I DREAM.
ISN'T IT?
PLEASE, TALON, I WON'T TELL ANYONE.
I JUST NEED TO KNOW.

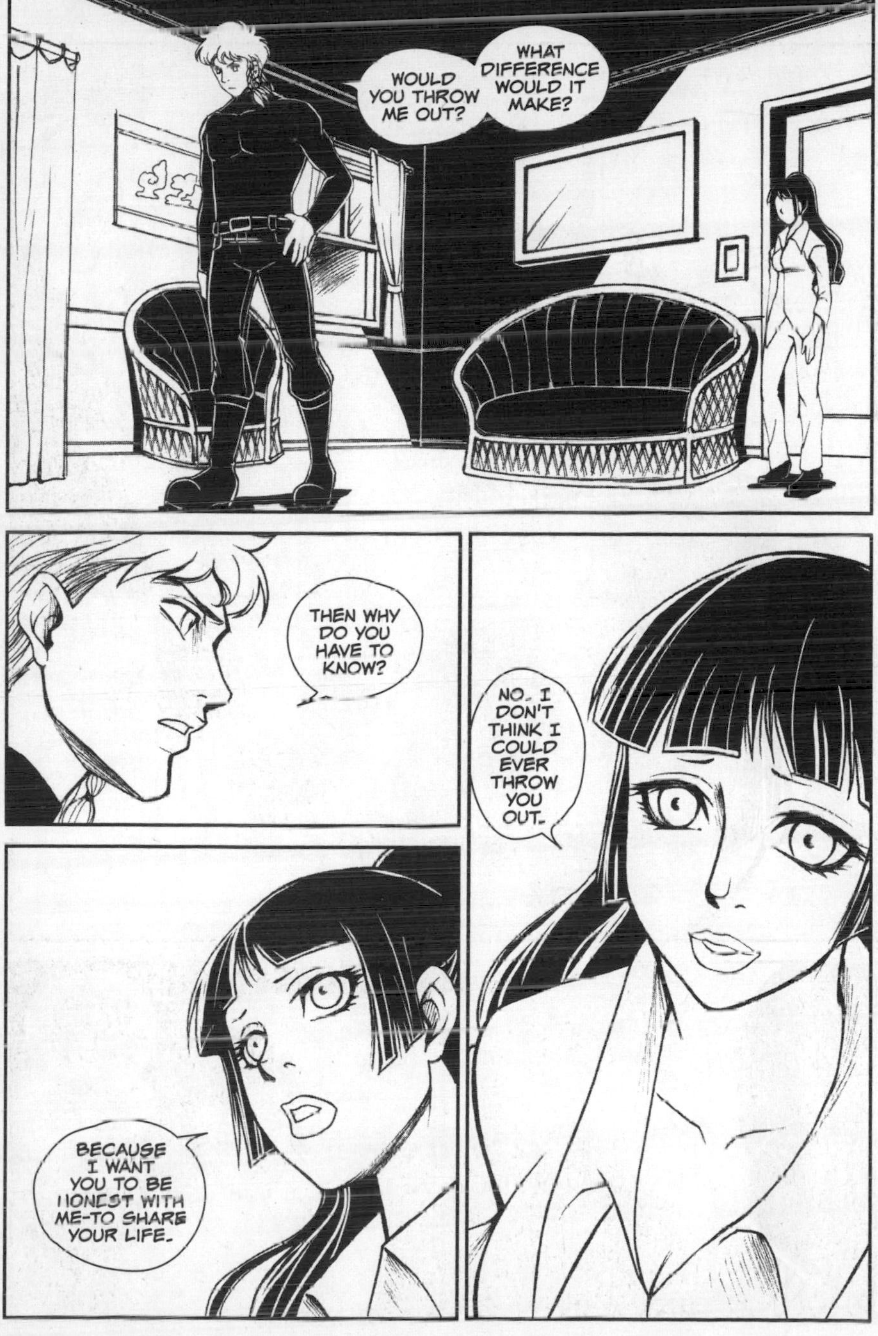
WHAT DIFFERENCE WOULD IT MAKE?
WOULD YOU THROW ME OUT?
THEN WHY DO YOU HAVE TO KNOW?
NO. I DON'T THINK I COULD EVER THROW YOU OUT.
BECAUSE I WANT YOU TO BE HONEST WITH ME-TO SHARE YOUR LIFE.

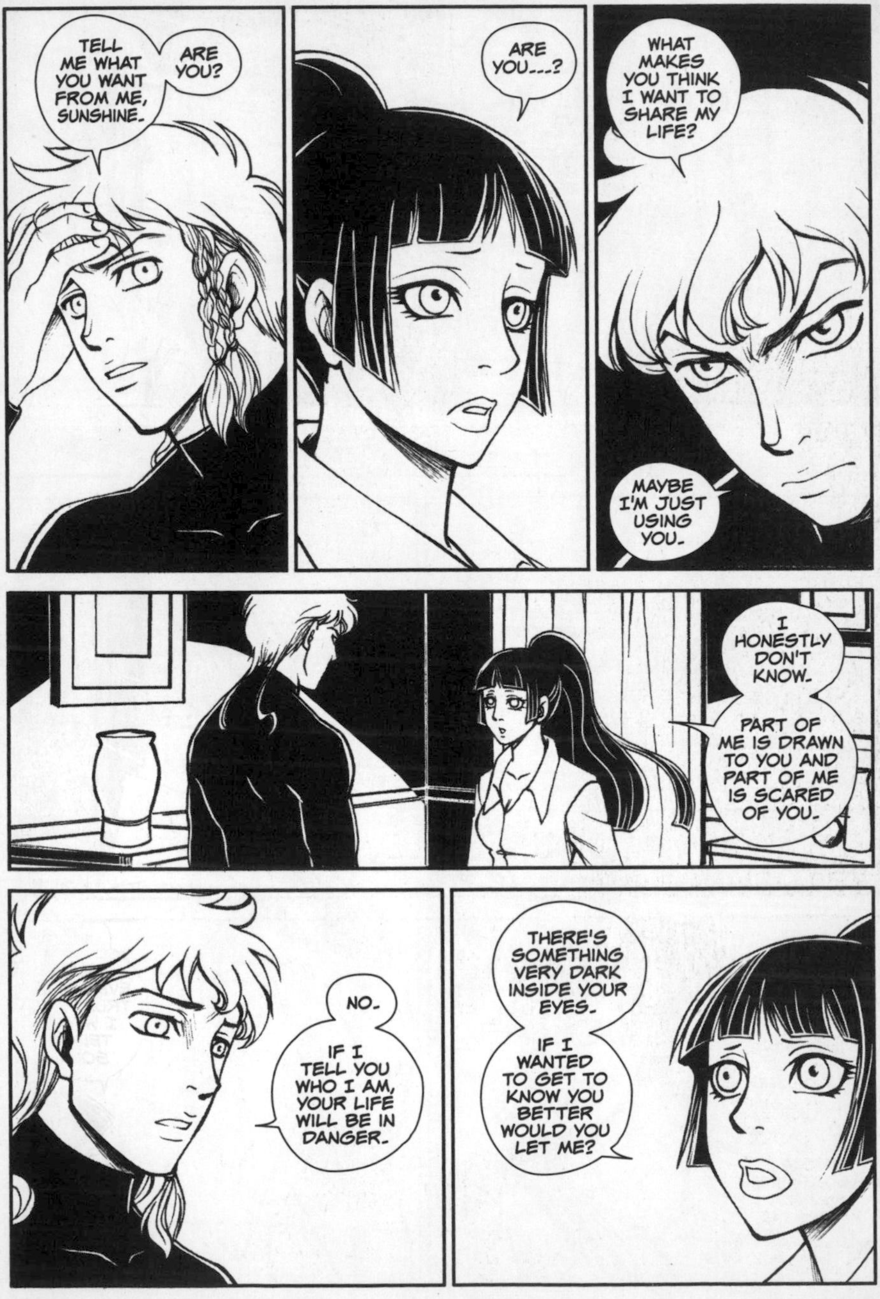
TELL ME WHAT YOU WANT FROM ME, SUNSHINE.
ARE YOU?
ARE YOU...?
WHAT MAKES YOU THINK I WANT TO SHARE MY LIFE?
MAYBE I'M JUST USING YOU.
I HONESTLY DON'T KNOW.
PART OF ME IS DRAWN TO YOU AND PART OF ME IS SCARED OF YOU.
NO.
IF I TELL YOU WHO I AM, YOUR LIFE WILL BE IN DANGER.
THERE'S SOMETHING VERY DARK INSIDE YOUR EYES.
IF I WANTED TO GET TO KNOW YOU BETTER WOULD YOU LET ME?

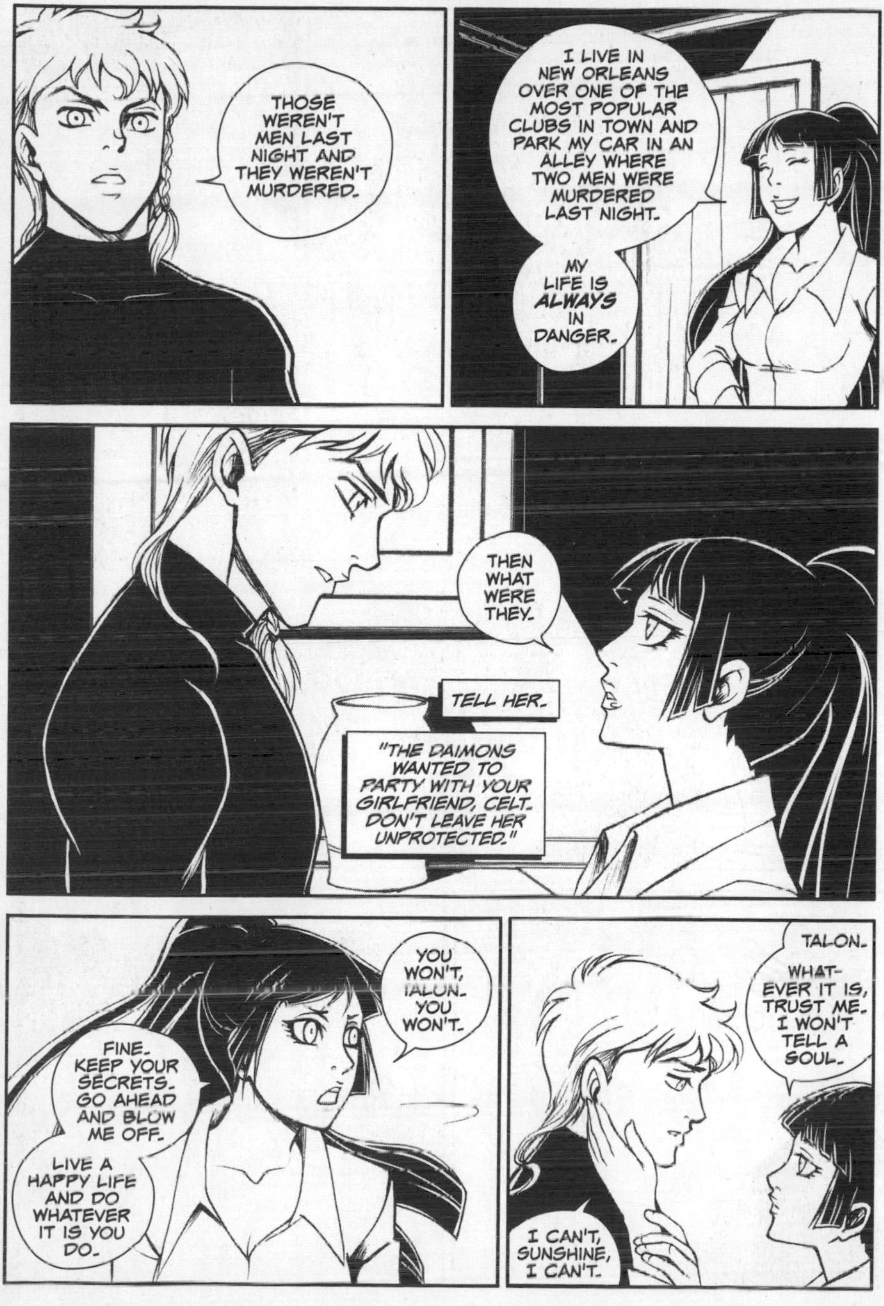

THOSE WEREN'T MEN LAST NIGHT AND THEY WEREN'T MURDERED.
I LIVE IN NEW ORLEANS OVER ONE OF THE MOST POPULAR CLUBS IN TOWN AND PARK MY CAR IN AN ALLEY WHERE TWO MEN WERE MURDERED LAST NIGHT.
MY LIFE IS ALWAYS IN DANGER.
THEN WHAT WERE THEY.
TELL HER.
"THE DAIMONS WANTED TO PARTY WITH YOUR GIRLFRIEND, CELT. DON'T LEAVE HER UNPROTECTED."
YOU WON'T, TALON. YOU WON'T.
FINE. KEEP YOUR SECRETS. GO AHEAD AND BLOW ME OFF.
LIVE A HAPPY LIFE AND DO WHATEVER IT IS YOU DO.
TALON.
WHAT-EVER IT IS, TRUST ME. I WON'T TELL A SOUL.
I CAN'T, SUNSHINE, I CAN'T.

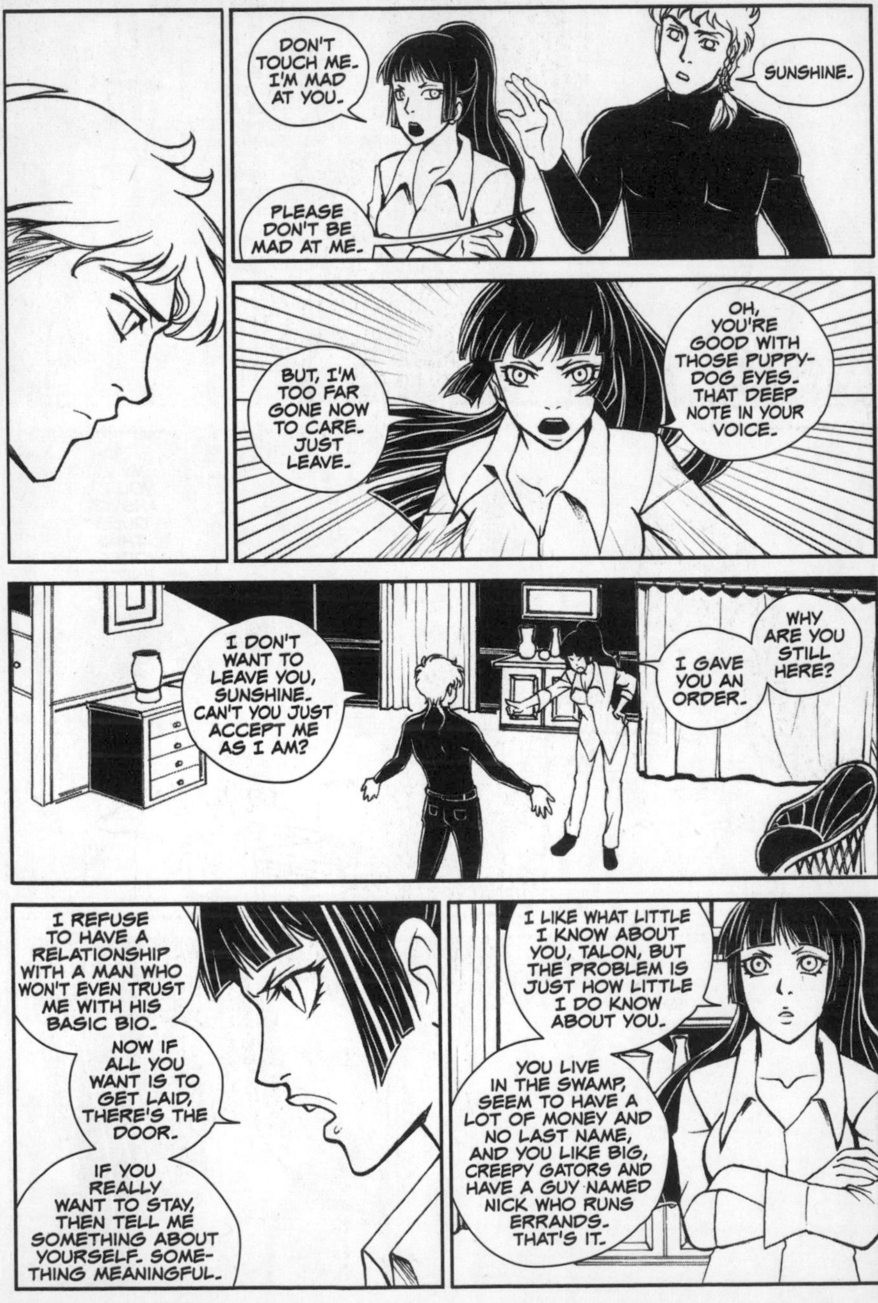
DON'T TOUCH ME. I'M MAD AT YOU.
SUNSHINE.
PLEASE DON'T BE MAD AT ME.
OH, YOU'RE GOOD WITH THOSE PUPPY-DOG EYES. THAT DEEP NOTE IN YOUR VOICE.
BUT, I'M TOO FAR GONE NOW TO CARE. JUST LEAVE.
WHY ARE YOU STILL HERE?
I GAVE YOU AN ORDER.
I DON'T WANT TO LEAVE YOU, SUNSHINE. CAN'T YOU JUST ACCEPT ME AS I AM?
I LIKE WHAT LITTLE I KNOW ABOUT YOU, TALON, BUT THE PROBLEM IS JUST HOW LITTLE I DO KNOW ABOUT YOU.
YOU LIVE IN THE SWAMP, SEEM TO HAVE A LOT OF MONEY AND NO LAST NAME, AND YOU LIKE BIG, CREEPY GATORS AND HAVE A GUY NAMED NICK WHO RUNS ERRANDS. THAT'S IT.
I REFUSE TO HAVE A RELATIONSHIP WITH A MAN WHO WON'T EVEN TRUST ME WITH HIS BASIC BIO.
NOW IF ALL YOU WANT IS TO GET LAID, THERE'S THE DOOR.
IF YOU REALLY WANT TO STAY, THEN TELL ME SOMETHING ABOUT YOURSELF. SOME-THING MEANINGFUL.

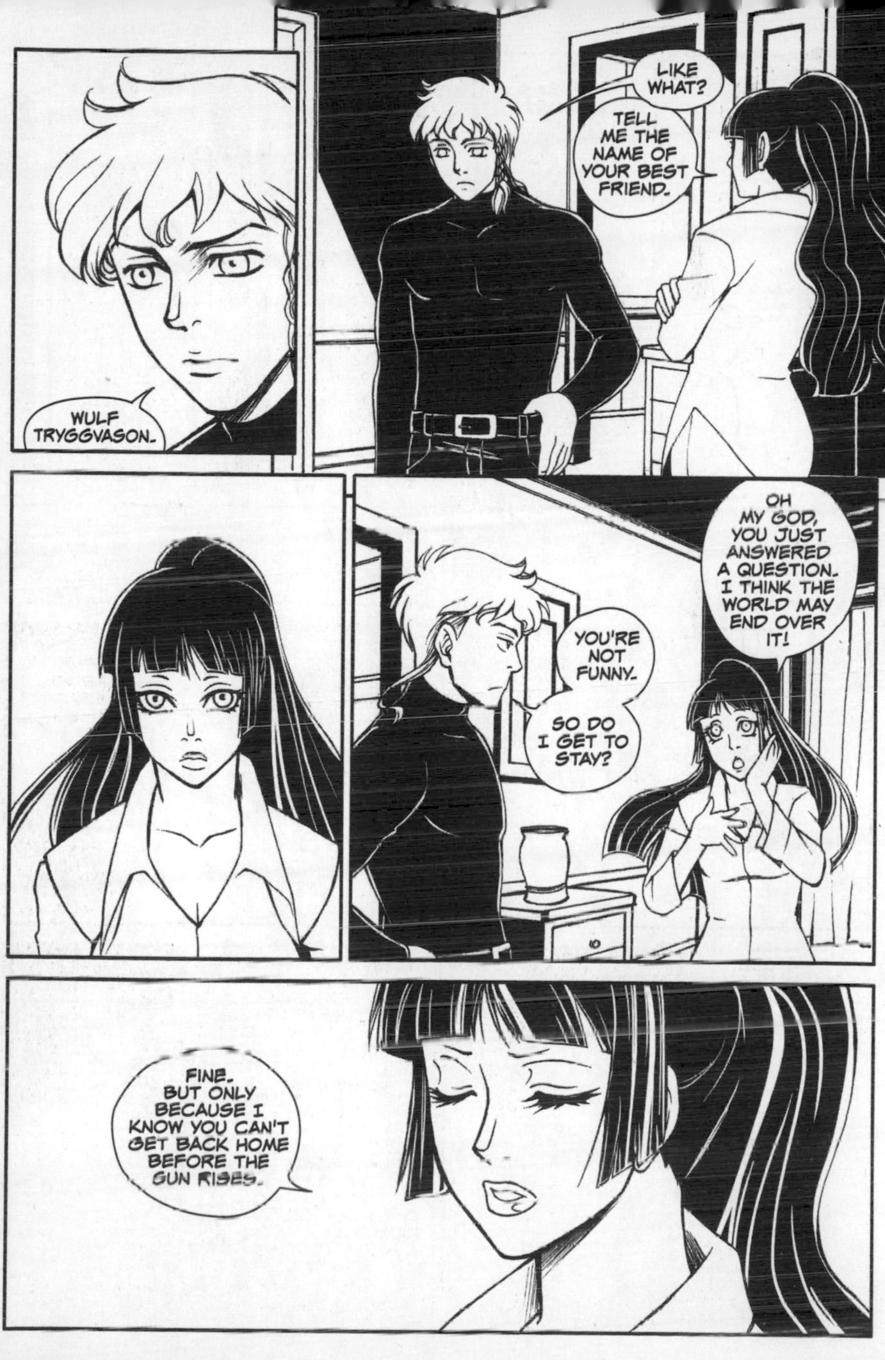
LIKE WHAT?
TELL ME THE NAME OF YOUR BEST FRIEND.
WULF TRYGGVASON.
OH MY GOD, YOU JUST ANSWERED A QUESTION. I THINK THE WORLD MAY END OVER IT!
YOU'RE NOT FUNNY.
SO DO I GET TO STAY?
FINE. BUT ONLY BECAUSE I KNOW YOU CAN'T GET BACK HOME BEFORE THE SUN RISES.

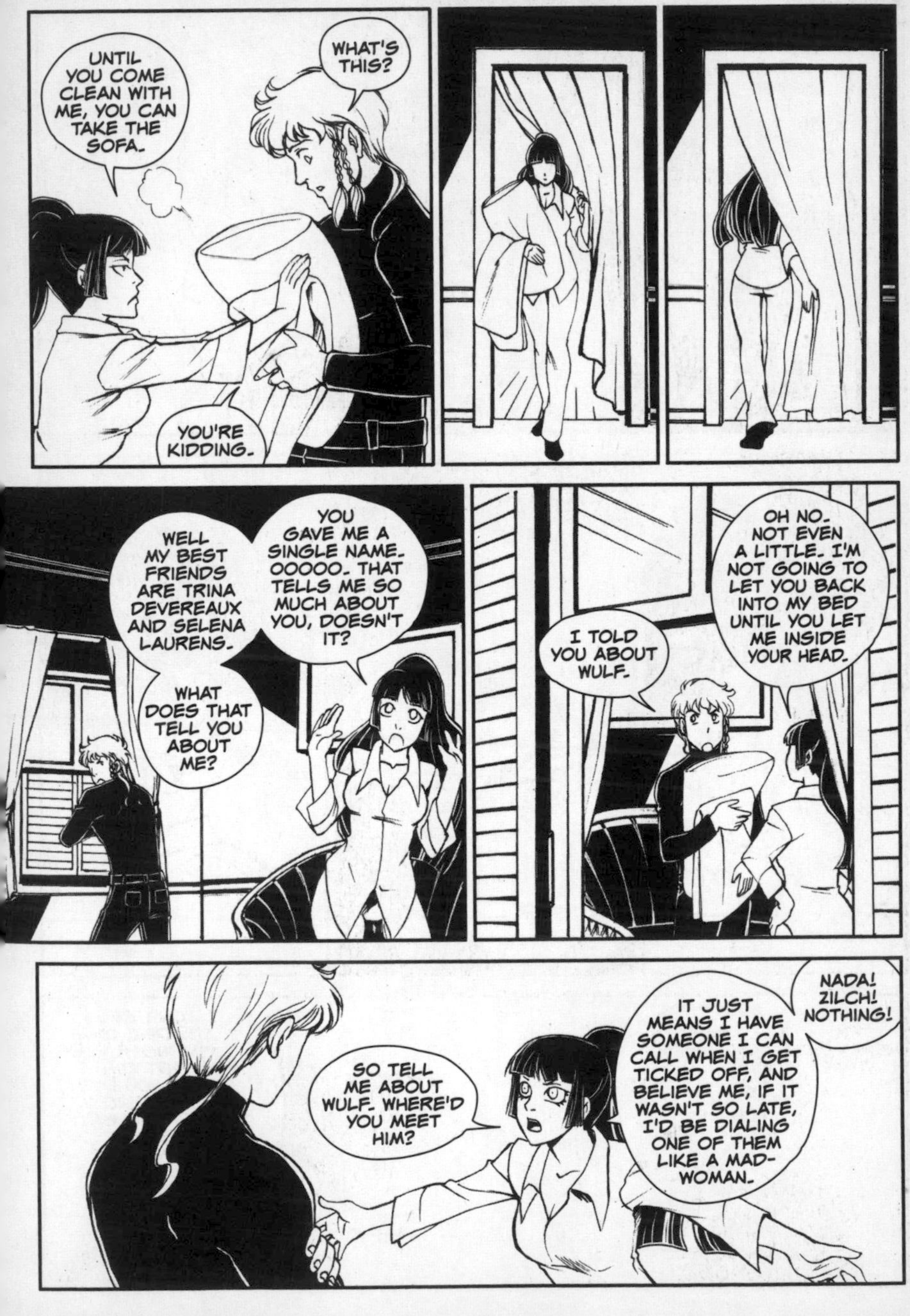
UNTIL YOU COME CLEAN WITH ME, YOU CAN TAKE THE SOFA.
WHAT'S THIS?
YOU'RE KIDDING.
WELL MY BEST FRIENDS ARE TRINA DEVEREAUX AND SELENA LAURENS.
WHAT DOES THAT TELL YOU ABOUT ME?
YOU GAVE ME A SINGLE NAME. OOOOO. THAT TELLS ME SO MUCH ABOUT YOU, DOESN'T IT?
I TOLD YOU ABOUT WULF.
OH NO. NOT EVEN A LITTLE. I'M NOT GOING TO LET YOU BACK INTO MY BED UNTIL YOU LET ME INSIDE YOUR HEAD.
IT JUST MEANS I HAVE SOMEONE I CAN CALL WHEN I GET TICKED OFF, AND BELIEVE ME, IF IT WASN'T SO LATE, I'D BE DIALING ONE OF THEM LIKE A MAD-WOMAN.
NADA! ZILCH! NOTHING!
SO TELL ME ABOUT WULF. WHERE'D YOU MEET HIM?

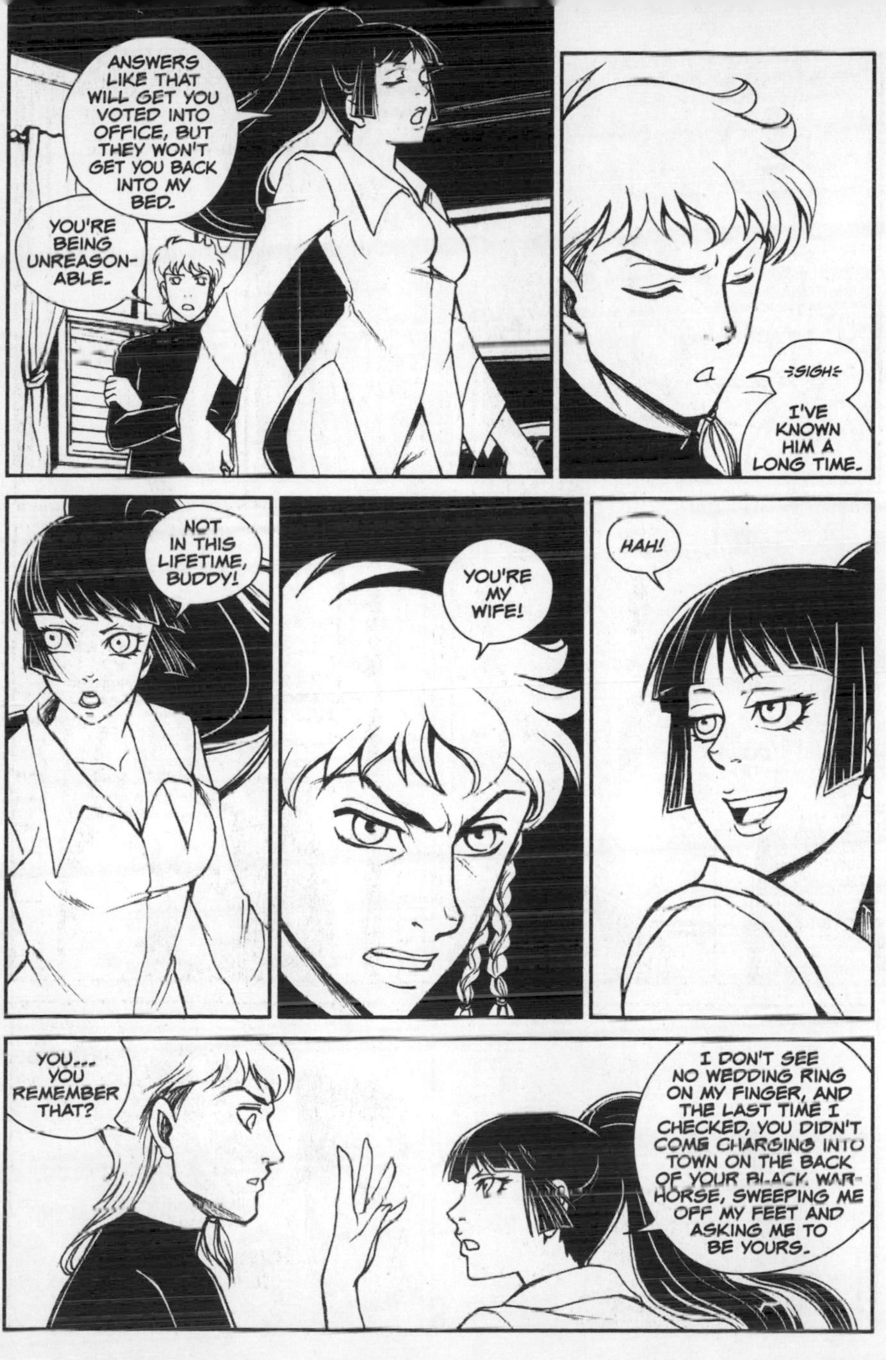
ANSWERS LIKE THAT WILL GET YOU VOTED INTO OFFICE, BUT THEY WON'T GET YOU BACK INTO MY BED.
YOU'RE BEING UNREASON-ABLE.
=SIGH=
I'VE KNOWN HIM A LONG TIME.
NOT IN THIS LIFETIME, BUDDY!
YOU'RE MY WIFE!
HAH!
YOU... YOU REMEMBER THAT?
I DON'T SEE NO WEDDING RING ON MY FINGER, AND THE LAST TIME I CHECKED, YOU DIDN'T COME CHARGING INTO TOWN ON THE BACK OF YOUR BLACK WAR-HORSE, SWEEPING ME OFF MY FEET AND ASKING ME TO BE YOURS.

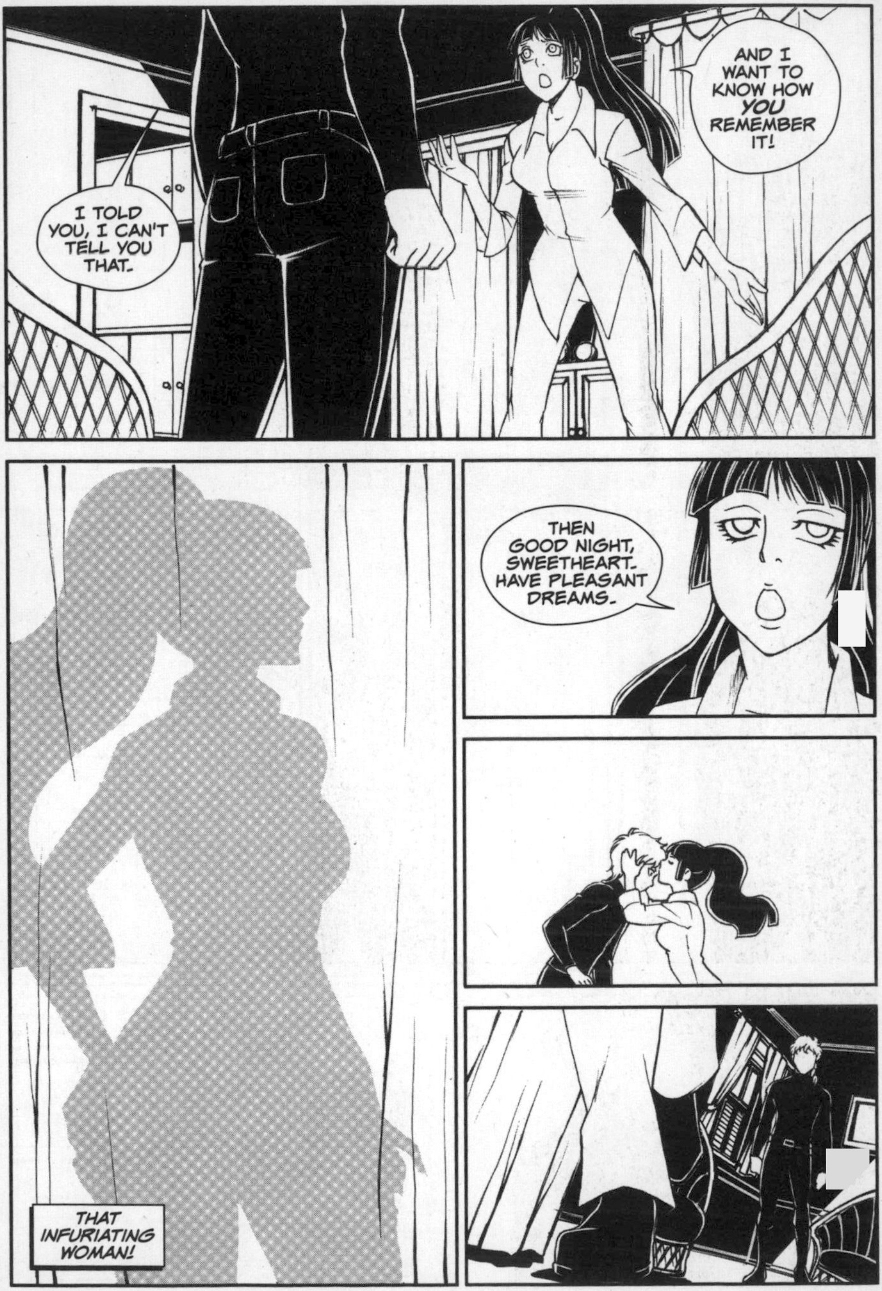
AND I WANT TO KNOW HOW *YOU* REMEMBER IT!
I TOLD YOU, I CAN'T TELL YOU THAT.
THEN GOOD NIGHT, SWEETHEART. HAVE PLEASANT DREAMS.
THAT INFURIATING WOMAN!

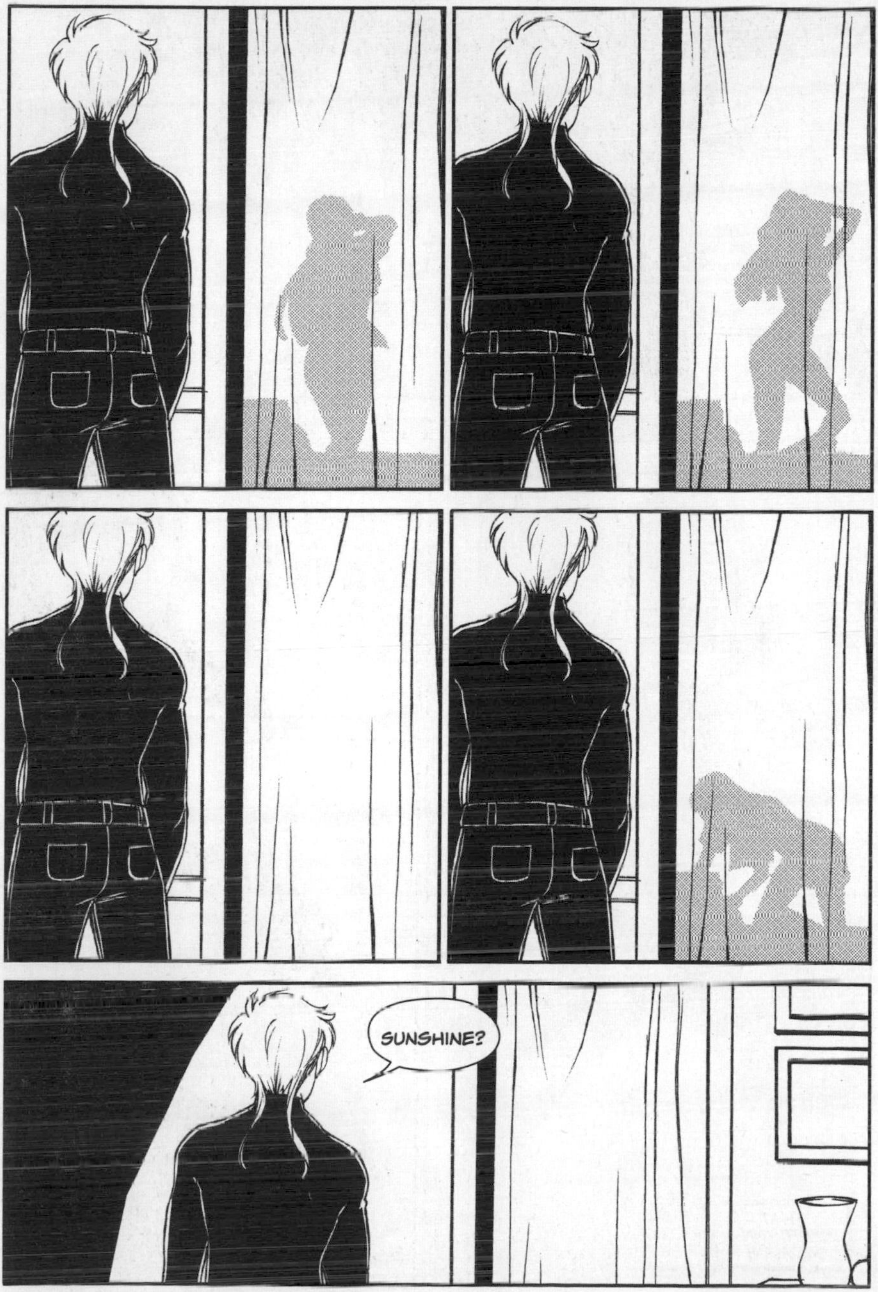
SUNSHINE?

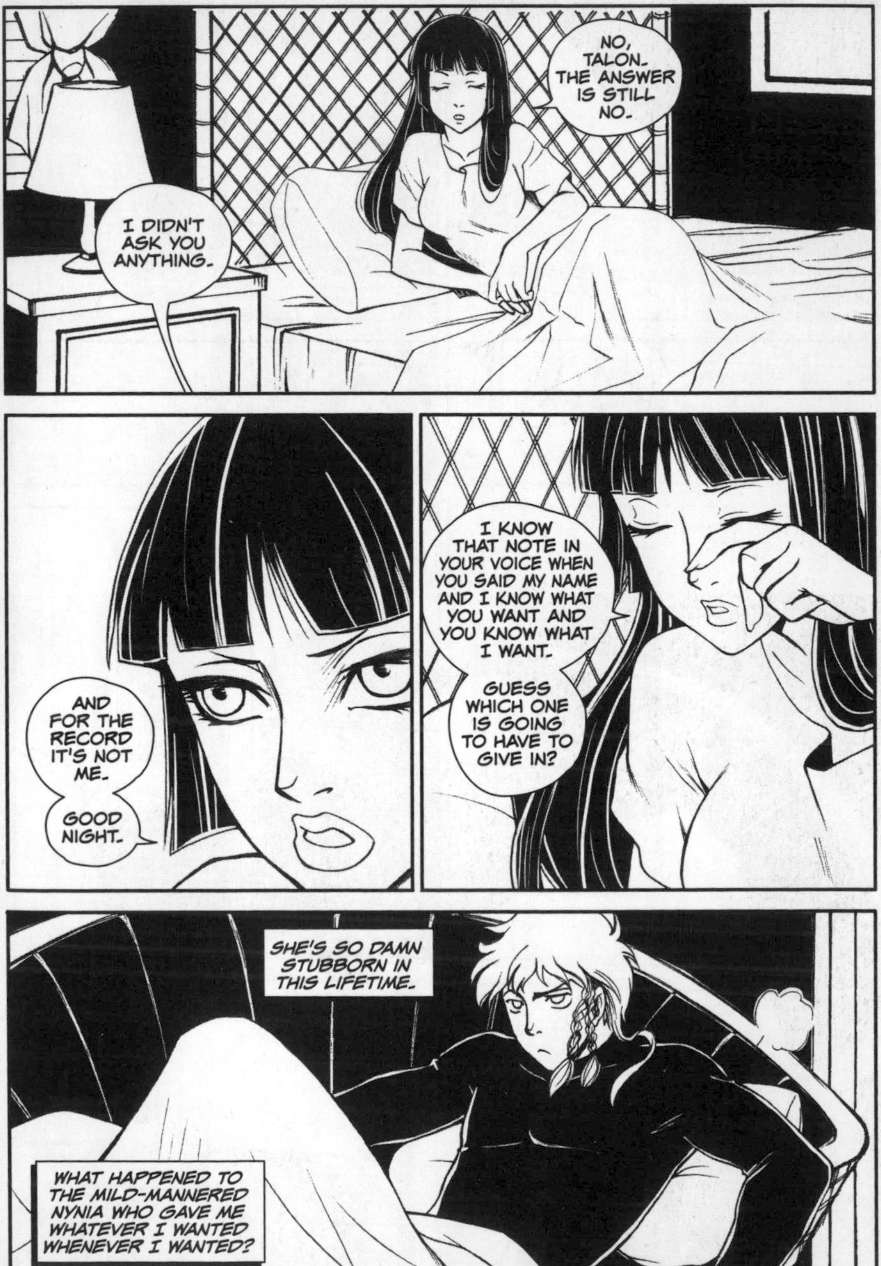

NO, TALON. THE ANSWER IS STILL NO.
I DIDN'T ASK YOU ANYTHING.
I KNOW THAT NOTE IN YOUR VOICE WHEN YOU SAID MY NAME AND I KNOW WHAT YOU WANT AND YOU KNOW WHAT I WANT.
GUESS WHICH ONE IS GOING TO HAVE TO GIVE IN?
AND FOR THE RECORD IT'S NOT ME.
GOOD NIGHT.
SHE'S SO DAMN STUBBORN IN THIS LIFETIME.
WHAT HAPPENED TO THE MILD-MANNERED NYNIA WHO GAVE ME WHATEVER I WANTED WHENEVER I WANTED?

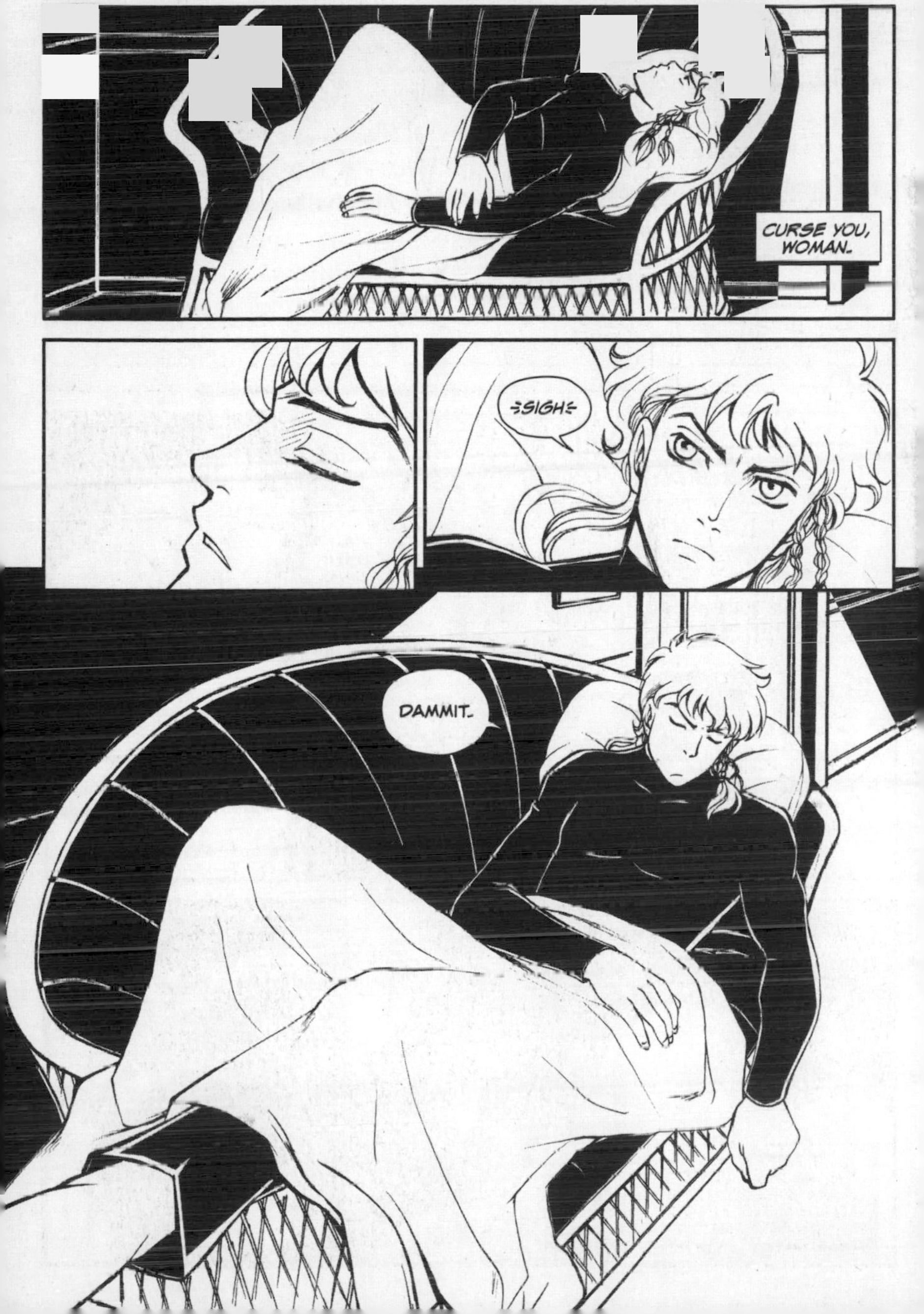
CURSE YOU, WOMAN…
SIGH
DAMMIT…

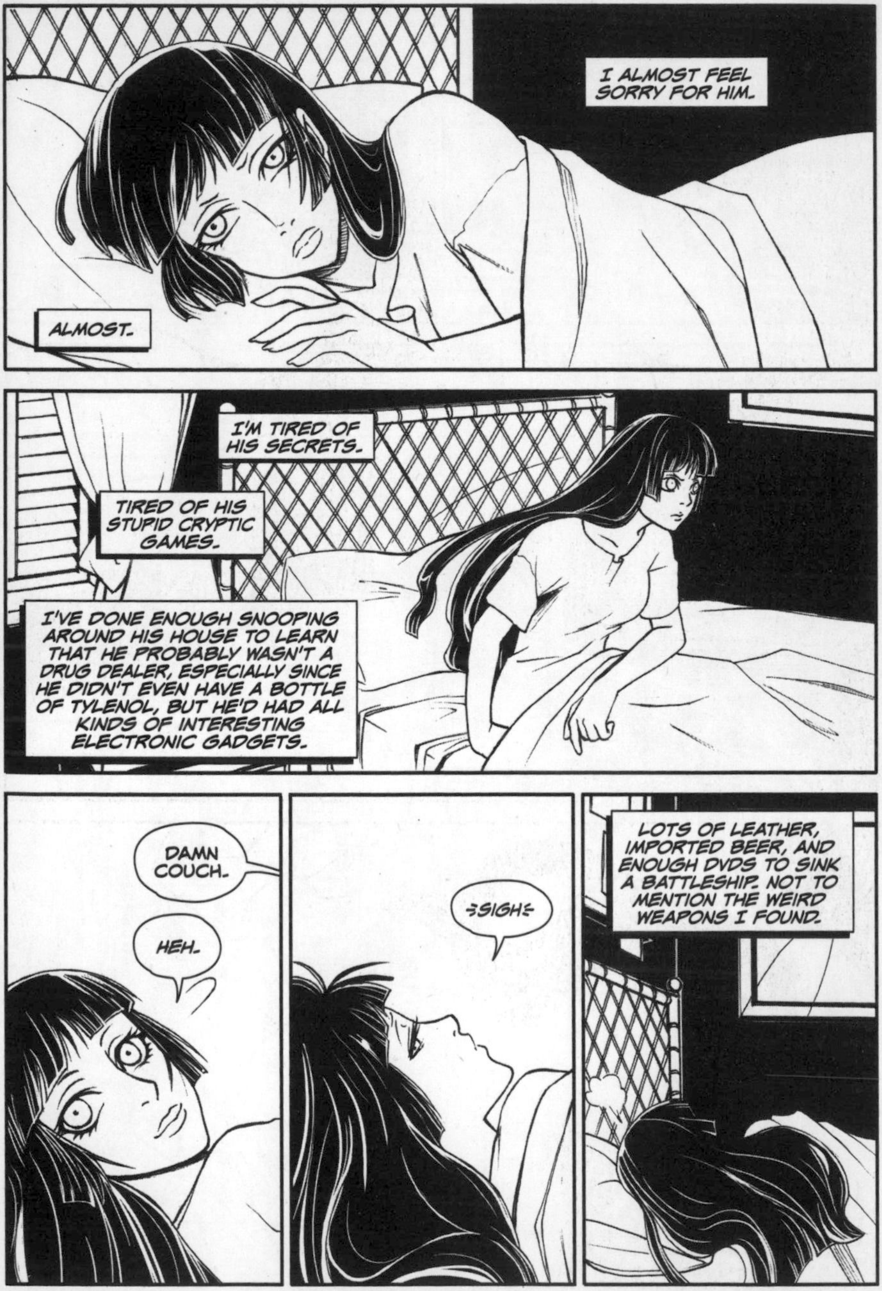

I ALMOST FEEL SORRY FOR HIM.
ALMOST.
I'M TIRED OF HIS SECRETS.
TIRED OF HIS STUPID CRYPTIC GAMES.
I'VE DONE ENOUGH SNOOPING AROUND HIS HOUSE TO LEARN THAT HE PROBABLY WASN'T A DRUG DEALER, ESPECIALLY SINCE HE DIDN'T EVEN HAVE A BOTTLE OF TYLENOL, BUT HE'D HAD ALL KINDS OF INTERESTING ELECTRONIC GADGETS.
DAMN COUCH.
HEH.
=SIGH=
LOTS OF LEATHER, IMPORTED BEER, AND ENOUGH DVDS TO SINK A BATTLESHIP. NOT TO MENTION THE WEIRD WEAPONS I FOUND.

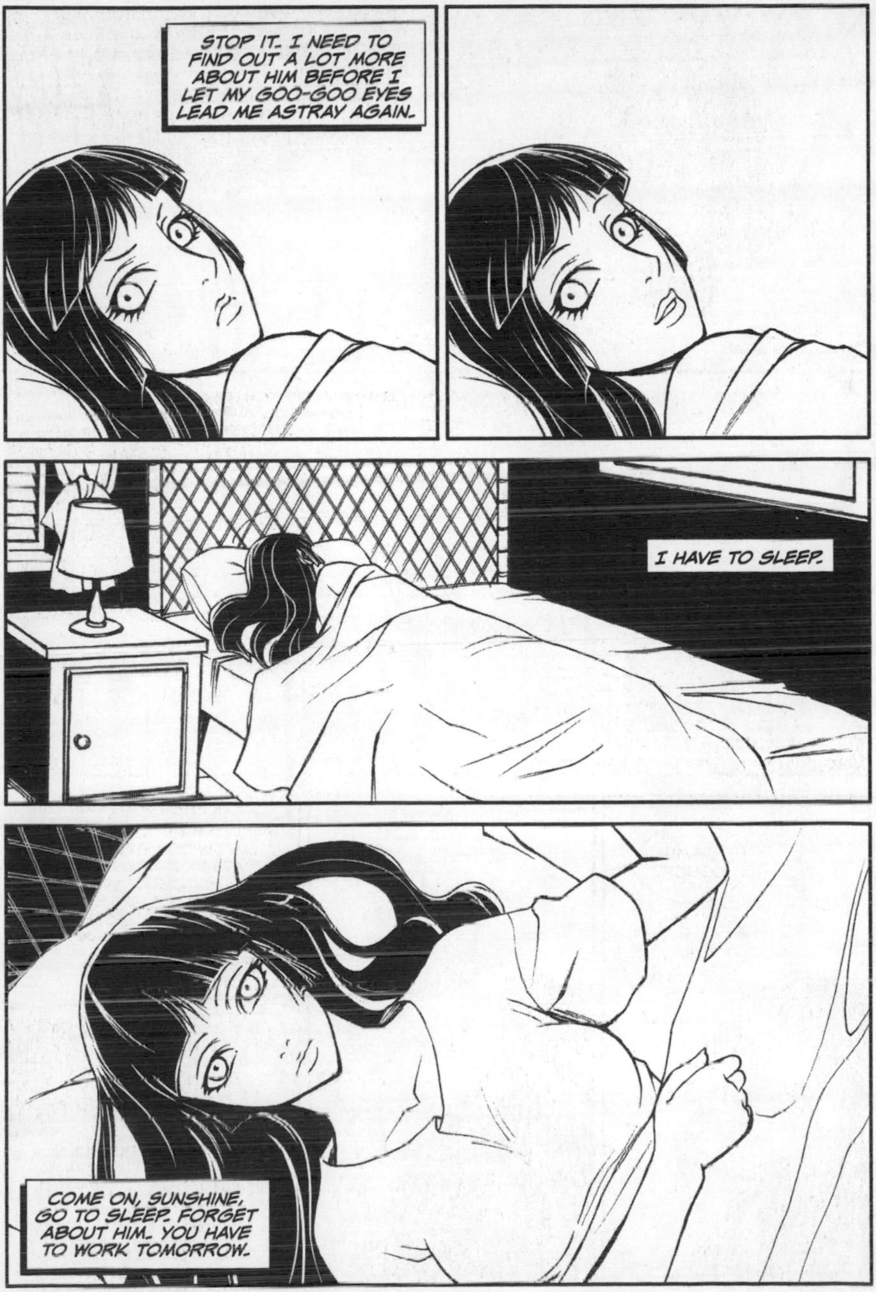
STOP IT. I NEED TO FIND OUT A LOT MORE ABOUT HIM BEFORE I LET MY GOO-GOO EYES LEAD ME ASTRAY AGAIN.
I HAVE TO SLEEP.
COME ON, SUNSHINE, GO TO SLEEP. FORGET ABOUT HIM. YOU HAVE TO WORK TOMORROW.

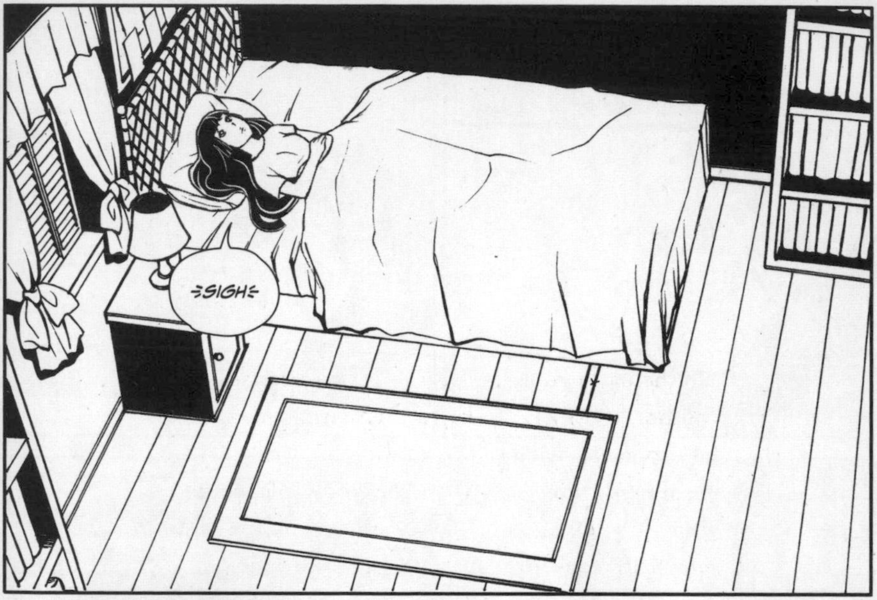
SIGH

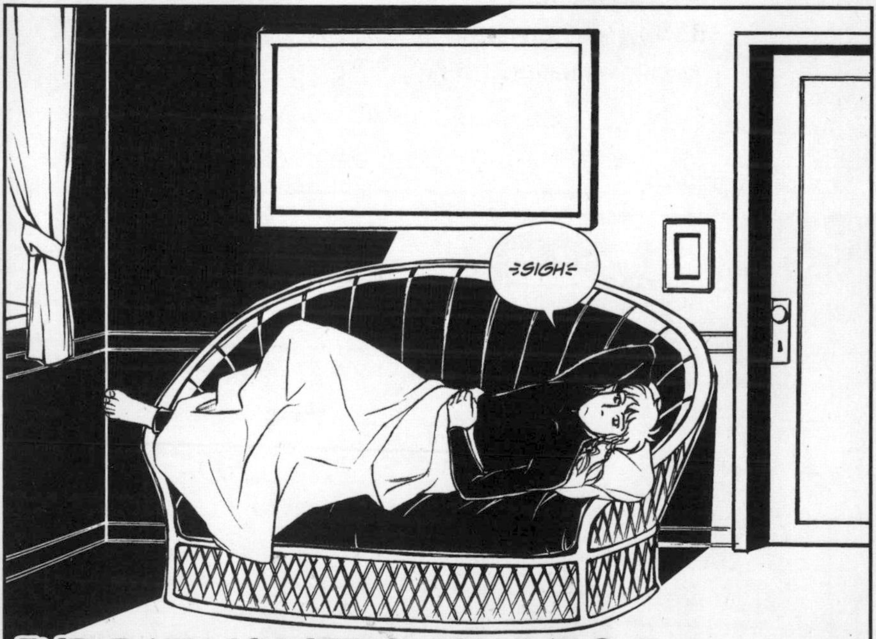
SIGH
END DARK-HUNTERS VOLUME 3

In the past two years, *New York Times* bestselling author SHERRILYN KENYON has claimed the #1 spot twelve times. This extraordinary bestseller continues to top every genre she writes. With more than 22 million copies of her books in print in over 30 countries, her current series include: The Dark-Hunters, The League, Lords of Avalon, BAD Agency, Chronicles of Nick and the forthcoming Nevermore.

MARCH 2011—

the DARK HUNTERS

ARE BACK IN VOLUME 4!

In the war against vampires, mankind has only one hope: The Dark-Hunters. Ancient warriors who died of brutal betrayal, the Dark-Hunters have sworn themselves into the service of the goddess Artemis to protect us.

It's a pact with pretty good perks—immortality, power, psychic abilities, wealth and a cool wardrobe. But it comes with a few drawbacks: fatal sun poisoning and a new, irreparable dental problem. But aside from the fangs and nocturnal lifestyle, it's not so bad...when you don't have to save the world...again.

Talon, an ancient Celtic warrior, commands the elements and knows no fear. He has also lived under a dark curse for longer than he can remember. Hundreds of years ago, he killed the son of the god Camulus. In return, Camulus decreed death for everyone Talon was close to. Now a Dark-Hunter in modern-day New Orleans, Talon meets Sunshine, who is the key to ending his curse once and for all. Unfortunately for both of them, it's Mardi Gras, and New Orleans is teeming with a complex plot of ancient gods, including Camulus, who are now out to re-conquer the world. The gloves are off and it's time for a rematch with Talon out to save everyone.

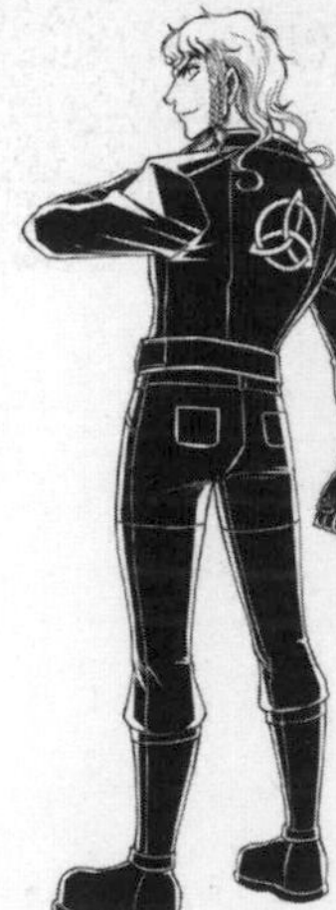

St. Martin's Griffin

Starting high school was tough.
And that was before the DEMONS,
WEREWOLVES, and ZOMBIES showed up...

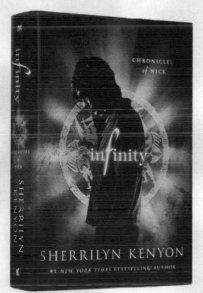

At fourteen, Nick Gautier thinks he knows everything about the world around him, until the night when his best friends try to kill him. Saved by a mysterious warrior who has more fighting skills than Chuck Norris, Nick is sucked into the realm of the Dark-Hunters.

Nick quickly learns that the human world is only a veil for a much larger and more dangerous one. A world where the captain of the football team is a werewolf and the girl he has a crush on goes out at night to stake the undead...

Live fast. Fight hard.
Make your enemies cry.

NO MERCY

⚔ A DARK-HUNTER® NOVEL

Shape-shifter Dev Peltier thought he knew it all. But one night when not just a Dark-Hunter, but an official member of the Dogs of War, sashays into his bar, he realizes that he might have met his match.

Sam was one of the fiercest Amazon warriors in her tribe. But when an act of brutal betrayal made her a Dark-Hunter, she's been pissed ever since. And now old and new enemies alike are moving into New Orleans—and Dev just might be the only hope she and mankind have to save the world.

**AVAILABLE
SEPTEMBER 2010**

They are Darkness.

They are Shadow.

They are the Rulers of the Night.

THEY ARE THE DARK-HUNTERS.®

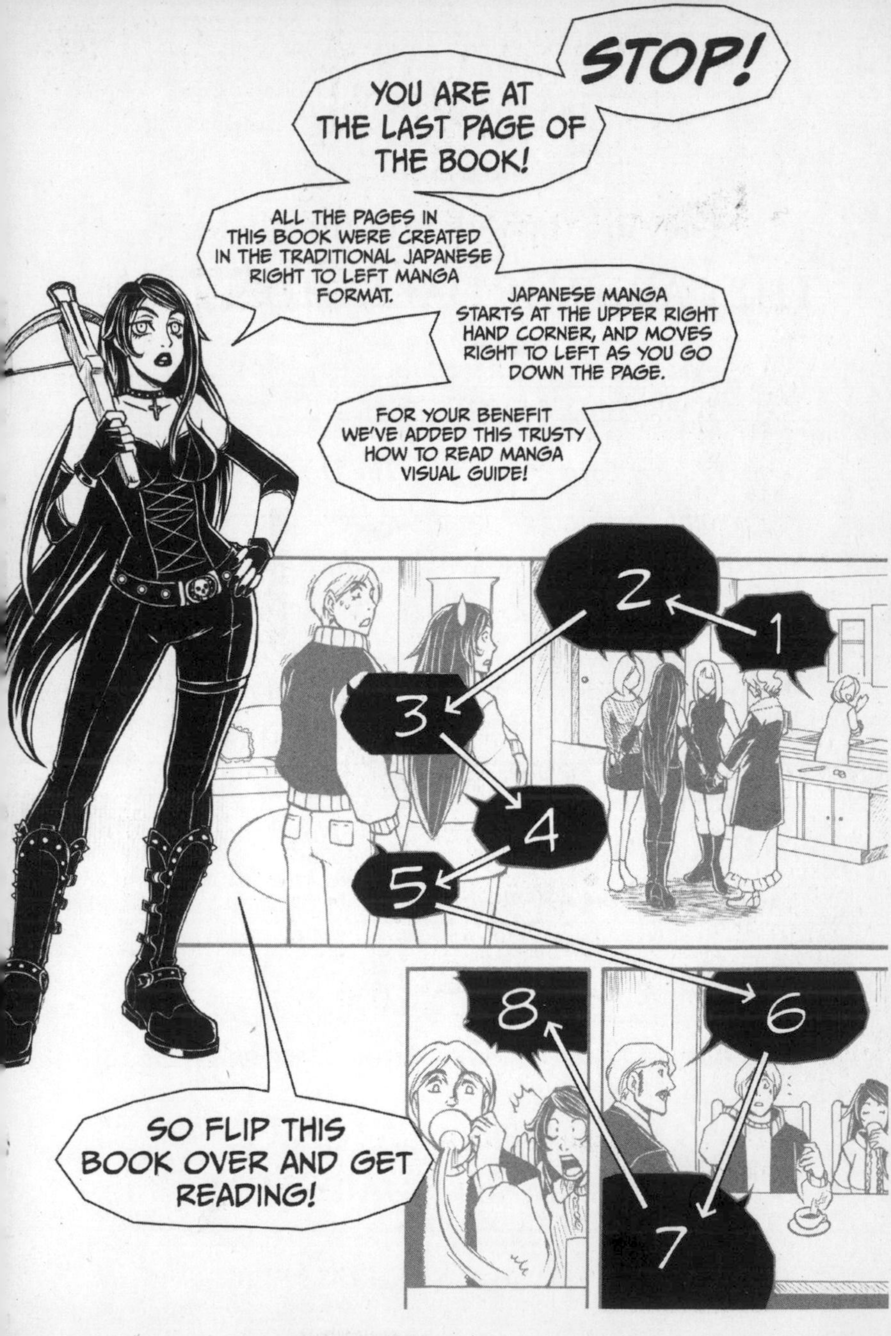
STOP!
YOU ARE AT THE LAST PAGE OF THE BOOK!
ALL THE PAGES IN THIS BOOK WERE CREATED IN THE TRADITIONAL JAPANESE RIGHT TO LEFT MANGA FORMAT.
JAPANESE MANGA STARTS AT THE UPPER RIGHT HAND CORNER, AND MOVES RIGHT TO LEFT AS YOU GO DOWN THE PAGE.
FOR YOUR BENEFIT WE'VE ADDED THIS TRUSTY HOW TO READ MANGA VISUAL GUIDE!
1
2
3
4
5
6
7
8
SO FLIP THIS BOOK OVER AND GET READING!